San
Sebastián

VASCO

FRANCIA

CORDILLERA PIRENAICA

Pamplona

NAVARRA

LA
RIOJA

Tudela

Huesca

CATALUNYA

Gerona

Soria

ARAGÓN

Zaragoza

Lérida

Barcelona

Cariñena

San Sadurni de Noia

Alcañiz

Río Ebro

Vilafranca del Penedès
Tarragona

Río Tajo

Teruel

PAÍS VALENCIANO

ISLAS BALEARES

MENORCA

Cuenca

Castellón
de la Plana

MALLORCA

Palma

Valencia

LAKE ALBUFERA

Río Júcar

Albacete

IBIZA

Alicante

Mar Mediterráneo

Murcia

MAR MENOR

MURCIA

N

ESPAÑA

ería

0   MILES   100

KM   100

THE SPANISH TABLE

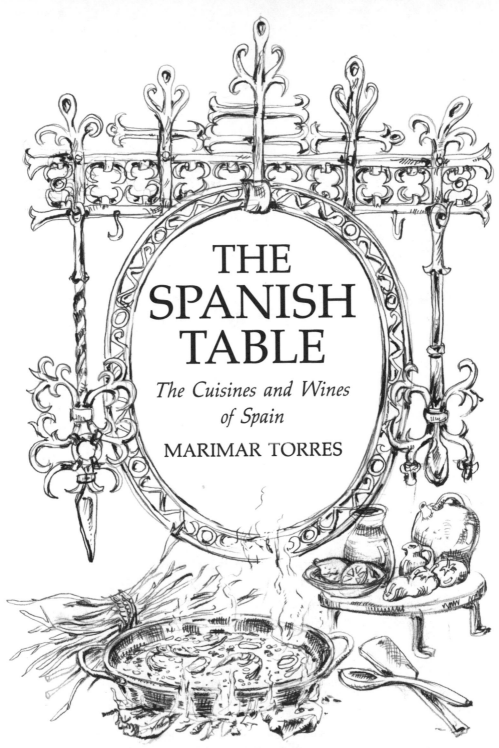

THE
SPANISH
TABLE

*The Cuisines and Wines
of Spain*

MARIMAR TORRES

DOUBLEDAY & COMPANY, INC., GARDEN CITY, NEW YORK
1986

Index prepared by Maro Riofrancos

Library of Congress Cataloging-in-Publication Data
Torres, Marimar.
The Spanish table.
Includes index.
1. Cookery, Spanish.
2. Wine and wine making—Spain.   I. Title.
TX723.5.S7T66   1986   641.5946   85–29241
ISBN 0-385-19402-1

To Rosalía,
my parents' cook,
who allowed me to follow her
around as a child,

and
To Ann Walker,
with whom I have shared
many hours of fun and experimentation
in the kitchen

A WORD OF ACKNOWLEDGMENT

This book has been the culmination of a long-time dream to bring today's Spanish cuisine to North America. And perhaps more important, it has given me the opportunity to learn, during the years I devoted to it, a lot about my home country and its people. In my travels through Spain I found the most incredible cooperation from restaurant and winery owners, chefs and winemakers, all of whom are mentioned in the book.

In the United States, there are a great number of people who made the book possible. First of all, Ann Walker, with whom I made my first gastro-nomic-culinary journey around Spain, surveying the key restaurants; she has collaborated with me from the beginning in developing and double-testing all the recipes. Together we endeavored to keep intact the idea of the chef who inspired the recipe while making it work with our ingredients —even to improve it, whenever possible. And for all this, I will never be able to thank Ann enough.

Throughout the testing of the recipes, two women were by my side, providing invaluable help: Bonnie Whyte, a great cook and patient friend; and Patricia Riquelme, who since 1980 has helped me with many of the dishes. And of course, I have to thank all my friends who acted as "guinea pigs" and gave me their opinions about the numerous dishes they had to try at one dinner—often compensating by dieting the entire next week. In particular I want to thank Robert Finigan, for the great influence he has had on my appreciation of food since I came to live in America.

Another person in the United States who faithfully contributed her skills is Joann Shirley. She not only typed the book but helped immeasur-ably to improve my English—a much needed assistance, considering that I came to live here just ten years ago. And indeed, I have to thank my editor at Doubleday, Marie Kratsios, for her kind advice and assistance whenever I needed it, as well as my copy editors, Estelle Laurence and Elaine Chubb, for their outstanding job, and especially my agent, Charlotte Sheedy and her associate Regula Noëtzli, for their invaluable help at all times.

One person without whom I might never have written this book is Dr. Pierre Mornell, a writer himself who inspired and supported me in the project from the day I conceived the idea, and stood behind me convincing me that I could do it.

The book would have been an impossible task without Montse Painous, my assistant at my family's winery in Spain, who has been with me ever since I started to work there twenty years ago. Montse's devotion to this project ranged from helping me research the best restaurants and wineries to scheduling my trips, coordinating my visits and contacts—and patiently answering, by telex or telephone, my myriad of questions from here. Besides her, everybody at the winery and our representatives throughout Spain helped me with their contacts and experience.

There are many acknowledgments due to people in Spain. First, all the members of my family searched for the best recipes in their repertoire and also undertook endless—though wonderful—meals at Catalan restaurants, often paying for it with strict diets afterward (my father paid by picking up the bill, too). My mother, especially, provided me with recipes galore from her voluminous files. My brother Miguel shared not only his many contacts in the wine and food world but also his wealth of knowledge, patiently answering the endless questions of a younger sister and allowing me to use the information contained in the wine books he has written.

Rosalía, the family cook, deserves special thanks. At eighty-six her memory is still vivid; she has often recounted for me the wonderful meals she cooked for my family since she started working for my grandmother at the age of nineteen.

Then there is a long list of Spanish wine and food authorities who gladly shared their knowledge and time with me. My good Catalan friend Mauricio Wiesenthal, a living encyclopedia on gastronomy and wine, helped me throughout the book but especially in the part about Catalan wines, for which he willingly wrote the Spanish draft. In Madrid, Dr. Manuel Martínez Llopis, another gastronomic encyclopedia, opened for me his incredible recipe files and gave me much advice and information. Juan José Lapitz, a Basque who knows and loves food, helped me to understand his region's cuisine by taking me to the "food sanctuaries" there and meeting the top chefs. José Carlos Capel, a *madrileño* who has lived in Andalucía and written about its cuisine, introduced me to the importance of the Andalusian cooking heritage. Lorenzo Millo helped me with the chapter about Valencia. Enric Canut, the young president of the Association for the Promotion of Farmhouse Cheeses, provided information about the incredible array of Spanish cheeses.

In the wine chapter, my mentors and guides were Antonio Larrea in Rioja, Xosé and Carmen Posada in Galicia, Isabel Mijares in Valdepeñas, José Antonio Mijares in La Mancha, and all the wineries that are mentioned in the section on sherry. Wine writer José Peñín also provided useful information about the Spanish wine regions.

In Spain's gastronomic world, Madrid publisher Miguel Rodríguez helped me with his advice and introduced me to the books' authors from his series about the cooking of each Spanish region. Catalan publisher Jaume Beltrán also provided me with numerous contacts and information. Clara María González de Amezúa, director of Spain's most renowned cooking school, Alambique, in Madrid, shared her knowledge and her mastery of Spanish regional cooking. Many great writers, among them Lluís Bettonica, Manuel Vázquez Montalbán, Jorge Victor Sueiro, Carmen Casas, Ana Lorente, Carlos Delgado, Nines Arenillas, Antonio Vergara, Esperanza Gallego, Ana María Calera, Mann Sierra and José María Busca Isusi, have provided me with excellent information, points of view and inspiration. And I should also mention Spain's best restaurant guide, *Gourmetour*, which steered me through the country with its sound, unbiased advice.

Last but not least, I owe this book to *a place*—Rancho La Puerta, a fitness resort in the Mexican desert, near San Diego, away from the world and from telephones, which provided me with peace and quiet, good exercise, excellent instructors who became supportive friends, and healthful food, all of which allowed me to concentrate and get the book written.

CONTENTS

Whenever the name of a recipe is capitalized, the recipe is included elsewhere in the book and can be found by consulting the Index. Whenever a method is marked with an asterisk, detailed information is given elsewhere in the book; see Index for page numbers.

INTRODUCTION

When I was growing up in Catalonia, the kitchen was always a place of fascination. I remember how I would sneak in and ask Rosalía, the family cook, if there was any job she could give me. Sometimes she would say, "Well, you can scrub the floor," but if I had been especially good she would let me get my hands into the flour—and that I loved.

This was rare, however, because in our home, as in many Spanish homes, the kitchen traditionally was the cook's domain. I was never allowed there without Rosalía's permission. My mother, Margarita, had little interest in cooking, although she did like making desserts. How she raised her eyebrows when I announced at age five or six that when I grew up, I wanted to be either a cook or a dancer.

My aunt Oriola is the real cook of the family. Some of the recipes in this book are ones I've taken from her and adapted. Aunt Oriola and Rosalía were really my mentors, although my love of cooking took a while to flower. For most of the twenty-nine years that I lived in Barcelona, I attached very little importance to cooking. Until I came to the United States, in fact, I rarely ventured into the kitchen at all; at that time it was felt that young women should spend their time at more "elevated" pursuits. Cooking in Spain, until very recently, was laborious and unfashionable; it was the cook's chore.

America was a revelation to me. Here I found cooking upgraded to an art which most of my friends, both male and female, took pride in mastering. It wasn't considered a waste of time to spend two days preparing a lavish dinner. It was looked on as a labor of love, and one fully appreciated by guests who knew all the effort and creativity that had gone into the production. The first time I made paella, I remember the astonishment expressed by my friends—they loved it and raved about it. For me, it was just a simple paella, the same dish I had watched my grandmother's cook, Adriana, prepare numerous times. Whenever I entertained, I prepared traditional Spanish dishes and the response was always the same. People were delighted and fascinated by *real* Spanish cooking.

The enthusiastic reactions soon led friends who owned cooking schools to invite me as a guest instructor. That, too, was a revelation for me. What a surprise to learn that Americans thought of Spanish food as something spicy hot to be washed down with beer and tequila! It was gratifying to see their delight in discovering the flavors and food combinations in Spanish cooking, so different from those of Latin America, which were more familiar to them.

My life in America has been liberating for me in more ways than one. I have always, in terms of my country's social conventions, been something of a nonconformist and my working in the family business represented a break with established traditions. The Torres family has owned vineyards in Spain since the seventeenth century, and has been actively involved in the wine business since 1870. My father, Miguel, is the fourth-generation proprietor, my two brothers and I are the fifth. When my brother Miguel, Jr., and I were in school, my father was already grooming him for the business. Something inside me said, I would like to do that, too.

Instead, my mother always arranged for me to study languages during the summer; that was more lady-like. By the time I was sixteen I was fluent in German, French and English, which is an enormous help today, of course. But I wanted to work with wine. When I was about ten, after really insisting, I was able to get a summer job at the winery, handing dirty bottles to the men who washed them for reuse.

I made my first trip to America with my father in 1967, when he came to visit American distributors and wine merchants. As his assistant/secretary, I learned a great deal and tried to persuade him to make me the family representative for our wines here in America. He simply wouldn't hear of it. Later on, however, he allowed me to travel by myself to promote Torres wines in Canada, where our distribution was just getting started. The liquor boards were very conservative and having a woman visit them was unheard of—it earned me a lot of publicity, and our sales began to soar. When I later married an American wine and food critic and came to live in California, I started Torres Wines North America in a corner of our living room. At that time, in 1975, our sales volume in the United States was 15,000 cases a year. Today it is well over 100,000—and the office is no longer in my home.

Food and wine go so naturally together that, for me, each reinforces the other. Cooking has become my joy; I love working in the kitchen, I love the feel of the ingredients. I even like to clean squid for paella, one of the dishes I most enjoy preparing because you get to work with so many things. Basically it's like a painting—you have all these different components and assembling them all is kind of a thrill; you feel like you are really creating something and it never comes out quite the same.

These experiences eventually led quite naturally to the idea of doing this book. As I delved more deeply into the history and lore of Spanish cooking, I realized how much it could appeal to the American palate. Americans have such a wonderful curiosity about food. The inventiveness of American cooks has led them to explore many different cuisines and many styles of cooking. I also have sensed recently a growing awareness of

Spain through travel and the media, which has come about at the same time as the increasing interest in Spanish food. Certainly it is a cuisine that easily adapts to the bounty of American ingredients and the American appetite for interesting flavors.

THE
FLAVOR
OF
SPAIN

In order to understand the cuisine of Spain, it is important to realize that it is a country of 200,000 square miles and 37 million people (smaller than Texas and one and a half times the population of California) with a tremendous variation in climates, people, history, cuisines, wines and culture. Spain has four *real* languages, as well as various dialects: Basque, spoken in north-central Spain and in southwest France; Galician, the language of the Peninsula's northwest region; Catalan—from Catalonia, my home region—also spoken in Valencia and the Balearics; and Castilian, the official Spanish language.

It always amuses me that people refer to my way of pronouncing my hometown, Barcelona (Barth-elona), as my "Castilian accent," when there is no such thing in Spain. *Castellano* or Castilian is a language, and from it emanate numerous dialects and different accents, throughout Spain and in Latin America, such as Andalusian, Mexican, and Argentinian. They all stem from the same language—*castellano.*

More and more Americans visit Spain every year, and I must confess that my proud Spanish heart fills with joy as I hear reports of "the highlight of our trip." Hospitality is one quality I believe inherent in the Spanish nature; we truly love to receive visitors. And indeed, if people make the effort to travel across an entire ocean from America, then we can't do enough to show them a good time.

The main meal in Spain is the midday *comida* or *almuerzo,* which is eaten rather late by American standards. At home we never had *comida* until three o'clock in the afternoon. Restaurants in Madrid and Barcelona are rarely filled before 3:00 P.M., or before 10:30 P.M. The evening meal, *cena,* at home was more of a light supper: a soup, some grilled fish with boiled vegetables, a piece of fruit for dessert. If we were entertaining or it was a special occasion, the meal would be more elaborate. If going out for dinner, we would often begin with drinks and *tapas,* the special Spanish version of hors d'oeuvres. In Spain the *tapas* bars are loaded with little dishes that include everything from salted almonds to kidneys in sherry sauce. It is great fun to go *de tapas,* the Spanish equivalent of bar-hopping, often making a meal of these appetizers in the evening.

We use lots of olive oil in cooking, which gives Spanish food much of its unique flavor. But since we are all health- and weight-conscious these days, I have found ways to use less fat in my recipes and make them lighter, retaining the flavor with fresh ingredients and herbs and seasonings. For instance, I usually drain off the oil or fat as much as possible, and often deglaze with wine or brandy, which add an extra flavor of their own.

Wine is something I don't measure; it has flowed freely in our family since the seventeenth century.

A GASTRONOMIC TOUR THROUGH THE REGIONS OF SPAIN

There is not one Spanish cuisine; there are many. And they reflect the Spaniards' pride of regional identity and heritage, a legacy we are seeking to express and preserve with new enthusiasm in the Spain of today.

To know and understand the variation in the different cuisines of Spain, we will travel through the fifteen regions of the Peninsula. We will visit the cities and small towns, from the beaches to the mountains, exploring the meals and produce from the villagers as well as sophisticated restaurateurs. And best of all, their tastiest recipes will then follow!

CATALUNYA (CATALONIA)

While the many and varied cuisines of Spain are a delight to explore, I am naturally happiest cooking the dishes of Catalonia, or Catalunya, my home region. Catalan cuisine is one of the oldest, and most individual, of Spain—typical of the Catalonians themselves. We have always had a strong sense of our own identity that expresses itself in many ways—in our art, in our language, in our politics, in our lifestyle.

Catalonia is a region of 12,000 square miles sweeping down from the green and rugged Pyrenees to the beaches of the beautiful Costa Brava, north of Barcelona, and, to the south, the golden sands of the Costa Dorada. The land is a mixture of mountains and plains, which makes the climate and agriculture very varied.

Basically, there are two well-defined cuisines in Catalonia: the fisherman-style dishes of the coast, based on the bounty of seafood found only in the Mediterranean; and the more solid, sturdy preparations of the inland areas. In the Pyrenees the cooking is warm and comforting; I have some great memories of earthy, delicious meals by the fire after a day of skiing in the mountains, with the wind blowing outside over the snow-covered slopes.

The Pyrenees also provide the right environment for some of Catalonia's best cheeses, such as Serrat, dry or semi-dry with a classic, intense taste of the sheep's milk from which it is made; and de Arán, a slightly smoked, ball-shaped cow's milk cheese, its rind rubbed with rum. Another excellent cow's milk cheese is La Selva, made near Gerona; it can be fresh (white) or tender (pale yellow), both soft, creamy and delicate. A favorite Catalan dessert is the white fresh Mató, soft and moist, made from goat or cow's milk, eaten with honey and walnuts. A true delicacy!

The wealth of Catalan cuisine relies on the wide range of produce available, from the alpine-type mushrooms—especially the unique, delicious *rovellons*—and herbs grown in the Pyrenees to the rice, fruits and vegetables grown south in the fertile Ebro River valley. The classic Mediterranean trilogy of olives, vineyards and wheat dominates in Catalonia. We also have a lot of game, from the small wild birds like partridges and quail to rabbit and hare, dove, duck, goose (a Catalan specialty) and even deer. Basic staples also are fowl, veal, baby goat and, above all, pork, whose fat has been used as a cooking element throughout the centuries.

The History of Catalonia

The Greeks founded the city of Ampurias, on the Mediterranean, north of Barcelona. Today that district, L'Empordà (or Ampurdán in Castilian), with its dramatic Costa Brava, is one of Catalonia's main gastronomic centers and according to my friend, gastronomic historian Manuel Martínez Llopis, it has the finest and most elaborate of all Spanish cuisines. The Romans later established in Tarragona—south of Barcelona—the capital of their Spanish empire, Hispania. Both Greeks and Romans had great influence in the cuisine of Catalonia, and in all of Spain. Remnants of many ancient cuisines, such as the Arab and Jewish custom of using lemon, honey and cinnamon in certain dishes, can be found in modern Catalonia. And spice traders from the Far East introduced a variety of other spices.

Catalan cuisine is Spain's oldest on record. The first Spanish cookbook (and one of the most ancient surviving in all of Europe) is the *Llibre de Sent Soví*, written in the Catalan language in the first half of the fourteenth century.

Barcelona is the commercial capital of all Spain. This as much as anything has given Catalonia its sophisticated, cosmopolitan character; it is much more European than the rest of the country. During the Renaissance, Barcelona ranked with Venice and Genoa as a great center of trade and banking. Today it is still one of the most important ports on the Mediterranean. It was through Barcelona that pasta arrived in Spain, as Naples, Milan and Sicily belonged to the Spanish Crown during the fourteenth and fifteenth centuries. And Roussillon and Provence, today in southern France, were also part of Catalonia from 1160 to 1659—hence the similarities among these cuisines.

The nineteenth century saw the development of Barcelona as a city of great restaurants. Today, it has over 10,000 eating establishments! The oldest of them, Can Culleretes, dates back to 1786. It was originally a *chocolatería* or chocolate house, which is similar to a coffee shop. Patrons would go there in the afternoon and drink hot chocolate with rolls or sweets. It was Spain that introduced chocolate to Europe from the New World, and in fact monopolized it until the seventeenth century. Chocolate is used a lot in Catalonia, but rather than as a basic ingredient for rich desserts, Catalans have traditionally used it to flavor and thicken savory dishes.

Catalan Cuisine Today

There are six primary ingredients in Catalan cooking: olive oil, garlic, onions, tomatoes, nuts (almonds, hazelnuts and pine nuts) and dried fruits, particularly raisins and prunes. In addition, the four traditional herbs are oregano, rosemary, thyme and bay leaves.

The five essentials in Catalan cuisine are:

1. *Sofrito,* meaning long sautéing, consists of onion and tomato slowly sautéed in olive oil, sometimes with garlic, peppers or other ingredients. It is used as a basis for many dishes and sauces.

2. *Picada,* which literally means pounded, is usually a mixture of garlic, parsley, nuts, some toasted or fried bread and sometimes saffron or other spices. The ingredients are traditionally ground or "pounded" with a mortar and pestle, then added raw to the preparation while the cooking is in progress. *Picada* is used as a thickening and flavoring agent, and in a way is a complement to *sofrito.*

3. *Allioli,* an emulsion of pounded garlic and olive oil traditionally mixed together in a mortar, is one of the most widely used sauces in Catalan cooking. It enhances grilled meats or fish, and can also enliven the flavor of a dish by stirring in just a spoonful at the end.

4. *Romesco* today is a sauce that evolved from a fish dish, Fish Stew, Tarragona Style (Romesco de Pescados), typical of the Tarragona area where there are lots of almond groves. A favorite accompaniment to grilled fish and vegetables, it is usually a paste of toasted almonds, garlic, sweet red peppers or *nyoras* (a type of dried mild red pepper), bread and tomatoes.

5. *Samfaina* is a mixture of onion, tomato, pepper, eggplant and zucchini, cut into small pieces and sautéed in olive oil. It is served to accompany meats, codfish, fowl, fish, even fried eggs or as an omelet filling.

A very basic utensil in the Catalan kitchen is the mortar and pestle. Despite the availability of modern conveniences like the blender and food processor (which I use for the most part), it is still frequently used to grind nuts and spices—as in the case of *picada*—and to prepare sauces such as *allioli* and *romesco.*

Catalans also like to cook with fruit, as in chicken with prunes, goose with pears, Duck with Figs (Pato con Higos), Squab with Peaches (Pintada al Melocotón) or Spinach with Pine Nuts and Raisins, Catalan Style (Espinacas a la Catalana). In fact, any dish prepared *a la catalana* is likely to contain pine nuts and raisins or prunes.

Finally, Catalans love grilled dishes, especially cooked outdoors on an open fire. *Parrillada,* a combination of grilled shellfish, seafood or meats, is a great favorite. We even barbecue vegetables, as in Assorted Grilled Vegetables, Catalan Style (Escalivada) or Baked Young Onions or Leeks (Ceballots).

PAÍS VALENCIANO

South of Catalonia, bordering the Mediterranean, is the País Valenciano—the home of paella, undoubtedly the most famous dish of Spanish origin known in America.

This region is the number one rice producer in Spain, and the grain has been cultivated there since Arab times. The Romans introduced the hydraulic system, and the Arabs expanded and perfected the irrigation in the low, swampy lands around Lake Albufera, south of the city of Valencia.

The cuisine of the coast is very different from that of the inland areas. The terrain is quite varied, since the region originated for political reasons rather than geographical unity. While the coastline has many small, fertile *huertas* or vegetable gardens and is heavily populated, the inland is mountainous and almost uninhabited, with rivers flowing through narrow canyons. Its cuisine is therefore earthy, solid and high in calories—hardy food for a rigorous climate. It uses mountain products including aromatic herbs such as rosemary, thyme and savory, game such as partridge, hare or mountain rabbits. The flavorful snails are a traditional ingredient in many dishes, including the original Paella Valenciana (Classic Paella with Shellfish, Chicken and Pork). *Ollas* or stews, where everything—beans, potatoes, pork and sausages—is cooked together, are very popular.

The coastline of País Valenciano starts on the north with the town of Vinaroz, renowned for its delicious shrimp. Some say they are the finest in Spain (though on the southwest coast, Sanlúcar assuredly claims that honor). Just south of Vinaroz are the seaside resorts of Benicarló and Peñíscola, also well known for their shellfish.

The area around Castellón de la Plana is an ocean of orange trees and great agricultural wealth. The cooking here is quite similar to Catalonia's in its fisherman-style dishes, such as Fish Stew with Potatoes, Costa Brava Style ("Suquet" de Pescado), a stew of many varieties of fish, with a *sofrito* and *picada.*

One great dish from La Plana is *arròs a banda* (rice on the side), so called because the rice is cooked in a stock made from the local fish and shellfish, and is then served "on the side." As with all seafood rices *a la marinera,* or "fishermen's style," this is accompanied by a Garlic Mayonnaise (Allioli) sauce. I personally find that the powerful taste of garlic rather overwhelms the delicate flavors of the dish; but the tradition comes from the old days, when *arròs a banda* was a two-course meal and the fish was served after the rice. Of course, it had very little flavor left after cooking for a long time to make the stock—hence it needed a strong sauce.

The area around the city of Valencia is called La Huerta, or the vegetable garden. It is the birthplace of paella and has the most representative gastronomy of the region. Despite its worldwide fame the dish is not very old, probably no more than 200 years. In the early days it was a Lenten dish made with vegetables, codfish and snails. Some inventive farmer must have come up with the idea of adding a little meat from his barnyard to make it more festive. As it became adopted by restaurants, other more sophisticated ingredients were added, such as shellfish and even lobster, thus reaching the peak of refinement (and price!). Originally it was prepared over a wood fire, often made with vine cuttings. Even today, a *true* paella party is cooked outdoors—always by men—and served right from the paella pan.

The name paella originates from the utensil in which the dish is cooked—the Catalan word for skillet. Made of iron, it is round and shallow with two handles, and usually quite large, since paella is a dish for many. At home, it should always be cooked on top of the stove, though restaurants often bake it because it is faster.

The secret to a successful paella is the rice. Some cooks seem to attribute more importance to the other ingredients, but it is these that must contribute their flavor to the rice. It is essential to use short-grain rice, which is tastier than long-grain; the Italian-style rice, particularly the Arborio, works very well. Valencia's cuisine abounds with rice dishes other than paella, and recipes for some are included in this book.

Lake Albufera, just south of Valencia, is a source of excellent fish, especially its unique eels, which are the basis for some delicious preparations. One of my favorites is *all-i-pebre d'anguilas* (garlic-and-pepper of eels), where the eels are simply poached with garlic, hot pepper and paprika *(pebre roig)*, accompanied by potatoes. The area is also well known for the quality of its ducks, and another classic dish is *arròs al forn amb ànec de l'Albufera* (baked rice with Albufera duck).

Alicante is the home of *turrones,* those terrific candies which become an obligatory treat at Christmas. The cities of Jijona and Alicante—capital of the province—gave the name to *turrón de Jijona* and *de Alicante,* the two most typical. The basis for *turrón* is almonds, honey and egg white, but there are many different variations. *Alicante,* my favorite, is similar to the French nougat but harder.

Farther south is the historic city of Elche, the date capital of Spain. Indeed, it has more than a million date palms, the highest concentration in all of Europe.

MURCIA

A small region nestled between Valencia and Andalucía, Murcia is best known for the cooking of its coastal area—especially the Mar Menor in the north—and of its Huerta Murciana, the fertile vegetable gardens along the banks of the Segura River. A third cuisine, of the Serranía or mountain range inland, is less important; it is shepherd style, with close ties to La Mancha. The best part is its sausages and meats, which combine to make *pastel murciano*—a pie dating to the sixteenth century, filled with chopped meats, onion and spices, and covered with puff pastry—quite reminiscent of the Moroccan *bastilla*.

The Mar Menor (smaller sea), at the mouth of the Segura River, provides the area with its famous salt flats. A specialty here is *pescado a la sal*, or fish baked in salt, derived from a very ancient method of cooking. A whole fish is packed in a thick coating of coarse salt and baked; the salt forms an insulating cover and keeps the fish moist inside. The system is very simple but requires absolutely fresh fish. I particularly enjoy it with the tasty Mediterranean *dorada* and *lubina* (sea bass). The dish is found all over Spain, so if you have an opportunity, you must try it!

Also worth tasting is *arroz en caldero*, named after the deep cauldron, *caldero*, used by the fishermen to cook it. It is a fish rice similar to the Valencian *arròs a banda* but with the dried red peppers *nyoras*.

While the cooking of Mar Menor consists of simple preparations of the excellent local produce, that of the Huerta Murciana is more elaborate. It is based mostly on vegetables, for this is probably the wealthiest vegetable garden of Spain. Its red peppers, *pimientos morrones*, are the ones usually canned and exported. Great salads abound; I have fond memories of boat rides along the Murcian coast and of the salads we made, which the rocking of the boat seemed to mix in a special way—they were unparalleled!

Gazpacho murciano is a variation of the classic cold Andalusian soup. The ingredients are not puréed but cut in small dice, mixed with water, vinegar and olive oil, and sprinkled with dried oregano.

Finally, one of my favorite Murcian dishes is *cordero en ajo cabañil:* lamb and thinly sliced potatoes fried in olive oil are combined with a *majado* (mashed mixture) of raw chopped garlic, hot paprika and vinegar. Disarmingly simple, earthy and delicious.

A landmark of Murcian cuisine is Rincón de Pepe, a restaurant in the city of Murcia where you can try an array of the local produce and specialties. Raimundo González-Frutos has done a fantastic job of gathering and developing the classic recipes from the region's cuisine.

ANDALUCÍA

This southernmost region is the only one in Spain with a coast on both the Mediterranean Sea and the Atlantic Ocean. Separated from the central plateau of Castile by the mountain range of Sierra Morena, it is full of light and sunshine.

Andalusian cuisine is, together with Catalan, the oldest in Spain, documented since the thirteenth century; yet its cuisine has been neglected until recently.

The Arabic Influence

Probably the most important fact in Andalucía's gastronomic history is that it developed from the Arabic culture (with Roman roots). The tenth through the twelfth centuries saw the greatest splendor in the history of the Islamic world, and of Europe, in Córdoba—headquarters of the Califato or seat of the Arabic empire in Spain until the mid-thirteenth century—and later in Granada. Moreover, almost simultaneously, Jewish culture reached its peak in Spain.

At one point, all of Spain except the northern belt was under Islamic domination and influence. The part of the country occupied by the Arabs was known as Al-Andalus, hence the name Andalucía. This was the region where they stayed the longest (800 years) and which they loved the most. The great poets of Al-Andalus have left us a beautiful legacy of poems in praise of wine, women and ephebes (young boys), three of life's pleasures they thoroughly enjoyed—the last two in the open, the first discreetly, as it was forbidden to them.

The Desserts

The Arabic influence is perhaps most notable in the desserts. It is because of the Arab tradition that Spanish pastry making today is based 90 percent on almonds. *Mazapán,* or marzipan, originally an Arab product, is made with almonds and sugar. Another of their legacies is *almíbar,* or sugar syrup, which made their desserts especially sweet.

The use of egg yolks in Spanish desserts seems to have originated in Jerez, because the egg whites were used to clarify sherry wines. The yolks were traditionally given as charity to convents, where nuns made their little custards, *natillas,* Egg Caramel Tarts (Tocinillos de Cielo), and so on, with them.

Oranges, perhaps the most Spanish of all fruits, were brought to Spain by the Arabs. Not only meant for desserts, they were also used in savory dishes such as Chicken in Orange and Mint Sauce (Pollo con Salsa de Naranja y Menta).

Sevilla, Port of Entry from the New World

Sevilla welcomes the traveler with the charm of its baroque buildings, a reminder that in the sixteenth and seventeenth centuries it was one of the most opulent cities in Europe. After the discovery of America, its harbor on the Guadalquivir River was the gateway to Europe. It was through Sevilla that America's products, such as potatoes, corn, peppers, tomatoes, most dried beans, pineapple, avocado, peanuts and chocolate, arrived in Europe.

One famous old dish that evolved after America's discovery is gazpacho. It was originally the white Ajo Blanco de Málaga (Cold White Gazpacho from Málaga with Garlic and Almonds), made with bread, garlic, olive oil, vinegar and almonds; then tomatoes were substituted for almonds in Salmorejo de Córdoba (Thick Gazpacho from Córdoba), and later peppers and cucumbers were added for the classic Gazpacho Rojo de Sevilla (Cold Soup from Seville with Tomatoes and Vegetables) recipe.

Sherry wine vinegar is an ingredient I find irreplaceable in gazpacho as well as in some salads and marinades for the distinct flavor and fragrance it imparts. It has been used in Spain, especially in Andalucía, for many years. Fortunately, it has recently caught on in international cuisine, so today it is widely available in specialty stores and fine markets.

Andalucía and Its Tapas

Sevilla is also the place to go for *tapas,* which may be the most fun part of Andalusian cuisine. Before lunch and dinnertime, you will see bars and taverns fill up with friendly groups who carry on animated conversations while nibbling on small portions of anything edible, from almonds and olives to tiny fried fish or boiled shellfish, *serrano* ham or sausages, fried fish roe, potato omelet, small casseroles of stews such as kidneys and tripe and any combination imaginable. They are having *tapas*—tasting the establishment's specialties while chatting with friends over a glass of wine, often a chilled fino sherry.

The origin of the word *tapa,* which literally means cover, seems to go back to the middle of the last century, from the name given to the slice of ham, cheese or bread used to cover the wineglass served to the horsemen as they arrived at the roadside inn tired and thirsty. The *tapa* protected the wineglass from dust or rain. In fact, the *tapa* was free—the patron paid only for the wine, which of course would be the famous *jerez* or sherry, the perfect accompaniment.

The variety of *tapas* is almost as extensive as the entire Spanish gastronomy. A whole dinner may be turned into a *tapas* menu, simply by making smaller portions; I usually call *all* of my Spanish buffet meals *tapas* dinners! Many recipes in this book can be prepared as *tapas.* Try some of the dishes in the Appetizers and First Courses chapter, any cold salads, seafood preparations like Prawn Toast (Tosta de Gambas) or Mediterranean Fish Cake (Pastel de Pescado Mediterráneo), meat stews such as Bean Stew with Sausages, Asturian Style (Fabada Asturiana) or Tripe with Garbanzo Beans, Ham and Sausage, Galician Style (Callos a la Gallega), vegetables like Artichoke Stew with Pine Nuts (Alcachofas con Piñones) or Cabbage Torte (Pastel de Col), and serve them at your next buffet dinner with one or two of the breads found in the chapter on Breads and Pastry Doughs. Assuredly, you will have a successful *tapas* party.

Of course you can enjoy *tapas* all over Spain, from Andalucía to Basque Country, but perhaps Sevilla is the only city where the best restaurants are *tapas* bars, offering an amazing assortment. I've never seen faster waiters; they need to be, because of the small portions and the variety one patron alone will consume. To keep track, trust prevails; the waiter will just ask what you had and charge for whatever you say. Some bars have a selection of small *tapas (pinchitos* or *banderillas,* combinations of three or four tidbits skewered with a toothpick) all priced the same, and the waiter will count the toothpicks at the end to add up your check. Sometimes he will draw a line on a chalkboard for every portion you order, adding up the lines at the end.

The art of frying reaches the peak of perfection in the *tapas* bars of the cities of Cádiz and Málaga. Nowhere else will you find the tiny fish deep-fried to a dry, crunchy outside and moist inside without any trace of oil. Indeed, not even the best tempura I have had in Japan can match the extraordinary taste of the Andalusian *pescadito frito.*

The King of Hams: Jabugo

Pork has been a staple of Spanish gastronomy since Roman times, and curing its meat to make ham and sausages is an art that enjoyed a high social status in Spain for generations. In fact, for centuries pork was the only source of protein in many areas of Spain; the survival of a whole family often depended on preserving its meat to make it last throughout the year.

Jabugo is a little village seventy-five miles north of Huelva, nestled in the high peaks of the western end of the Sierra Morena mountain range. The name *jamón serrano* is given to the excellent Spanish cured mountain hams, for which Jabugo has the best reputation. Around the village there are plenty of leafy oak forests which provide the acorns the black Iberian pig, *cerdo ibérico,* loves to eat, and a cool mountain climate indispensable for curing the hams. The placid Iberian pig, originally related to the wild boar, at one time was found all over the Peninsula and the Balearic Islands; but today this breed abounds only in some areas of Andalucía and Extremadura. It produces the best hams because it has more veins of fine fat intermingled in its meat than any other kind of pig.

January and February are the best months to visit Jabugo: it's the peak season for the *matanza,* the pig butchering, an occasion for great festivities in the whole area. As a child, I never quite understood why there was a big party centered around the killing of a pig—until I read about its historic and religious connotation: it was a way for the Christians to differentiate themselves from the Jews and Arabs.

The *matanza* is an important gastronomic event which usually lasts three days. The *mataor* or butcher and the *matancera,* his female partner, are the orchestrators of the task, which calls for the help of everybody in the family and more. Everyone gets a job, from washing the tripe and intestines (a delicate chore assigned to the *matancera)* to chopping onions and garlic, baking bread for the sausages, building a fire or even making coffee. And intertwined with the work is the partying at night, feasts with classic, earthy, rather indigestible menus, all of it washed down with generous amounts of wine and spirits, notably the rough *aguardientes* obtained from pure unmatured distillation.

The process of curing the hams takes at least fifteen months and up to three years. First they are stored in salt for fifteen to twenty days, then washed and hung in drying rooms to exude the fat, and finally transferred to dark, humid cellars for maturing. *Chorizos, caña de lomo* and all sausages except the salami-style ones are smoked for about two months in dark rooms with terracotta-tile floors, watered down to maintain an 80 to 85 percent humidity, and an oak fire in the middle. The smell of those thousands of appetizing sausages hanging from the ceiling is irresistible!

Bullfights

Another animal unique to Spain and native to Andalucía is the Iberian bull or *toro ibérico*. The origin of *corridas* or bullfights is obscure; some historians attribute it to the Cretan bullfighting, but that had a different purpose. While in old Crete it was purely an acrobatic game, in Spain the goal has always been to confront man and beast in a deadly struggle. The *corridas* started in the sixteenth or seventeenth century as a horseman's game, a legacy of the medieval jousts, for the *matador* or bullfighter was on horseback. The eighteenth century saw the great development of cattle ranches in Andalucía, and with it the peak of bullfighting. *Rejoneadores,* or bullfighters on horseback, were until the late eighteenth century much more popular than *toreros,* the bullfighters on foot. Today it is the other way around.

The bull's meat is highly appreciated in Spain and quite in demand after a *corrida. Estofado de rabo de toro* is a bull-tail stew which I have enjoyed especially at El Caballo Rojo restaurant in Córdoba. One popular delicacy is *criadillas,* euphemistically called here Rocky Mountain oysters and in France *rognons blancs*—they are in fact the bull's testicles.

EXTREMADURA

Situated to the far west of the country, north of Andalucía, this region is one of the least inhabited of Spain. Many of the Spanish *conquistadores*— Pizarro, Hernán Cortés, Orellana, Cabeza de Vaca—came from Extremadura. It is a land of mountains and oak forests, dry climate in the summer and little rain in the winter.

The cuisine of Extremadura was chronicled as early as the sixteenth century by the monasteries. A very important cookbook of the time, that of the Benedictine monks of the Alcántara Monastery in Cáceres, was stolen and taken to France during the Napoleonic invasion of 1808. In fact, one of Auguste Escoffier's classic recipes, partridge *à la mode d'Alcántara,* has its origin in that cookbook. Another French classic, consommé, is also said to have developed from a recipe in the book, *consumido.*

Sheep are plentiful in the mountains around Badajoz; they are the basis for the shepherd-style lamb stew *caldereta de pastor.* Another shepherd's dish, *migas* (literally, bread crumbs), found all through La Mancha to Murcia, is also very popular here, especially for breakfast. It is made in an iron pot, where some chopped garlic and green peppers have previously been sautéed. Day-old bread soaked in water is drained and crumbled, added to the pot and sautéed until golden. The dish is served with olives, grapes, uncured bacon, chorizo or other pork sausages. In Murcia I've indulged in it for breakfast with hot chocolate. Delicious!

The little town of Villanueva de la Serena, east of Badajoz, held the famous archives of La Mesta, which governed the routes of the nomadic shepherds from the thirteenth to the seventeenth or eighteenth century. In 1248, King Alphonse X the Wise established the "Honorable *Mesta* Council of Castile's Shepherds" to protect the shepherds and their flocks from thieves during their periodic migrations to the north and south of Spain in summer and winter. A shepherd-style cuisine developed along these routes, and its influence in the area's gastronomy has remained to this day.

My favorite Extremaduran cheese is *queso de los Ibores,* a buttery, rich and mellow fresh goat cheese made in the area of Los Ibores in northeast Cáceres. It is also called *pimientonado* because the rind is usually brushed with oil and coated with paprika.

CASTILLA–LA MANCHA

The Shepherd's Cuisine: Lamb and Game

The shepherd's legacy is most notable in this extensive region. La Mancha has an old, sturdy, dry-land farming cuisine, with pastoral recipes dating from the thirteenth century.

Gazpachos de pastor or *gazpachos manchegos,* found all over La Mancha, Extremadura and west Valencia, have nothing to do with the Andalusian cold vegetable soup gazpacho. They are made from whatever game the shepherds have on hand—hare, rabbit, partridge—together with ham, some mountain herbs, mushrooms, tomatoes and peppers. They are eaten with the *torta,* a heavy flour-and-water dough cooked on a stone hot from the fire; half the *torta* is broken into the pot and mixed with the gazpachos, and the other half is used as a spoon, in pieces. It is not a light meal—but certainly tasty.

The cuisine of La Mancha is limited, yet you can eat magnificently; it has the most abundant small game of all Spain. It is said that one good reason why King Philip II established Madrid as Spain's capital in the sixteenth century was because it was a convenient meeting point for his hunting parties.

Pisto manchego, a La Mancha classic, is found in many areas of Spain. It is the equivalent of the Catalan *samfaina* and the French ratatouille, only the vegetables are cut smaller and cooked longer. *Pisto* can be a delicious accompaniment to scrambled eggs or white rice, or to salt codfish in *bacalao a la manchega.*

Don Quijote, the "Man of La Mancha"

La Mancha is the land of Cervantes' Don Quijote, and the influence of this character in the area's history is extraordinary. Cervantes was, in fact, a satiric genius; he ridiculed his society and the establishment in a most subtle and effective way. The *hidalguía* or nobility was such that the hidalgos (noblemen) were not supposed to work, for they regarded work as improper; so they were mostly poor, but had to pretend to wealth. They were thin, like Don Quijote, because they starved. Paradoxically, while Spain dominated the world in the sixteenth and seventeenth centuries, there was tremendous hunger among its people. To conceal it, some hidalgos would sprinkle bread crumbs over their beards before leaving home, as if they had just finished a banquet, and they would walk around with a toothpick.

Marzipan

Mazapán de Toledo is quite famous all over Spain. Legend has it that marzipan originated in the thirteenth century in the San Clemente nuns' convent of Toledo, during a siege of the city. Since bread was scarce, the nuns made a dough as a substitute for it, using the staples they had on hand—almonds and sugar. They called it *mazapán* or club bread, because it was hard as a club!

Little nuns' stories aside (Italians wouldn't agree with it anyway), the origin of marzipan is definitely Arab; their *maysaban* was a confection made with dried fruits and sugar, a very Islamic combination. But the craftsmanship of Toledo confectioners gave *mazapán* its fame and prestige. It is a treat to visit a marzipan shop there—my favorite is La Positiva, in Bargas—and watch the little figurines being shaped. They are baked briefly in a hot wood-fired oven, dipped in a sugar syrup *(almíbar)* and dried.

Manchego Cheese

Manchego is La Mancha's—and maybe Spain's—most famous cheese. It is made from sheep's milk and can range from *tierno* or tender—fresh, mellow and snow-white—to *seco* (dry), dark yellow and hard, with intense sheep taste and a little piquant. The one mostly found in this country is the *semiseco,* mild and very tasty.

Saffron, "the Gold of La Mancha"

This is also the land of saffron, the costliest spice in the world. Traveling through the plains of La Mancha in late October, you will see the fields covered with a colorful purple hue. It is from the hundreds of thousands of saffron flowers growing in small plots, alternating with the naked, just-harvested vineyards.

The world's finest-quality saffron is produced in Spain—mainly in the provinces of Albacete, Ciudad Real, Cuenca and Toledo—and the best is

Mancha Superior. The harvest of "the rose," as the saffron flower is called, lasts approximately twenty days starting around October 15, the feast day of St. Theresa—and it is the occasion for great celebrations. The little towns organize competitions, and the old men judge the youngsters' skill in peeling "the rose."

Native to the Orient, saffron arrived in Spain via the Arabs (azafrán, Spanish for saffron, derives from the Arabic word za'faran or yellow) although the Romans were already using it as a dye and spreading it on the floor to perfume their orgy rooms. Today, the red pistils of the purple saffron flower are highly appreciated in fine cuisine. And maybe the price won't seem as high when you consider the enormous amount of labor necessary to produce saffron.

Each flower has 3 pistils, and they have to be harvested daily, early in the morning, or the sun will spoil them. The men harvest the flowers, their backs bent over for hours, and the women peel them the same day—an exhausting task they perform while singing around a table. An experienced "peeler" will do a maximum of 2 to 3 ounces a day, or about 10,000 flowers. Then the pistils must be dried in the evening without delay, a process which will reduce the crop to one quarter of its size.

If kept in airtight containers, away from heat and cold, light, and above all humidity, saffron will keep for several years. The La Mancha farmers treat it just like gold; they store it and sell it in time of need.

I always prefer to use saffron in threads—I buy it in Spain at about $1/gram—rather than powdered, as the latter is more likely to be adulterated. Besides, the visual effect of the threads is much better. It is a good idea to mash it a bit with a mortar and pestle, and always cook it in a warm liquid for at least 5 minutes, to release the flavor further. Never use it in excess, or it will impart a medicinal flavor; a small amount will go a long way. And when you do use it, you will appreciate it even more if you think of the La Mancha farmers who went through so much effort to produce it.

MADRID

The capital of Spain, itself a small autonomous region as of 1982, is the center of all the regional cuisines of the country; all, that is, except Catalan. Catalonia has traditionally kept its cooking within its boundaries, and its representation in Madrid restaurants is quite minimal.

Madrileños love to wine and dine and have a good time. They make friends easily; it is said that in Barcelona it takes you much longer to make a friend, but when you do it's a friend forever—in Madrid you make a friend in a minute, but the friendship may only last for the day. The city has excellent restaurants and hotels as well as great entertainment, from cabarets and flamenco dancing to theater and museums. Chateo (meaning chato-hopping, from chato or small glass) is a favorite pastime. I've always had a terrific time in Madrid, and can happily use any excuse to spend a few days there.

A classic dish of Madrid cuisine is *cocido madrileño,* a delicious stew pot from the nineteenth century which blends meats, marrow and sausages *(chorizo* and *morcilla)* with cabbage, carrots, chick-peas and potatoes for a three-course meal of soup, vegetables and meats. *Besugo al horno* (baked sea bream) is a simple preparation with lemon and oil, designed to enhance the fresh taste of this excellent fish. *Callos a la madrileña,* a favorite *tapa* as well as a main course, is tripe stewed with ham and sausages, onion, garlic, paprika and spices.

Madrid has as much tradition in *tapas* as Andalucía; a *tapas* tour of Madrid can be an unforgettable experience. There are still, in the downtown quarter near the Plaza Mayor, old inns *(mesones)* and hostelries *(posadas)* from the sixteenth and seventeenth centuries, with an entrance for the horse-drawn carriages, since the guests came in stagecoaches. The typical streets Cava Baja, Cuchilleros and Arco de Cuchilleros are full of earthy *tapas* bars, among them the popular Cuevas de Luis Candelas (Caves of Luis Candelas, a legendary bandit of the time); the delightful Posada de la Villa, an old three-story inn, beautifully restored and a fine restaurant, too; and Casa Botín, home of Madrid's most celebrated roasted suckling pig and a haunt of Hemingway, who made it famous in *Death in the Afternoon.*

Other Madrid landmarks in that area are Lhardy, which has been serving *cocido madrileño* since 1920, along with an array of wonderful *tapas;* and the old *Valentín,* started in 1899 by Valentín Fernández and run today by his son Félix, where you will eat the best *cocido* in the entire city. No matter how many wonderful new restaurants Madrid has, I always treasure the experience of a *tapas* dinner in the picturesque old section of the city.

CASTILLA-LEÓN

This region embraces the ancient kingdoms of Old Castile and León, a vast land rich in history and tradition which extends through the northern part of the Castilian Plateau. To the northwest, it is flanked by the Montes de León, a mountain range where good cheese abounds.

The *hornos de asar* (literally, baking ovens), establishments specializing in serving *asados,* the roasted local meats, are probably the most important gastronomic heritage of the region. They are particularly typical of three provinces: Segovia, Valladolid and Burgos. Originally, *hornos de asar* were bread bakeries which used the Arabic *hornos de bóveda,* conically shaped adobe ovens where the fire is banked on one side and the heat circulates around. It was the custom, and still is, to take a young lamb to the bakery for roasting; bakeries use dried vine shoots to heat the fire and do a much better job of roasting than can be done in most homes, where ovens are often either too small or nonexistent.

Roasted young animals such as lamb or suckling pigs are a true delicacy here. Nowhere can they bake a *lechazo,* the tender baby lamb fed only with its mother's milk, the way they do in Old Castile. And *tostón* or *cochinillo,* a suckling pig of about 8 pounds, is a specialty of the region, enjoyed by the Castilian kings of the fifteenth century. The quality test was—and still is—to carve it with the edge of a plate to prove its tenderness.

Segovia is well known for its Roman aqueduct, the finest example of Roman construction in Spain, as well as for its almost-as-famous restaurant alongside it, Mesón de Cándido. Cándido López, the "Great Innkeeper of Castile," has served delicious roasted suckling pig and other specialties at his restaurant since 1931. Duque, the oldest *mesón* or country restaurant in Segovia, started by Dionisio Duque in 1895, is another favorite.

Sepúlveda, just northeast of Segovia and seventy miles from Madrid, is a particularly lovely town. I have enjoyed many a dish of roast lamb in its casual *hornos de asar;* my favorites are Cristóbal and Tinín. Also worthy of a visit is the charming village Pedraza de la Sierra, just a two-hour ride from Madrid. Walking through the beautifully kept cobblestone streets and peeking through the windows of the old farmhouses is a journey to days long past. Pedraza is the second residence of many wealthy *madrileños,* who have fortunately guarded it from being spoiled.

Castile is also the land of bread. The round loaves, crusty and golden on the outside and pure white inside, are made from the high-quality wheat grown all over the region. It is a compact bread, very tasty and quite different from any other I've had.

A legacy from the Arabs is *escabeche,* a way of sautéing and marinating fish or fowl with lemon or vinegar to preserve it. Originally *escabeches* were made along the Mediterranean coast, using the local fish; gradually they moved inland and today they are a specialty of northern Castile. The word comes from the Arab *sikbaj,* a word of Persian origin meaning acid food, as mentioned in the book *Thousand and One Nights.* I've had the best *escabeches* ever at Mesón de la Villa in Aranda de Duero, where Eugenio and Seri Herrero serve their famous *escabechados*—chicken, partridge, quail, rabbit, or whatever is in season. Mussels and trout also make excellent *escabeches,* and so do vegetables such as zucchini.

The area around Palencia, Valladolid and Zamora, north of the Duero River, is the fertile Tierra de Campos. The wide variety of vegetables provides the raw material for the delicious *menestra de verduras,* which I have enjoyed here as much as farther east, in Navarra and Rioja. This same area is a paradise for small game such as doves and pigeons; they are stewed like larger game, in their own blood, and cooked with vegetables.

An important specialty of Tierra de Campos is its fresh white or dry cheese de Villalón or Pata de Mulo (donkey's leg, named after its shape), made from raw sheep's milk and native to the town of Villalón, near Valladolid. Other Castilian cheeses worth mentioning are the fresh white Burgos, made from sheep's milk, soft and moist; León, a cured cheese from sheep's milk found all over Old Castile, with a characteristic almondy flavor; and Zamora, a Manchego-style cheese which is more available and less expensive than the original Manchego.

In sum, the pantry of Old Castile is humble and sparse, yet tasty and hearty, preserving the natural flavors in a simple but nutritious way.

GALICIA

Galicia may be the most striking region of all Spain. To start with, the Galicians are Celts, therefore different from the rest of the Peninsula, which is of mostly Iberian ancestry. Their character is also unique: they are individualistic, epicurean, tradition-bound, cynical and great conversationalists. They are more Irish than Spanish! They are also good drinkers; while Spain's wine consumption is 15 gallons per capita, Galicia's is 35. The region even has its own language, *gallego* or Galician, similar to Portuguese.

Situated in the farthest northwest corner of the Iberian Peninsula, Galicia still maintains its ancestral purity, the small villages and country farms that add a colorful note to the green landscape. Driving around the region, one is startled by the lush, extraordinarily green and beautiful countryside. It has a very high rainfall and mild climate, tempered by the ocean currents. Everything grows there—from kiwis and avocados to *grelos,* the delicious greens that are a specialty of their cuisine.

The Camino de Santiago

Santiago de Compostela is the political, spiritual, religious and educational center of the region—a city full of history, named after Santiago or St. James the Greater, the patron saint of Spain. The city's origin goes back to the early days of the Reconquista, the Christians' "reconquest" of Spain from the Moors, who had invaded the country in the year 711. The Reconquista started soon after in Asturias, the region next to Galicia, and lasted nearly eight centuries, until 1492. The Arabs never established themselves in northern Spain; hence they left no influence on that area's gastronomy.

In the beginning, the Reconquista was not progressing very well. The Moors had a strong motivation, their religion; the Christians didn't—until, in the year 813, some fishermen claimed to have found the remains of the Apostle Santiago. The impact was great, and it gave the Christians a symbol, a spiritual reason to fight the Moors.

Around the eleventh century the Church issued a bull granting dispensation for all sins to those who would travel to Santiago and revere the Apostle's remains. This created the Camino de Santiago, or route followed by the pilgrims through northern Spain and France, and even from Germany. The Camino was a very important means of cultural and gastronomical communication; it brought foods and customs back and forth from other parts of Spain—and most important, from Europe.

The Gastronomy: A Wealth of Shellfish

With its 800 miles of winding coastline, Galicia has the longest exposure to the ocean of any Spanish region; thus its cuisine is based on seafood. Galician shellfish, in fact, is the most appreciated all over Spain.

The Galician coast also provides some spectacular landscapes, with its *rías* or deep bays similar to the Norwegian fiords. The tiny island of La Toja, inside the Arosa *ría,* is a paradisaical spot. A little farther south lies the village of Bayona and its famous Parador Nacional, with a breathtaking view over the Vigo *ría* and the ocean. It is a real treat to let an afternoon go by while sitting enjoying the scenery together with a sampling of the marvelous local shellfish—especially the *vieiras* (scallops), which in Galicia are a true delicacy. They are always eaten with the coral (roe), and served in their own shell; the most traditional way to prepare them is *a la gallega,* or Galician style, baked with oil, wine, onions and bread crumbs, a simple recipe based on the freshness of the scallop itself.

Shellfish in Galicia is prepared very simply, so as to enhance its high quality. The most wonderful crab, lobsters, mussels, squid, *percebes* (goose barnacles), *cigalas,* which are similar to a Mediterranean lobster but the size of a large prawn, *zamburiñas* (small scallops) and many others are simply grilled, steamed or boiled. There is also an array of clams and oysters of many types, which are for the most part eaten raw, sprinkled with some lemon juice.

An experience I'll never forget was going to gather oysters from their own beds in the *bateas,* in the Arosa *ría* near Villagarcía. *Bateas* are like large stationary barges, made from cement and wood, with ropes hanging from them where mussels or oysters grow. We took a small boat early in the morning and, armed with a knife and some lemons, cut the oysters out and ate them with lemon juice right on the boat. A bottle of fresh *alvarinho* wine proved an exceptional accompaniment.

Another very popular mollusk in Galicia is *pulpo* or octopus. Probably the thought of eating an animal with many slippery legs is unappetizing to the American mind; but in fact Spanish octopus is much tastier than any I've tried here. The preparation requires quite a bit of work, for you have to pound octopus vigorously for a long time to tenderize it. I remember when, in my childhood, my brothers would catch octopus in the summertime—it was much to the family cook's distress, as she knew hard work was in store for her!

One of the most common ways to cook octopus is *a feira,* or festive style—so called because it is eaten traditionally at village fairs—just dressed with some olive oil and paprika.

Inland, the peasant cooking uses the basic farm produce in the nourishing *caldo gallego* (Galician broth), a homey meal-in-a-pot that combines pork and other local meats with potatoes, dried beans and vegetables. In the Galician specialty *lacón con grelos,* the greens are cooked with the famous *lacón,* or foreleg of the tasty local pork.

Empanada gallega (Galician pie) is another classic preparation, perhaps their best-known dish. It can be filled with meats such as chicken, veal, rabbit or pork; with fish such as sardines, eel or tuna; or with any shellfish. One of my favorites, and a little more unusual, is Anchovy and Onion Pie (Empanada de Anchoas).

Some of the best Spanish cheeses come from Galicia, all made from cow's milk. My favorites are Tetilla (little breast, after its shape), pale yellow, semi-soft, mild and flavorful; and San Simón, pear-shaped, semi-firm and creamy, delicately smoked, white and with reddish orange rind.

Two of my favorite Galician desserts are the almond tart *(tarta de almendras)* and Santiago Almond Torte (Tarta de Santiago); both have an almond base, but the first is different in that it has no flour, just a rich filling of ground almonds mixed with egg, sugar and grated lemon peel. And an excellent end to any meal is Witch's Brew (Queimada), with or instead of coffee.

ASTURIAS

East of Galicia is the Principality of Asturias, from which the heir to the Spanish crown gets his name. The current Prince of Asturias is King Juan Carlos's son, Felipe. The title dates back to 1388, when King Juan I of Castile granted it to his son as a wedding gift, and it has been handed down ever since to the heirs of the Kingdom of Castile. Asturias is also famous as the place where the Reconquista started: in Covadonga, a mountain refuge 50 miles east of Oviedo.

This is dried beans country, and the best-known dish is Bean Stew with Sausages, Asturian Style (Fabada Asturiana), a hearty stew which combines dried beans *(fabes)* with the *compango*—pork, chorizo and blood sausages. There is a definite resemblance between *fabada* and the French cassoulet of Carcassonne—one more influence from the Camino de Santiago pilgrims.

Asturias is rich in apples and cider, used to delicately garnish and flavor their excellent fish in the classic preparation *merluza a la sidra* (hake in a cider sauce).

The greatest variety of cheeses in the country is found all along the northern belt of Spain, in Galicia, Asturias, León, Cantabria and País Vasco; but Asturias is probably the country's single top producer. Its most famous cheese is named Picón after the Picos de Europa, and it is made in several little villages in that part of the Cantabrian mountain range. It is an outstanding blue-veined cheese made from a mixture of cow's, sheep's and goat's milk, wrapped in chestnut leaves and kept in humid caves where air circulates naturally. It is creamy and soft, with intense aroma and sharp taste, ranking right up there with Gorgonzola and Roquefort in quality. The best known is Cabrales-Picón, made in the village of Cabrales.

Asturian cows also provide the best milk in Spain, a basic ingredient in *arroz con leche* (rice pudding). This is a very popular dessert throughout Spain, but particularly famous in this area.

CANTABRIA

Santander, the capital of Cantabria—the region east of Asturias—is an important port and fishing center. Sardines, tuna, bonito and anchovies are among the best in Spain. The charming seaside village of Laredo, just east of Santander, is the main fishing center as well as the tourist capital of the beautiful Costa Verde (Green Coast), now also known as the Cornisa Cantábrica. It is home as well of the excellent Risco restaurant, high on a hill overlooking the entire village, where I enjoyed an old dish from the Laredo fishermen: *pollo marino* (sea-style chicken), a euphemism for a tuna or bonito preparation from a time when chicken used to be more expensive than fish—certainly the other way around today!

Laredo is particularly well known for its *besugo* (sea bream), which, in the old days, was shipped to Madrid in carts, packed with lemon for preservation. From this derives the custom practiced all over Spain of baking that fish with half slices of lemon stuck on top of it.

If you are in the area during the hunting season, don't miss trying venison from deer of the local reserve, which is marinated and cooked in red wine with a rich, dark sauce.

PAÍS VASCO (BASQUE COUNTRY)

Spanish Basque Country and its language are today known throughout Spain by their original Basque names—Euskadi and *euskera*. This is one of the most significant regions in the country, with a long history and great gastronomic tradition.

Basque and Catalan are undoubtedly the main cuisines in Spain today. But one big difference between them is that, while Basques have always exported theirs, we Catalans never took ours outside of the region. There are Basque restaurants all over Spain, and in the United States too, but few Catalan ones.

Fish has traditionally been very important in Basque cuisine. For centuries the people have lived off the ocean's produce, not only from the nearby waters but farther away too. First fishing for whales and then for cod, they arrived in Newfoundland—even before Columbus discovered America. The old dish *marmitako* originated from the way Basque fishermen cooked tuna, bonito and other fish on board. In the beginning it was made with bread. After America's discovery, potatoes were substituted for bread and later peppers and tomato were added. A great restaurant in which to eat *marmitako* is the long-established Nicolasa in San Sebastián.

Tiny squid *(calamares* or *chipirones)* are made into the only truly black dish in the world, squid in its own ink *(calamares en su tinta).* Here in the United States it is difficult to make the dish *really* black, for the squid are not caught on a hook, as they are in Spain, but with drag nets, and while they are in the net, the squid exude most of their ink.

Bilbao, capital of the Basque province of Vizcaya, is well known for its *bacalao* (salt codfish). I've had the best *bacalao* dishes ever at Genaro Pildaín's historic Guría restaurant. His *bacalao a la vizcaína,* an old recipe for salt codfish cooked in onions and dried red peppers, is famous. There are about 200 recipes to prepare *bacalao,* and you will find at least some in every Bilbao restaurant.

A wonderful Basque dish is *angulas* (baby eels), often prepared *al ajillo* —with garlic and hot peppers, served in boiling hot oil. The best known throughout Spain are those from Aguinaga, a small town 6 miles west of San Sebastián. *Angulas* are found only along the coast of the Bay of Biscay, in Spain and France. The reason is that eels lay their eggs in the Sargasso Sea, and the brood is transported by the Gulf Stream to Europe; they grow up to become adult eels *(anguilas)* in the rivers that flow into the Bay of Biscay, from where they swim back to the Sargasso Sea, and the process starts again. This is why there are no *angulas* in the United States, unfortunately; they are available only frozen or canned—and it just isn't the same thing.

San Sebastián, capital of the Guipúzcoa province, is the tourist as well as gastronomic capital of Basque Country, where the most renowned restaurants are located. It was here in the seventies that a group of young, innovative chefs started the "New Basque Cuisine," promoting their novel ideas with great success. Juan Mari Arzak took charge of Arzak restaurant in the late sixties, and in a few years he made his cuisine famous throughout Spain and abroad. Pedro Subijana opened Akelaŕe restaurant in 1972, and has today become one of Spain's top chefs. Both of these restaurants have a double star in the French Michelin Guide—the only two in Basque Country to have been accorded such an honor.

It was also in San Sebastián that, on January 1, 1900, the first *sociedad gastronómica* (gastronomic society) was born. These are enormously popular in the matriarchal Basque society because they are reserved exclusively for men, who have there a place to gather, a kitchen to cook their own meals and a cellar in which to keep their best wines. The idea has prospered, especially in the last 25 years; in 1950 there were about 200 "gastronomic societies" in the region, and today there are over 1,000!

The atmosphere in these societies is one of equality and harmony. All members have the same status: the mayor may cook for the janitor, and the manager for the laborer. There are no political ideas discussed; fine cooking is enjoyed and friendship promoted.

The area near the French border—notably the village of Zugarramurdi, some 30 miles from San Sebastián—was famous in the old days for its *akelarres*. Witches and sorcerers gathered around a male goat, invoking the devil, during their Saturday evening rituals—which always ended in an orgy. While the *akelarre* was being celebrated, the attendants roasted veal using a cooking method that had its origin in America. It is called *lindo*, a derivation of the name "Indians" given to the region's emigrants who came back from the New World bringing not only silver but American customs as well. Several legs of veal are stuck in the ground around a large fire and turned by hand to cook evenly.

The variety of cheeses in the area is wide and excellent. They are mostly made with sheep's milk and range from the fresh, white and tender curd cheeses, to those cured from raw milk. An array of smoked cheeses is also made there; the most famous—and my favorite—is Idiazábal, yellowish white, firm, with golden rind and an intense smoky flavor with a hint of mountain herbs.

NAVARRA

Traveling south from San Sebastián, you will drive along a winding road through green lush landscapes to Pamplona, the capital of Navarra, immortalized by Hemingway in his book *The Sun Also Rises*. I have enjoyed his wonderfully vivid description of the Sanfermines and the excitement of the running of the bulls the week of July 7 to celebrate the day of San Fermín, the city's patron saint. It is a marathon week of eating and drinking and staying out in the streets all night.

The area around Lodosa, in the south of Navarra, is famous for its red peppers, notably the *pimientos del pico* (peppers of the beak, named after their beak-shaped ends). In September and October, a delicious smell perfumes the air of the little towns as the women roast peppers in front of their houses over wood fires; then they peel and can them, selling the jars for additional income.

Other types of fine red peppers grown in Spain are *choriceros* and *del cuerno*, found mostly in Basque Country, and *morrones* in Aragón and Murcia; but reputedly the finest in all of Spain are *pimientos del pico*.

The northern mountain areas, in the Pyrenees, are a paradise for mushrooms and game, such as dove and quail. Quail are combined with some very special beans, the tender *pochas*—available only at the beginning of the hunting season—in the wonderful fall dish *codornices con pochas*.

One memorable cheese in Navarra is Roncal, named after the Pyrenees valley where it is made, from raw sheep's milk. It is firm, of ivory color, slightly piquant, with a characteristic aroma and flavor.

Pamplona is renowned for its chorizos and other sausages, notably the narrow flavorful *chistorra*. Ever since my first visit there I have been fascinated by the strings of sausages which hang outside the balconies of the homes, together with the red peppers, to dry. A truly colorful sight!

South of Pamplona, the banks of the Ebro River form the fertile area of La Ribera. Here vegetables and fruits grow abundantly, and the easy access to irrigation has made this area very fruitful. The cuisine is primarily based on vegetables; artichokes and asparagus, simply boiled and accompanied by a *vinagreta* sauce, are unique because of the natural flavor of the fresh ingredients.

La Ribera has a famous dish, *caldereta ribereña*, a country-style stew named after the cauldron in which it is made: deep, with three legs so a fire can be built underneath. Obviously an outdoors dish, it is cooked by the peasants and shepherds, and includes anything the land provides: meat and potatoes, maybe a few birds hunted in the morning, eels or trout caught in nearby rivers, some snails, and seasonal vegetables.

The city of Tudela—center of La Ribera—had Hebrew, Islamic and Catholic communities living together from the tenth century on. The Arab and Mediterranean influence is still visible in the way they stuff their morcillas (blood sausages) with pine nuts and raisins, flavoring them with cinnamon.

LA RIOJA

Logroño, the region's capital, is only three miles from Basque Country and the same from Navarra—hence La Rioja's cuisine is intimately joined to that of its two neighbors.

The name Rioja evokes wine; its reds are known all over the world. Curiously, though, *a la riojana* (Rioja-style) dishes do not use any wine, but always some kind of peppers—either red bell peppers, fresh or dry, whole or ground (paprika), or the hot chiles called *guindillas*—and often chorizo.

Patatas a la riojana are a staple of the region. The potatoes are served with enough broth to almost make a soup; generous amounts of paprika and the delicious local chorizo provide a lot of flavor. Other classic *a la riojana* dishes are snails, tripe, pork loin, and salt codfish cooked with tomatoes, onions and potatoes besides the peppers and the tasty chorizo.

The Rioja gardens are well known for their vegetables, and peppers are as important here as they are in Navarra. They are often charbroiled and served as an accompaniment to grilled meats or to the favorite Riojan dish, lamb chops roasted over a fire made with vine cuttings. A wonderful combination are quails stuffed in red peppers *(pimientos rellenos de codornices)*.

Pork is excellent, often cooked quite simply, grilled or charbroiled. The cuisine here is earthy and country style, not too varied but very tasty.

The combination of the Riojan Ribera's fruits and the region's great wines makes for the delicious *melocotones al vino,* whole peaches cooked in red wine. And speaking of wine, the local Spiced Red Wine (Zurracapote) is worth a try.

ARAGÓN

This is a large region, bordering Catalonia and Valencia as well as the Pyrenees and France, Navarra and Castile; therefore its cuisine reflects the influence of these areas. Northern Aragón, around Huesca, is cold and mountainous. I've had many a warming meal there which tasted like heaven after a long day of skiing—peasant-style cooking at its best.

South in the Teruel province, the mountains of Serranía de Albarracín provide ideal conditions to make excellent *serrano* hams, which dry well in the cold mountain winds.

The region's central province, Zaragoza, in the Ebro River Valley, is flat and fertile. Vegetables and fruit trees are plentiful, and the candied fruits made here are very famous. Vineyards and olive trees grow very well, too; Cariñena makes sturdy, full-bodied wines, and Alcañiz produces excellent olive oil. Almond trees provide the basis for *guirlache,* the delicious candy made with caramelized sugar and almonds.

One of the most distinctive preparations is *salmorrejo*—which has nothing to do with the *salmorejo* or gazpacho-style thick soup of Andalucía. Here the name is given to a number of dishes with eggs such as *tortilla al salmorrejo,* an omelet with potatoes and rice covered with a garlic sauce, and *huevos al salmorrejo,* eggs poached with white wine and pork filets, sausages, chorizo, ham and asparagus.

The roasted meats can be excellent, and lamb is plentiful. A traditional way to roast meats, still used today with small animals like rabbits or hare, is *al entierro* or burial style. The animal is not skinned but cleaned, and stuffed with chopped garlic, onion, pork fat, ham and chorizo. Then it is placed in a hole in the ground, covered with earth, and a fire is built over it. When this turns into red-hot coals, an onion is placed on top; as soon as the onion is tender, the animal is cooked. It is then skinned and ready to eat.

BITS
AND
PIECES

OLIVE OIL

Olive oil is indispensable in preparing many of the recipes in this book. It will impart a more authentic "Spanish" flavor to the food than a vegetable oil.

It is the fat most used along the Mediterranean for cooking, a heritage from the Greeks and Romans; the first records of its cultivation date back 6,000 years to the Middle East. It came to Spain through Tarragona from eastern Mediterranean traders, especially the Greeks, in the first millennium B.C. But in northern Spain it was not used until the eighteenth century; before that, Galicia used mostly lard and Basque Country used butter.

Together with Italy, Spain heads the list of olive oil producers in the world; over 5 million acres are dedicated to its cultivation, with an average annual production of 500,000 tons. Most of it is produced in the Andalusian provinces of Jaén, Córdoba and Sevilla, although some of the best olive oil is obtained in Catalonia. The area around the village of Borjas Blancas, east of Lérida, is particularly famous for the quality of its oil and is one of only four olive-producing areas in the country covered and controlled by an Appellation of Origin. So is the area of Siurana, west of Tarragona. Both oils are made from the *arbequina* olive, a small, round, greenish variety which stands out for its low acidity and fine, fruity flavor. The other two Appellations of Origin are in Andalucía: Sierra de Segura and Baena, north and west of Jaén respectively. The first uses the *picual* olives, dark and small; the second grows mostly the *picudo* variety, lighter in color and pointed at the end.

Olive oil is extracted from its fruit by pressing; an olive contains between 18 and 30 percent oil, depending on its ripeness, and an average of 20 to 22 percent oil is obtained in the process. Olive oil can be consumed virgin, which means it has been obtained by cold pressing and not refined; virgin oil has the lowest acidity, from under 1 percent in the extra virgin to under 1.5 percent in the superfine virgin. It has a darker, greener color and much fruitier taste; it is excellent for seasoning salads, but I find it too strong for cooking. Extra virgin olive oil is a special treat and well worth seeking out, even if expensive; buy it from a retailer you trust, so he can guide you to one that will suit your taste.

Refined olive oil has a higher acidity and limpid yellow color. The so-called pure olive oil is a mixture of refined and about 5 to 10 percent of virgin. It is much less expensive, and I find it best for cooking.

When storing olive oil, it is important to keep it away from direct sunlight and at a temperature between 50 and 60 degrees F.

ORANGE AND LEMON ZEST

Zest is the rind of an orange or lemon, without any of the white pith. Whenever a recipe calls for grated orange/lemon peel or rind, I recommend you use a zester rather than grating the peel, as this releases the oils. If you don't have one, use a vegetable peeler to make very thin strips, and then chop them.

BREAD CRUMBS

Using soft white bread crumbs as a binder in a stuffing is very common in Spanish cuisine. A filling made with all meat tends to be too heavy; adding bread crumbs lightens the filling, and I find that the final product is much tastier.

Bread crumbs can be made from white or whole wheat bread, but my recipes call for white bread because that is what we mostly use in Spain. I have indicated when commercial dry bread crumbs should be used. These are grated much finer and are good for coating food, but not for a stuffing.

To make bread crumbs it is better to use day-old bread, if possible. Remove the crusts and mince bread in the food processor. A 1-pound loaf of bread will give you about 1/2 pound of bread crumbs, after removing crusts. When measuring, don't pack it; the directions in my recipes are intended for loose measurements.

ROASTING AND PEELING PEPPERS

Red and green peppers are used a lot in Spanish cuisine, and many recipes in this book include them. Very often they are roasted and peeled—which may seem like a difficult task. But here are a few tips on how to do it easily.

Preheat oven to 400 degrees F.

Place the peppers on an ungreased baking sheet in the oven for 30 minutes, turning them around occasionally, until they scorch and the skin blisters and puffs up, starting to blacken. Immediately put them in a paper bag and twist it shut; leave the peppers in it for 15 to 30 minutes. While they are still warm it will be fairly easy to skin them, scraping them with a small, sharp knife. Do not do this under running water, or the peppers will lose some of their flavor; and don't worry about getting every last bit of skin off.

This procedure will just precook the peppers; if they are to be baked later, they will not be overcooked. In fact I prefer peppers on the well-done side, not only because they are easier to digest but also because their flavors come through more fully. Roasted peppers are simply delicious as an accompaniment to grilled meats; in this case I like to sprinkle on some olive oil and salt after peeling and seeding them, maybe a touch of minced garlic, and put them back in the oven for another 15 minutes.

If you only have to peel 2 or 3 peppers, you may find it faster to skewer each pepper on a fork and hold it over a flame until the skin starts to blacken, turning it around so it scorches evenly all over. After each pepper has blistered, place it in a paper bag as directed above.

In Spain, peppers are often roasted over a wood fire, which naturally provides wonderful flavors. A barbecue is a great substitute for that here, especially if you are going to serve them roasted.

FLAMBÉING

Spanish chefs—and Catalans in particular—are very fond of flambéing foods when cooking. This is done not as a decorative presentation but as part of the actual preparation, to add flavor and a bit of color to the dish. The harsh alcohol flavors burn off quickly, and what is left is the essence of the brandy or other spirit used.

It is important to use a liquor with high alcohol content; you cannot flambé with wine. Both the liquor and the ingredients should be hot, and you should use a shallow pan. Pour in the liquid, shake the pan and, as soon as the liquor is hot, ignite with a match—but be very careful and do not stand too close to the pan, as it will burst forth in flames right away. This method will not only improve your dish but it is also dramatic and fun to do.

CARAMELIZING

My recipes often call for caramelizing, whether to line a flan mold or to add color and flavor to a savory dish. The method simply consists of combining sugar with a little water in a saucepan over a brisk heat. (You can actually caramelize sugar by itself, without water, but I find it easier to do when the sugar is dissolved in about 1 tablespoon water to 1/4 cup sugar.) Don't stir the mixture, just shake the pan gently; in about 4 minutes, the water will evaporate and the sugar will first melt, then turn to a thick golden liquid. At this point you must decide how dark a caramel you want—and quickly, since the color goes from light golden to burnt brown very fast.

When used to line a mold, caramel will not only add a nice color and flavor to your dessert but will also make it easier to unmold. In savory dishes, the caramel is added to a hot liquid; it will hiss and smoke, but don't let that deter you—the caramel will soon dissolve, contributing a nice color and extra flavor.

EQUIVALENTS

1 small onion	=	1/3 pound
1 large onion	=	1/2 pound
1 medium carrot	=	1/4 pound
1 large carrot	=	6 ounces
1 large tomato	=	1/2 pound
1 large pepper	=	6 to 8 ounces
1 small pepper	=	4 to 6 ounces
1 cup chopped onion	=	1 medium
1 cup chopped carrot	=	2 medium
1 cup chopped tomato (unpeeled)	=	1 large
1 cup chopped tomato (peeled and seeded)	=	2 large
1 cup chopped pepper	=	1 large
1 cup chopped leek	=	1 small (white part with 1/3 of the green part)
1 tablespoon minced garlic	=	3 large cloves
1 tablespoon minced shallots	=	1 medium
1/4 cup minced shallots	=	2 large
1 cup grated Parmesan or Gruyère cheese	=	4 ounces
1/4 cup lemon juice	=	1 large lemon
1/2 cup orange juice	=	1 or 1 1/2 large oranges
1 tablespoon orange zest	=	1 large orange
1 tablespoon lemon zest	=	2 medium lemons
2 teaspoons lemon zest	=	1 large lemon
1 large (1/2-inch) slice white bread	=	1 ounce
1 cup white bread crumbs (without crusts)	=	3 ounces white bread (before trimming crusts)
1 cup sugar	=	1/2 pound
1 cup unsifted confectioner's sugar	=	4 1/4 ounces
1 cup unsifted flour	=	4 ounces (1/4 pound)
1 cup mashed potatoes	=	3/4 pound
1 cup blanched almonds	=	5 1/2 ounces
1 cup whole almonds	=	5 ounces
3/4 cup whole almonds	=	4 ounces
1 cup ground almonds	=	3 1/2 ounces

1 cup hazelnuts	=	4½ ounces
1 cup walnuts	=	3½ ounces
1 cup pine nuts	=	6 ounces
½ cup pitted olives	=	4 ounces
1 cup unpitted olives	=	⅓ pound

FOOD AND WINE MENU PLANNING

Perhaps the most important thing to realize about matching food and wine is this: almost any wine tastes better with food and almost any food tastes better with wine. It's that simple. Don't be misled by self-appointed experts who tell you at great and boring length that you *must* drink a particular wine with a particular food.

In Spain, for example, wine is usually served with meals and, most often, you drink the wine of the particular area you are in, be it red or white; if it is red, you drink it straight through the meal and no nonsense about white wine with fish and red wine with meat.

However, the pairing of food and wine is fun and often rewarding, since different foods *do* change one's appreciation of the wine, and vice versa. As wine writer Larry Walker maintains, "The integrity of neither should be violated. That is, the food should not be molded to the wine, nor the wine be so homogenized that it becomes a kind of bland and universal 'food wine.' My only other quibble is that wine *is* food and should be part of the menu planning process from the beginning, designed to harmonize (not necessarily blend) with the rest of the menu."

The only rule to follow is that you should try to find a balance and a harmony between the food and wine you are serving, almost as if you were composing a painting or planning a garden. You might begin with a specific dish, a main dish, something that is in season or maybe just on sale at the local market. Plan the rest of the menu around that dish, be it lamb or fish or eggplant. Then try to remember the taste of some of your favorite wines —will they harmonize? Will they be too acidic? Too sweet? Too heavy? As you can see, the more experience you have in tasting different wine and food combinations, the better you will be able to pair them. Some people enjoy keeping a kind of kitchen diary to help jog palate memory; I keep a record of all my dinners, guests, menus and wines, and make notes of what worked.

There are very few golden rules in serving wines; one I always follow is never to serve a wine of lower quality than the one which has gone before. The second is to suit the wines to the guests; if they are connoisseurs they should be offered fine wines, for even if the differences are small they will be able to appreciate the subtler overtones. With guests who are not experts, serve wines whose differences they can appreciate at once. The third rule is not to attach too much importance to old vintages; a wine that is too old is nothing but a memory, a museum piece.

I hope that through these pages you will learn to enjoy and use the exciting foods (and wines) of Spain; I believe they will add a strong, vivid note to your culinary repertoire.

APPETIZERS AND FIRST COURSES

Huevos Rellenos de Anchoa
(Eggs Filled with Anchovies)

Stuffed eggs are as popular in Spain as they are in America; but these are out of the ordinary because of the interesting mixture of flavors. They make a delightful appetizer and are also very good in a salad, or with cold sausages and tomatoes, etc.

To serve 6

> 6 small eggs, or 12 quail eggs

For the filling:

> 1 (2-ounce) can flat anchovy
>   fillets, drained
> 2 medium cloves garlic
> 1/8 teaspoon hot red pepper
>   flakes

> 1/4 cup olive oil
> 3/4 cup grated Parmesan cheese
> 2 tablespoons lemon juice

As a garnish:

> 6 Niçoise olives, or other small
>   black flavorful olives, with pits
>   (if using quail eggs, use 12
>   olives)

To cook the eggs: Place eggs in a saucepan, cover with cold water and bring to a boil. Immediately reduce heat to very low and simmer, covered, for 10 to 15 minutes. (If you use quail eggs, they will cook faster.) Place eggs under cold water to stop the cooking. Peel eggs, cut them in half and carefully remove the yolks.

To prepare the filling: In a food processor, purée anchovies with garlic and pepper flakes; add olive oil and Parmesan, and whirl until a thick paste is formed. Add egg yolks and lemon juice, and mix thoroughly. Taste for seasoning.

To assemble the eggs: Using a pastry sleeve, pipe the filling into the whites of the eggs. Cut olives in half and remove the pits; place half an olive on top of each egg. Refrigerate for at least 1 hour before serving.

Zanahorias Aliñadas
(Carrots Seasoned with Herbs)

This is a classic dish served in Andalucía at tapas bars, and each cook takes pride in having the best recipe. One of the tastiest preparations I've had comes from Las Golondrinas, a wonderful place in the quintessential tapas city, Sevilla. Owner Luis Ribera never gives out his recipe, so I was very lucky to get it.

I serve these carrots usually as an appetizer, with toasted baguette rounds; but they also make a delightful, light first course.

To serve 6

2 pounds long thin carrots
4 large cloves garlic
1½ teaspoons dried oregano
¾ teaspoon cumin seeds
1 teaspoon dried coriander
   (cilantro)
¼ teaspoon crushed hot red
   pepper flakes

¼ teaspoon freshly ground black
   pepper
1 teaspoon salt
1½ tablespoons sherry wine
   vinegar
½ cup olive oil
2 teaspoons chopped fresh
   parsley leaves

Peel carrots and slice into 1-inch-thick rounds (if they are large, cut in half lengthwise). Bring a large pan of salted water to a boil; add carrots and cook over medium heat for 8 to 10 minutes, or until carrots are tender but still firm. Drain and place in a serving bowl.

In a food processor, grind together garlic, oregano, cumin, coriander, pepper flakes, pepper and salt. Add vinegar to form a paste. Add oil in a thin stream and blend it all together. Transfer to the bowl with the carrots, add parsley and mix well to coat carrots with the dressing. Let carrots marinate for 2 hours or longer. Serve at room temperature.

Champiñones Rellenos al Jerez
(Stuffed Mushrooms with Sherry)

Mushrooms are very often eaten as a tapa *in Spain, and we frequently combine them with sherry in a sauce. But in this recipe sherry adds zest to the filling, an interesting variation on more traditional preparations.*

To serve 6

18 large mushrooms (1 to 1½ pounds)
½ cup whole almonds
¼ cup white bread crumbs, without crusts (see Bread Crumbs*)
½ pound medium-ground pork
1 teaspoon orange zest*

6 tablespoons flavorful dry or semi-dry Spanish sherry, such as amontillado or oloroso
½ teaspoon salt, or to taste
¼ teaspoon freshly ground black pepper, or to taste
1 or 2 tablespoons olive oil

Preheat oven to 350 degrees F.

Wipe mushrooms clean; remove mushroom stems and chop them finely. Set aside mushroom caps. Toast almonds in the preheated oven for 12 minutes, and chop them coarsely in the food processor.

In a mixer or by hand, combine mushroom stems, chopped almonds, bread crumbs, pork, orange zest, sherry, salt and pepper. Pack mushroom caps with the stuffing.

Increase oven temperature to 400 degrees F.

In a large skillet, heat enough olive oil just to coat the bottom of the pan. Add mushroom caps, filling side down, and sauté over medium-low heat until the filling is golden brown, 2 or 3 minutes. Remove them with a spatula and place on an oiled baking sheet, filling side up. Bake for about 20 minutes. Serve immediately.

A WORD ABOUT SNAILS

Snails are eaten in Spain quite often, but traditionally they have been cooked as a peasant dish—not as an elegant preparation, as it is the case in France, for example. It is only recently that Spaniards have elevated snails to the status of a delicacy! The following recipes reflect both attitudes: the first one is an earthy, peasant-style dish; the other two are refined and delicate—one Catalan, and one Basque.

Snails have been popular along Spain's Mediterranean coast for a long time. Later on, the custom of eating snails expanded inland, and not long ago to the Basque Country. Custom has it that snails were eaten in the old times on vigil days, especially Holy Thursday, Good Friday and Christmas Eve, when Catholics were not allowed to eat meat—and snails were not considered to be meat. According to popular belief, the tastiest snails are those that grow up in the vineyards, but where there are no vineyards, those found in cemeteries are just as good. This was earnestly told to me by Pedro Subijana, owner of Akeláre restaurant in San Sebastián, who is one of the most progressive chefs in Spain. His Effortless Snails in a Watercress Sauce (Caracoles sin Trabajo con Salsa de Berros) has become a classic of the New Basque Cuisine. A more traditional way to prepare snails is with tomato sauce or red peppers, combined with meats such as chorizo or ham.

Caracoles Picantes
(Catalan: Cargols Picants)
(Snails in a Piquant Sauce)

This recipe comes from El Celler del Penedès, a country restaurant near Vilafranca del Penedès where chef/owner Pere Valls serves wonderful earthy dishes typical of Catalonia. A special feature of this dining spot is a huge porrón *which they keep outside, full of wine, to welcome thirsty visitors. Used in the Catalan countryside, the* porrón *is a wine-drinking container with two spouts: a larger one through which you fill it, and a smaller one through which you pour the wine into your mouth, raising the* porrón *high with your hand. If you can raise it with one hand only, you are allowed to drink as much as you want free!*

This gives you an idea of the kind of restaurant this is—friendly, hospitable and very Catalan. And so is this peasant-style snails recipe, with its classic Catalan sofrito *and* picada, *flavorful and spicy. It can be served as an appetizer or first course, and would be terrific as a* tapa *at a buffet dinner, served in a clay casserole as we do in Spain. In any case, make sure to accompany it with good crusty bread.*

To serve 6

For poaching the snails:

1 cup dry white wine
1 cup Brown Veal Stock
1/2 teaspoon fennel seeds
2 sprigs fresh thyme (or 1/4 teaspoon dried)

36 large snails, frozen or canned (about 1/2 pound, drained weight)

For the *sofrito*:

3 tablespoons olive oil
3 large cloves garlic, minced
1 small onion, chopped
1 pound tomatoes, peeled, seeded and chopped
1/2 teaspoon hot red pepper flakes

1/2 pound ham hock (or a ham bone), cut into 3 or 4 pieces
1 cup Enriched Veal Stock or 2 cups Brown Veal Stock
1 cup full-bodied dry red wine

For the *picada:*

> 1 tablespoon olive oil
> 1 medium slice white bread
>   (about 1/2 ounce)
> 10 almonds, ground

> 1/2 sweet red pepper or canned
>   pimiento, chopped (or 1/2 cup)
> 2 sprigs parsley, stems removed,
>   chopped (or 1 tablespoon)

To poach the snails: In a saucepan, combine the wine, stock, fennel and thyme; cook for 20 minutes on medium-low heat, to reduce by about half. Drain the snails and rinse them under running water. Add them to poaching liquid and cook for 5 minutes. Drain snails and remove any fennel seeds that cling to them. Discard liquid and reserve snails.

To prepare the sofrito: In a skillet, heat oil and add garlic and onion; cook until soft, stirring. Add tomatoes, pepper flakes and ham hock pieces; cook on low heat for 1/2 hour, to obtain a concentrated thick sauce.

Add stock and wine, increase heat to medium and cook until reduced to 1 cup—about 1/2 hour. Remove and discard ham hock pieces.

To prepare the picada: Heat oil in a skillet. Add bread slice and fry over medium heat until golden on both sides. In a food processor, finely grind the bread slice with the almonds, red pepper (or pimiento) and parsley.

To assemble the dish: Add the *picada* to the *sofrito* in the skillet and cook, stirring, for a few minutes until warm. Add snails and cook just to heat them through. Taste for seasoning, and serve warm.

Tartaletas de Caracoles a las Hierbas Aromáticas
(Catalan: Tartaletes de Cargols a las Herbes Aromàtiques)
(Snail Tartlets with Mushrooms and Aromatic Herbs)

This delicate and sophisticated Catalan recipe will be enjoyed even by those who don't like snails—unless you tell them what's in it (I speak from experience!).

A creation of chef/owner Toya Roqué, of Azulete restaurant in Barcelona, it is a good example of her inventive, new approach to turning a "peasant" food into an elegant dish.

For this recipe you need 6 individual shallow tartlet molds about 4 1/2 inches in diameter. It is best if they have a removable rim, as it will be easier to take them out after they are cooked. The Press-in Pastry, however, is not difficult to detach from the mold, because of its high butter content and absence of water.

To serve 6

For the tartlets:

> 1 recipe Press-in Pastry

For the filling:

13 1/2 ounces canned snails
   (drained weight)
2 tablespoons butter
1/2 cup minced shallots
1 1/2 cups finely chopped
   mushrooms (about 6 ounces)
1 teaspoon finely chopped fresh
   chervil (or 1/4 teaspoon dried)

3/4 teaspoon finely chopped fresh
   tarragon (or 1/4 teaspoon dried)
1 pound tomatoes, peeled,
   seeded and finely chopped
1 cup heavy cream
3/4 teaspoon salt
1/2 teaspoon freshly ground black
   pepper

As a garnish:

2 tablespoons snipped fresh or
   dried chives

Preheat oven to 425 degrees F.

To prepare the tartlets:　Divide pastry into 6 equal parts (2 ounces each) and, with your hands, press it into each mold. Refrigerate for at least 15 minutes. Immediately bake in the preheated oven for 10 to 15 minutes, or until golden. When slightly cooled, remove pastry from molds and set aside.

    Reduce oven temperature to 375 degrees F.

To prepare the filling:　Rinse snails under cold running water and chop them. Heat butter in a skillet; add shallots and sauté over medium-low heat until translucent. Add mushrooms and continue cooking until liquid evaporates. Add chervil and tarragon, stir and cook for about 1 minute; add tomatoes and cook over medium heat until liquid evaporates. Add cream, salt and pepper; continue cooking for a few minutes until mixture thickens a bit. Add snails and cook for 5 minutes. Taste for seasoning.

To assemble the tartlets:　Fill the tartlets with the mixture, distributing it evenly. Place the tartlets on a baking sheet in the oven and bake for about 10 minutes, or until tartlets are golden brown.

    Serve warm, sprinkling some chives over the center of each tartlet.

Caracoles sin Trabajo con Salsa de Berros
(Effortless Snails in a Watercress Sauce)

Pedro Subijana is one of the most representative chefs of modern Basque cuisine; he deserves much credit for the simplicity and delicacy of his recipes, such as this one.

    Dining at his beautiful Akelaŕe restaurant in San Sebastián, high on a hill overlooking the Bay of Biscay, is an experience not to be forgotten. I particularly enjoyed these "effortless snails"; he gave them this name because they are served without shells and are easy to eat. The dish may be effortless for the eater—but not so much for the cook. Yet I assure you, it is worth all the work you put into it, and will delight even those guests who wrinkle their noses at the thought of eating snails.

To serve 6

For the pastry shells:

> 1/2 recipe Puff Pastry, chilled
> 1 egg, beaten

For poaching the snails:

> 1 cup dry white wine
> 1 cup Brown Veal Stock
> 1/2 teaspoon fennel seeds
> 2 sprigs fresh thyme (or 1/4
>   teaspoon dried)

> 41/2 ounces snails, frozen or
>   canned (drained weight)

For the sauce:

> 2 tablespoons butter
> 6 large cloves garlic, minced
> 1/2 pound unpeeled tomatoes,
>   chopped
> 1 cup Enriched Veal Stock or 2
>   cups Brown Veal Stock

> 1/4 cup heavy cream
> 1/2 cup coarsely chopped
>   watercress leaves
> 1/4 teaspoon salt, or to taste
> 1/8 teaspoon freshly ground
>   white pepper, or to taste

As a garnish:

> A few sprigs watercress

Preheat oven to 425 degrees F.

To prepare the pastry shells: Roll out pastry to about 1/8-inch thickness. Using a cookie cutter of about 3-inch diameter, cut 12 rounds out of the pastry. Place 6 of the rounds on an ungreased baking sheet. Dip your finger in water and moisten a 1/2-inch ring around the edge of each round. Using a sharp-pointed knife or a 2-inch-diameter cookie cutter, make a line 1/2 inch in from the edge of the other 6 rounds. (Don't cut all the way through the dough, however, or it will not rise.) Place these 6 rounds on top of the others on the baking sheet. Brush the tops with the beaten egg. Bake in the preheated oven for 8 minutes, then reduce heat to 375 degrees F. and bake for an additional 10 to 15 minutes, or until biscuits are golden and the bottom starts to darken.

Remove pastry shells from the oven and immediately cut through the round line you made earlier, lifting out the "lid" carefully with a knife. If there is any soft puff pastry inside, scoop it out with a spoon and discard it. You now have 6 round little boxes with lids for your snails.

These pastry shells can be made up to 3 days ahead, stored in an airtight tin and warmed up at the last moment in a preheated 300-degree F. oven for 5 minutes.

To poach the snails: Proceed as directed in the recipe for Snails in a Piquant Sauce (Caracoles Picantes).

To prepare the sauce: Heat butter in a skillet; add garlic and sauté over low heat for 2 minutes, or until soft. Add tomatoes and cook over low heat for 15 minutes. Add stock and purée in a food processor or blender. Strain through a fine mesh strainer, pushing the contents with the back of a spoon. Return sauce to skillet and reduce to about 1 cup. Add cream and cook over medium heat for 5 to 10 minutes, to thicken slightly. Add snails, watercress, salt and pepper, and taste for seasoning.

To assemble the dish: Gently heat snails in the sauce for just a couple of minutes, so they don't toughen. Place 1 pastry shell on each individual plate. Distribute snail mixture among the shells, letting the sauce overflow the top. Put the lid on at an angle—like a cocked hat. Decorate with sprigs of watercress on the side.

Tartaletas de Riñones
(Kidney Tartlets)

It is very common in Spain for tapas *bars to serve little tartlets filled with anything from chopped mushrooms to meats. The idea for these comes from Bar Oquendo, a popular* tapas *bar in San Sebastián which is famous for them and has been serving them since 1963, as owner José Mari Iriondo told me.*

Makes 12 (1½-inch) tartlets

For the tartlets:

> ½ **recipe Press-in Pastry**

For the filling:

> 1 large veal kidney (10–12 ounces), fresh if possible
> 4 tablespoons butter
> ½ cup minced shallots
> ½ pound tomatoes, peeled, seeded and chopped
>
> ½ cup dry Spanish sherry, preferably fino
> ¼ teaspoon salt, or to taste
> ½ teaspoon freshly ground black pepper, or to taste

To prepare the tartlets: Press pastry into 12 pastry shells of about 1½-inch diameter. Refrigerate for at least 15 minutes.

Preheat oven to 425 degrees F.

Bake tartlet shells in the preheated oven for 15 minutes, or until golden. Lower oven temperature to 350 degrees F.

To prepare the filling: Cut excessive fat from kidneys, and finely chop them. Heat 2 tablespoons of the butter and sauté kidneys, over medium heat, for 3 to 4 minutes. Set them aside.

In the same pan, heat remaining 2 tablespoons butter and sauté shallots slowly, on low heat, until very soft and golden. Stir in the tomatoes, and cook until dry. Add sherry and reduce by half. Return kidneys and their juices to the pan. Add salt and pepper, and taste for seasoning. Set aside.

To assemble the dish: At the last minute, warm up tart shells for 5 minutes in a 350-degree F. oven. Distribute kidney mixture among them. Serve immediately, while still warm.

Tarta de Cebolla
(Onion Tart)

This recipe was inspired by a dish I had at Panier Fleuri, in San Sebastián. Chef/owner Tatús Fombellida is a young woman with a great restaurant family tradition; she has inherited the skill and taste of her parents—still alive but letting her run the show—while adding new ideas which reflect her own personality.

This onion tart is not "new" in style, but different in that it has no cream—and it is one of the best I have ever had. The secret is in the long cooking of the onions and their combination with the light, airy puff pastry.

To serve 6 to 8

For the tart:

> *1 recipe Puff Pastry*

For the filling:

1/4 pound bacon, thickly sliced	**1/2 teaspoon salt, or to taste**
3 tablespoons butter	**1/4 teaspoon freshly ground**
6 large onions, very thinly sliced	**white pepper, or to taste**

To prepare the tart: Roll out the pastry to fit a 9- or 10-inch removable-rim pan, adding 1½ inches to the diameter. Cut pastry in a circle with a sharp knife; handle the pastry as little as possible. (With puff pastry you will get more rise if you cut the pastry before fitting it into the pan.) Place pastry inside pan, allowing edges to drape a little over the sides. Keep it refrigerated until needed.

To prepare the filling: Cut bacon into tiny strips. Melt butter in a large skillet and sauté bacon, over low heat, for 10 minutes.

Preheat oven to 425 degrees F.

Add onions to the bacon in the pan, and sprinkle with salt and pepper. Cook over low heat until onions are very soft and a deep golden color; it will take 45 minutes to an hour. The onions must cook this long to get that mellow consistency which brings out their sweetness. Stir frequently while they are cooking.

To assemble the dish: Remove pastry from the refrigerator and fill with the onions. Place in the preheated oven and bake for 30 minutes.

Serve warm, cut into wedges.

Tarta de Puerros
(Catalan: Pastís de Porros)
(Leek Tart)

High in the Catalan Pyrenees Mountains, just a few miles from the French border, is Can Borrell, a unique inn and restaurant that blends old traditions of great Catalan cuisine with the personal style of Lola Pijoán. In 1976 she and her husband, Jaume Guillén, opened Can Borrell in the picturesque old village of Meranges, in one of the most beautiful regions of Catalonia, La Cerdanya. Can Borrell overlooks an endless bucolic valley, near two crystal-clear mountain lakes. The narrow winding roads you have to take to get there are well worth it. Lola and Jaume have achieved the impossible dream: living in an ideal place while attracting lovers of food and nature to eat and stay there.

This leek tart is one of Lola's favorite creations—and one of mine, too.

To serve 8 to 10

8 tablespoons butter
3 bunches leeks, thinly sliced,
  with 1/3 of the green part
  (about 3 pounds after cleaning)
1/4 teaspoon salt, or to taste
1/2 teaspoon freshly ground black
  pepper, or to taste

1/8 teaspoon cayenne, or to taste
1/4 teaspoon nutmeg, or to taste
4 eggs
1 cup heavy cream

For the tart:

1 recipe Pie Pastry*
1 cup grated Gruyère or
  Emmenthaler cheese

To prepare the filling: In a large pot, melt butter and, on very low heat, sauté leeks until they are dry and reduced to almost a paste; it will take 45 minutes to 1 hour. Season with salt, pepper, cayenne and nutmeg. Let it cool. In a bowl, beat eggs slightly. Add cream and leeks; mix well.

Preheat oven to 425 degrees F.

To prepare the tart: Roll out pastry thinly to fit a 9- or 10-inch removable-rim tart pan about 1½ inches deep. Discard excess dough on the sides. Place a piece of foil over the pastry, and fill it with rice or beans. Bake in preheated oven for 15 minutes. Pick up foil by its edges and carefully lift it out of the pastry shell. Bake another 5 to 10 minutes, until lightly golden. Remove from oven.

Reduce oven temperature to 375 degrees F.

To assemble the dish: Pour the leek mixture into dough-lined pan. Sprinkle cheese on top. Bake in preheated 375-degree oven for 45 minutes to 1 hour, until cheese turns golden. Serve warm.

Garum
(Roman Dip)

Garum *was a famous sauce used by the Romans, as we have learned from recipes of such Roman authors as Apicius, who lived in the days of Christ. We know it was obtained by the pressing of fish, herbs and salt in bronze cauldrons, which were placed in the sun with a stone weight on top. As time passed, the fish fermented, with the salt acting as a preservative. A wicker basket was dipped into the cauldron, and the solids gathered in the basket were* garum. *The strained liquid left was* liquamen, *similar to the fermented fish sauces of Southeast Asia—known in Vietnam as* ñuoc-mam—*used as a flavoring in many dishes and also as a dipping sauce. The Romans used* garum *to season many of their recipes. I suppose it was used much the way people use steak sauce today.*

In my travels through southern Spain I learned that the remains of some of the most important Roman garum *factories had been discovered near Cádiz, Granada and Cartagena; but I was unable to find a present-day* garum *preparation anywhere. It was in the Ampurdán restaurant in Figueras, capital of L'Empordà (Ampurdán) district in northern Catalonia, that I found* garum *served as a dip. And indeed, it was delicious—even if not quite like what the Romans used to flavor their cooking. I serve it as a dip with crackers, toast or raw vegetables.*

Ampurdán's owner, Jaume Subirós, is the son-in-law of the late Josep Mercadé, who has been called one of the fathers of Catalan cuisine. Jaume not only carries on the restaurant tradition but has contributed new ideas and great talent, following the family's guidelines: raw materials of impeccable quality, handled with care and skill, and a total dedication to the development of Catalan cooking.

Makes about 2 cups

4 anchovy fillets
2 hard-boiled eggs
2 tablespoons drained capers
1/2 pound drained purple olives
  (Greek kalamata type), pits
  removed
1/2 pound drained pitted black
  olives

1/4 teaspoon chopped fresh
  tarragon leaves (or a pinch, if
  dried)
2 tablespoons full-bodied
  Spanish brandy
2/3 cup olive oil
1/2 teaspoon freshly ground black
  pepper, or to taste

In a food processor or blender, purée the anchovies, egg yolks (reserve the whites), capers, olives, tarragon and brandy. With the motor running, add the olive oil in a thin stream. Season with pepper to taste. Chill until serving time.

At the moment of serving, stir to blend in the olive oil, which will have separated a little. Pour mixture into a little bowl and sprinkle the egg whites, finely chopped, on top.

Mousse de "Escalivada"
(Catalan: Escuma d'Escalivada)
(Eggplant, Pepper and Tomato Dip)

Escalivada is a typical way of preparing vegetables in Catalonia which enhances their fresh flavor; they are simply grilled or baked and served sprinkled with olive oil, salt and pepper. Making a mousse out of it is a new version, in the classic style of the great Ampurdán restaurant in Figueras which has created so many dishes based on traditional Catalan recipes.

This attractively colored purée is delicious served with cold or grilled meats, or as a dip with thin toasted rounds of a narrow baguette.

To serve 6 to 8

> *About 1 tablespoon olive oil, for rubbing vegetables*
> *1 pound eggplant, preferably the long, thin Japanese variety, or a small regular eggplant (see Note below)*
> *2 large red peppers*
> *1 large ripe tomato*
> *1 large potato (1/2 pound)*
>
> *2 large heads garlic*
> *1 small onion*
> *1/4 teaspoon crushed hot red pepper flakes*
> *3 tablespoons red wine vinegar, or to taste*
> *1 teaspoon salt*
> *1/2 teaspoon freshly ground black pepper*

(Note: The long and thin Japanese-style eggplants are very similar to the Spanish ones—and much more flavorful than the usual kind found in the markets. It really will make a difference if you use them in this recipe.)

Preheat oven to 400 degrees F.

Without peeling them, rub with oil the eggplant, peppers, tomato and potato. Place on an ungreased baking sheet in the preheated oven, with the garlic heads and whole onion. Remove tomato after 15 or 20 minutes; eggplant after 30 minutes (45 if using a regular eggplant); peppers after 45 minutes; potato, garlic and onion after 1 hour. They have to be well done; leave them in longer if necessary.

Cut potato in half, scoop out the flesh and mash with a fork; discard the skin. Peel eggplant and onion and cut them up. Squeeze garlic cloves, discarding the peel. Stem, seed and peel peppers. Pull skin from tomato and seed it. Reserve juices from peppers and tomato.

Purée onion, potato and pepper flakes in a blender or food processor. Blend in remaining vegetables with juices until smooth. Add remaining ingredients. Taste for seasoning.

Allow to rest, unrefrigerated, for at least 2 hours, to let flavors mingle. Serve at room temperature or chilled.

Mousse de Endibias con Salsa de Cabrales
(Catalan: Escuma d'Endívies amb Salsa de Cabrales)
(Endive Mousse with Blue Cheese Sauce)

Big Rock is one of the most "in" restaurants on the fashionable Costa Brava, the coastal area north of Barcelona which many call the Spanish Riviera. Carles and Mari Carmen Camós opened Big Rock in Palamós in 1973, and from a simple little restaurant serving good honest Catalan home-style cooking, it has evolved into a gastronomic haven specializing in traditional dishes of L'Empordà district.

Most of Carles' recipes are perfect reproductions of old classics; but some, like this delicate mousse, show his inventive, newer approach to great cooking. Carles is a big, friendly, affable man who loves to chat with anybody interested in his food or his wines. He also told me he loves anything American or British—hence the name of his restaurant.

To serve 8 to 10:   Makes 1 (5-cup) ring mold

For the mousse:

3 tablespoons butter
1 large leek, chopped, with 1/3 of the green part
1 medium onion, chopped
1 pound Belgian endive, stems trimmed, chopped

2 ounces creamy blue cheese, such as Danish or Oregon blue
6 eggs
Salt and freshly ground white pepper to taste, if necessary

For the sauce:

2 ounces blue cheese (same as above)

1/3 cup half-and-half
3 tablespoons Mayonnaise

As a garnish:

2 heads Belgian endive, stems trimmed and leaves separated
Toasted rounds of a baguette

To prepare the mousse: Heat butter in a large skillet. Sauté leek with onion over low heat, stirring occasionally, until very soft and beginning to color—at least 20 minutes. Stir in endive; cover and cook for 10 or 15 minutes, until very soft. Purée in the blender or food processor, together with the cheese and eggs. Taste for seasoning, adding salt and pepper if necessary (depending on the saltiness of the cheese).

Preheat oven to 350 degrees F.

Butter generously a 5-cup ring mold and fill with the mixture. Place mold inside a larger pan filled with boiling water halfway up the mold. Bake in the preheated oven, uncovered, for 45 minutes or until firm.

To prepare the sauce: While mousse bakes, purée cheese with cream and mayonnaise until smooth. Chill for an hour or two, to let flavors mingle.

To assemble the mousse: When mold is cool, turn mousse out onto a round platter. (Don't worry if it doesn't come out perfect; scoop up with a rubber spatula any mousse that may have been pulled off and patch the surface to even it out.) Spread the sauce over and around the mousse.

Serve garnished with endive leaves around it, and pass the toast.

Corona de Gazpacho
(Gazpacho Mousse)

Prepare 8 hours ahead, or the day before

An interesting variation of the classic Spanish dish, gazpacho, this colorful mousse is a perfect summer recipe, best made at the peak of the tomato season and when the vegetables have the most flavor. It makes a neat appetizer; I always serve it with toasted thin rounds of a narrow baguette.

To serve 12 (as an appetizer)

1 small red bell pepper, cut up (or green, if red is not available)
1 teaspoon chopped garlic
3/4 teaspoon chopped seeded canned jalapeño chile pepper
1/2 small red onion, cut up
1 1/2 pounds unpeeled ripe tomatoes, cut up
1/2 English-type cucumber (about 1/2 pound), peeled and cut up

3 tablespoons olive oil (preferably extra virgin)
2 tablespoons sherry wine vinegar or a good red wine vinegar
1/2 teaspoon salt, or to taste
1/2 teaspoon freshly ground black pepper, or to taste
1 cup canned tomato juice
3 envelopes unflavored gelatin (or 3/4 ounce)

As a garnish:

1 lemon, cut into thin slices
A few sprigs parsley

In a blender or food processor, purée the bell pepper with the garlic and the jalapeño. Add the onion, tomatoes and cucumber, processing until very smooth. Blend in olive oil, vinegar, salt and pepper.

In a small saucepan, heat the tomato juice and, over low heat, whisk in the gelatin until it is completely dissolved. With the motor running, immediately pour the dissolved gelatin-tomato mixture into the bowl. Taste for seasoning.

Pour the gazpacho into a 5- or 6-cup ring mold, lightly oiled, and let set in the refrigerator for 6 hours or overnight.

To unmold, dip the bottom of the mold for just 2 or 3 seconds into a basin of warm water, and immediately invert onto a serving plate. Garnish with the lemon slices and parsley.

Mousse de Salmón y Aguacate
(Salmon and Avocado Mousse)

Smoked salmon is served often in Spain at fine restaurants or at elegant dinners in homes. El Amparo, one of Madrid's most creative restaurants and a particular favorite of mine, has added a new twist by introducing avocado, which blends very well with the flavor of smoked salmon and adds an interesting texture. It also provides a dramatic visual effect, a classic example of chef Ramón Ramírez's inventive approach to cooking.

Depending on the size of the avocados, this recipe will yield 5 or 6 cups; and if they are large, you may need only 3 avocados instead of 4. Use a rectangular pâté terrine or glass loaf pan that holds about 6 cups, with a lid if possible.

To serve 8:   Makes 1 (5- or 6-cup) terrine

2 packages (or 1/2 ounce)
  unflavored gelatin
1 egg
2 tablespoons minced onion
1 teaspoon dry mustard
1 cup vegetable oil
2 tablespoons lemon juice
8 ounces smoked salmon pieces
  (see Note 1 below)

1 cup heavy cream
4 small, ripe avocados,
  preferably the Haas variety
  (see Note 2 below)
3 tablespoons snipped fresh
  chives (about 1/8 inch long)

As a garnish (optional):

A few fresh chive tops

(Note 1: Some markets sell chips or smoked salmon pieces; if you can find them, these are a lot less expensive and will work just as well.)
(Note 2: I prefer to use the more flavorful Haas variety of avocados; these are small, dark and have a rough skin.)

In a small saucepan, soften gelatin in 3/4 cup water. Gently heat it, just until it is completely dissolved. Set aside to cool.

In a food processor or blender, combine the egg, onion and dry mustard; whirl to blend well. In a container with a pouring lip, mix the oil and lemon juice together. With the motor running, gradually add the oil mixture to the food processor bowl; whirl for another 10 seconds. Add the smoked salmon and purée. With the motor running, add the dissolved gelatin.

Refrigerate the mixture until it begins to set on the surface; it should take between 15 and 25 minutes (if you find that it has set too much, just whisk it).

Meanwhile, whip the cream until it stands in soft peaks. Peel the avocados; cut them in half lengthwise and remove the pits. Cut a slice from both ends of each avocado, so you will be left with just the center part, which has the hole from the pit. (This is just for looks; when you slice into the mousse, you will get a beautiful design from the avocado curve which you would not have if you used the whole fruit.)

Fold the cream and chives into the salmon mixture. Rinse the pâté terrine or glass loaf pan with water. Pour some of the salmon mixture into the mold, to about 1 inch. Place 4 of the avocado halves, cut side up, in a line down the center of the mousse. Press avocados down, so there will be no air pockets. Cover with some more mousse, to about 1/4 or 1/2 inch over the avocados. Place remaining 4 avocado halves, cut side up, over the first row. Cover with the rest of the mousse mixture. Cover mold and refrigerate until serving time.

To serve: Dip the mold into a basin of warm water for just a few seconds. Invert the mold onto a cutting board; the mousse should come out easily. Cut into slices served on individual plates, to show the attractive design of the mousse. If desired, serve decorated with a few fresh chive tops.

This mousse can be prepared a day ahead, as long as it is not cut in advance. The avocado slices will darken when they are in contact with the air, but not as long as they are completely encased in the mousse.

Pâté de Salmón Ahumado
(Smoked Salmon Pâté)

This recipe was inspired by a salmon pâté I had at Sacha in Madrid, a great restaurant which combines good food with a wonderful feeling of dining in someone's living room— largely as a result of the earthy personality of owner Pitila Mosquera. She serves this pâté as a little appetizer while you wait for your meal. The capers were not in her recipe; I have added them as I find they contribute an interesting note of texture and flavor. I would suggest serving this pâté as Pitila does, with toasted bread rounds.

To serve 10 to 12:   Makes 2 1/2 cups

1/2 medium onion
8 ounces smoked salmon pieces
1 cup heavy cream

1/2 teaspoon freshly ground
* white pepper*
1 tablespoon small capers

Finely chop onion in a food processor or blender. Add salmon and purée. With the motor running, pour in the cream. Blend in pepper. Transfer to a bowl, fold in capers and taste for seasoning. Refrigerate until serving time.

Pâté de Anchoa con Caviar
(Anchovy Pâté with Caviar Mayonnaise)

This dish makes an elegant first course, interesting and light. The touch of caviar in the mayonnaise provides a nice contrast with the pungency of the anchovies in the pâté.

*   The idea came from a dish I had at Risco, a charming country-style restaurant in a hotel high on a hill overlooking the beach town of Laredo, in the northern region of*

Cantabria. Owners Zacarías and Inés Puente are warm, hospitable hosts, as proud of their domain as they are of their cuisine.

To serve 6:   Makes 2 cups

For the pâté:

2 (2-ounce) cans flat anchovy fillets, drained	1 cup heavy cream
4 eggs	1/4 teaspoon freshly ground white pepper

For the caviar mayonnaise:

1 whole egg	1/4 cup vegetable oil
1 egg yolk	2 teaspoons lemon juice
1 teaspoon prepared Dijon-style mustard	1 (2-ounce) jar black lumpfish caviar (small eggs)
1/4 cup olive oil	

Preheat oven to 350 degrees F.

To prepare the pâté: In a blender or food processor, finely purée anchovies; whirl in eggs, cream and pepper. Taste for seasoning. Butter a shallow 3-cup rectangular or round ovenproof mold. Line bottom of mold with buttered wax paper. Pour mixture into mold.

Cover mold and place it in a larger pan filled with boiling water halfway up the sides of the mold. Place in the preheated oven for 50 or 60 minutes, until a cake tester comes out clean (it should be slightly firm to the touch). When cool, pass a knife around the edges and unmold onto a platter. Remove the wax paper. Refrigerate.

To prepare the caviar mayonnaise: In a blender or food processor, beat egg, egg yolk and mustard together. In a pouring jar, combine oils and lemon juice. With the motor running, slowly add oil mixture to eggs and mustard; the mixture will thicken and become a mayonnaise. (If the mixture separates, see Mayonnaise [Salsa Mayonesa] recipe for how to correct it.) Fold caviar into the mayonnaise. Refrigerate until serving time.

To assemble the dish: When you are ready to serve, whisk mayonnaise and pour some over and around the pâté, passing the rest in a sauceboat. Serve slightly chilled.

Pâté de Cabrales a la Manzana
(Blue Cheese Pâté with Apples)

Start preparation at least 1 day ahead, by marinating chicken livers

I had this pâté at La Máquina restaurant in Madrid, which specializes in Asturian cuisine. This northern Spanish region produces the finest blue cheese in Spain, Cabrales-Picón; unfortunately that is hard to find here, but a very good substitute is a flavorful Oregon or Danish blue, or a good Roquefort. Make sure not to get a salty or creamy cheese, but a fine zesty type.

The combination of the blue cheese with the other ingredients in this pâté is interesting and different; the apples provide a refreshing contrast in taste and texture. I serve it with peeled apple wedges or toasted bread rounds; I personally prefer to spread it on the apple wedges, as they combine very well with the subtle taste of the blue cheese.

Makes about 4 cups

1 pound chicken livers	2 eggs
6 tablespoons dry flavorful Spanish sherry, such as amontillado	1/2 cup heavy cream
	1/2 teaspoon salt
	1/4 teaspoon freshly ground white pepper
6 tablespoons full-bodied Spanish brandy	1 large Pippin or Granny Smith apple (6 to 8 ounces)
1/2 cup (4 ounces) flavorful blue cheese	

In a nonmetallic bowl, marinate the livers in 1/4 cup each sherry and brandy. Cover and refrigerate for at least 24 hours.

Preheat oven to 350 degrees F.

Transfer livers with their marinade to a saucepan. Bring to a boil, cover and reduce heat to very low. Cook gently for 10 minutes. With a slotted spoon, remove livers from the liquid and transfer to food processor or blender. (Discard liquid in saucepan.) Purée livers with the cheese. Add eggs and cream, remaining 2 tablespoons each sherry and brandy, salt and pepper; blend until smooth. Pour through a fine sieve into a bowl. Peel, core and grate the apple; immediately fold it into the pâté mixture.

Butter the sides and bottom of a terrine, and pour in the pâté mixture. Cover tightly with foil and a lid. Place in a larger pan filled with boiling water about halfway up the sides of the terrine. Bake in the preheated oven for 60 minutes, or until the pâté is firm and pulls away from the sides of the terrine.

Let pâté cool before refrigerating. Serve at room temperature. (It is always a good idea to let pâtés sit in the refrigerator for a day before serving.)

Terrina de Conejo con Ciruelas
(Catalan: Terrina de Conill amb Prunes)
(Rabbit and Prune Terrine)

Start preparation 1 day or at least 10 hours ahead

This is another recipe inspired by the Ampurdán restaurant in Figueras. You can serve it as an appetizer, with toasted thinly sliced baguette rounds, or as a first course, as Jaume Subirós does. It goes very well with Apple Garlic Mayonnaise (Allioli de Manzana).

The combination of flavors in this dish is as successful as the presentation is attractive. The prunes and fresh herbs complement the rabbit and other meats, and the carrots add pretty spots of color.

Makes 1 (7-cup) terrine

1/3 pound carrots, peeled and cut into 1/4-inch dice
1/2 pound boneless rabbit meat
1/2 pound lean pork meat, such as boneless pork loin
1/2 pound pork fat, including whatever fat is trimmed from the pork loin or other pork cut used
1/2 pound boneless boiled ham, cut into 1/2-inch dice
1 large onion, finely chopped
3 large cloves garlic, finely chopped

3/4 cup (6 ounces) coarsely chopped pitted prunes
1/2 cup full-bodied Spanish brandy
2 teaspoons minced fresh rosemary leaves
2 teaspoons minced fresh thyme leaves
1 teaspoon salt
1 teaspoon freshly ground black pepper
1/2 cup fino sherry, or another dry Spanish sherry

In a pan, bring about 1 quart salted water to a boil. Blanch carrots for 2 minutes; drain and set aside.

Cut rabbit meat, pork and pork fat in pieces, and grind them coarsely together. (If using a food processor, do it in small batches and don't grind to a paste; only pulse enough to chop.)

In a nonmetallic bowl, mix ground meats with ham, onion, garlic, prunes, reserved carrots and brandy. Let the mixture marinate at room temperature for 2 hours or longer.

Preheat oven to 325 degrees F.

Add rosemary, thyme, salt and pepper to the meat mixture; mix well. Oil a 7- or 8-cup terrine mold and pack mixture into it. Pour sherry over. Cover terrine with foil and put lid on top. Set mold inside a larger pan filled with boiling water halfway up the mold. Bake in the preheated oven for 2 hours. Let cool, covered, at room temperature, then refrigerate overnight or for at least 4 hours. Serve at room temperature.

Pastel de Jamón
(Ham Terrine)

This is a favorite recipe from my mother's buffet parties; it is easy to whip up, and can be prepared the day before. She made this terrine with truffles, which in Spain are more affordable than in the United States. I tried it once and certainly enjoyed the delicacy—but it was hard to recuperate from paying the grocery bill. So I found that adding a fresh herb such as sage in place of the truffles is an excellent switch. Some fine commercial duck liver pâtés with truffles and brandy are not too expensive and also work very well.

This dish has the consistency of a pâté, but I like it best served as a first course. The tomato sauce adds an interesting fresh flavor; it should be made shortly before serving.

To serve 8

For the terrine:

2 tablespoons butter
2 tablespoons flour
1 cup milk
3/4 pound baked ham, fat
   trimmed, finely chopped
1/4 pound duck or pork liver pâté
1/2 tablespoon finely chopped
   fresh sage (or 1 teaspoon
   dried)

4 eggs, beaten
2 or 3 tablespoons amontillado
   or another flavorful Spanish
   sherry
1/2 teaspoon freshly ground black
   pepper, or to taste

For the tomato sauce:

1/4 cup fresh parsley leaves
11/2 pounds ripe tomatoes (3
   large), peeled and seeded
11/2 tablespoons tomato paste
2 tablespoons sherry wine
   vinegar or red wine vinegar

3 tablespoons fine olive oil, extra
   virgin if possible
1/2 teaspoon salt, or to taste
1 teaspoon freshly ground black
   pepper, or to taste

As a garnish:

24 long, thin green beans,
   steamed to tender crispness
16 cherry tomatoes

Preheat oven to 350 degrees F.

To prepare the terrine: In a small saucepan, melt butter; add flour and cook for about 1 minute. Add milk and continue cooking over medium heat, whisking constantly until sauce thickens or comes to a boil. Cook for 1 minute and remove from heat. Set aside.

In a bowl, mix the ham, pâté, sage, eggs, sherry and pepper. Add white sauce and blend well. Taste for seasoning; salt will probably not be necessary.

Butter a 5-cup rectangular mold and a piece of wax paper cut to fit the bottom. Pour mixture into the mold, cover and place it inside a larger pan filled with boiling water halfway up the mold. Bake in the preheated oven for 1/2 hour; remove it from the water, uncover and bake for another 25 to 30 minutes, until a cake tester comes out clean. Let it cool.

To prepare the tomato sauce: Finely mince parsley in a blender or food processor. Add remaining ingredients and purée. Taste for seasoning; the sauce should have a sharp flavor.

To assemble the dish: Unmold terrine onto a board and cut it into 16 slices. Spoon some tomato sauce on each dish, place 2 slices of terrine on top, arrange 3 green beans on one side of the terrine and 2 tomatoes on the other. Serve at room temperature.

Pastel de Tortillas
(Three-Layer Omelet Torte)

This triple-layered omelet, with its fresh tomato sauce, was a favorite at home; my mother often served it as a festive first course for lunch on Sundays. I find it can be a lunch by itself, accompanied by a salad. While not difficult to prepare, it is unusual and visually very attractive.

To serve 6

For the omelets:

1 large potato (3/4 pound), peeled and sliced into thin nickel-size pieces (can be done in food processor)
3/4 teaspoon salt
3/4 teaspoon freshly ground black pepper
About 1/2 cup olive oil

1 large onion, thinly sliced
12 eggs
1 pound red bell peppers, stemmed, seeded and coarsely chopped
3/4 pound green beans, ends trimmed, finely diced

For the sauce:

2 tablespoons olive oil
1 small onion, chopped
2 pounds unpeeled ripe tomatoes, chopped
1/2 tablespoon tomato paste

1/4 teaspoon salt, or to taste
1/4 teaspoon freshly ground black pepper, or to taste
Dash of cayenne (optional)

As a garnish:

About 1/2 cup grated Parmesan cheese

To prepare the omelets: Season potatoes with 1/4 teaspoon each salt and pepper. Heat about 1/2 cup oil in a nonstick skillet and, over medium heat, sauté potatoes until golden brown and crispy. Drain. Leave 1 or 2 tablespoons oil in the skillet (reserve rest) and add onion; sauté over low heat until soft, about 10 minutes. Beat 4 eggs in a bowl; stir in potatoes and onions.

Wipe skillet clean and heat 1 tablespoon of the reserved oil. Pour in egg mixture and cook over low heat just until omelet is barely set, about 3 minutes. Place on top of the skillet an inverted plate slightly larger than the skillet, and turn out the omelet onto it; slide the omelet back into the skillet. Cook until eggs are cooked throughout, about 2 more minutes. Slide omelet onto a round serving plate.

Pour 2 tablespoons oil in the skillet and add peppers; cook over medium heat until dry, about 15 minutes. Beat 4 eggs with 1/4 teaspoon each salt and pepper; stir in peppers. Wipe skillet clean and add 1 tablespoon oil. Pour in egg mixture and cook omelet in the same way as the former one. Slide it onto potato omelet.

Meantime, bring a large amount of salted water to a boil. Add beans and cook until crisp-tender, 5 minutes; drain. Beat remaining 4 eggs with 1/4 teaspoon each salt and pepper. Stir in green beans. Wipe skillet clean and add 1 tablespoon oil. Pour in egg mixture and make omelet the same way as the former ones. Slide it onto pepper omelet.

To make the sauce: Heat oil in a skillet and sauté onion over low heat until soft, about 5 minutes. Add tomatoes and cook over medium heat for 15 minutes. Stir in tomato paste, salt, pepper and cayenne, if desired. Transfer to a blender or food processor and purée. Strain through a fine sieve.

To assemble the dish: Preheat oven to 350 degrees F. Reheat omelet torte in the oven and pour sauce over, drizzling over the sides. Sprinkle some cheese on top and pass the rest in a bowl. Serve warm.

SOUPS

Gazpacho Rojo de Sevilla
(Cold Soup from Sevilla with Tomato and Vegetables)

Gazpacho is undoubtedly the most popular cold soup in Spain, one you will find in many restaurants during the hot summer months—especially in the south, where it originated. An Andalusian grand lady, Eugenia de Montijo, took it to France in the nineteenth century when she married Napoleon III, and there it became very fashionable, along with many other cold Andalusian soups.

There are numerous variations of gazpacho: white and red, thick and thin, puréed and diced—even warm ones for the wintertime, although I don't find them as interesting as the cold soups. In the old days it was hard work to make gazpacho, for the ingredients had to be puréed by hand; I remember having it very seldom at home—until my mother brought back a blender from a trip to the United States!

The following recipe is my own adaptation of the classic red gazpacho, original to Sevilla and the most widespread of all. After making it many times over the years, I find this the perfect recipe for my taste.

To serve 6

For the soup:

3 pounds very ripe tomatoes,
 peeled, seeded and cut up
1/2 large red pepper, stemmed,
 seeded and cut up
1/2 large English-type cucumber,
 peeled and cut up
1 teaspoon finely chopped garlic

4 tablespoons fine olive oil,
 preferably extra virgin
1/3 cup sherry wine vinegar, or to
 taste
1/2 teaspoon salt, or to taste
1/2 teaspoon freshly ground black
 pepper, or to taste

For the garnish:

> 2 tablespoons olive oil
> 2 (1/2-inch) slices of bread,
>   without crusts, diced small
> 1 large tomato, peeled, seeded
>   and diced small (by hand)
> 1/2 large red pepper, seeded and
>   diced small (by hand)

> 1/2 large English-type cucumber,
>   peeled and diced small (by
>   hand)
> 1/2 red onion, diced small (by
>   hand)

To prepare the soup: Purée the vegetables in the blender or food processor with the garlic, oil, vinegar, salt and pepper. Add 1 cup water, or more if you prefer a thinner soup. Refrigerate for at least 5 hours.

To prepare the garnish: In a small skillet, heat 2 tablespoons oil and sauté the bread over medium-high heat until golden; drain on paper towels. Place vegetables and croutons in separate bowls and pass them as garnishes with the chilled soup.

Ajo Blanco de Málaga
(Cold White Gazpacho from Málaga with Garlic and Almonds)

This is an understated, light cold soup, original to Málaga but found all over Andalucía, perfect for the hot summer days of this southern region. The recipe is of Arab origin, going back to the tenth century. It is made from the produce of the Andalusian soil: almonds, bread, garlic, sherry vinegar and grapes. When grapes are not in season, you can substitute other fruits, such as apples, pears or melon.

One of the best ajo blancos *I had in southern Spain was at El Fogón, the delightful restaurant run by Lalo Grosso and her family in Puerto de Santa María, near Cádiz. Her daughter, María José, manages El Fogón and also lives in the little villa where the restaurant is. This naturally makes for the pleasant, comfortable feeling of dining in someone's home.*

To serve 6

> 1/3 cup blanched almonds
> 3/4 pound white bread,
>   preferably not sourdough,
>   crusts removed (about 11/2
>   pounds before trimming
>   crusts)

> 3 large cloves garlic
> 2 eggs
> 1 cup olive oil
> 1/3 cup sherry wine vinegar
> 1 teaspoon salt, or to taste

As a garnish:

> 18 sweet seedless green grapes
>   (or 1 cup diced peeled apple,
>   pear or melon)

Place almonds in a bowl and cover with boiling water; let them soak for 1 hour. Soak bread in 6 cups cold water.

In the food processor or blender, purée the drained almonds until they are reduced to a fine paste. Add garlic and eggs; whirl to combine well. In a pouring jar, mix oil and vinegar; with the motor running, add mixture in a thin stream. Drain bread, squeezing it with your hands; reserve the water. Add bread to other ingredients and purée. Add salt and taste for seasoning.

Transfer the mixture to a large nonmetallic bowl and add reserved water; you may dilute it with more water, to the consistency you desire. Cover the soup and chill it for 3 to 4 hours or longer; it will keep in the refrigerator for at least 2 or 3 days.

To serve, place 3 grapes in each bowl and ladle soup on top. If you used other diced fruits, pass them around separately.

Salmorejo de Córdoba
(Thick Gazpacho from Córdoba)

Salmorejo is a gazpacho soup without water, original to the city of Córdoba but now found all over Andalucía, with minor variations in the ingredients and garnish. This is the classic recipe, as served by Pepe García Marín at El Caballo Rojo, an excellent restaurant in Córdoba where Pepe features the most authentic and interesting dishes of Andalusian cuisine. He has done a fantastic job researching old Arab recipes which were practically lost, and adapting them to today's cooking methods and ingredients.

To serve 4 to 6

*1/4 pound white bread,
    preferably 1 or 2 days old,
    crusts removed (about 1/2
    pound before trimming crusts)
2 pounds ripe tomatoes, peeled
    and seeded
1 teaspoon minced garlic
2 egg yolks*

*11/2 tablespoons sherry wine
    vinegar or a fine red wine
    vinegar
1/2 teaspoon salt
1/4 teaspoon freshly ground
    white pepper
1/3 cup fine olive oil, preferably
    extra virgin*

As a garnish:

*1 hard-boiled egg, chopped
2 ounces thinly sliced prosciutto,
    cut in 1-inch strips*

In a bowl, soak bread in about 3/4 cup cold water. With your hands, squeeze excess water from bread; purée it in the blender or food processor with tomatoes and garlic. Add egg yolks, vinegar, salt and pepper. With the motor running, add the olive oil and blend well. Chill the soup for at least 4 or 6 hours before serving.

Pass hard-boiled eggs and prosciutto in separate bowls, as a garnish.

Crema Fría de Melón a la Hierbabuena
(Cold Melon Cream Soup with Mint)

El Cenador del Prado has been a success since it opened in Madrid in 1984. It is a delightful, bright and cheerful restaurant, new in style and in its approach to cooking, owned by the young Herranz brothers: Tomás, the chef, and Ramón, the manager.

Tomás is never afraid to experiment with new ideas; yet many of his recipes have a very traditional, even old-fashioned background. This cold melon soup has a perfect balance of ingredients; he serves it garnished with tiny prawns and julienned fresh mint, but I usually garnish it with just a whole mint leaf and 3 melon balls in each bowl.

To serve 6

2 large, ripe cantaloupes (5 or 6 pounds)
1 tablespoon cornstarch
1 cup plus 6 tablespoons port wine

1/4 teaspoon salt
1 cup heavy cream

As a garnish:

18 cantaloupe balls (cut from the 2 melons)
6 fresh mint leaves
12 tiny precooked bay shrimp (or

6 small shrimp, boiled and peeled, sliced in half lengthwise) (optional)

Cut cantaloupes in half and remove the seeds. Using a small melon-baller, scoop out 18 balls; set aside for the garnish.

Peel melons and cut them up. Place in a saucepan with 1 cup water, and bring slowly to a boil. Dissolve cornstarch in 1 cup of the port and add to cantaloupe as soon as the water boils. Cook over low heat, stirring, until thickened—about 15 minutes. Season with the salt. Purée and strain through a medium sieve. Chill. When the soup is very cold, add cream and remaining 6 tablespoons port.

Serve cold, garnishing each bowl with 3 melon balls, a fresh mint leaf and, if desired, the shrimp.

Sopa de Tomate y Hierbabuena con Almendras
(Catalan: Sopa de Tomàquet i Menta amb Ametlles)
(Cold Tomato Mint Soup with Almonds)

On a warm summer evening in Barcelona, this was the perfect starter for a family feast at El Racó d'en Binu, an outstanding restaurant in Argentona, near Barcelona. It is refreshing, light and interesting.

Chef/owner Francesc Fortí has risen to the top echelon of new Catalan cuisine in Spain, combining the finest local produce with his creative ideas. He represents the third generation since Albino Forti, "Grandpa Binu"—after whom the restaurant was named when it opened in 1970—started the great family cooking tradition.

To serve 4 to 6

4 tablespoons butter
3/4 pound onions, finely chopped
1 pound unpeeled zucchini,
  coarsely chopped
1 pound unpeeled ripe tomatoes,
  puréed
31/2 cups Chicken Stock

1 teaspoon salt
1/2 teaspoon freshly ground
  white pepper, or to taste
6 large fresh mint leaves,
  chopped
1/4 cup sliced almonds

In a medium-large skillet, heat butter and sauté onions on low heat until soft and golden, about 20 minutes. Add zucchini and cook until tender, about 15 minutes. Purée in the blender or food processor. Transfer to a large saucepan. Add tomato purée and stock. Bring to a boil, and immediately turn off heat. Strain through a fine-mesh strainer. Add salt, pepper and mint; taste for seasoning. Chill.

Preheat oven to 350 degrees F. Toast almonds for 3 to 4 minutes, or until golden.

Serve the soup cold, sprinkling sliced toasted almonds on each bowl.

Crema de Hinojo
(Catalan: Sopa de Fonoll)
(Cream of Fennel Soup)

Martinet is a picturesque little town nestled in the Catalan Pyrenees. In 1975, on a paradisaical spot in the outskirts, Josep and Dolores Boix opened an inn with an exceptional restaurant, Can Boix. Their cuisine aims at enhancing the finest produce of the bountiful area, La Cerdanya, and the dishes are prepared with care and imagination—the work of a great chef.

I had this soup there on a warm summer day, and it was served cold; but at home I've made it warm and found it just as good. When making it cold, I have substituted yogurt for cream and found this added a fresh, zesty flavor (and decreased the calories a bit, too!). I also thinned it some more, adding another cup of stock at the end.

To serve 6

4 tablespoons butter
1 teaspoon minced garlic
2 medium onions, minced
2 heads fennel (about 2 pounds),
  stems and leaves trimmed,
  chopped
4 cups Chicken Stock (5 cups, if
  served cold)

1 tablespoon orange zest*
1/2 cup heavy cream (or yogurt, if
  served cold)
2 teaspoons salt, or to taste
1/2 teaspoon freshly ground
  white pepper, or to taste

In a large pot, melt butter and sauté garlic with onion over low heat for 10 minutes. Add fennel and continue cooking for 20 or 30 minutes, stirring occasionally. Add chicken stock and orange zest. Bring to a boil, reduce heat and cook over very low heat, covered, for 30 minutes or until vegetables are very tender. Purée and strain through a medium sieve. Stir in cream and season with salt and pepper. Reheat and serve warm. (If served cold, add yogurt when chilled.)

Crema de Remolacha
(Beet Cream Soup)

This flavorful soup is another creation of Lalo Grosso, one of many delicacies she serves at her charming restaurant in Puerto de Santa María, El Fogón. I like beets, but I've never had them taste as good as in this recipe!

To serve 4 to 5

4 tablespoons butter
1 medium onion, chopped
1 large leek (about 1/2 pound), finely chopped, with 1/3 of the green part
1 teaspoon minced garlic
1 large bunch beets (about 2 pounds before trimming), peeled and finely chopped

1 tablespoon sherry wine vinegar
1 cup fino sherry, or another flavorful dry Spanish sherry
4 cups Chicken Stock
1 teaspoon sugar
1/2 cup heavy cream
1/2 teaspoon salt, or to taste
1/4 teaspoon freshly ground white pepper, or to taste

Heat butter in a large pan or flameproof casserole. Over low heat, sauté onion, leek and garlic until very soft and golden—30 to 45 minutes, to get as much flavor as possible. Add beets, stir and sauté for about 4 minutes. Add vinegar, sherry, stock and sugar. Bring to a boil, reduce heat to low and cook, partially covered, for 45 minutes. Uncover and cook for another 15 to 20 minutes, until beets are very tender.

Purée in the blender or food processor, and strain through a medium sieve. Return the soup to the pan; add cream, salt and pepper. Taste for seasoning. Serve warm or chilled.

Crema de Tomillo
(Catalan: Sopa de Farigola)
(Thyme Cream Soup)

I have enjoyed this soup at two restaurants: Lola Pijoán's Can Borrell in Meranges, in the Catalan Pyrenees, and Montse Guillén in Barcelona. That is no wonder, because Lola is Montse's mother!

This is a classic Catalan soup made with fresh thyme, earthy and heartwarming; it was Montse's idea, though, to add the quail eggs as a garnish—her note of "new" style, and one that goes very well here.

To serve 4 to 6

For the vegetable stock:

2 tablespoons olive oil
1 large onion, chopped
1 medium stalk celery, chopped
2 large carrots, chopped
1 large leek, chopped, with 2/3 of
  the green part

1 small bunch fresh thyme
2 bay leaves
10–12 black peppercorns

For the soup:

1 large bunch fresh thyme
1 large head garlic or about 40
  unpeeled cloves, crushed
1/2 cup heavy cream

1 teaspoon salt
1/8 teaspoon freshly ground
  white pepper

As a garnish, per serving:

2–3 thin baguette slices, rubbed
  with garlic, sprinkled with
  olive oil and toasted in the
  oven

2 quail eggs, poached (optional)
1 fresh sprig thyme

To prepare the stock: Heat oil in a large skillet and sauté onions, celery, carrots, leek and small bunch of thyme over very low heat until soft and very brown, about 45 minutes. Stir occasionally so the vegetables don't burn, but let them turn quite golden.

Add bay leaves and peppercorns, and cover with 8 cups water. Bring to a boil, immediately reduce heat to very low and simmer, covered, for an hour. Strain the stock into another pot, pushing down gently with a spoon against the colander.

To prepare the soup: Add the large bunch of thyme and garlic cloves to the stock. Increase heat and cook briskly at a boil for 20 minutes. Strain soup. Add cream and heat through. Season with salt and pepper. Taste for seasoning.

To assemble the dish: Place 2 or 3 toasted bread rounds at the bottom of each bowl; put poached eggs, if desired, on top, and pour soup over. Add a sprig of fresh thyme and tell each guest to swish it through the soup before eating; this will intensify the thyme flavor.

Sopa de Hierbabuena
(Mint Soup)

This recipe was given to me by a young woman from Extremadura, Cristina Tristancho. At nineteen, she not only is a superb cook but has been doing a terrific job of revitalizing old recipes from her native region which have been forgotten, and incorporating them in today's cuisine.

A perfect example is this shepherd-style soup, which will surprise you with the simplicity and compatibility of its ingredients. It also has an attractive presentation, especially when served in a round clay casserole, 8 or 9 inches in diameter.

To serve 6 to 8

> 8 cups Chicken Stock
> 6 large cloves garlic, minced
> 1/2 cup (packed) chopped fresh
>   mint leaves
> 1 teaspoon salt

> 1 (1-pound) loaf of white bread,
>   at least 1 day old, crusts
>   removed, and sliced thin
> 3/4 cup (packed) grated Gruyère
>   cheese

In a pan, combine the stock with the garlic, 1 teaspoon of the chopped mint leaves and the salt. Bring to a boil, reduce heat to low and simmer for 5 or 6 minutes.

Preheat broiler.

In a shallow ovenproof casserole, preferably of clay, place bread slices in a layer. Sprinkle some chopped mint over and continue alternating layers, ending with a layer of bread. Pour hot stock over the bread. Sprinkle with the cheese and place under the broiler until cheese is golden. Serve immediately.

Sopa de Pescadores
(Catalan: Sopa de Pescadors)
(Fishermen's Soup, Mediterranean Style)

Practically every restaurant along the Mediterranean coast of Spain serves wonderful fish soups; they have the raw materials right at hand. To reproduce them here I have found it essential to make a double fish stock (that is, use a Fish Fumet instead of water as a basis to make the second fumet), and to use only fresh white fish.

One restaurant that comes to memory when I think of great fish soup is Mare Nostrum, in the seaside resort of Sitges, south of Barcelona, where my parents have had their summer home since 1950—the same year Josep Martí opened Mare Nostrum. And it has been one of the top restaurants in town ever since, particularly noted for its fisherman-style cuisine.

To serve 8

For the second fumet:

2 tablespoons olive oil
1 large onion, chopped
3 large garlic cloves, chopped
2 1/2 pounds unpeeled ripe
   tomatoes, chopped
Fish heads and bones reserved
   from filleting 2 pounds of fish,
   or about 4 pounds of fish
   trimmings (see Note below)
1 cup dry white wine
2 or 3 leeks, sliced or coarsely
   chopped, with about 2/3 of the
   green part

1 large onion, sliced
1 medium unpeeled carrot, sliced
   or coarsely chopped
3 or 4 unpeeled cloves garlic,
   crushed
Bundle of herbs made with some
   fresh parsley (with plenty of
   stems), 2 bay leaves and 1
   teaspoon dried thyme,
   rosemary, savory or sage (if
   fresh, use a few sprigs)
1 tablespoon orange zest*
1 recipe Fish Fumet

For the soup:

2 pounds fresh white fish fillets
8 large shrimp, in their shells
1/2 cup dry white wine
16 live mussels or small clams,
   shells scrubbed
1 cup short-grain rice

1/2 teaspoon (.2 gram) saffron
   threads (or 1/4 teaspoon
   powdered saffron)
3/4 teaspoon salt, or to taste
1/2 teaspoon freshly ground black
   pepper, or to taste

(Note: You may buy the whole fish and have the fish market fillet it for you, giving you the heads and bones for the second fumet. You will need about 6 pounds whole fish to get 2 pounds of fillets. Discard skins, fins and intestines. Clean and rinse well fish heads and bones to remove all blood and gills.)

To prepare the second fumet: Heat oil in a large casserole or stock pot; sauté chopped onion and chopped garlic over low heat for about 10 minutes. Add tomatoes and cook over medium heat until dry. Add fish heads and bones and wine. Bring to a boil, stir and cook over high heat for 5 minutes to evaporate the alcohol. Add leeks, sliced onion, carrot, crushed garlic, bundle of herbs, orange zest and fish fumet; bring to a boil, immediately reduce heat to very low and skim the scum from the surface. Simmer, partially covered, for 35 minutes. During this time, skim off the scum as it rises to the surface.

To prepare the soup: Pluck all bones from fish fillets with tweezers or pliers, and cut fillets in chunks. Rinse and pat dry shrimp. Set aside.

In a large pot, bring wine to a boil. Add mussels or clams, on a rack, and steam, covered, until they open—about 4 to 5 minutes for mussels, 5 to 10 for clams. Set them aside and reserve steaming liquid. Discard any that have not opened.

Strain the second fumet through a colander, pressing down the bones and vegetables gently with a spoon. Add mussel or clam steaming liquid to the fumet. Strain again through a fine sieve into a large pot. Bring to a boil and add rice, saffron, salt and pepper. Gradually add fish fillets and shrimp. Bear in mind that rice takes about 20 minutes to cook, fish fillets 7 or 8 minutes, medium shrimp 3 or 4 minutes—all depending on size. At the last minute, add mussels or clams. Taste for seasoning. Serve immediately.

Fideos con Almejas
(Noodles with Clams)

I found the best version of this traditional Galician dish at Chocolate, the outstanding restaurant in the fishermen's village of Vilaxoán, near Pontevedra. Josefa Cores, the friendly chef and owner, feels that women play an important role in Galician cooking. Yet their work is understated and behind the scenes, while the man is up front and does the P.R. Josefa's husband, Manolo, is a great cook too—though often away running their restaurant in Caracas, Venezuela!

Meanwhile, the women in the family run the show. The restaurant, however, is named after Manolo's nickname, "Chocolate."

To serve 6

7 tablespoons olive oil
4 large cloves garlic, minced
1 small onion, minced
1 large red bell pepper, stemmed, seeded and chopped
1 pound ripe tomatoes, peeled and chopped
7 cups Fish Fumet
1/2 teaspoon (.2 gram) saffron threads
2 tablespoons chopped fresh parsley leaves

1 bay leaf
1 teaspoon salt, or to taste
3/4 teaspoon freshly ground black pepper, or to taste
8 ounces spaghetti egg noodles, broken into 2-inch pieces
1 cup dry white wine
3 pounds small live clams, shells scrubbed (about 8 to a pound)
1 (10-ounce) package frozen green peas

Heat 4 tablespoons oil in a large casserole; sauté garlic and onion over low heat for about 10 minutes, until soft. Add pepper and tomatoes and sauté slowly for another 20 minutes, stirring occasionally. Add fumet and bring to a boil. Stir in saffron, parsley, bay leaf, salt and pepper. Set aside.

Heat remaining 3 tablespoons oil in a large skillet with high sides. Over medium-high heat sauté noodles, stirring, until golden. Add 4 cups of broth from the casserole, a cup at a time, stirring, to let the pasta gradually absorb it. Remove from heat.

In a large pan, bring wine to a boil. Add clams, on a rack, and steam them, covered, over medium-high heat for 5 to 10 minutes or until they open. Set clams aside and keep warm. Discard any that do not open. Strain liquid from pan into the casserole with the broth.

Remove bay leaf from casserole and pour contents into skillet with pasta; stir in peas and cook for 5 minutes. Add clams and taste for seasoning. Serve immediately.

VEGETABLE SALADS

Zanahoria Rallada con Naranja y Piñones (Shredded Carrot Salad with Orange and Pine Nuts)

The famous Zalacaín restaurant in Madrid serves this refreshing salad as a little nibble before the meal. I also find it very nice as a light first course.

To serve 6

1½ pounds young, thin, tender carrots
¼ cup fresh orange juice

1 tablespoon fresh lemon juice
1 tablespoon olive oil
¼ cup pine nuts

Peel and shred the carrots; you should have about 4 cups. (You can shred them in the food processor.) Place them in a bowl with the orange and lemon juice. Allow to marinate anywhere from 10 minutes to ½ hour.

Meanwhile, heat oil in a small pan and sauté the pine nuts, stirring, until golden. Drain them on paper towels. Just before serving, toss the nuts with the carrots.

Ensalada de Zanahoria al Jerez
(Carrot Salad with Sherry)

The idea for this flavorful salad came from Rincón de Pepe restaurant in Murcia, where chef/owner Raimundo González-Frutos has developed a number of recipes based on the local produce.

To serve 4 to 6

For the dressing:

1/2 tablespoon Dijon-style mustard
1/4 cup sherry wine vinegar

1/4 cup amontillado or another full-flavored dry Spanish sherry

For the salad:

1 bunch watercress, rinsed and drained

1 pound thin young tender carrots, peeled and grated

In a bowl, mix together ingredients for the dressing, beating with a fork or whisk. Trim the watercress of all stems, keeping only the leaves; you should have about 1 cup of leaves. At the last minute, toss watercress and carrots with the dressing.

Ensalada de Naranja y Aguacate
(Orange and Avocado Salad)

This salad could be a California recipe—yet I had it as an appetizer at Els Capellans, a restaurant in the lovely hotel Huerto del Cura in the town of Elche, near Alicante, in the País Valenciano region.

To serve 6

For the salad:

3 oranges
3 avocados, preferably the Haas variety (see Salmon and Avocado Mousse, Note 2)

1 tablespoon chopped fresh tarragon (or fresh mint)

For the dressing:

1/2 tablespoon lemon juice
1 1/2 tablespoons sherry wine vinegar or red wine vinegar
5 tablespoons olive oil

3/4 teaspoon Dijon-style mustard
1/4 teaspoon salt
1/2 teaspoon freshly ground black pepper

Peel the oranges and cut them in sections, discarding the membrane. Peel the avocados and cut into sections approximately the same size as the oranges. (Don't peel avocados more than 1/2 hour prior to serving time, or they will get dark—unless you pour the vinaigrette over them.) Arrange decoratively in circles on individual plates, alternating orange and avocado slices. Sprinkle tarragon or mint on top.

Whisk together all dressing ingredients and drizzle over each plate.

Ensalada de Aguacate con Tomate
(Avocado and Tomato Salad)

La Gabarra restaurant opened in Madrid in October 1982, and it has been a hit ever since. Owner Fernando Jover enjoyed cooking all his life, although he grew up in an upper-class environment in northern Spain where it was not considered appropriate for a man to cook. He started his first "serious" restaurant in Bilbao. A boat lover, he named La Gabarra after the word for barges in Bilbao and northern Spain.

Fernando features a cuisine that mixes traditional Basque preparations with superb novelties such as this salad, which successfully combines textures and flavors.

To serve 6

3 small avocados, preferably the Haas variety (see Salmon and Avocado Mousse, Note 2)
4 tablespoons sherry wine vinegar
4 large tomatoes, peeled
8 large basil leaves, finely shredded
1 small head Romaine lettuce, finely shredded (you need only half a lettuce, so use just the inner leaves, which are paler and more tender)
6 tablespoons olive oil
1 teaspoon salt
1/2 teaspoon freshly ground black pepper

Cut avocados in half lengthwise, remove seeds and peel the fruits. With your hand or a brush, rub about 1 tablespoon of the vinegar over the avocados so they won't darken.

Seed and dice 3 of the 4 tomatoes; in a bowl, toss with the basil leaves. Thinly slice remaining tomato, and cut each slice in quarters.

Just before serving, line 6 salad plates with the shredded lettuce. Using the small side of a melon-baller, scoop out 4 balls from the seed side of each half avocado; set these aside. In a bowl, mix olive oil, remaining 3 tablespoons vinegar and salt and pepper; pour mixture over tomatoes and basil, and toss. Fill avocado halves with this mixture, and arrange avocado balls on top. Place 1 avocado half over the lettuce on each plate, and garnish with 3 or 4 quartered tomato slices around the avocado.

Ensalada de Aguacate y Pimientos Rojos
(Avocado and Red Pepper Salad)

It was at Wallis—a new, very creative restaurant in Madrid—that I had ensalada de aguacate y pimientos del piquillo, *a delightful combination of very fine red peppers roasted over a wood fire, with thin slices of avocado. Also in Madrid, the outstanding restaurant Cabo Mayor serves anchovies with avocados in a very elegant dish—so both of these ideas inspired me to create this recipe.*

To serve 8

4 large sweet red bell peppers
About 1 tablespoon olive oil for
  rubbing peppers
2 ripe avocados, preferably the
  Haas variety (see Salmon and
  Avocado Mousse, Note 2)
10 canned flat anchovy fillets
  packed in oil, drained

2¹/2 tablespoons balsamic vinegar
1/2 teaspoon freshly ground
  white pepper
3 tablespoons snipped fresh
  chives (about 1/8 inch long)

Preheat oven to 400 degrees F. Rub peppers with oil. Roast and peel them according to directions for roasting and peeling peppers.*

Cut the peppers in half along their natural seams and remove the seeds. If some peppers break up a bit while peeling them, don't worry; just try to keep them as whole as possible. Place half peppers (or quarters, or even strips, if they have broken up too much) on an ungreased baking sheet and put them back in the 400-degree F. oven for 15 minutes.

Remove the pits from the avocados and scoop out the flesh into the blender or food processor. Purée with the anchovies and vinegar. Add white pepper and taste for seasoning; it will probably not need any salt, as the anchovies are quite salty themselves.

Place half a pepper on each plate. Arrange a spoonful of avocado purée at the base of the pepper. Sprinkle the chives over the peppers and serve immediately.

Ensalada de Endibias y Aguacates a la Salsa de Cabrales
(Catalan: Amanida d'Endìvies i Alvocat amb Salsa de Cabrales)
(Endive and Avocado Salad with a Blue Cheese Sauce)

The Font brothers' Sa Punta restaurant, opened in 1976, is one of the prettiest in Spain. High up on a rock in the village of Pals, in the northern Catalan district of L'Empordà, near Gerona, it overlooks the Mediterranean through beautiful pine woods; a small white sandy beach is just 200 yards away. In the pleasant summer season of the Costa Brava, you can dine outside as well as in an elegant indoor dining room.

Jaume Font, the chef, is an artist. His cooking, basically Catalan, features some classic recipes from L'Empordà to which he adds his own personality and imagination. His wife, Mari Carmen, and his brother José run the dining room with charm and efficiency.

I loved this salad, one of their ideas, because of the flavor combinations as well as its attractive presentation.

To serve 8

For the dressing:

> *2 ounces blue cheese (preferably a flavorful creamy Oregon or Danish blue; don't use a salty cheese)*
> *1/3 cup half-and-half*
> *1/2 tablespoon dry Spanish sherry, preferably fino*

> *1/2 tablespoon sherry wine vinegar*
> *1/4 teaspoon salt, or to taste*
> *1/4 teaspoon freshly ground black pepper, or to taste*

For the salad:

> *3 medium heads Belgian endives (3/4 pound)*
> *3 medium carrots, peeled*

> *2 large avocados, preferably the Haas variety (see Salmon and Avocado Mousse, Note 2)*

To prepare the dressing: In a bowl, mash blue cheese with a fork in 2 tablespoons half-and-half. Add remaining dressing ingredients and mix well.

To prepare the salad: Cut endives into very thin strips crosswise. Cut carrots into thin strips, or thickly grate them using the food processor. Toss endives and carrots with the dressing in the bowl.

Shortly before serving (so they won't darken), cut the avocados in half lengthwise and remove the seeds. Peel them and cut them into quarters lengthwise. Make a "fan" of each quarter, by making 3 or 4 slices not quite all the way through at the base and fanning the slices out.

To serve, arrange an avocado fan on one side of each individual plate, and endive/carrot mixture at the base of the avocado.

Barquitos de Ensalada
(Colorful Salad Boats)

This is a recipe from my mother which makes a very nice fall or winter salad, as it uses fennel, apple and red cabbage. The orange adds a touch of color as well as nice flavor contrast. I often served it in Spain at buffet parties, for it looks very pretty and is a perfect palate cleanser between courses.

To serve 6 to 8

For the dressing:

2/3 cup olive oil
2 tablespoons sherry wine
  vinegar or red wine vinegar
1 teaspoon prepared Dijon-style
  mustard
2 teaspoons fresh tarragon

leaves, coarsely chopped (or 3/4
  teaspoon dried tarragon,
  crumbled)
1/2 teaspoon salt, or to taste
1/4 teaspoon freshly ground black
  pepper, or to taste

For the salad:

1 cup finely shredded red
  cabbage
1 cup finely diced sweet anise or
  fennel (see Note below)
1/2 cup finely diced celery
1 small tart apple, such as
  Pippin or Granny Smith, finely
  diced (about 1 cup)

2 small oranges, peeled, seeded
  and finely diced (1 scant cup)
1 small red onion, very thinly
  sliced (about 1 cup)
6 or 8 large, round-shaped leaves
  Boston (butterhead) lettuce, all
  about the same size

(Note: If fennel is not available, omit and increase celery to 1 cup instead of 1/2.)

In a salad bowl, combine dressing ingredients and beat well. Toss dressing with the cabbage, fennel, celery, apple, orange and onion. Arrange lettuce leaves on individual plates and spoon mixture on each. Serve chilled.

Ensalada de Col Lombarda con Boquerones
(Catalan: Amanida de Col Llombarda amb Seitons)
(Red Cabbage Salad with Anchovies)

Start preparation 1 day ahead

The idea for this salad came from a lovely little restaurant in Barcelona, L'Olivé. Owner Josep Olivé uses the small fish boquerones, *which don't exist here; they are white and less pungent than anchovies. But the recipe works really well with anchovies, too.*

To serve 8

2 pounds red cabbage, finely
  shredded
6 tablespoons sherry wine
  vinegar or red wine vinegar
2 teaspoons salt

1 (2-ounce) can flat anchovy
  fillets, drained
1/2 cup olive oil
6 tablespoons chopped fresh
  parsley leaves

In a large saucepan, combine cabbage with vinegar, salt and 2 cups water. Bring to a boil, reduce heat to medium-low and cook, covered, for 15 minutes. Let it stand, covered and unrefrigerated, for about 24 hours.

Purée the anchovies in a food processor or blender with the olive oil.

Drain and squeeze excess moisture from the cabbage; place it in a large bowl. Toss with the anchovy–olive oil mixture and the parsley. Serve cold or at room temperature.

Ensalada de Habas a la Hierbabuena
(Catalan: Amanida de Faves a la Menta)
(Fava Bean Salad with Mint)

This salad has become a classic of Catalan cuisine. It is an original recipe from the late master chef Josep Mercadé, featured by his son-in-law Jaume Subirós at the great restaurant Ampurdán in Figueras, near Gerona. Fava beans go very well with prosciutto, and the mint provides a touch of freshness.

Fava beans are widely available in Spain, fresh and frozen; but here the season in the spring is usually quite short. You can buy them while they are available and store them shelled and blanched in your freezer; if the skins are too tough, peel them after blanching. This salad also works very well with frozen lima beans.

To serve 8

For the salad:

1½ pounds shelled young fava beans (about 4 pounds before shelling), or 2 (10-ounce) packages frozen large lima beans
¼ pound lean, good-quality

prosciutto, sliced medium-thin, cut into ¼-inch-wide strips
1 small head Romaine lettuce, finely shredded
5 large fresh mint leaves, cut into thin strips

For the dressing:

2–3 tablespoons herbed or Dijon-style mustard
½ cup olive oil
3–4 tablespoons red wine vinegar, to taste

1 teaspoon freshly ground black pepper, or to taste
½ teaspoon salt, or to taste

Bring a large amount of salted water to a boil. Add fava beans and cook until tender, 5 to 7 minutes. Drain and let cool. Transfer beans to a large salad bowl. Add ham, lettuce and mint.

Combine all the dressing ingredients in a bowl and whisk until well blended. Taste for seasoning.

Just before serving, pour dressing over salad and toss gently until lettuce is evenly coated. Serve at room temperature.

FISH AND MEAT SALADS

"Xatonada"
(Catalan Tuna Salad with a *Romesco*-Style Sauce)

This is a classic recipe from the Catalan district of El Vendrell, in the Low Penedès. El Celler del Penedès, the excellent country-style restaurant near Vilafranca del Penedès, serves a delicious xatonada, *and chef/owner Pere Valls was more than happy to share his recipe with me.*

The name xatonada *is derived from the word* xató, *the* romesco-*style sauce which is basic to the dish. It makes a delightful cold luncheon salad as well as a first course for dinner. In Catalonia it is traditional to serve it on Ash Wednesday.*

To serve 6

1 medium head escarole lettuce
1 (7-ounce) can albacore tuna, packed in olive oil
2 small tomatoes (Italian-style are best), each cut into 6 wedges
2 hard-boiled eggs, each cut into 6 wedges

12 large flat canned anchovy fillets (1 [2-ounce] can)
3/4 cup (1/4 pound) small black olives with pits (Niçoise-style or dried oil-cured olives are best)
1 recipe "Xató"

Separate, wash and dry the escarole leaves; arrange them as a bed on individual plates. In a bowl, crumble tuna very finely with your fingers; distribute it evenly on each plate, mounding it in the center. Arrange 2 tomato wedges on the sides of each plate, and 2 egg wedges; put 1 anchovy fillet across each egg wedge. Sprinkle olives on top.

Place a small mound of *xató* on each plate, and pass remaining sauce in a bowl. Serve at room temperature.

Ensalada Templada de Bonito
(Warm Bonito Salad with Vegetables)

This is one of the most imaginative and delicate fish salads I have had in Spain. It comes from one of my favorite restaurants in San Sebastián, Akelaŕe, inspired by chef/owner Pedro Subijana. I have made it with bonito, tuna and small scallops, and it has always been a success.

To serve 6

For the fish marinade:

1 pound fresh bonito or tuna fillets (or 3/4 pound fresh small bay scallops)

3 tablespoons apple cider vinegar
1 teaspoon coriander seeds, lightly crushed

For the dressing:

2 tablespoons apple cider vinegar
1/2 teaspoon prepared Dijon-style mustard
1/2 teaspoon salt

1/8 teaspoon freshly ground black pepper
6 tablespoons finest-quality olive oil, extra virgin if possible

For the salad:

1 cup finely shredded red cabbage
1/2 cup packed alfalfa sprouts
1 cup thinly julienned carrots (about 2 inches long)
1 cup mâche lettuce (also called

lamb's quarter or corn salad), or shredded inner leaves of Romaine
2 heads Belgian endives, leaves separated and soaked in cold water

To marinate the fish: Toss bonito, tuna or scallops with the vinegar and coriander seeds for 10 minutes. Drain.

To prepare the dressing: In a food processor or blender, mix well vinegar, mustard, salt and pepper. Add oil slowly in a thin stream.

Preheat broiler.

To prepare the salad: Toss the cabbage, sprouts, carrots and lettuce together with 2 tablespoons of the dressing. Use half of this mixture to line 6 salad plates. Drain and pat dry the endive spears; arrange them in a circle on top of the cabbage mixture. Sprinkle the remaining cabbage mixture over the endive spears.

Place the fish on an oiled heatproof pan under the broiler. The cooking time for the bonito will vary according to the thickness of the fillet; for a 1/2-inch-thick fillet, allow about 7 minutes. The scallops will take only 1/2 minute.

Peel the skin off the bonito. When fish is cool enough to handle, with your fingers, shred the fish and place a small heap in the middle of the vegetables on each plate.

Heat the remaining 6 tablespoons of dressing in a small pan, stirring. Pour some of the hot dressing over each salad plate and serve immediately.

Ensaladilla de Bonito
(Bonito Salad with Peppers, Onions and Tomatoes)

This refreshing salad was inspired by a dish I had at Los Remos restaurant, in the beach town of San Roque, near the southern city of Cádiz. As I sat down on their lovely patio waiting for a meal which promised to be memorable, owner Alejandro Fernández brought me this salad as an unpretentious little tapa. *I thought it could make a delightful summer lunch dish.*

To serve 4 to 6

For the poaching liquid:

1 cup dry white wine
1 medium unpeeled carrot, sliced
1 large onion, sliced
1 bay leaf
3 sprigs fresh parsley
1–2 sprigs fresh thyme (or 1/4 teaspoon dried)

1–2 sprigs fresh tarragon (or 1/4 teaspoon dried)

1 1/2 pounds fresh bonito fillets (or another firm fish such as tuna, red snapper or mahimahi)

For the vegetables:

1 large green pepper, stemmed, seeded and finely diced
1 medium onion, finely chopped

2 large firm ripe tomatoes, peeled, seeded and finely diced

For the dressing:

1/2 cup olive oil
4 tablespoons red wine vinegar
1 teaspoon salt

3/4 teaspoon freshly ground black pepper

Combine all ingredients for the poaching liquid with 1 quart water in a pot large enough to hold the fish. Bring to a boil, reduce heat to low and simmer, partially covered, for 30 minutes. Add fish, cover and poach for 8 to 10 minutes, depending on the size and type of fish—just enough to barely cook it.

Remove fish from liquid, drain and let it cool. Trim fillets of all fat and skin, and cut them into 1/4-inch cubes. Place vegetables in a large bowl, and toss with the fish.

Combine all the dressing ingredients in a bowl, beating with a fork or whisk. Pour over salad and let it sit, unrefrigerated, for 1 or 2 hours. Serve slightly chilled.

"Esqueixada"
(Catalan Shredded Codfish Salad)

Start preparation 2 days in advance, by soaking codfish in water

Catalonia is the only region in Spain where you will find salt codfish served cold and uncooked, in this very traditional salad. It makes a delicious first course; even those who are not used to salt cod have found this a favorite at my dinner parties.

Recently I had an excellent version of esqueixada *at Tritón in Barcelona, a very home-style, traditional restaurant, which features country Catalan cooking. Owner Joaquín "Quimet" Vidal, always friendly and attentive, has built a reputation for the quality and consistency of his food.*

To serve 6 to 8

1 pound boneless dried salt codfish (see Salt Cod*)

1 small red (or green) pepper, seeded and sliced into thin rings

1/2 large red onion, thinly sliced, rings separated

1 large unpeeled firm ripe tomato, thinly sliced

3/4 cup fruity olive oil, preferably extra virgin

1/4 cup red wine vinegar

4 large cloves garlic, minced

1/2 teaspoon freshly ground black pepper, or to taste

Salt to taste, if necessary

As a garnish:

2 ounces black unpitted olives

2 hard-boiled eggs, quartered

Cover the salt cod with water and soak for 48 hours, changing the water several times—5 or 6 if possible. Drain and press the cod with your hands to remove excess water. Discard any skin or bones. With your fingers, shred the cod into thin strips and place in a salad bowl.

Toss the pepper, onion and tomato with the cod. In a bowl combine the oil, vinegar, garlic and black pepper, beating to blend well. Pour over the cod and, with your hands, mix and toss to coat the cod and vegetables. Taste for seasoning.

Arrange on a platter or in a bowl, and garnish attractively with olives and hard-boiled eggs.

"Trinxat" de Rape
(Catalan: Trinxat de Rap)
(Catalan Shredded Monkfish Salad)

This recipe comes from a top restaurant in Catalonia and, for that matter, in Spain: Eldorado Petit, which Lluís Cruañas opened 12 years ago as a "small" ("petit" in Catalan) restaurant in the seaside village of Sant Felíu de Guíxols, in the heart of the famed Costa Brava. I remember Eldorado Petit as a tiny dining spot where everything on the limited menu was great. Today, Lluís is a brilliant representative of Catalan cooking, and in 1984 he opened another restaurant of the same name in Barcelona, which has very quickly established itself among the best in the city.

I had this dish for lunch on a hot summer day, and it couldn't have been more appropriate. It can make a delightful first course, too.

To serve 6

For the fish:

> 2 pounds fresh monkfish, in
>   whole pieces
> 1 tablespoon sherry wine vinegar
>
> 1 bay leaf
> 6 black peppercorns

For the dressing:

> 1 pound ripe tomatoes, peeled,
>   seeded and diced very small,
>   by hand
> 1/4 cup snipped chives (fresh, if
>   possible)
> 1/2 cup heavy cream
> 1 tablespoon dry Spanish sherry,
>   such as amontillado
>
> 3 tablespoons sherry wine
>   vinegar, or to taste
> 2 teaspoons salt, or to taste
> 1 teaspoon freshly ground white
>   pepper, or to taste

For the salad:

> 2 large ripe tomatoes, peeled and
>   thinly sliced
> 1/2 small red onion, very thinly
>   sliced
>
> 1/2 large English-type cucumber,
>   peeled and thinly sliced

To cook the fish: Place monkfish in a pan with vinegar, bay leaf and peppercorns. Add water to cover, bring to a boil and immediately reduce heat to low; simmer for 10 to 12 minutes, or until fish is cooked. Drain.

To prepare the dressing: In a nonmetallic bowl, combine all the dressing ingredients and let stand for at least 30 minutes.

To assemble the salad: Press fish with your hands to squeeze out as much water as possible. Remove the loose grayish skin and membranes from the fish. With your fingers, shred it very finely. Once more, squeeze water out of it with your hands. Toss fish with the dressing in the bowl and refrigerate until serving time, between 1 and 3 hours.

To serve, arrange a bed of the thinly sliced tomatoes, onion and cucumber, and place a mound of fish salad on top.

Ensalada de Verduras con Dos Gustos de Salmón (Vegetable Salad with Fresh and Smoked Salmon)

Cabo Mayor restaurant in Madrid is one of the most interesting exponents of new cuisine in Spain. Víctor Merino and his son-in-law, Pedro Larumbe, have created a number of fascinating recipes; I was particularly impressed with this one. The combination of fresh and smoked salmon is perfectly balanced with the other ingredients, and the presentation is most attractive as well.

To serve 6

For the salad:

1 pound fresh salmon fillets, skin removed
1 tablespoon tarragon or sherry wine vinegar
1/2 teaspoon salt
1/3 pound smoked salmon
6 ounces young thin green beans, ends trimmed (or 24 long ones)

1/4 pound young thin carrots, peeled
1 large turnip, peeled
1/2 cup stemmed watercress leaves
2 tablespoons snipped fresh chives

For the dressing:

3 tablespoons olive oil
2 tablespoons tarragon or sherry wine vinegar

1/2 teaspoon salt
1/4 teaspoon freshly ground white pepper

As a garnish:

A few sprigs watercress

To prepare the salad: Julienne the salmon fillets in very thin strips about 2 inches long. In a bowl, combine vinegar with salt and toss fresh salmon strips in it. Let stand for about 10 minutes (don't leave it much longer or the vinegar will cook the salmon). Drain and set salmon aside.

Julienne the smoked salmon in strips about the same size as the fresh salmon. Set aside.

Julienne beans, carrots and turnip in very thin strips about 2 inches long—again, about the same size as the salmon. In a pot, bring salted water to a boil and cook each vegetable separately until tender but still crisp (2 or 3 minutes after the water has returned to a boil; the turnip usually takes the shortest time to cook). Drain each vegetable and refresh under cold running water. Pat dry and set vegetables aside in a glass or wooden bowl. Add watercress leaves and chives.

To prepare the dressing: Beat together dressing ingredients.

To assemble the salad: In a salad bowl, combine fresh and smoked salmon with vegetables. Toss with the dressing. This is a scantily dressed salad, but the sharpness of the dressing mingles nicely with the sweetness of the fish and the crunchiness of the vegetables.

Serve on individual plates, arranging the salad in loose little heaps with a sprig of watercress on the side.

Ensalada Templada de Lentejas y Conejo al Curry (Catalan: Amanida de Llentíes i Conill al Curry) (Warm Curried Lentil and Rabbit Salad)

This recipe was inspired by a dish I had at Azulete, one of Barcelona's most innovative and exciting restaurants. Chef/owner Toya Roqué represents the current wave of women cooks who have made headlines in Spain. This is one of her creations—a dish as original as it is representative of Catalonia's new style of cooking.

To serve 8

For the salad:

2 bunches watercress or mâche lettuce (also called lamb's quarter or corn salad)
4 medium carrots (about 1 pound), peeled

3/4 cup lentils
6 cups Chicken Stock or rabbit stock

For the rabbit:

2 tablespoons butter
1 stalk celery, chopped
1 medium onion, chopped
1 tablespoon curry powder
1/2 cup dry white wine

Hind and forelegs of 1 rabbit (see Note below)
1 teaspoon salt
1/2 teaspoon freshly ground black pepper

For the dressing:

2 teaspoons chopped garlic
1/4 cup apple cider vinegar
2 tablespoons apple juice
1 teaspoon sugar
1 teaspoon dry mustard

1 teaspoon curry powder
1/2 teaspoon salt
1/2 teaspoon freshly ground black pepper
2/3 cup vegetable oil

(Note: For this recipe you will need only a rabbit's hind legs and forelegs. You can use the body or saddle for Stuffed Rabbit Saddle with Vegetables [Silla de Conejo Rellena con Verduras].)

To prepare the salad: Trim stems from watercress or mâche lettuce, saving only the leaves. Set aside in refrigerator. Dice very finely 3 carrots. Chop the fourth carrot and set aside.

Wash the lentils and remove any pebbles. Bring stock to a boil in a large pan. Add lentils, bring to boil again and reduce heat to simmer. Cook, uncovered, for 15 minutes. Add diced carrots and cook another 15 minutes, or until lentils are soft but not mushy. Strain lentils and carrots and set aside. Reserve stock.

To cook the rabbit: Melt butter in a medium-deep skillet. Add chopped carrot, celery and onion and sauté until soft, about 5 minutes. Stir in curry powder. Add wine and cook over medium heat for another 5 minutes, or until liquid has evaporated. Add 1 cup of reserved stock (use remainder in another recipe), and bring to a boil. Season rabbit with salt and pepper. Reduce heat to very low and place rabbit legs on top of the vegetables; cover and cook on low heat for 45 minutes. Turn rabbit pieces several times as they cook. Remove rabbit and dice meat to about the size of the diced carrots. Set aside.

To prepare the dressing: In a blender or food processor, combine all the dressing ingredients except oil. With the motor running, slowly add the oil; the dressing should thicken. Transfer it to a pan and heat gently.

To assemble the dish: In a bowl, mix the rabbit with carrots and lentils. Toss mixture with the dressing in the pan. Line 8 salad plates with the greens; heap the rabbit mixture in the middle of the greens, and serve immediately. The combination of warm and cold adds to the interest of this salad.

FISH AND SHELLFISH

Mejillones en Escabeche
(Mussels Marinated in a Wine, Vinegar and Herb Sauce)

This is a recipe from my mother, who made it at home, usually with sardines—a classic Spanish recipe of Arab origin. Since fresh sardines are not as common in the United States as they are in Spain, I found that mussels work very well here.

This dish can be served as a first course, as an appetizer or even as a light lunch entrée. In any case, be sure to accompany it with lots of crusty bread to dip in the delicious sauce— Peasant Bread (Pan de Payés) is perfect with it.

To serve 6 to 8

1 cup dry white wine
3 pounds live mussels, shells scrubbed
1/4 cup olive oil
6 large cloves garlic, minced
2 tablespoons finely chopped fresh thyme leaves (or 2 teaspoons dried)
2 tablespoons finely chopped fresh parsley leaves

2 bay leaves, middle vein removed, crushed
3/4 cup balsamic vinegar
1 teaspoon Spanish paprika
1 teaspoon lemon zest*
1/4 teaspoon salt, or to taste
1/2 teaspoon freshly ground black pepper, or to taste
Pinch of cayenne

In a large pot, bring wine to a boil. Add mussels, on a rack, cover and steam over medium-high heat for 4 or 5 minutes. Transfer them to a plate. (Discard those that have not opened.) Reduce liquid in the pot to 3/4 cup. Strain and reserve.

Heat oil in a skillet and cook garlic over low heat until golden. Add thyme, parsley and bay leaves; cook for 2 or 3 minutes, stirring. Turn off heat; add reserved liquid from steaming the mussels, vinegar, paprika, lemon zest, salt, pepper and cayenne. Taste for seasoning.

Remove mussels from their shells, reserving half of each shell. Place mussels in a nonmetallic bowl, add sauce and let them marinate for at least 2 hours before serving. (If longer, cover and refrigerate; but bring to room temperature before serving.)

To serve, arrange mussels on a serving plate in their half shells. Pour some sauce over, and pass remaining sauce separately.

Guisantes Estofados a la Menta Fresca con Almejas
(Catalan: Pesols Estofats a la Menta Fresca amb Copinyas)
(Pea Stew with Fresh Mint and Clams)

The idea for this dish came from Sa Punta restaurant in Pals (Costa Brava, near Gerona) where Jaume Font features classic and new dishes of Catalan cuisine. Mixing peas with mint is a traditional combination of L'Empordà, the district where Pals is. The freshness of the mint comes through perfectly with the peas, blending very well with the clams.

This is not a very soupy stew, but I serve it in soup bowls—and always accompanied with good crusty bread.

To serve 4 to 6

3 tablespoons butter
1 large onion, minced
1/2 cup finely chopped fresh mint
  leaves
1 pound shelled peas, fresh or
  frozen

1/2 teaspoon salt
1/2 cup dry white wine
4 pounds live small clams (try to
  get 10 to 12 per pound), shells
  scrubbed

As a garnish:

1 sprig fresh mint per person

In a large casserole, heat butter and sauté onion with mint leaves until very soft, about 20 minutes. Add peas and salt, cover and cook until peas are tender—about 15 minutes for fresh peas, 5 minutes for frozen.

Meanwhile, in a large pot, bring wine to a boil. Add clams, on a rack, and steam them until they open, 5 to 10 minutes. Add them to the pea stew. Discard any that do not open. Strain wine and juices drained from steaming the clams through a fine-mesh strainer into the stew. Taste for seasoning. Serve warm in soup bowls, garnished with a fresh mint sprig.

Trucha Escabechada
(Trout Marinated in Vinegar with Onions and Carrots)

Start preparation the day before

Fish en escabeche *make delightful cold luncheon dishes, and trout is a favorite in Spain for this type of preparation. O'Pazo restaurant in Madrid, which owner Evaristo García has made famous for its fresh fish and shellfish, serves an excellent* trucha escabechada *in the style of this recipe.*

To serve 6

For the trout:

> 6 (5–6-ounce) whole fresh trout
> About 1/2 cup olive oil
> 1/2 cup flour
>
> 1 teaspoon salt
> 1/4 teaspoon freshly ground black
>   pepper

For the marinade:

> 12 large cloves garlic, very thinly
>   sliced (by hand)
> 1 medium carrot, peeled and
>   sliced very thin
> 1 medium onion, sliced thin
>
> 1 1/2 cups white wine vinegar
> 1 bay leaf
> 1 or 2 sprigs parsley
> 1/2 teaspoon hot red pepper
>   flakes

As a garnish:

> Parsley sprigs
> Lemon slices
>
> 1/4 cup chopped fresh parsley
>   leaves

To cook the trout: Rinse trout and pat it dry. Heat oil in a large skillet. Combine flour, salt and pepper in a brown paper bag; add trout, one at a time, shaking the bag to coat it. Place trout in the skillet and cook over high heat until golden, about 3 minutes on each side, turning only once. Remove the trout to a glass, enamel or clay casserole.

To prepare the marinade: Add garlic to the oil in the skillet and sauté until golden; remove with a slotted spoon and drain on paper towels. Add carrot and onion to skillet and sauté over low heat for 10 minutes. Add vinegar, bay leaf, parsley, hot pepper flakes and 1 cup water. Cover and simmer on very low heat for 20 minutes.

Pour marinade over the trout, and arrange garlic over them; save 2 or 3 tablespoons garlic to use later as a garnish. Cover the casserole and refrigerate for 24 hours. During this time, turn the trout several times in the marinade.

Remove trout from the refrigerator 2 hours before serving. Arrange them on a serving platter (or serve directly from the casserole). Pour the marinade, garlic, onion and carrot over. Garnish with the sprigs of parsley and lemon slices; sprinkle reserved garlic slices and the chopped parsley on top.

Tosta de Gambas
(Prawn Toast)

Koldo Lasa, in his early thirties, is the youngest offspring of a great dynasty of cooks, which began when Francisco Lasa started a roadside inn in 1929. He had many children, who all devoted themselves to cooking—as did the grandchildren, too! Since the mid-seventies, Koldo has been running Hostal Lasa in Bergara, near San Sebastián, my favorite of all the various restaurants the family has scattered around northern Spain. Koldo has given his own creative touch to the Lasas' traditional Basque recipes.

Tosta de gambas *makes a delightful first course or a light luncheon entrée. It is perfect accompanied by a vegetable salad.*

To serve 4

> **1 pound small raw prawns, in**
> **their shells (if you can get**
> **them with the heads, these**
> **will add more flavor to the**
> **dish; in this case, buy 1½**
> **pounds)**
> **3 tablespoons butter**
> **1 cup full-bodied Spanish**
> **brandy**

> **2 cups Fish Fumet**
> **½ cup heavy cream**
> **1 tablespoon finely chopped**
> **fresh parsley leaves**
> **½ teaspoon salt**
> **½ teaspoon freshly ground**
> **white pepper**
> **6–8 (½-inch) slices Loaf Bread**
> **(see Note below)**

As a garnish:

> **1 tablespoon snipped fresh**
> **chives**

(Note: Loaf Bread [Pan de Molde] is ideal for this recipe. You will need only a few slices for this dish, but you can serve the bread throughout the meal, or use it later—it makes wonderful toast! Or you can use any white bread, sliced and toasted.)

Peel the prawns, reserving the shells. Sauté the shells (and heads, if you have them) in 2 tablespoons of the butter for 1 or 2 minutes. Add ½ cup brandy; when hot, flambé.* When the flames subside, add the fumet; bring to a boil, reduce heat to low and cook, uncovered, for 15 minutes, pushing down the shells with a spoon from time to time. Strain through a fine-mesh strainer, pushing down the shells with a spoon, and reserve the sauce.

Sauté the prawns on medium-high heat in the remaining tablespoon butter for 1 minute; add remaining ½ cup brandy, increase heat and, when hot, flambé. After 1 or 2 minutes, douse with the reserved sauce. Remove the prawns with a slotted spoon and reserve.

Over high heat, cook sauce until reduced to about ¾ cup. Add cream, parsley, salt and pepper, and cook over medium heat for about 5 minutes. Taste for seasoning.

Trim the crusts from the bread slices; cut them in half and toast them; place on individual plates. Return the prawns to the pan, just to heat through. Arrange the prawns on top of the toast and pour sauce over; make sure the sauce soaks the bread. Sprinkle chives on top. Serve warm.

Langostinos a la Crema de Perejil
(Catalan: Llagostins a la Crema de Julivert)
(Shrimp in a Parsley Cream)

The secret of the great Cal Isidre restaurant is that every morning Isidre Gironés goes to the best market in Barcelona, La Boquería, and personally selects the produce for the day's menu. His wife, Montserrat, is the charming hostess. This recipe was inspired by a delightful dish I had there.

Serves 6

1¹/₂ pounds medium or medium-small prawns, in their shells
4 tablespoons butter
1 cup dry white wine
1 cup Fish Fumet
1 cup packed chopped fresh parsley leaves

4 or 5 large cloves garlic, minced
1/2 cup heavy cream
1/2 teaspoon salt
1/4 teaspoon freshly ground black pepper

Shell the prawns and set them aside. In a medium skillet, heat butter and sauté the prawn shells over low heat for 20 to 30 minutes. Stir occasionally and push the shells with the back of a spatula to get as much of their flavor into the butter as possible. Add wine, increase heat to medium-high and cook, stirring, until the wine is reduced to about 1/2 cup. Strain through a fine-mesh strainer into a medium-size pan, pushing shells down with a spoon to get all the juices through. Add fumet to the skillet, stirring and scraping with a wooden spatula to release any particles left in the skillet. Pour fumet through the strainer (with the shells) into the pan with the wine mixture. Discard shells.

Scald the parsley: put it in a strainer and dip it for just a few seconds into a pan of boiling water. Drain and stir it into the sauce. Add garlic and cook over low heat for 2 minutes. Add cream and cook over medium heat until reduced by about one third or to desired consistency. Season with salt and pepper. Add the prawns and cook them, stirring, for 2 to 3 minutes or until done (depending on their size). Serve immediately.

Pastel de Pescado Mediterráneo
(Catalan: Pastís de Peix Mediterrani)
(Mediterranean Fish Cake)

This is a recipe from my sister-in-law, Mahle, one of the first I made in the United States—and a hit from day one. It is easy to make, and all you need is good fish.

Mahle serves it often at buffet dinners or as a first course. It also works very well as an appetizer on toast, because it is like a fish terrine. I guess it is a precursor of "new-style" fish mousses; not your usual mousse type but meatier, more country style.

To serve 8

4 tablespoons olive oil
1 1/2 pounds flavorful fresh fish,
  such as rock cod, monkfish,
  halibut or sea bass
1/4 cup full-bodied Spanish
  brandy
1 large onion, minced
3 cloves garlic, minced
2 pounds tomatoes, peeled,
  seeded and chopped
1 tablespoon chopped mixed
  fresh herbs, such as thyme,
  oregano or rosemary (leaves
  only)

1/4 cup dry white wine
1 teaspoon salt
1/2 teaspoon freshly ground black
  pepper
1/2 pound peeled prawns,
  coarsely chopped
1/4 pound crab meat, shredded
6 eggs, beaten
About 1/4 cup commercial dry
  bread crumbs

As a garnish:

1/4 cup drained large capers
8 prawns, cooked and peeled,
  leaving the tail intact

Heat 2 tablespoons oil in a skillet and, over medium heat, sauté the fish for 3 minutes. Add the brandy and, when hot, flambé.* When the flames subside, remove the fish and let cool.

Add remaining 2 tablespoons oil to the same skillet and, over low heat, sauté onion and garlic until golden. Add the tomatoes, herbs, wine, salt and pepper; increase heat to medium-high and cook until thick. Purée half of the sauce and reserve. Transfer the remaining sauce to a bowl.

Preheat oven to 350 degrees F.

Peel, bone and crumble fish. Add to bowl, together with the raw prawns and crab meat. Taste for seasoning. Stir in the beaten eggs and mix well.

Oil a 6- or 7-cup loaf pan (an 8 × 5-inch bread pan works well) or a round mold. Add bread crumbs and shake to coat the bottom and sides; discard excess. Pour in the fish mixture. Place the mold inside a larger pan filled with boiling water halfway up the mold. Bake in the preheated oven for 30 minutes. Remove from the larger pan and bake for another 60 minutes or until a cake tester comes out clean.

Unmold and serve either hot or cold, covered with the tomato sauce. Garnish with the capers around the edges, and arrange the whole prawns around the cake.

Pastel de Krabarroka
(Basque Fish Mousse)

Juan Mari Arzak is today one of Spain's most renowned chefs. His excellent Arzak restaurant in San Sebastián—the gastronomic center of the Basque Country—is enhanced by his charming personality. He has developed many interesting dishes found today in restaurants throughout Spain, among them this fish mousse, which has become a classic of "New Basque Cuisine."

The fish used by Arzak for this dish is krabarroka, *the Basque name for the fish known in the rest of Spain as* gallineta, *in France as* rascasse, *and in the United States as* cabezone. *It is a rockfish, ugly and with many bones, yet very tasty. But you can use any moist, flavorful white fish, such as rock cod, monkfish or orange roughy. I must say I have changed the recipe somewhat—adding, for instance, a little saffron, which Arzak does not use but which contributes a lovely note of flavor. This delicate dish will make an elegant first course or a delicious luncheon entrée.*

To serve 8

> *1 pound fillets of cabezone or*
> *another moist, firm white fish*
> *(see above)*

For the poaching liquid:

> *1 cup dry white wine*
> *1 medium unpeeled carrot, sliced*
> *1 small onion, sliced*
> *1 small stalk celery, sliced*
>
> *1 bay leaf*
> *1 sprig parsley*
> *1 sprig thyme (or 1/4 teaspoon*
> *dried)*

For the mousse:

> *About 2 tablespoons fine dry*
> *bread crumbs*
> *1 tablespoon butter*
> *2 tablespoons minced onion*
> *1 pound tomatoes, peeled but*
> *not seeded, chopped*
> *1/2 teaspoon (.2 gram) saffron*
> *threads*
>
> *1 bay leaf*
> *1/2 tablespoon tomato paste*
> *1 cup heavy cream*
> *8 eggs*
> *1/2 teaspoon salt, or to taste*
> *1/2 teaspoon freshly ground*
> *white pepper*

As an accompaniment

> *1/2 recipe Mayonnaise; make*
> *whole recipe and use half*

To poach the fish: In a pot large enough to hold the fish, combine all ingredients for the poaching liquid. Add 3 cups water, bring to a boil and simmer, partially covered, for 30 minutes. Add fish to the liquid, cover and simmer just until cooked through, 8 to 10 minutes. Clean the fish by removing skin, dark spots and any bones. (You can strain the liquid and save to use as a light fumet.) Set the fish aside.

Preheat oven to 400 degrees F.

To prepare the mousse: Butter an ovenproof 6-cup mold (the mousse will yield about 5 cups) and put the bread crumbs in it, shaking and turning to cover all the sides and bottom. Shake out any excess crumbs. Refrigerate the mold to set the crumbs, about 10 minutes, while you prepare the mousse.

Heat butter in a medium skillet and sauté onion until soft. Add tomatoes, saffron and bay leaf; cook over medium-low heat until liquid evaporates. Remove bay leaf. Purée in the food processor or blender. Whirl in tomato paste, cream, eggs, salt and pepper. Add the fish and blend, pulsing just a few times, until it is medium ground. Taste for seasoning. Remove mold from refrigerator and pour mixture into it.

Place the mold in a larger pan filled with boiling water halfway up the mold. Bake in the preheated oven until a cake tester comes out clean. The timing will depend on the mold you have used; about 1¼ hours for a rectangular cake pan, about ¾ hour for a ring mold.

When cool, run a knife around the edges and unmold onto a serving plate. Serve at room temperature, with the mayonnaise on the side.

Crêpes de Txangurro
(Thin Pancakes Stuffed with Crab)

This is another dish that Juan Mari Arzak has made into a classic of "New Basque Cuisine" by adding his personal touch to a traditional recipe. Txangurro *is a Basque preparation of shredded crab with an "American" sauce; but it is his idea to stuff it in a pancake and add a delicate sauce to it.*

I have served this dish as a first course for dinner and as an entrée for lunch, accompanied by a salad.

To serve 6

For the pancakes:

3 eggs
¾ cup flour
1 cup milk
1 tablespoon full-bodied Spanish brandy

About 2 tablespoons butter for cooking

For the filling:

6 tablespoons butter
2 medium carrots, peeled and
  finely chopped
3/4 cup minced shallots
2 1/2 tablespoons minced garlic
1 1/2 pounds tomatoes, peeled,
  seeded and chopped

1/2 cup full-bodied Spanish
  brandy
1 1/2 cups Fish Fumet
1 cup heavy cream
Salt and freshly ground black
  pepper to taste, if necessary
1 pound crab meat

For the sauce:

1 cup Fish Fumet

To prepare the pancakes: In a blender or food processor, combine all the ingredients except the butter, and blend until very smooth. Let the batter rest for about 30 minutes before cooking.

In a crêpe pan or a 7-inch heavy-bottomed skillet, heat a tiny bit of butter until quite hot. Add about 2 tablespoons of the batter and, over medium heat, very quickly swirl the batter around so that it coats the bottom of the pan. The pancake should be as thin as possible. Cook the pancake until the edges start to pull away from the sides of the pan; the bottom should be golden. Invert the pan over a firm surface—a wooden board, for example—and give it a sound whack to release the pancake. (Don't worry if the first pancake takes a little longer and doesn't come out perfectly; the rest of them will be faster and better.) Set the pancakes aside. You should have at least 12 pancakes.

To prepare the filling: In a heavy-bottomed skillet, melt butter and add carrots, shallots and garlic. Sauté over low heat until very soft and golden, about 15 minutes. Add tomatoes, increase heat and cook until dry. Add brandy and flambé.* When the flames subside, add fish fumet and reduce by half. Add cream and cook over medium heat until slightly thickened—2 or 3 minutes. Taste for seasoning, adding salt and pepper if necessary. Reserve 1 cup of this sauce. Add crab to the skillet, stir and heat through.

To assemble the pancakes: Distribute crab mixture among the pancakes, and roll them up. Place them, seam side down, on an ovenproof serving platter or baking dish.

Preheat broiler.

To prepare the sauce: Purée reserved sauce with 1 cup fumet, and strain through a fine-mesh strainer into a saucepan. Heat through and pour over the crab pancakes. Place platter under the broiler just until the tops turn golden, and serve immediately.

SALT CODFISH

Salt codfish dishes, found all over Spain, are among the best offerings of the Mediterranean countries. In the following pages you will find several of my favorite recipes, as well as Catalan Shredded Codfish Salad ("Esqueixada") in the Fish and Meat Salads chapter.

Codfish was originally a northern product, first found in Norway in the ninth century. Yet Spain and Portugal are the main creators of recipes for salt codfish, which paradoxically we have always imported, at least since the fifteenth century. The best comes from Newfoundland, and also from Scotland and Norway. Basques were the first to eat it in Spain, as they caught it when fishing for whales in northern Europe; but Basque cuisine kept within its boundaries until well into the nineteenth century— while since the fifteenth, salt codfish has been cooked in Catalonia. It probably came there from the South of France, which has old dishes such as *brandade de morue* (shredded salt codfish with olive oil, garlic and milk), original to Nîmes and also found in Spain.

Salt codfish, dry and hard as a wooden board, can be turned into a juicy, exquisite delicacy. Not all salt codfish is the same quality, though; when buying it, be sure the fillets are thick and the flesh white. If they are thin and yellowish, they are old and will be stringy. If you are not going to use it right away, store it in your refrigerator and it will keep for at least 2 or 3 months.

Salt codfish needs to be soaked in cold water for about two days before using it, changing the water 5 or 6 times during the process, as directed in my recipes. After this operation, the cod will no longer be salty. If you are short of time and the recipe calls for shredded cod, shred it before soaking; it will take less time to freshen.

Salt cod has a distinct flavor, very different from fresh cod, which I personally enjoy very much. Even though today we have other methods of preserving fish, the unique flavor of salt cod is important in the following recipes; you will not get the same results with fresh cod.

Pimientos Rellenos de Bacalao
(Red Peppers Stuffed with Cod)

Start preparation 2 days in advance, by soaking codfish in water

Stuffed red peppers are a dish found very often all over Spain. Meat-stuffed peppers are more traditional and old-fashioned; to prepare them with seafood is a newer approach. My favorite stuffing is salt codfish, as served at Rekondo restaurant in San Sebastián. And yet this is not a "New Basque Cuisine"–style restaurant; Chomín and Mari Carmen Rekondo serve sound, classic Basque cooking. Besides its excellent food, the restaurant is famous for Chomín's amazing cellar, which he built in 1975 and today has 80,000 bottles!

To prepare this dish, any small sweet red peppers will work; but the kind called pimientos are perfect for stuffing, because they are meatier and it is easier to keep them from breaking. Whatever peppers you use, don't worry if they fall apart a bit; the stuffing will help to hold them together—and when you arrange them on the plate they will look fine.

When red peppers are not in season, you can also use green peppers—although I find that the red ones are sweeter and more colorful.

To serve 8

For the peppers:

1 pound boneless dried salt codfish
8 medium red bell peppers
1 cup white bread crumbs, without crusts (see Bread Crumbs*)
1/3 cup milk
2 tablespoons olive oil

6 large cloves garlic, chopped
1 medium onion, chopped
3/4 teaspoon freshly ground black pepper, or to taste
Salt to taste, if necessary
2 eggs, beaten
1 tablespoon chopped fresh parsley leaves

For the sauce:

2 tablespoons olive oil
1 onion, sliced
1/2 pound carrots, peeled and coarsely chopped
1 cup dry white wine
1 tablespoon tomato paste

2 tablespoons chopped fresh parsley leaves
1 tablespoon Spanish paprika, or to taste
Pinch of cayenne
1 1/2 cups Chicken Stock

To prepare the cod: Soak codfish in water to cover for 48 hours, changing the water 5 or 6 times during this period. Drain and press the cod with your hands to remove excess water. Discard any skin or bones left and, with your hands or a knife, shred cod into small pieces. Set aside.

To stuff the peppers: Preheat oven to 400 degrees F. Roast and peel peppers according to directions for Roasting and Peeling Peppers.* Stem each pepper and remove the seeds, trying to keep peppers whole as much as possible. Turn oven down to 350 degrees F.

Soak bread crumbs in milk. Heat oil in a skillet; add garlic and onion, and sauté over low heat until soft, about 5 minutes. Add codfish and cook over medium heat for 5 minutes. Squeeze bread crumbs dry and discard milk. Add crumbs to skillet; stir in pepper, taste for seasoning and add salt if necessary. Off heat, add beaten eggs and 1 tablespoon chopped parsley.

Using a spoon or a pastry sleeve filled with the cod mixture, distribute filling evenly among the 8 peppers. Set them in an oiled baking dish.

To prepare the sauce: In a saucepan, heat oil and add onion and carrots; sauté over medium-low heat for 10 minutes. Add white wine, increase heat to high and cook for about 5 minutes, until dry. Stir in tomato paste, 1 tablespoon chopped parsley, paprika, cayenne and stock. Simmer on low heat for ½ hour, uncovered. Purée mixture in a blender or food processor. Taste for seasoning.

To assemble the dish: Pour the sauce on top of the peppers, covering them evenly. Bake in preheated 350-degree oven for 20 minutes. At the last moment, sprinkle the remaining tablespoon parsley on top.

Bacalao al Ajoarriero
(Codfish in a Tomato and Red Pepper Sauce)

Start preparation 2 days in advance, by soaking codfish in water

This is a very old dish, original to the northern region of Navarra. The name literally translates as "garlic muleteer," because it was often prepared for muleteers as they arrived at the roadside inns, carrying their goods in mule-drawn carts. It was a handy preparation; the sauce was ready, and the shredded codfish was added quickly.

A dish of such humble origin is today served at many fancy restaurants, sometimes refined by the addition of expensive shellfish. Iñaqui Oyarbide, who is from Navarra, has made his ajoarriero *with lobster famous at Madrid's superb Príncipe de Viana restaurant. I also enjoy it with prawns, as it is served in Basque Country at Dos Hermanas restaurant in Vitoria.*

But the only shellfish that could originally have been part of ajoarriero *is crayfish, from the nearby rivers. One recipe I treasure is Hemingway's favorite, given to me by Manuel Martínez-Llopis, a gastronomic historian who has the greatest collection of recipes and their stories. It includes crayfish and prawns, besides other untraditional ingredients such as white wine, mushrooms and various herbs. Traditional or not, it is delicious!*

The following is a classic recipe, the way I've had it at Pamplona's top restaurant, Josetxo. You will find it an instant success, whether served as a first course or as an appetizer, accompanied by croutons.

To serve 4 to 6

1 pound boneless dried salt
  codfish
2 tablespoons olive oil
12 large cloves garlic, minced
1 medium onion, chopped
2 medium red bell peppers (12
  ounces), stemmed, seeded and
  thinly sliced

1 pound unpeeled tomatoes,
  chopped
1/8 teaspoon hot red pepper
  flakes
1/4 teaspoon freshly ground
  white pepper, or to taste
Salt to taste, if necessary

Soak codfish in water to cover for 48 hours, changing the water 5 or 6 times. Drain and press cod with your hands to remove excess water. Discard any skin or bones, and shred it finely with your fingers.

Heat oil in a flameproof clay casserole or pan. Add garlic and onion; when soft, add red peppers and sauté for 5 minutes over medium heat, stirring. Add tomatoes, red pepper flakes and white pepper. Cook over medium heat until the mixture becomes very thick, about 15 minutes. Purée this sauce in a blender or food processor.

Return sauce to the casserole or pan. Add shredded codfish and cook over medium-low heat for about 10 minutes. It should have a thick consistency, with all the flavors mingled. Taste for seasoning; salt will probably not be necessary.

Bacalao a la Catalana con Pasas y Piñones (Catalan: Bacallà a la Catalana amb Panses i Pinyons) (Catalan-style Codfish with Pine Nuts and Raisins)

Start preparation 2 days in advance, by soaking codfish in water

This dish has the classic ingredients of Catalan cuisine: sofrito, picada, *even pine nuts and raisins, which automatically qualify the dish to be named* a la catalana. *I have served it with equal success as a first course, a main course and an appetizer or* tapa, *cutting the cod in smaller pieces. Moreover, it can be made ahead and reheated at the last moment.*

The following two codfish recipes come from Jaume de Provença, one of my favorite restaurants in Barcelona not only for its high standards but because it is Catalan to the bone. Owner/chef Jaume Bargues has contributed a lot to bringing my region's cuisine to the top rank it enjoys today. He is imaginative and talented, always creating new dishes but also keeping some great old traditionals, such as this one.

To serve 4 to 6

> 1 pound boneless dried salt
>   codfish

For the *sofrito:*

> 2 tablespoons olive oil
> 1 large onion, finely chopped
> 4 large cloves garlic, minced
> 2 pounds ripe tomatoes, peeled
>   and chopped
> 1 tablespoon chopped fresh
>   parsley

> 1 tablespoon olive oil
> 1/4 cup pine nuts
> 1/4 cup raisins

For the *picada:*

> 1 tablespoon olive oil, if
>   necessary
> 1 large (1/2-inch) slice white
>   bread
> 12 blanched almonds
> 12 hazelnuts (filberts)
> 3 large cloves garlic
> 1 tablespoon fresh parsley leaves

> 1 cup dry white wine
> 2 cups Fish Fumet
> 1/2 teaspoon salt
> 1/4 teaspoon freshly ground black
>   pepper

Soak the codfish in water to cover for 48 hours, changing the water 5 or 6 times. Drain and press the cod with your hands to eliminate excess water. Remove any skin and bones, and cut it in 4 or 6 serving pieces.

To prepare the sofrito: Heat 2 tablespoons oil in a skillet or, preferably, in a flameproof clay casserole (this develops better flavors and allows the *sofrito* to cook longer without burning). Add onion and garlic and cook slowly, for at least 20 minutes, until quite golden. Add tomatoes and parsley and sauté until dry, about 30 minutes or longer.

Meanwhile, heat 1 tablespoon oil in a small skillet and sauté pine nuts and raisins, until nuts are golden and raisins plump up. Remove them and set aside. Reserve oil in the skillet.

Preheat oven to 350 degrees F.

To prepare the picada: Add another tablespoon oil to skillet if necessary, and sauté bread until golden. Toast almonds in the preheated oven for 15 minutes, and hazelnuts for 12; rub hazelnuts in a damp towel to remove most of the skins. In the food processor, finely grind fried bread with garlic, almonds, hazelnuts and parsley.

Add white wine to tomato mixture, increase heat and cook until dry. Add fumet, bring to a boil and stir in *picada*. Season with salt and pepper. Add the codfish and cook, uncovered, over medium-low heat for 10 minutes. Taste for seasoning. Add pine nuts and raisins. Serve warm.

Bacalao a la Mousse de Allioli
(Catalan: Bacallà a l'Escuma d'Allioli)
(Codfish in an Allioli Mousse)

Start preparation 2 days in advance, by soaking codfish in water.

This recipe is based on an old Catalan combination, salt codfish with allioli. *Yet the idea of making an airy mousse out of a garlic mayonnaise is new and exciting—characteristic of Jaume Bargues's style. The dish has become a classic of new-style Catalan cuisine. It is easily prepared and can be served as an entrée or first course, depending on the portions.*

To serve 4 to 6

  1 pound boneless dried salt
  codfish

For the mousse:

  2 large heads garlic
  2 eggs, separated
  1 cup olive oil

  1 tablespoon lemon juice
  1/4 teaspoon salt
  Pinch of cayenne

Soak the fish in water to cover for 48 hours, changing the water five or six times. Drain and press the cod with your hands to eliminate excess water. Remove any skin or bones left. Set aside.

Preheat oven to 400 degrees F.

Bake whole garlic heads in the preheated oven for 45 minutes. When cool, cut off about one third of the garlic head tops, up to where you can see the cloves, and squeeze them out with your fingers. You should have about 3 tablespoons.

In a blender or food processor, beat garlic with egg yolks until thick. In a container with a pouring lip, mix oil, lemon juice, salt and cayenne, beating with a fork. With the motor running, add oil mixture to the egg yolks and garlic very slowly, in a thin stream; the mixture will thicken and acquire the consistency of a thick mayonnaise. (If the mixture separates or curdles or does not thicken, see the Mayonnaise (Salsa Mayonesa) recipe for a way to correct it.)

Transfer *allioli* to a bowl. Beat the egg whites until stiff, and fold them into the *allioli*.

Cut the codfish into 4 or 6 serving pieces, making sure they are all the same thickness; if some of them are too thin, put 2 thin ones on top of each other to level out all the pieces. Lay codfish in an oiled ovenproof casserole and cover with the mousse. Just before serving, bake in a preheated 400-degree F. oven, uncovered, for 10 to 15 minutes, or until the mousse is golden on top.

Atún Mechado al Horno
(Braised Tuna Studded with Anchovies)

A few miles outside Granada is the little village of Dúrcal, with an old mill owned for generations by the Carrillo family. In 1978, young Manuel Carrillo decided to restore it and made it the home of the Gastronomic Academy of Granada. He has since devoted himself to researching old Arab recipes, developing them with chef Luis Rico.

Manuel made the old mill into a beautiful restaurant, appropriately called El Molino (The Mill), where he serves those old specialties. But he does not like it to be called a restaurant; in fact, it is more like a working museum, and a wonderful place to visit. The mill provides the flour for their crusty breads, which are made daily in the old oven. The kitchen is also from the old days, with wood and coal stoves—and a silver-haired, grandmotherly cook named Aurora who fits perfectly into the environment.

To serve 6

For the fish:

9 large flat canned anchovy   *1 tablespoon lemon juice*
fillets (less than a 2-ounce can)   *1/4 teaspoon salt*
2 pounds fresh tuna, cut into 6   *1/4 teaspoon freshly ground black*
fillets   *pepper*

For the vegetables:

2 tablespoons olive oil
1½ pounds onions, thinly sliced
4 large cloves garlic, minced
½ pound carrots, peeled and
* thinly sliced into rounds*
½ pound ripe tomatoes, peeled,
* seeded and chopped*
1 large green pepper, cut into
* thin strips lengthwise*

¼ cup finely chopped fresh
* parsley leaves*
1 teaspoon salt
¼ teaspoon freshly ground black
* pepper*
2 bay leaves

To stud the tuna: Cut each anchovy into 3 pieces. With the point of a sharp knife, make a slit in the tuna flesh and stick 4 or 5 pieces of anchovy into each tuna fillet at different points; press into the opening with your finger. Sprinkle the fillets with lemon juice, salt and pepper. Set aside.

To prepare the vegetables: In a large skillet, heat oil and slowly sauté the onions, garlic and carrots over low heat until very soft, about 45 minutes. Add tomatoes, pepper strips, parsley, salt and pepper; cook until peppers are soft and tomatoes are dry, about 15 minutes.

To assemble the dish: Preheat oven to 350 degrees F.
  In an ovenproof lidded casserole that can accommodate the tuna fillets in a single layer, place half the vegetables in a layer; put the tuna fillets on top, tuck the bay leaves in beside the tuna and cover with remaining vegetables. Cover and bake in the preheated oven for about 30 minutes, or until fish is cooked.

Chicharro con Juliana de Verduras
(Mackerel with Julienned Leeks and Carrots)

In the old part of San Sebastián there is a small restaurant, Kokotxa, which in recent years has become a star in Basque Country. It is run by three young men: chef Iñaki Muguruza and brothers Guillermo and Gastón Nogués. Their cuisine is modern and rather Basque-French in style, as attested by this recipe.

I like to serve this dish in small portions as a first course; it provides a colorful, appetizing beginning for an elegant dinner.

To serve 6

For the sauce:

6 tablespoons butter
½ cup minced shallots
2 medium leeks (1½ pounds),
* green part trimmed, thinly*
* julienned (see Note below)*
3 medium carrots, peeled and
* thinly julienned*

½ cup heavy cream
½ teaspoon salt, or to taste
⅛ teaspoon freshly ground
* white pepper, or to taste*

For the fish:

> 3 mackerel (about 1½ pounds
> each), cut into 2 fillets each,
> with the skin on
> 2 tablespoons olive oil

> 2 tablespoons sherry wine
> vinegar or a good red wine
> vinegar

As a garnish:

> 1 tablespoon minced fresh
> parsley leaves

(Note: To thinly julienne the leeks, cut them in half lengthwise, separate the leaves and, one by one, roll them up lengthwise and slice across horizontally.)

Preheat oven to 350 degrees F.

To prepare the sauce: Heat butter and sauté shallots over low heat until golden. Add the leeks and carrots and sauté until soft, 15 to 20 minutes. Add cream, salt and pepper. Taste for seasoning. Reserve sauce.

To cook the fish: Oil a glass baking pan or ovenproof clay casserole. Place the fillets in a single layer, skin side down. Pour oil and vinegar over. Bake, uncovered, in the preheated oven for 8 minutes.

To assemble the dish: Pour sauce over the fish fillets and sprinkle with parsley. Serve immediately.

Pescado "Koskera"
(Fish in a Parsley and Pea Sauce, Basque Style)

This recipe is a perfect example of the simple, tasty cooking in the Basque "gastronomic societies." It was prepared for me by the president of the Cofradía Vasca de Gastronomía (Basque Gastronomic Society) in San Sebastián. These societies are reserved exclusively for men, so I was very honored to be invited!

To serve 6

> 4 tablespoons olive oil
> 1 large onion, sliced
> 3 large cloves garlic, minced
> ½ cup dry white wine
> 2 cups Fish Fumet
> 1 cup fresh or frozen small green
> peas

> ½ cup packed finely chopped
> fresh parsley
> ½ teaspoon salt, or to taste
> ½ teaspoon freshly ground black
> pepper, or to taste
> 2 pounds fresh fish fillets, such
> as turbot, snapper, cod, etc.

Heat 2 tablespoons oil in a skillet and sauté onion with garlic over low heat for about 15 minutes, until very soft and starting to color. Add wine, increase heat and cook rapidly until wine evaporates. Add fumet and cook over medium heat for 5 minutes. Purée the mixture and return it to the pan. Stir in peas, parsley, salt and pepper.

Heat remaining 2 tablespoons oil in a flameproof clay casserole or a skillet large enough to hold the fish fillets in 1 layer. Sauté the fish over medium heat, until golden. Pour sauce over the fish and cook for about 3 minutes, or until the fish is done. Serve from the casserole, or on individual dishes.

Pescado Braseado en Hojas de Col con Salsa al Cava (Braised Fish Wrapped in Cabbage Leaves with a Champagne Sauce)

One of Madrid's most reputable, traditional and consistently good restaurants over the years is Jockey. Founded by Clodoaldo Cortés in 1945, it has flourished under his son, Luis Eduardo, and director Félix Rodríguez, who runs the elegant dining room with the efficiency of a great professional.

From the beginning, chef Clemencio Fuentes has shown his mastery of the art of cooking. This delicate dish with a "new" touch is adapted from one of his creations.

To serve 6

1 large (2-pound) green cabbage, preferably Savoy
1½ pounds fresh rock cod or snapper, cut into 12 thin fillets
¾ teaspoon salt
½ teaspoon freshly ground black pepper
4 tablespoons butter

⅓ cup minced shallots
½ pound mushrooms, finely chopped
2 cups champagne, preferably a brut *Spanish* cava
2 cups Fish Fumet
½ cup heavy cream

Core the cabbage and cook it, whole, in boiling salted water to cover for 15 minutes. Drain and separate the leaves. Lay 12 leaves flat (if necessary, 2 leaves can be patched together). Arrange 1 fish fillet on top of each leaf, and sprinkle them with ¼ teaspoon each salt and pepper.

Heat the butter and sauté shallots for 5 minutes over low heat. Add the mushrooms, ½ teaspoon salt and ¼ teaspoon pepper; cook for 15 minutes. Add 1 cup champagne and cook over high heat until evaporated.

Distribute mushroom mixture over the fish pieces. Fold the fillets over and wrap 1 cabbage leaf around each fillet. Place them seam side down in a skillet large enough to hold all of them in 1 layer.

In a pan, bring the fumet and remaining cup of champagne to a boil, and reduce to 1 cup. Add cream and cook over medium heat for 5 minutes. Pour over the cabbage rolls. Bring to a boil, reduce heat to low, cover and cook for 15 minutes. Remove the cabbage rolls to a serving platter and reduce the sauce to desired consistency. Taste for seasoning. Pour over the fish and serve immediately.

Rodaballo Soufflé a la Albahaca
(Catalan: Turbot Soufflé amb Alfàbrega)
(Turbot with Basil Soufflé)

Another creation of the outstanding Ampurdán restaurant in Figueras (near Gerona, in the northern Catalan district of L'Empordà) is this superb combination of a fine fresh fish— turbot from the Mediterranean is excellent—with aromatic basil in a light, airy sauce.

If you don't have turbot, I have found that the recipe works very well with any firm white fish, as long as it is fresh. The sauce will accent the flavor!

To serve 6

For the poaching liquid:

1 cup dry white wine
6 black peppercorns
2 sprigs parsley
2 sprigs fresh basil

2 pounds fresh turbot fillets (or another fresh firm white fish, such as red snapper or rock cod), cut into 6 pieces
1 cup heavy cream

3 eggs, separated
1/2 cup chopped fresh basil leaves
1/2 teaspoon salt
1/4 teaspoon freshly ground white pepper
1 tablespoon butter
1 pound firm ripe tomatoes, peeled, seeded and finely diced (by hand)

Combine ingredients for the poaching liquid in a pan large enough to hold the fish; bring to a boil. Reduce heat and simmer, covered, for 30 minutes. Add the fish fillets and poach for 6 or 7 minutes, just until cooked through. Remove any skin or bones. Discard poaching liquid.

In a small saucepan, cook cream on medium heat until reduced by half. In a large bowl, beat egg yolks; add hot cream slowly, stirring. Add basil leaves, salt and pepper. Beat egg whites until stiff, and fold them into the mixture.

Preheat broiler.

In a skillet, heat butter and add tomatoes; cook 1 minute, just to heat them through. Transfer tomatoes to an ovenproof plate, arranging them in a bed. Place fish fillets on top, and pour cream sauce over. Place under the broiler until golden, and serve immediately.

Salmón al Vapor con Salsa de Vino Tinto
(Catalan: Salmó al Vapor amb Salsa de Vi Negre)
(Fresh Salmon in a Red Wine Sauce)

This recipe comes from a restaurant in Barcelona—one of the city's best, too—but I'm not sure how Catalan it is because Neichel is owned by a great Alsatian chef, Jean-Louis Neichel. He is in fact a disciple of French master Alain Chapel, and his recipes show a creative refinement worthy of the finest international cuisine. For me, more important than regional cuisines are personal styles, and good chefs and poor chefs; Jean-Louis is an extraordinary one, and I'm glad he decided to establish his restaurant in Barcelona.

I prefer this dish as an entrée, in which case the recipe should serve 4 rather than 6. Because of the red wine in the sauce, it goes very well with an elegant, medium-bodied red wine. Neichel serves it garnished with thinly sliced, slightly sautéed mushroom caps and a poached spinach leaf on top of each salmon piece, which I find adds a lovely note of color and flavor; you can use the spinach leaves on which the salmon was poached.

To serve 4 to 6:

For the sauce:

> 2 tablespoons olive oil
> 1 small onion, minced
> 1 small stalk celery, minced
> 1 medium carrot, topped but
>   unpeeled, minced
> 1/2 small leek, minced
> 1 1/4 cups plus 1 tablespoon
>   medium-bodied dry red wine

> 1 cup Enriched Veal Stock or 2
>   cups Brown Veal Stock
> 1 cup Fish Fumet
> 1 tablespoon lemon juice
> 6 tablespoons butter, cut in small
>   pieces
> Salt to taste

For the salmon:

> Several large spinach leaves, to
>   line the steamer
> 2 pounds salmon fillets, skinned,
>   cut into 4 or 6 pieces
> Salt for sprinkling the salmon

To prepare the sauce: Heat oil in a large pan and sauté vegetables over low heat until soft and golden, about 30 minutes. Add 1/4 cup of the red wine and increase heat until wine is cooked away, scraping the pan with a wooden spatula to release any browned bits stuck to the bottom. Add 1 cup red wine, veal stock and fumet. Increase heat and cook briskly to reduce by about half. Purée and strain through a fine-mesh strainer. Return to the pan and cook further, until reduced to 1 cup.

Turn heat to low; stir in lemon juice and remaining tablespoon red wine. Whisk butter pieces, one by one, into the sauce, being careful the sauce does not come to a boil. Taste for seasoning, and add salt if necessary. This sauce may be prepared ahead and heated up in a double boiler at the last moment.

To prepare the salmon: Line a steamer with spinach leaves. Place the salmon fillets on top, and sprinkle lightly with salt. Place the steamer over a pot with 1 inch of boiling water. Cover, and cook over low heat for 5 to 10 minutes, depending on the thickness of the fillets, just until done.

To serve the dish: Arrange the fillets on a serving platter or individual plates, pour some of the sauce over and pass remaining sauce separately in a sauceboat.

Escalopas de Salmón con Vieiras y Pimientos Verdes (Salmon with Scallops in a Green Pepper Sauce)

The brilliant idea for this combination of flavors is a good example of the style of Peñas Arriba, a new restaurant in Madrid that is the team effort of two men in their twenties: José Luis Seco—"Chiqui" to everybody—and Javier Otaduy, the chef. Some of their recipes are inspired by the cuisine of Cantabria, the northern region where Chiqui lived and learned to cook before going to Madrid.

This dish can be served as a main course or, cutting the recipe in half, as an elegant appetizer.

To serve 6

For the sauce:

2 tablespoons olive oil
1 pound green peppers,
    stemmed, seeded and cut into
    strips lengthwise

1/2 cup heavy cream
1/2 teaspoon salt
1/4 teaspoon freshly ground
    white pepper

For the seafood:

2 tablespoons butter
1/4 cup minced shallots
1/2 cup dry white wine
2 pounds salmon fillets, cut into
    12 pieces

12 large scallops (between 1 and
    1 1/2 pounds)

As a garnish:

2 tablespoons snipped fresh
    chives
1/4 cup salmon roe

To prepare the sauce: Heat oil in a skillet; over low heat sauté green peppers for about 20 minutes, stirring occasionally, until very tender and golden. Stir in cream, salt and pepper; bring to a boil and turn off heat. Set aside.

To prepare the seafood: Heat butter in a skillet wide enough to hold the salmon fillets in 1 layer. Sauté shallots over low heat for 5 minutes. Add wine and bring to a boil. Add the salmon fillets, reduce heat to low and cover. Cook for 7 to 10 minutes, or until salmon is cooked through. Transfer the salmon to a serving platter and keep warm.

Pour contents of skillet into a blender or food processor and purée, together with green peppers and their sauce. Return to skillet, heat through and add scallops. Cook over low heat, covered, for 3 minutes or until scallops are just cooked through; they should feel barely firm to the touch.

To assemble the dish: Place 1 scallop on top of each salmon piece and pour sauce over. Sprinkle scallops with chives and arrange salmon roe on top.

Rape con Romero
(Monkfish with Rosemary)

Pedro Subijana shows again in this recipe his flair for simplicity, characteristic of many dishes he serves at his Akelaŕe restaurant in San Sebastián. It is based on the freshness of ingredients and on his skill in combining them in a way that works extraordinarily well.

To serve 6

> *2 pounds fresh monkfish, in whole large pieces*
> *1 tablespoon olive oil*
> *1 tablespoon butter*
> *3 tablespoons minced shallots*
> *2 tablespoons minced garlic*
> *1 cup dry white wine*
> *1/2 teaspoon salt*
>
> *1/4 teaspoon freshly ground black pepper*
> *1 scant tablespoon coarsely chopped fresh rosemary*
> *1 pound ripe firm tomatoes, peeled, seeded and diced small (by hand)*

Preheat oven to 350 degrees F.

Remove loose grayish skin and membranes from the monkfish. Place the fish in a buttered baking pan and bake for 15 minutes. When cool, cut large part of the fish into medallions, and the narrow tail section into fillets. Discard juices in pan.

In a wide skillet, heat oil and butter. Add shallots and garlic, and sauté over low heat until soft. Pour in the wine and cook briskly for 2 to 3 minutes. Add the fish to the pan, turning it to coat with the sauce. Add salt and pepper, sprinkle with the rosemary and add the diced tomatoes. Cook, uncovered, just to heat the tomatoes through—about 1 minute—so the sauce retains a very fresh tomato taste. Taste for seasoning. Serve immediately.

Rape con Nueces
(Monkfish in a Walnut Cream Sauce)

Alejandro Fernández and his staff at Los Remos, a delightful restaurant on a tiny beach in the Bay of Algeciras—right across from the African coast—have created, over the 25 or more years it has been opened, a well-deserved reputation for having one of the top cuisines in the south. He has assembled a variety of recipes featuring local produce, such as this great combination of monkfish with the richness of walnuts in a cream sauce. Because of its complexity, I usually serve it as a main course; in that case, the recipe should be for 4 rather than 6.

To serve 4 to 6

> **2 pounds monkfish, in whole large pieces**
> **2 tablespoons olive oil**
> **3 tablespoons butter**
> **3 large cloves garlic, finely chopped**
> **3/4 cup finely chopped onion**
> **1 cup finely chopped leek**
> **1 1/2 cups walnuts, coarsely chopped**

> **1/4 cup Pernod liqueur**
> **1/4 cup full-bodied Spanish brandy**
> **2 cups Fish Fumet**
> **1/4 cup heavy cream**
> **3/4 teaspoon salt, or to taste**
> **1/2 teaspoon freshly ground white pepper**

Preheat oven to 350 degrees F.

To cook the fish: Remove loose grayish skin and membranes from the monkfish. Place on a buttered baking pan and bake in the preheated oven for 15 minutes. Let cool for about 10 minutes. Cut fish into medallions and reserve juices in pan.

To prepare the sauce: In a skillet, heat oil and 2 tablespoons butter. Over medium-low heat, sauté garlic, onion and leek until very golden, almost brown—about 20 minutes. Add 1/2 cup walnuts and cook slowly for 10 minutes, stirring. Pour in Pernod and brandy, increase heat and, when hot, flambé*; cook until flames subside, shaking pan. Transfer to blender and purée with the reserved pan juices, fumet, cream, salt and pepper. Strain through a fine sieve into a skillet large enough to hold the fish. Sauté remaining cup of chopped walnuts slowly in 1 tablespoon butter for about 5 minutes, stirring; add to skillet. Taste for seasoning.

Add fish medallions to skillet and heat through, coating with the sauce; transfer to a serving plate, and serve immediately.

Pescado "a l'All Cremat"
(Catalan: Peix a l'All Cremat)
(Fish in a Burned Garlic Sauce)

Cremat *in Catalan means burned—but don't let this turn you off from trying this country-style Catalan recipe. You won't find the sauce garlicky, just very flavorful. It is an old fisherman's dish, according to Xavier Mestres, chef/owner of L'Avi Pau restaurant in Cunit, south of Barcelona. And he should know, for his grandfather Pau was a fisherman —besides being a great cook and restaurateur. This is why Xavier named the restaurant after him,* avi *being Catalan for grandfather.*

Peix a l'all cremat is a very popular dish in Catalonia, but L'Avi Pau's rendition is the inspiration for this recipe. It makes a nice first course, and is light enough to carry over to the main dish. I usually prefer to serve it accompanied by a medium-bodied red wine.

To serve 6

> 4 tablespoons olive oil
> 1 large head garlic (or about 20 large cloves), peeled and thinly sliced by hand lengthwise
> 1/2 pound unpeeled ripe tomatoes, seeded and finely chopped

> 1 1/2 pounds red snapper or sea bass fillets (or another firm, white, fresh fish) cut into 6 pieces
> 1/2 teaspoon salt

In Spain, this dish traditionally would be cooked and served in a clay casserole; but if you don't have that, use any flameproof casserole or non-metallic skillet with high sides, large enough to hold the fish fillets in a single layer.

Heat oil and add garlic; cook slowly on low heat until garlic is dark brown, 10 to 15 minutes. Keep stirring so it does not turn black and burn— but it should be really dark brown (this will give the color and wonderful flavor to the sauce). Add tomatoes and continue to cook, over medium-low heat, until dry. Add 2 cups water, bring to a boil and reduce by about half. Add fish fillets in a single layer and sprinkle with salt. Reduce heat to medium and cook fish, turning it only once, 3 to 4 minutes on each side, depending on the thickness of the fillets. Serve immediately, from the same casserole.

Zarzuela de Mariscos
(Catalan: Sarsuela de Marisc)
(Shellfish Stew, Barcelona Style)

Catalans are known for their love of music, as are most Spaniards. There is a Catalan saying, "Pinch a man on the streets of Barcelona—if he doesn't cry out in pitch he's not Catalan." Our love of music and food combine in this dish, a classic recipe from the area around Barcelona. Zarzuela is the Spanish term for light opera or operetta. As most seafood lovers would agree, the dish is a colorful production worthy of Gilbert and Sullivan.

Zarzuela is featured in a number of seafood restaurants in Barcelona. One of them, Casa Costa (a lively place in the popular seaport quarter), serves a special rendition with lobster, called "Ópera" to signify that it's even better—the ultimate.

One of my favorite places for zarzuela is Peixerot, a delightful old restaurant in the fishing village of Vilanova i la Geltrú, south of Barcelona, owned by brothers Jordi, Joan and Josep Mestres. I have spent many a lovely summer evening dining on the restaurant patio, enjoying their excellent fish preparations.

To serve 6

1/4 cup olive oil
2 large onions, minced
2 large red or green bell peppers (preferably red), stemmed, seeded and cut in thin strips lengthwise
2 ounces lean prosciutto, cut in strips
3 pounds tomatoes, peeled, seeded and chopped
4 large cloves garlic, minced
1/2 cup whole almonds, ground
1/2 teaspoon (.2 gram) saffron threads
3 bay leaves
1 teaspoon dried thyme
1 teaspoon fresh rosemary leaves (or 1/3 teaspoon dried)

2 teaspoons salt, or to taste
1/2 teaspoon freshly ground black pepper, or to taste
1/2 teaspoon hot red pepper flakes
1 cup dry white wine
3 cups Fish Fumet
1 tablespoon lemon juice
12 small live clams, shells scrubbed
12 small live mussels, shells scrubbed
6 large prawns, in their shells
1 pound scallops
1 1/2 pounds squid, cleaned and cut into rings (see Rice in a Casserole with Shellfish)

As a garnish:

6 lemon wedges

In a large flameproof casserole, heat oil and sauté the onions and peppers for 5 minutes or until soft. Stir in the prosciutto and cook for 3 to 4 minutes. Add tomatoes and cook rapidly until dry. Stir in garlic, almonds, saffron, bay leaves, thyme, rosemary, salt, pepper, pepper flakes, wine, fumet and lemon juice. Bring to a boil. Add the clams and mussels; cover, reduce heat to moderate and cook 10 minutes. Add prawns, scallops and squid and cook 5 more minutes. Taste for seasoning and serve from the casserole, garnished with lemon wedges.

Romesco de Pescados
(Catalan: Romesco de Peix)
(Fish Stew, Tarragona Style)

Tarragona and the nearby district of El Vendrell are the home of romesco, *the sauce which originated from the fisherman-style preparation for the local fish. Practically all restaurants in the area serve* romesco *as a sauce, but only a few serve the dish* romesco de pescados; *one of my favorites is Casa Morros in Torredembarra, near Tarragona, where it is one of Juan Morros's specialties.*

The dried nyoras *peppers, found all along the Mediterranean coast from Catalonia to Murcia, are the key to this dish. They are round, small, dark red peppers, with just a trace of spiciness and extremely flavorful. Unfortunately they do not exist in the United States, but I have found that* ancho *or* pasilla *chiles (also called dried* poblanos *or* pisados) *work very well. If you cannot find these, any other kind of sweet-mild, flavorful dried chile peppers will do.*

To serve 6 to 8

2 ancho chile peppers, or another type of sweet-mild dried chile peppers (see above)
1/2 cup whole almonds
3–5 tablespoons olive oil
2 large (1/2-inch) slices of white bread
4 large cloves garlic, finely chopped
1 medium onion, finely chopped

1 cup dry white wine
2 cups Fish Fumet
1 teaspoon salt, or to taste
1/4 teaspoon freshly ground black pepper, or to taste
3 pounds fresh fish fillets, cut in 18 chunks (you may use one or more types of fish: red snapper, cod, sea bass, etc.)

Preheat oven to 350 degrees F.

Place the chiles in a saucepan and cover them with water. Bring water to a boil, reduce heat to low and simmer for 10 minutes. Turn off heat, cover and soak them for 45 minutes. Reserve 1 cup of the soaking water. Stem, seed and peel the chiles. Set aside.

Toast almonds in the preheated oven for 15 minutes. Grind them very finely. Set aside.

Heat 2 or 3 tablespoons oil in a skillet and fry bread until golden. Set aside.

Sauté garlic and onion in 1 or 2 tablespoons oil over very low heat until soft and golden, at least 20 minutes. (You may add small amounts of water if they dry out.) Add wine, increase heat and cook briskly until reduced to 1/4 cup. Purée in the food processor or blender with the chiles, almonds, bread, 1 cup of the reserved water from soaking the chiles and the fumet. Season with 1/2 teaspoon salt and the pepper.

Pour sauce into a large skillet and heat through. Season the fish with remaining 1/2 teaspoon salt, add to the sauce and turn to coat. Reduce heat and cook over low heat, covered, for about 10 minutes or until the fillets are done. Taste for seasoning. The sauce should not be further reduced; this is a rather soupy stew. Serve with lots of bread to dip in the sauce!

"Suquet" de Pescado
(Catalan: Suquet de Peix)
(Fish Stew with Potatoes, Costa Brava Style)

This is an old classic dish from the fishermen of the Costa Brava, the dramatic coast north of Barcelona. Many restaurants serve it, and each recipe is very different; this comes from Big Rock, in the fishing village of Palamós, where Carles Camós serves some truly authentic local fisherman dishes.

As is traditional with fisherman-style preparations, this is served with Garlic Mayonnaise (Allioli) on the side, which indeed offers a nice contrast between the sweetness of the red peppers and onions in the dish and the sharpness of the garlic in the sauce.

To serve 6

For the *sofrito:*

1/2 cup olive oil
4 large onions, minced
2 large red bell peppers, minced

1 pound ripe tomatoes, peeled,
   seeded and chopped

For the fish and potatoes:

3 tablespoons olive oil
2 pounds fresh firm white fish
   fillets, such as red snapper, cut
   into pieces
Flour for coating the fish
3 large cloves garlic, minced
2 tablespoons chopped fresh
   parsley

1/2 cup full-bodied Spanish
   brandy
4 cups Fish Fumet
1 pound white potatoes, peeled
   and sliced thin
1 teaspoon salt, or to taste
1/2 teaspoon freshly ground black
   pepper, or to taste

For the *picada:*

1/4 cup whole almonds
1 tablespoon olive oil
1 thin slice of white bread (about
   1/2 ounce)
2 large cloves garlic

As an accompaniment:

1 recipe Garlic Mayonnaise

To prepare the **sofrito:**   In a large flameproof casserole, preferably of clay, heat oil and sauté onions and peppers over medium-low heat. The secret to this dish is in sautéeing the onions and peppers for a very long time, 45 minutes to an hour, until the onions are almost caramelized. Toward the end you may have to reduce the heat to low, perhaps even add a little water so the vegetables don't burn—but they must be very brown. Add tomatoes and cook until dry.

To cook the fish and potatoes: Heat oil in a skillet large enough to accommodate all of the fish. Flour the fish and sauté it over medium heat very briefly on both sides. Set the fish aside, draining on paper towels. Add garlic and parsley to the same skillet and sauté until garlic is soft. Add brandy and cook over high heat until almost dry. Transfer contents of the skillet to the casserole with the vegetable mixture; add fumet and potatoes. Bring to a boil and cook over medium-low heat for about 20 minutes or longer, until potatoes are tender. Season with salt and pepper.

To prepare the picada: Preheat oven to 350 degrees F. Toast almonds for 15 minutes. In a small skillet, heat olive oil and, when quite hot, fry bread slice until golden on both sides. In the food processor, grind very finely the almonds, fried bread and garlic.

When potatoes are tender, stir in the *picada*. Add fish fillets and cook about 7 more minutes, just until fish is cooked.

Serve warm, passing the *allioli* around so guests can have as much or as little as they want—depending on how much they like garlic.

Langosta con Pollo "Mar y Montaña"
(Catalan: Llagosta amb Pollastre "Mar i Muntanya")
(Lobster and Chicken with Nuts and Chocolate)

This unusual combination, with its picada *which includes not only the traditional hazelnuts, garlic and herbs, but also chocolate, is a specialty of Catalan cuisine and specifically of L'Empordà. It is a classic dish from the Costa Brava, north of Barcelona, where it originated at the beginning of this century.*

One of my favorite versions is that of Eldorado Petit, the great restaurant in Sant Feliu de Guíxols. Lluís Cruañas calls the dish mar i muntanya, *or "sea and mountain," because of the combination of produce from both areas in L'Empordà. Lluís feels it is one of the most elegant and interesting Catalan recipes—and I certainly agree with him.*

To serve 8

> *3 or 4 live lobsters (about 6*
>   *pounds total)*

For the broth:

> *2 tablespoons olive oil*
> *3/4 pound unpeeled carrots,*
>   *sliced or coarsely chopped*

> *1 large onion, sliced*
> *1/2 cup celery leaves*
> *2 bay leaves*

For the chickens:

2 chickens (about 3 pounds
   each), cut into 8 pieces (reserve
   chicken livers)
1 teaspoon salt

1/2 teaspoon freshly ground black
   pepper
2 tablespoons olive oil

For the *sofrito*:

1 pound onions, chopped
1 1/2 pounds tomatoes, peeled,
   seeded and chopped
1 cup dry white wine

For the *picada*:

1/2 cup hazelnuts (filberts)
4 ounces unsweetened baking
   chocolate
6 large cloves garlic
1/2 cup fresh parsley leaves
2 tablespoons fresh thyme leaves
   (or 2/3 tablespoon dried)

2 tablespoons fresh oregano
   leaves (or 2/3 tablespoon dried)
1/2 tablespoon orange zest*
1/2 teaspoon (.2 gram) saffron
   threads (or 1/4 teaspoon
   powdered saffron)
1/2 teaspoon powdered cinnamon

To prepare the lobsters: In a large pot, bring about 4 quarts water to a boil. Drop in 1 lobster at a time—it will turn pink. As soon as it stops moving, a minute or two, remove lobster from the pot and set aside. Bring the water back to a rapid boil before dropping in the next lobster. Let lobsters cool, and reserve the water.

When lobsters have cooled enough to handle, remove their tails: grasp the body in one hand and the tail in the other, twist the tail and pull; it will come free easily. Remove the claws in the same manner. Cut each tail (complete with shell) crosswise into 2 or 3 pieces (depending on size). Set aside tails and claws. (In order to make it easier to remove the tail meat from the shell at the table, you may cut off the inner membrane/shell with a pair of scissors.)

To prepare the broth: Heat 2 tablespoons oil and sauté carrots and onion until soft, 6 to 8 minutes. Add to the pot with the reserved water, together with lobster bodies, celery and bay leaves. Bring to a boil, reduce heat to low and simmer, partially covered, for 30 minutes. Strain the broth and pour it back in the pot. Cook it over high heat until reduced to 6 cups. Set aside.

To prepare the chickens: Poach chicken livers in simmering water to cover for 10 minutes; drain and reserve livers. Pat dry chicken pieces, and season with salt and pepper. In a large skillet, heat 2 tablespoons oil and sauté chicken pieces, over medium heat, until golden. Set them aside. Pour off fat, leaving just about 2 tablespoons in the skillet.

To cook lobsters and chickens in the sofrito: Add chopped onions to the fat in the skillet, and sauté over low heat until soft. Add chopped tomatoes and cook until dry. Add white wine and cook until it has evaporated. Transfer this mixture to the large pot with the reduced broth. Add chicken pieces and cook for 20 minutes over medium heat, covered. Add lobster tails and claws; cook for 10 minutes.

Remove chicken and lobster pieces from the sauce (reserve sauce) to a large ovenproof platter with at least a 2-inch lip; in Spain we traditionally use a clay casserole. Arrange lobster and chicken pieces decoratively, except for the claws. Transfer these to a cutting board, and remove the meat from the claws by cracking the shells soundly with a hammer. Add meat from the claws to serving platter; keep warm.

To prepare the picada: Preheat oven to 350 degrees F. Toast hazelnuts for 12 minutes and rub them in a damp cloth to remove most of the skins. In the food processor, grind together hazelnuts with chicken livers and remaining *picada* ingredients.

To assemble the dish: Stir *picada* into reserved sauce. Cook for 5 minutes, stirring; taste for seasoning. Pour the sauce over the chicken and lobster pieces on the platter, and serve immediately.

POULTRY AND GAME

Pollo Escabechado
(Chicken Marinated in Vinegar and Wine, Spices and Herbs)

Start preparation 1 or 2 days in advance

Aranda de Duero is a small town between Burgos and Segovia, in the middle of the northern Castilian Plateau. One good reason for going there is to dine at Mesón de la Villa and visit with its hospitable owners, Eugenio and Seri Herrero; he with his colorful moustache and she with her warm, motherly disposition are the friendliest hosts you can imagine.

Escabeche is an old way of cooking and preserving food, a legacy from the Arabs; although originally introduced along the Mediterranean, today it is most representative of northern Castile—and one of Seri's specialties. She prepares escabechados of fowl and small game, such as quail, partridge, rabbit and chicken; I chose this recipe because chicken is most widely available here.

To serve 4 to 6

1 (3¹/₂-pound) chicken
¹/₂ cup olive oil
3 large onions, thinly sliced
1 head garlic, peeled, left in
 whole cloves
2 cups red wine vinegar
2 cups medium-bodied dry red
 wine

1 teaspoon salt
1 tablespoon dried thyme
6 bay leaves
8 whole cloves
15 black peppercorns, lightly
 cracked

As a garnish:

12 sprigs watercress

Clean and truss the chicken. Poke holes all over it with a skewer. Pat it dry.

Heat oil in a large heatproof lidded casserole. Over medium-high heat, sauté chicken on all sides until lightly golden. Remove chicken from casserole and set aside.

In the same oil, sauté onions on medium heat until soft and golden. Return chicken to the casserole, breast side down. Add all remaining ingredients and bring to a boil. Reduce heat to low, cover and cook for 45 minutes, turning it once.

Cut up chicken into serving pieces and place them in a glass container. Pour contents of casserole over the chicken. Cover and refrigerate for at least 1 day and up to 4 days.

Remove fat from surface; bring to room temperature before serving. Arrange chicken pieces, onions and herbs in one layèr on a platter or, preferably, in a clay casserole. Garnish with watercress sprigs around.

Pollo en Pepitoria de Rosalía
(Rosalía's Chicken Stew with Vegetables)

This is a homey, good chicken stew recipe dating from the sixteenth century, when the Provence region of southern France was a part of Catalonia. It was the favorite chicken recipe of Rosalía, my parents' cook—and I think her best.

To serve 4

1 (3- to 4-pound) chicken, cleaned and cut into 8 serving pieces	16 small boiling onions, peeled
1³/₄ teaspoons salt	³/₄ pound carrots, peeled and sliced into ¹/₂-inch rounds
³/₄ teaspoon freshly ground black pepper	8 small unpeeled red potatoes
2 tablespoons olive oil	1 bay leaf
	1 cup dry white wine
	2 cups Chicken Stock

For the *picada*:

¹/₂ cup whole almonds	threads (or ¹/₄ teaspoon
3 large cloves garlic, peeled	powdered saffron)
¹/₂ teaspoon (.2 gram) saffron	3 hard-boiled eggs

Pat dry chicken and season with ¹/₄ teaspoon each salt and pepper. Heat oil in a skillet and, over medium-high heat, brown chicken pieces. Transfer them to a large lidded flameproof casserole. Add onions and carrots to the skillet and cook them, stirring, for 10 minutes or until they start to brown. Add them to the casserole, and arrange potatoes around the chicken. Nestle bay leaf in the middle, and sprinkle with remaining salt and pepper.

Remove most of the fat in the skillet and deglaze with wine. Cook over high heat, stirring and scraping, for 2 or 3 minutes; pour liquid over chicken in casserole. Add stock and bring to a boil. Reduce heat to very low, cover and simmer for 45 minutes. Set chicken and vegetables aside. Discard bay leaf.

To prepare the picada: In the food processor, finely grind the almonds with the garlic; add saffron and egg yolks (reserve the whites). Add enough liquid from the casserole to form a paste.

Whisk *picada* into the casserole, and reduce liquid to about 2 cups. Taste for seasoning. Return chicken and vegetables to casserole, covering with sauce. Chop egg whites by hand and sprinkle over as a garnish.

Pollo con Salsa de Naranja y Menta
(Chicken in Orange and Mint Sauce)

The Arabs brought mint and oranges to Spain, and this dish combines both ingredients in an unusual recipe of definite Arab influence.

To serve 4 to 6

3 whole chicken breasts, cut in half, skinned and boned
1/2 teaspoon freshly ground black pepper
1/2 teaspoon salt
2 tablespoons olive oil
1/2 cup oloroso or another
medium-dry, flavorful Spanish sherry
1 cup orange juice
2/3 cup Chicken Stock
2 tablespoons orange zest*
2 tablespoons chopped fresh mint leaves

As a garnish:

4 or 6 thin orange slices
A frew sprigs fresh mint

Season chicken breasts with pepper and salt. Heat oil in a large skillet and, over high heat, sauté chicken pieces very briefly, just until they start to brown, to sear in the juices. Transfer chicken to a plate.

Deglaze pan with sherry. Add orange juice, chicken stock and orange zest. Bring to a boil, turn heat down to low and add chicken breasts with their juices. Simmer, uncovered, for 10 minutes or until chicken pieces are done. Turn them over once while cooking. Transfer chicken to a serving platter and keep warm.

Bring liquid to a high boil and add chopped mint. Reduce to about 3/4 cup. Taste for seasoning.

Pour sauce over chicken. Serve garnished with orange slices and mint sprigs.

Pollito de Grano al Vino de Jerez
(Chicken Flavored with Sherry, in a Sherry Sauce)

Start preparation 9 hours ahead or the day before, by injecting chicken with the sherries

Here is another outstanding creation from Madrid's El Amparo, the restaurant where Ramón Ramírez has developed some of the most imaginative recipes of today's Spanish cuisine. Ramón is from Málaga, and this dish has a clear Andalusian inspiration.

To prepare it you will need a flavor injector—and if you've never used one, you are in for a treat. I find it so much fun to inject the sherry into the chicken that I always have trouble sticking to the maximum 1/2 cup indicated in the recipe!

To serve 4

For the chicken:

> 1 (3- to 4-pound) whole chicken
> 1/3 to 1/2 cup oloroso or another flavorful medium-dry Spanish sherry
> 1/3 to 1/2 cup fino or another flavorful dry Spanish sherry
> Salt and pepper for sprinkling chicken

For the sauce:

> 1/2 cup sherry wine vinegar
> 1 1/2 cups Chicken Stock
> 1 cup heavy cream
> 1/2 cup oloroso or another flavorful medium-dry Spanish sherry
> 1/2 teaspoon salt
> 1/4 teaspoon freshly ground white pepper

To prepare the chicken: At least 8 hours before cooking (or the day before), clean chicken and inject it with the sherries, using a flavor injector fitted with a needle, making several punctures. Inject the oloroso sherry into the breast and wings, and the fino into the legs. Turn chicken over, to inject back of thighs. Cover and refrigerate until 1 hour before cooking time.

Preheat oven to 400 degrees F.

Rub inside of the chicken with salt and pepper. (Reserve any sherry and juices drained from the chicken.) Place chicken in a roasting pan (without a rack) in the preheated oven, breast side up, and bake for 45 minutes; it should be slightly underdone. Transfer chicken to a board and cut it into 4 serving pieces.

To prepare the sauce: With a spoon, remove most of the fat from the pan. Add vinegar and deglaze pan over high heat; transfer to a skillet or casserole large enough to accommodate the chicken quarters. Cook vinegar down to a glaze; add stock and reserved chicken juices, and reduce to 1/2 cup. Add cream and oloroso; reduce by half, over medium heat. Add salt and pepper.

To assemble the dish: Add quartered chicken and its juices, turning to coat with the sauce, and cook until chicken pieces are done. If sauce is too thin, remove chicken to a serving platter and reduce to desired consistency. Taste for seasoning. Pour sauce over chicken and serve.

Pintada al Melocotón
(Squab with Peaches)

This is one of those recipes from my mother's file "for special occasions." Pintada is Spanish for the French pintade *or* pintadeau, *a game bird similar to a guinea hen. I have found that squab works beautifully in this recipe—or you can also use Rock Cornish hens.*

To serve 6

6 (3/4- to 1-pound each) squabs or Rock Cornish hens	1 (3-inch) cinnamon stick
Salt and pepper for seasoning birds	1/4 cup full-bodied Spanish brandy
2 tablespoons olive oil	1/4 cup orange brandy liqueur, such as Gran Torres or Grand Marnier
3 tablespoons butter	
1 large carrot, sliced	1 bay leaf
1 large onion, sliced or coarsely chopped	3 sprigs parsley
	1 or 2 sprigs fresh thyme
6 large, firm but ripe yellow peaches	1/3 cup balsamic vinegar or a fine red wine vinegar
4 cups Brown Veal Stock	6 tablespoons pine nuts
4 large unpeeled cloves garlic, crushed	

Clean birds, pat them dry with paper towels and season lightly with salt and pepper. Truss. In a flameproof lidded casserole large enough to hold all the squabs, heat oil and 2 tablespoons butter; brown squabs over medium heat. Set squabs aside. Add carrot and onion and sauté until golden.

Meanwhile, peel peaches; first dip them briefly—4 or 5 seconds—in boiling water to loosen the skin. Halve peaches and reserve them with their pits.

Preheat oven to 325 degrees F.

Place squabs back in the casserole, over carrot and onion; add veal stock, garlic, cinnamon, brandy, liqueur, herbs and peach pits. Cover squabs tightly with double foil, and place lid over casserole. Braise in the preheated oven for 30 minutes. Turn squabs over and add peaches; cover again with foil and lid, and braise for another 30 minutes.

Remove squabs and peaches; cut off strings. Strain braising liquid through a fine-mesh strainer into a saucepan. Return squabs and peaches to casserole; keep warm. Reduce braising liquid to desired consistency (by about one third). Add vinegar, and cook for 2 or 3 minutes to dissipate its strength. Taste for seasoning.

Meanwhile, heat remaining tablespoon butter in a small skillet and sauté pine nuts until golden. Add them to the finished sauce. Pour over peaches and squabs, and serve immediately.

Capones al Agridulce
(Catalan: Capons a l'Agredolç)
(Game Hens in a Sweet and Sour Sauce)

Start preparation 9 to 10 hours ahead or the day before, by marinating hens

The idea for this recipe came from one of Barcelona's oldest and most prestigious restaurants, Reno. For 30 years it has blended classic and new concepts in traditional cooking under the direction of Josep Juliá. Reno is a serious, elegant restaurant: attentive service, select ingredients and skillful preparation have combined to assure continuity of quality over the years.

The sweet and sour combination, found all over the Mediterranean, is a legacy from the Arabs. It enhances a mild bird, such as a Rock Cornish hen, giving it a spicy, flavorful appeal.

To serve 4

> *4 (about 1½ pounds each) Rock*
> *Cornish hens*

For the marinade:

> *2 cups red wine vinegar*
> *½ tablespoon powdered cloves*

> *½ cup (packed) coarsely*
> *chopped fresh mint leaves*

For the hens:

> *2 tablespoons olive oil*
> *2 tablespoons butter*
> *2 medium onions, chopped*
> *1 teaspoon salt*
> *½ teaspoon freshly ground black*
> *pepper*

> *2 cups Chicken Stock*
> *½ cup sugar*
> *½ cup red wine vinegar*
> *½ cup full-bodied Spanish*
> *brandy*

As a garnish:

> *A few sprigs fresh mint*

Wash and pat dry the hens; remove the innards and cut off wing tips. Tie legs together with string. With a skewer, poke holes all over each hen.

To prepare the marinade: Place hens in a nonmetallic bowl and pour the vinegar over them. Add cloves and mint leaves; toss to coat. Cover and refrigerate for at least 8 hours. During this period, turn hens in the marinade several times.

Remove hens from the refrigerator 2 hours before cooking. Discard the marinade, and wipe each hen dry with a paper towel. Set aside.

To prepare the hens: In a flameproof lidded casserole, large enough to hold all the hens, heat oil and butter. Over medium-low heat, sauté onions until soft. Add hens to casserole and sprinkle with salt and pepper; pour stock over the hens. Bring stock to a boil and immediately reduce heat to low; cover hens tightly with double foil, place lid over casserole and simmer gently for 30 minutes.

Preheat oven to 350 degrees F.

Remove hens from casserole, reserving the stock; brush off onions that cling to them and put hens in a baking pan. Brush them with olive oil and bake in the preheated oven, uncovered, for 30 minutes.

Meanwhile, strain the stock from casserole and discard onions. Defat stock and return it to the casserole. In a small saucepan, caramelize (see Caramelizing*) sugar: dissolve the ½ cup sugar in 1 or 2 tablespoons water; over medium-high heat, cook until it turns golden brown. Pour caramelized sugar into the casserole with the stock; it will hiss and solidify, but don't worry—it will melt later. Add the red wine vinegar and cook sauce over high heat until reduced to 1½ cups.

When the hens are baked, place them on a serving platter and keep warm. Pour off fat from the baking pan and deglaze with the ½ cup brandy; add this glaze to the sauce.

To assemble the dish: Pour some sauce over hens and garnish with sprigs of mint. Pass remaining sauce separately in a sauceboat.

MAKING AN "ESSENCE" OF MEAT FOR POULTRY AND GAME DISHES

In the following recipes I have incorporated a cooking technique from my friend and teacher Madeleine Kamman, who has mastered the concept of "essences" of meat. It involves making a double stock—that is, cooking the necks, wings, backs and other bones in a basic brown veal stock for a long time. If you do not feel up to the task, you can simply simmer these in water for 25 minutes to make a broth, defat it and reduce to 1 cup. But if you appreciate the little extra flavor in your sauces, the additional effort involved in making a veal stock to prepare the "essence" will be worthwhile.

Pato con Aceitunas
(Catalan: Ànec amb Olives)
(Duck with Olives)

This recipe was given to me by Xavier Grifoll, chef of a little restaurant in Barcelona called Tiró Mimet. Tiró in old Catalan means duck, and that's Xavier's specialty. He once owned a restaurant in La Cerdanya, the northern region of Catalonia bordering on France at the Pyrenees Mountains, where one of the classic dishes is duck with turnips; a special kind of turnips, though, not at all like ours, as I found out after several tries. So following his suggestion, I made it with olives—and it was a hit.

To serve 4

> 1 large (4- to 5-pound) duck, cut
> into 4 serving pieces (reserve
> fat, wings, back and neck)

For the "essence":

> Reserved wings, back and neck
> of the duck
> 2–3 cups Brown Veal Stock

For the duck:

> 9 large cloves garlic, minced
> 1 large onion, chopped
> 1 medium leek, chopped, with 1/3
> of the green part
> 2 medium red bell peppers,
> seeded and cut into thin strips
> lengthwise
> 1 1/2 pounds unpeeled tomatoes,
> chopped

> 1/2 cup full-bodied Spanish
> brandy
> 1/2 cup dry white wine
> 1 cup (1/3 pound) green flavorful
> olives with pits (avoid using
> canned olives, if possible)
> 1/2 cup chopped fresh parsley
> leaves

To prepare the "essence":   Remove fat from duck, and most of the skin from reserved wings, back and neck; cut these in small pieces. Sauté in a skillet with a couple of tablespoons of duck fat, stirring around until they are very brown. Transfer pieces to a medium pan. Pour off fat from skillet and deglaze with about 1/2 cup of stock. Pour glaze into pan. Add some more stock and simmer, uncovered, over very low heat. Keep turning pieces over and adding more stock, little by little, as it evaporates. Cook for about 2 hours, or until reduced to 1 cup. Strain "essence" and reserve. Discard bones.

To prepare the duck: In a large skillet or, better yet, a flameproof clay casserole, sauté duck breasts and legs on low heat until golden on all sides; it will take about 30 minutes. The duck exudes its own fat, so you will not need to add any to the pan. Set breasts and legs aside.

   Pour off all but 2 or 3 tablespoons of the fat. Add garlic, onion and leek; sauté slowly until soft, about 10 minutes. Add peppers and tomatoes, and cook over medium heat until dry. Add brandy and, when hot, flambé.* When flames subside, add wine and bring to a boil. Stir in olives and parsley. Return duck breasts and legs to the skillet or casserole, cover and simmer on very low heat for about 1 hour.

To assemble the dish: Add reserved "essence." If the sauce is too thin, remove duck to a platter and cook the sauce over high heat until reduced to desired consistency. Taste for seasoning, adding salt and pepper if neces-sary. Serve duck directly from the casserole, or arrange it on a serving platter, covering with the sauce.

Pato con Higos
(Catalan: Ànec amb Figues)
(Duck with Figs)

This is a delightful example of the traditional Catalan way to cook meats or poultry with fruits. Some of the finest ducks I've eaten come from L'Empordà, the bountiful region in northeast Catalonia, and are often cooked with pears, apples or other fruits.

Agut d'Avignon, the outstanding restaurant in the picturesque old part of Barcelona, near the Ramblas promenade, features duck with figs among other classic specialties of L'Empordà. Former owner Ramón Cabau told me he prefers to make the dish with dried figs, although I've made it with both fresh and dried and enjoyed them equally—but following his advice, my recipe calls for dried figs.

To serve 4

>8 ounces dried figs
>1 large (4- to 5-pound) duck,
>   quartered (reserve liver, fat,
>   wings, neck and back; see
>   Note below)

For the "essence":

>Reserved wings, back and neck
>   of the duck
>2½–3 cups Brown Veal Stock

For the duck:

>Salt and freshly ground black
>   pepper for seasoning duck
>1 cup dry Spanish sherry,
>   preferably amontillado or a
>   dry oloroso

For the sauce:

> *1 large orange*
> *2 tablespoons finest-quality*
>   *Spanish brandy*
> *Pinch of powdered cinnamon*

(Note: You will need the duck's liver for this recipe; if there isn't one, substitute 3 chicken livers.)

Cover figs with 1 cup boiling water and soak for 2 hours. Stem figs and reserve figs and water.

To prepare the "essence": Remove most of the skin from duck wings, neck and back, and cut them in small pieces. Sauté in a skillet on medium-high heat with some of the reserved fat, stirring around until they are very brown. Transfer pieces to a medium pan. Pour off fat from skillet and deglaze with about 1/2 cup veal stock; pour glaze into pan. Add another 1/2 to 1 cup of veal stock to the pan and simmer, uncovered, on very low heat. Keep turning pieces over and adding more stock, little by little, as it evaporates. This will give you an "essence" of duck, or a double reduction of duck stock in the veal stock, which will add a lot of flavor to your dish. It should cook for about 2 hours; the longer you cook it, the more flavorful a reduction you will obtain. You should end up with 1 cup of duck "essence."

To cook the duck: Pat dry the quartered duck pieces with paper towels and season with salt and pepper. In a lidded skillet, heat some of the duck's fat and, over medium-high heat, brown duck quarters. Pour off fat, add 1/2 cup sherry, cover tightly with double foil and put lid on top of skillet. Braise for 45 minutes over low heat.

To prepare the sauce: Simmer the liver in 1/4 to 1/2 cup water reserved from soaking figs—just about to cover—for 15 minutes. In a blender or food processor, purée the drained liver with 4 figs; add juice and zest of the orange (see orange zest*) brandy, cinnamon and liquid from simmering livers. Reserve sauce.

To assemble the dish: Set duck quarters aside and defat skillet. Add remaining 1/2 cup sherry and cook until reduced by about half. Stir in reserved sauce, duck "essence" and water from soaking figs. Return duck to skillet. Add remaining figs, cover and cook for 20 minutes. Remove duck and figs to a serving platter and keep warm.

Reduce sauce some more, if necessary, to desired consistency. Taste for seasoning. Pour some sauce over the duck and pass remaining sauce in a sauceboat.

Perdiz con "Farcellets" de Col a la Ampurdanesa
(Catalan: Perdiu amb Farcellets de Col a l'Empordanesa)
(Partridge with Cabbage Croquettes, L'Empordà Style)

Partridge with cabbage is one of the oldest dishes of classic Catalan cooking, traced back to the fifteenth century. In a very Catalan way, the cabbage is cooked with the birds and made into croquettes (farcellets), *which are absolutely delicious.*

Partridge is a game bird in Spain, prepared in many different ways all over Catalonia. In Barcelona, partridge with cabbage is served at several Catalan restaurants. I have particularly enjoyed it at Quo Vadis, an old, prestigious establishment which specializes in classic dishes of the area prepared with top-quality local produce; owner Martí Forcada, an enthusiast of Catalan cooking, willingly shared his recipe with me. The following is a combination of Martí's recipe and an old recipe from L'Empordà district in northern Catalonia, given to me by my friend gastronomic historian Manuel Martínez-Llopis.

Partridge is ideal for this dish, but I have also made it with squab and game hens; the latter are larger than squab or partridge (easier to eat, too—and more affordable), so you will need only 4 hens for this recipe.

To serve 8

For the birds:

4 cups Chicken Stock
1 large head green cabbage, cored and quartered
8 partridges or squab, or 4 Rock Cornish hens (reserve necks and feet)
1/2 pound pancetta, sliced medium thick (or 8 slices)
Salt, pepper and a dash of nutmeg, for seasoning the birds
2 tablespoons olive oil

1 pound unpeeled carrots, chopped
1 large onion, chopped
4 large cloves garlic, finely chopped
1 tablespoon chopped fresh oregano leaves
1 tablespoon chopped fresh thyme leaves
4 whole cloves
1 1/2 cups medium-bodied dry red wine

For the *farcellets*:

1 egg, beaten
Flour for coating the farcellets
Abundant olive oil for frying

To prepare the birds: In a large pot, bring stock to a boil and add cabbage. Reduce heat and cook for 20 minutes, covered. Drain cabbage and separate the leaves; reserve cabbage and stock.

Pat dry birds and truss them. Loosen the skin covering their breasts and slide 1/2 slice of pancetta (1 for game hens) under the skin of each bird. Season with salt, pepper and a small grating of nutmeg over each one. Heat olive oil in a large lidded flameproof casserole. Cut remaining pancetta in small strips and sauté over low heat for 5 minutes. Add birds, increase heat to medium-high and sauté until lightly golden. (Add feet and necks too, if you have them.) Set birds aside.

Reduce heat to medium-low and add carrots, onion and garlic; sauté for 15 minutes, or until soft and golden. Add herbs, cloves, wine and reserved chicken stock. Bring to a boil, place birds on top and cover with the cabbage leaves. Cover the casserole with a lid and cook over low heat for an hour (about 45 minutes for game hens).

Drain the cabbage leaves and set aside. Remove the birds to a serving platter and keep warm (if using game hens, cut them in half). Strain contents of casserole through a fine sieve and return sauce to casserole. Increase heat to high and reduce to about 2 cups.

To prepare the farcellets: Form cabbage leaves into 2-inch dumplings; don't roll the leaves, just press with the palms of your hands to shape them into tight balls. Put egg and flour in separate bowls. Dip each ball first into the egg and then into the flour to coat. Have a skillet ready with hot oil to a depth of 1 inch and, over medium-high heat, sauté cabbage dumplings until golden. Drain on paper towels.

To assemble the dish: Arrange *farcellets* around birds, pour some sauce over and pass the rest separately in a sauceboat.

Conejo con Hierbas al Vino Tinto
(Catalan: Conill amb Herbes al Vi Negre)
(Rabbit Cooked in Red Wine with Herbs)

Start preparation at least 8 hours ahead or the day before, by marinating rabbit

Here's a recipe from the great cook in my family, Aunt Oriola. You will love this dish; it is a classic Catalan combination, mixing chocolate and almonds with the traditional Catalan herbs: rosemary, thyme, oregano and bay leaves.

To serve 8

For the marinade:

1 (750 ml) bottle full-bodied dry
   red wine
3 large cloves garlic, minced
2 bay leaves
1/4 cup (packed) finely chopped
   fresh herbs, such as oregano,

rosemary and thyme (if dried,
   use 1 tablespoon)
3 large shallots, minced
2 rabbits (about 5 pounds total),
   cut into quarters

For the rabbits:

2 tablespoons olive oil
1/3 cup full-bodied Spanish
  brandy
1 (3-inch) stick cinnamon
2 ounces unsweetened baking
  chocolate, grated or chopped

2 1/2 pounds tomatoes, peeled,
  seeded and chopped
1/2 teaspoon salt, or to taste
1/2 teaspoon freshly ground black
  pepper, or to taste
2 tablespoons fresh lemon juice

As a garnish:

4 ounces (3/4 cup) sliced almonds,
  toasted

To prepare the marinade: In a large nonmetallic bowl, mix wine, garlic, bay leaves, herbs and shallots. Add rabbit and marinate for at least 6 hours, covered and refrigerated. Turn pieces occasionally. Pat rabbit dry and reserve marinade.

To cook the rabbit: Heat oil in a large lidded flameproof casserole. Brown rabbit pieces over medium heat. Set them aside.

Deglaze casserole with brandy. Add marinating liquid with herbs and bring to a boil. Stir in cinnamon stick, chocolate, tomatoes, salt and pepper. Reduce heat to very low and return rabbit to casserole. Cover and simmer for an hour, turning rabbit pieces occasionally.

To assemble the dish: Transfer rabbit to a serving platter and keep warm. Discard cinnamon stick and bay leaves. Increase heat to high and cook sauce until reduced by half. Stir in lemon juice. Taste for seasoning. Pour sauce over rabbit and sprinkle almonds on top just before serving.

Silla de Conejo Rellena con Verduras
(Catalan: Sella de Conill Farcida amb Verdures)
(Stuffed Rabbit Saddle with Vegetables)

Rabbit is eaten a lot in Catalonia, usually grilled, braised or prepared in some country-style fashion. But this is different; here is a truly elegant way of preparing rabbit. It is another recipe inspired by Toya Roqué, chef/owner of Azulete restaurant in Barcelona. She told me she came up with the idea from her days of cooking in southern France.

To serve 4

1 rabbit (about 2 1/2 pounds; see
  Note below)

For the "essence":

Reserved bones of the rabbit
1 tablespoon olive oil
About 2 cups Brown Veal Stock

For the stuffing:

1 tablespoon olive oil
1/2 cup minced onion
1/4 pound mushrooms, finely
   chopped
1/2 pound veal kidneys
3/4 teaspoon salt, or to taste
1/4 teaspoon freshly ground black
   pepper, or to taste

1/3 cup full-bodied Spanish
   brandy
1/2 cup white bread crumbs,
   without crusts (see Bread
   Crumbs*)

For the vegetable garnish:

20 small boiling onions, peeled
   (about 2 pounds)
3 medium slender carrots,
   peeled, quartered lengthwise
   and cut into 1-inch lengths
20 very small mushrooms (1/3
   pound), stems trimmed
1/2 pound green beans, ends
   trimmed, cut into 1-inch
   lengths

1/2 teaspoon salt
1/4 cup Madeira wine or a
   flavorful dry Spanish sherry
   such as amontillado or a dry
   oloroso

(Note: You will, in fact, need only the body of the rabbit, but you may use the legs for another dish such as Warm Curried Rabbit and Lentil Salad [Ensalada Templada de Lentejas y Conejo al Curry]. The rabbit must be boned, which you may do yourself as directed below, or prevail on your butcher to do. Reserve all fat and bones for later use in this recipe.)

Soak the top and bottom of an unglazed clay pot with a lid, of the Römertopf type, in cold water for at least 15 minutes before use.

To bone the rabbit: Cut off the front and back legs at the joint nearest the body. Using a sharp boning knife, cut and scrape away the meat from the rib cage and backbone so that you will have a large, thin, boneless piece of meat, about 8 or 10 inches long by 5 or 7 inches wide. If you can't separate the skin from the backbone and you end up with 2 half pieces, don't worry—just patch them together. If there are any holes in the skin, don't worry either. Place boned rabbit on top of a piece of wax paper, giving it a rectangular shape as much as possible. Overlap any holes, covering them with meat; you should not see the wax paper through the meat, or the stuffing will ooze out of the holes while the rabbit is cooking. Place another piece of wax paper on top and pound it gently to even out the surface.

To prepare the "essence": Cut up rabbit bones in small pieces and sauté in oil until very brown on all sides. Remove bones, pour off fat and deglaze skillet with 1/2 cup stock. Return bones to skillet and simmer, uncovered, over very low heat, turning pieces occasionally. As the liquid evaporates, gradually add remaining stock. Cook for about 2 hours, or until reduced to 1 cup. Strain "essence" and reserve. Discard bones.

To prepare the stuffing: Heat oil in a skillet and sauté onion over medium-low heat; after 2 or 3 minutes, add mushrooms. Meanwhile cut kidneys in half lengthwise, trim all fat and membrane and chop them finely; add them to the onions and mushrooms. Sprinkle with salt and pepper and cook over low heat for about 5 minutes, stirring often. Add brandy and, when hot, flambé.* When the flames subside, toss in the bread crumbs. Taste for seasoning. Transfer mixture to a food processor and pulse just 4 or 5 times (or chop coarsely by hand).

To assemble the rabbit: Place the stuffing in a row down the middle of the boned rabbit. Fold up the ends and sides to cover the filling—like wrapping a package. Line the reserved fat along the seams. Tie string tightly around the rabbit "package" at 1-inch intervals, and twice lengthwise. Tie it around again between the intervals. It should look like a tiny little bundle, long and narrow.

To cook the rabbit with the vegetables: Drain the water from the clay pot. Place vegetables in the pot, and put the rabbit over them; sprinkle with salt, and pour reserved "essence" and Madeira over. Cover with the top. Place pot on the middle shelf of a cold oven. Set the temperature at 480 degrees F. and bake for 40 minutes.

To serve the dish: Slice rabbit and place on a long serving platter, surrounded by the vegetables. Pour some sauce over rabbit, and pass remaining sauce in a sauceboat.

Pavo Relleno a la Catalana
(Catalan: Gall Dindi Farcit a la Catalana)
(Roast Turkey Stuffed with Dried Fruits, Nuts and Sausage)

Start preparation at least 7 hours in advance

Turkey is very seldom eaten in Spain, but it is traditional at Christmas. At home we always have it stuffed with prunes, apricots, apples, raisins, pine nuts and sausages: a delicious, very Catalan combination. Before turkey came from America, a rooster (gall in Catalan) was used; this tradition goes back to documents of the thirteenth century.

I always wished we'd have it more often than once a year—and by itself. At Christmas, you see, it comes after the Meat and Vegetable Stew with a Pasta Soup (Cocido Catalán or Escudella i Carn d'Olla), by which time I am never able to appreciate it!

There is a consolation, though: just as traditional and wonderful is the arroz de San Esteban (rice of St. Stephen, the patron saint on December 26), which naturally is made with all the turkey leftovers. And that is a very vivid memory of my childhood Christmases: looking forward to the next day's turkey rice.

To serve 8, with leftovers

> 1 (10- to 12-pound) turkey
> (reserve neck, liver and giblets)

For the stock:

> 1 large onion, chopped
> 2 medium unpeeled carrots,
> chopped
> 1 small stalk celery, chopped
> 3 sprigs parsley
>
> 2 bay leaves
> 1 sprig fresh thyme (or a pinch,
> if dried)
> 6 cups Chicken Stock
> (preferably) or water

For the stuffing:

> 3/4 pound pitted prunes
> 1/2 pound dried apricots
> 1/2 cup dark raisins
> 1/4 cup olive oil
> 1½ pounds mild Italian sausage,
> sliced into 1/2-inch pieces
> 1 cup pine nuts
>
> 2 large Pippin or Granny Smith
> apples (1 pound), peeled and
> cut into 3/4-inch dice
> 1 teaspoon salt
> 1/2 teaspoon freshly ground black
> pepper

For the turkey and its sauce:

> 2 teaspoons salt
> 1 teaspoon freshly ground black
> pepper
>
> 1/2 cup full-bodied Spanish
> brandy

To prepare the stock: Combine neck, liver and giblets from the turkey in a large pot with all the stock ingredients. Bring to a boil, immediately reduce heat to very low and cook, almost covered, for 2 hours. Strain stock and reserve. Discard neck and innards.

To prepare the stuffing: While the stock is cooking, place prunes, apricots and raisins in a bowl and cover with boiling water. Soak them for about 2 hours. Drain and reserve them. Discard water.

In a large skillet, heat oil and, over low heat, sauté sausage and pine nuts until sausage is cooked and pine nuts are golden. Add prunes, apricots, raisins and apples; cook, stirring, for about 5 minutes. Stir in salt and pepper. Remove stuffing to a bowl. Add 1/2 cup of the stock and deglaze pan. Stir this glaze into stuffing in the bowl.

Preheat oven to 350 degrees F.

To cook the turkey: Season the inside of the turkey with 1 teaspoon salt and 1/2 teaspoon pepper. Stuff it with the fruits, nuts and sausage filling. Truss.

Place the turkey, breast side up, in a baking pan without a rack. Pour a cup of the stock over the turkey and bake in the preheated oven for 2 or 2½ hours, or until the temperature reaches 170 degrees F. on a meat thermometer. Baste with the stock from time to time, adding more as needed (you may end up using it all—especially if you have an electric oven).

To prepare the sauce: Remove turkey to a cutting board and pour juices into a saucepan. Add brandy to the roasting pan and deglaze it, scraping the sides with a wooden spatula to release any bits stuck to the pan. Pour this glaze in the saucepan with the turkey juices, and add also any remaining stock which was not used for basting. You may reduce it to desired sauce consistency; if you used all or most of the stock for basting, you probably won't need to. Season with remaining teaspoon salt and 1/2 teaspoon pepper, or to taste. Strain sauce and pass in a sauceboat.

MEATS

Mollejas de Ternera al Oporto
(Veal Sweetbreads in a Port Sauce)

Young and talented, Pedro Subijana is a master and a pioneer in the art of cooking. His Akelare restaurant in San Sebastián is a great exponent of the "New Basque Cuisine." This recipe, delicate and elegant, is among my favorites. I usually serve it accompanied by Home-Style White Rice (Arroz Blanco Hervido).

To serve 4 to 6

For the sweetbreads:

*2¹/2 pounds fresh veal
  sweetbreads
1 tablespoon lemon juice
2 tablespoons butter*

*2 tablespoons olive oil
³/4 teaspoon salt, or to taste
¹/2 teaspoon freshly ground black
  pepper, or to taste*

For the sauce:

*2 cups port wine
2 tablespoons olive oil
1 cup thinly sliced leek (most of
  the green part removed)
¹/2 cup chopped celery*

*¹/4 cup chopped unpeeled carrot
1 pound unpeeled tomatoes,
  seeded and chopped
1 cup Enriched Veal Stock or 2
  cups Brown Veal Stock*

To prepare the sweetbreads: Soak sweetbreads in cold water for 2 hours, changing the water three times during this period. Drain sweetbreads and place them in a saucepan. Cover with cold water and add lemon juice. Bring water to a boil, reduce heat to low and simmer for 5 minutes. Drain sweetbreads and immediately plunge them into a bowl of cold water; this will make them firmer. After a few minutes, drain the sweetbreads and separate the kernels, removing tubes and connecting tissue. The pieces should be smaller than bite size. Pat dry with paper towels.

In a skillet that will accommodate all the sweetbreads in a single layer, heat butter and oil. When the butter is melted and the oil hot, add sweetbreads. Sprinkle with salt and pepper. Cook over medium-high heat, without stirring, for about 3 minutes. Turn them and sauté quickly until lightly browned, about 7 more minutes. With a slotted spoon, remove sweetbreads from the skillet and set them aside.

To prepare the sauce: Deglaze skillet with about 1/2 cup of the port, cooking over high heat until reduced to just a glaze. Add oil; sauté leek, celery and carrot until quite tender, 15 to 20 minutes. Add tomatoes and cook quickly until dry. Transfer to a blender or food processor, and purée with the veal stock.

Add remaining port wine to the skillet and cook over high heat until reduced by about half. Strain the puréed vegetable mixture through a fine-mesh strainer into the skillet with the port and cook over high heat until reduced to about 1 1/2 cups. Taste for seasoning.

To assemble the dish: Return sweetbreads to the sauce and heat through. Serve immediately.

Mollejitas a la Salsa de Miel y Vinagre de Jerez (Catalan: Pedrerets a la Salsa de Mel i Vinagre de Xerès) (Sweetbreads in a Honey and Sherry Vinegar Sauce)

The combination of vinegar and honey in a sauce is characteristic of southern Spain, where the Arab influence is most notable; but this recipe comes from a Catalan chef, Toya Roqué, owner of Azulete restaurant in Barcelona. Her menu features a wide variety of dishes with different influences, to all of which she has added her ingenious touch.

This dish will combine very well with the flavor of Saffron Rice (Arroz con Azafrán).

To serve 4 to 6

For the sweetbreads:

2 1/2 pounds fresh veal or lamb sweetbreads (see Note below)	2 tablespoons olive oil
1 tablespoon lemon juice	1/2 teaspoon salt
2 tablespoons butter	1/2 teaspoon freshly ground black pepper

For the sauce:

2½ tablespoons sherry wine
    vinegar, or to taste
¼ cup fino sherry, or another
    flavorful dry Spanish sherry
⅓ cup finely chopped shallots

⅓ cup finely chopped onions
1 cup Enriched Veal Stock or 2
    cups Brown Veal Stock
1 tablespoon honey

(Note: Toya uses lamb sweetbreads in her recipe, which are delicious if they can be found fresh. I have made this dish with both lamb and veal, and it comes out just as well with either; most important is that the sweetbreads be fresh. Lamb sweetbreads are smaller and firmer than veal.)

To prepare the sweetbreads: Soak sweetbreads in water for 2 hours and handle them as directed in Veal Sweetbreads in a Port Sauce (Mollejas de Ternera al Oporto).

In a skillet that will accommodate all the sweetbreads in a single layer, heat butter and oil. When the butter is melted and the oil hot, add sweetbreads. Sprinkle with salt and pepper. Cook over medium-high heat, without stirring, for about 3 minutes. Turn them and cook quickly until golden, about 7 more minutes. Set sweetbreads aside.

To prepare the sauce: Deglaze the skillet with vinegar and sherry; cook over high heat, stirring, until reduced to a glaze. Reduce heat to low and add shallots and onions; sauté for about 5 minutes, until soft. Add veal stock and cook over high heat until reduced to about 1½ cups. Stir in the honey and taste for seasoning.

To assemble the dish: Return sweetbreads to the pan and turn to coat with the sauce. Serve immediately.

Hojaldre de Mollejas al Aroma de Alcaparras
(Sweetbreads in Puff Pastry with a Caper Sauce)

Huelva, in the farthest western province of Andalucía, is probably not a city to which you would think of making a special gastronomic trip; yet La Muralla is a restaurant that could make you change your mind. Luis de la Osa and Bartolomé Albarracín opened it in 1982, and they have devoted themselves to reproducing local dishes which had been forgotten; a remarkable feat which has gained them a well-deserved reputation. Besides, both are tremendously friendly and hospitable—like true Andalusians—and they delight in receiving visitors who show an interest in their food and their accomplishments. This recipe is inspired by a memorable dish I had there.

To serve 6

For the biscuits:

>   1 recipe Puff Pastry
>   1 egg, beaten

For the sweetbreads:

>   1¹/2 pounds fresh veal
>   sweetbreads
>   1 tablespoon lemon juice
>   4 tablespoons butter
>   1/3 cup minced shallots
>   1/2 cup full-bodied Spanish
>   brandy
>   1 cup Enriched Veal Stock or 2
>   cups Brown Veal Stock

>   1/2 cup heavy cream
>   2 tablespoons olive oil
>   1/4 teaspoon freshly ground black
>   pepper, or to taste
>   1/4 teaspoon salt, or to taste
>   3 tablespoons whole capers

Preheat oven to 425 degrees F.

To prepare the biscuits: Roll out puff pastry into a rectangular shape about 1/8 inch thick. Using a sharp knife, cut into a rectangle exactly 12 × 16 inches. Cut this rectangle into 12 (4-inch) squares. Place 6 of these squares on an ungreased baking sheet. Dip your finger in water and moisten a 1/2-inch area around the edge of each square. Using a sharp pointed knife, make a line 1/2 inch from the edge of the other 6 squares. (Don't cut all the way through the dough, however, or it will not rise.) Place these 6 squares on top of the other squares on the baking sheet. Try to handle with your fingers as little as possible, and don't pat the edges; the pastry will rise better. Brush the tops with the beaten egg. Bake in the preheated oven for 8 minutes, then reduce heat to 375 degrees F. and bake for an additional 10 to 15 minutes, or until biscuits are golden and the bottoms start to darken.

Remove biscuits from the oven and immediately cut through the square line you made earlier, lifting out the 6 "lids" carefully with a knife. If there is any soft puff pastry inside, scoop it out with a spoon and discard it. You now have 6 neat square boxes with lids for your sweetbreads.

(These biscuits may be made up to 3 days ahead, and heated at the last moment in a preheated 300-degree F. oven for 5 minutes.)

To prepare the sweetbreads: Soak them in water for 2 hours and handle them as directed in Veal Sweetbreads in a Port Sauce (Mollejas de Ternera al Oporto).

In a skillet, heat 2 tablespoons butter and sauté shallots over low heat until soft. Add brandy and, when hot, flambé.* When the flames subside, add veal stock and reduce to about 2/3 cup. Stir in cream; bring to a boil and turn off heat. Cover and set aside.

In a skillet large enough to accommodate all the sweetbreads in a single layer, heat oil and remaining 2 tablespoons butter. When butter is melted and oil hot, add sweetbreads; season with salt and pepper and sauté over medium-high heat for about 3 minutes, without stirring. Turn sweetbreads over and cook another 7 minutes.

Heat sauce in skillet and add sweetbreads. Add capers and heat through, stirring. Taste for seasoning.

To assemble the dish: Divide sweetbread mixture among the biscuits and pour sauce over sweetbreads. Place "lids" on top and serve immediately.

Hígado Glaseado con Manzana y Naranja
(Glazed Liver with Apple and Orange)

Casa Alcalde, right in the heart of the colorful old quarter in San Sebastián, is an institution. I remember going there many years ago, while walking around that picturesque part of the city, and indulging in their marvelous Jabugo hams and other terrific tapas. *Since young Joseba Iraizoz took charge of the legendary establishment in 1981, there has been a resurgence in the kitchen. While you still can meander along the bar crowded with zillions of* tapas, *the small rustic restaurant in the back features superb traditional Basque cuisine as well as some novelties that have come out of Joseba's imagination.*

Such is this delicate dish, which he actually makes with fresh goose foie gras. *Since that is hard to find here, I followed his recommendation and tried it with calf's liver—it truly works! It is a brilliant combination, and also quick to prepare; but it has to be assembled at the last minute, so I usually make it for smaller parties. I have served it as an appetizer, and as a main dish preceded by a fish course.*

To serve 4

1 large navel orange, peeled and sliced into 4 (1/2-inch) rings, discarding the ends	*apple, peeled, cored and sliced into 4 (1/2-inch) rings, discarding the ends*
2 tablespoons butter	*1 pound calf's liver, cut on the diagonal into 4 thin slices*
2 tablespoons honey	*1/3 cup full-bodied Spanish brandy*
2 tablespoons sherry wine vinegar or red wine vinegar	*4 cornichons, sliced into fans*
1 large Granny Smith or Pippin	

Heat a heavy skillet and, when very hot, add the orange slices. Grill them quickly over high heat, on each side, until they scorch. Add 1 tablespoon each of the butter, honey and vinegar. Cook the oranges over medium heat in this sauce just until the butter melts. Place oranges on 4 individual plates.

Add apple rings to the skillet and cook over medium heat until tender, 5 to 7 minutes. Add about 2 tablespoons water to the pan during the cooking. Arrange apple slices next to orange slices.

Add remaining tablespoon butter to skillet and, when hot, sauté liver over medium-high heat, 1/2 minute on each side. Add brandy and flambé.* Cook quickly until liquid evaporates. Add the remaining tablespoon honey and vinegar. Cook until the liver is glazed, 1 minute on each side. Place liver over orange and apple slices. Arrange a cornichon fan on top of each liver piece and pour juices from the skillet over. Serve immediately.

Riñones al Jerez
(Kidneys in a Sherry Sauce)

Beasaín is a small town 30 miles south of San Sebastián, and probably its main claim to fame is its Castillo restaurant. The name is renowned in Basque gastronomy; José Castillo has been doing a fantastic job on behalf of the region's cuisine, researching and compiling old recipes in his books, and traveling all over to promote them. José Juan, his son, is the chef at Beasaín's Castillo, which he runs together with his wife, Ana Mari. José Juan's recipes are traditional and perfectly executed, such as this version of kidneys in a sherry sauce, a classic dish with his personal touch.

If served as a main course, Home-Style White Rice (Arroz Blanco Hervido) is an ideal accompaniment. In Spain it is often served as a tapa, *with good crusty bread to dip in the sauce.*

To serve 4 to 6

3 pounds fresh veal kidneys
1/2 cup milk
1/4 cup olive oil
3/4 teaspoon salt
1/2 teaspoon freshly ground black pepper, or to taste
1 cup dry Spanish sherry, preferably a fino or amontillado
9 large cloves garlic, minced

1 large onion, finely chopped
1/2 cup Enriched Veal Stock or 1 cup Brown Veal Stock
1 bay leaf, middle vein removed, crumbled
2 tablespoons finely chopped fresh parsley leaves
1/4 pound prosciutto, sliced not too thin, cut with scissors into 1-inch strips

Put kidneys in a bowl with milk. Add water to cover and let sit for an hour. Drain the kidneys and cut in half lengthwise; trim off the fat and cut into 1/2-inch pieces. Discard milk.

In a large pan, heat 2 tablespoons oil and sauté kidneys for 2 minutes over high heat. Stir in 1/4 teaspoon each salt and pepper. Remove kidneys with a slotted spoon and set aside. Add sherry to juices in pan and cook until liquid is reduced to about 1/4 cup. Set aside.

In a large skillet, heat remaining 2 tablespoons oil and sauté garlic with onion over low heat until soft, about 10 minutes. Add stock, reduced sauce from pan, bay leaf, parsley, prosciutto, 1/2 teaspoon salt and 1/4 teaspoon pepper. Cook over medium heat for 5 minutes (10 minutes if you used Brown Veal Stock). Stir in kidneys and their juices. Simmer over low heat for 5 more minutes. Serve warm.

Lengua Empiñonada
(Braised Tongue with Pine Nuts)

La Fragua is probably the most typical and best-known restaurant in Valladolid, northwest of Madrid, in the middle of Old Castile. Roasted suckling animals as well as great bread are among their specialties. The restaurant is beautifully decorated with Old Castilian motifs, and the kitchen reflects that approach; earthy stews, such as this one, are classics of the menu. Besides, José Antonio Garrote is a delightful host, always pleased to welcome anybody interested in Castilian cuisine. The pantry is excellent—and so is the cellar, José Antonio's pride, full of wonderful old vintages sure to warm your journey!

To serve 4 to 6

For the tongue:

1 (2½- to 3-pound) beef tongue	*4 large cloves garlic, unpeeled*
2 medium leeks, sliced	*and mashed*
1 large onion, sliced	*6 black peppercorns*

For the sauce:

2 tablespoons olive oil	*1 pound thin young carrots,*
1 large onion, minced	*peeled and cut into ½-inch*
4 large cloves garlic, minced	*diagonal slices*
⅛ teaspoon hot red pepper	*1 teaspoon salt, or to taste*
flakes	*½ teaspoon freshly ground black*
1½ pounds unpeeled tomatoes,	*pepper, or to taste*
chopped	*¼ cup pine nuts*
1 cup Brown Veal Stock	

To cook the tongue: Place tongue in a large stock pot with the leeks, onion, garlic and peppercorns. Pour over enough boiling water to cover (8 to 10 cups); bring to a boil again, reduce heat to low and cook, uncovered, for 2 hours.

Drain tongue, reserving the liquid. When tongue is cool enough to handle, peel it and remove the bone and fatty glands on each side. Cut into ¼-inch slices. Set aside.

To prepare the sauce: Skim fat from reserved cooking liquid; there should not be much fat, just lift it with a spoon. Transfer to a pan and, over high heat, reduce it to 1½ cups.

In a skillet, heat oil and over low heat, sauté onion and garlic with pepper flakes for 10 minutes or until soft. Add tomatoes and cook until dry. Transfer to food processor or blender, add reduced cooking liquid and purée. Strain through a medium sieve or a food mill. Transfer to a flame-proof casserole (preferably clay) and add veal stock, carrots and tongue slices. Bring to a boil, reduce heat to low and cook at a simmer, partially covered, until carrots and tongue are tender—about ½ hour to 45 minutes. Add salt and pepper to taste. The sauce should not be thick, and it will probably not need reducing; but if it is too thin, remove tongue and carrots to a platter and reduce to desired consistency.

In a small skillet, sauté pine nuts, stirring, until they turn golden; add to the casserole. Serve hot.

Fabada Asturiana
(Bean Stew with Sausages, Asturian Style)

Start preparation the day before, by soaking beans overnight

This is the greatest dish from Asturias: a hearty, nourishing stew very suitable for the cold winter days of that northern region. The meats used in Spain are not quite what we have here, but I have found that you can get excellent results with ham hocks and good pork sausages; my favorites are chorizo-style and blood sausages. I must add that I've served this good country dish many times, and it's always been a smashing success.

You are bound to find fabada *served at any restaurant in Asturias, but it is a particular specialty of La Máquina, an old farmhouse turned restaurant in Oviedo. María García-Rodríguez cooks, while her husband, Ramón, goes in search of the best local beans,* fabes, *and the* compango, *the mixture of pork meats and sausages that accompanies the beans.*

Like all bean stews, this will be even better the next day. I always keep it in a lidded clay pot, which brings out the best flavors.

To serve 6 to 8

1 pound large dry lima beans
1 tablespoon olive oil
1/4 pound sliced bacon, cut into
  thin strips
12 large cloves garlic, minced
4 onions, sliced
1 large leek (about 1 pound),
  sliced, with 1/3 of the green
  part
1 large carrot, peeled and
  coarsely chopped
2 ham hocks (about 2 pounds),
  cut into small pieces

1 pound flavorful, spicy pork
  sausages (preferably blood
  sausage, such as Italian blood
  pudding or boudin noir, and
  chorizo), cut into 3/4-inch
  pieces
2 bay leaves
1 tablespoon Spanish paprika
Salt and freshly ground black
  pepper to taste, if necessary

Place beans in a bowl and soak them in water overnight. Add water to cover by 2 inches, as beans will expand about twice in size. Next day, drain beans and reserve water.

In a very large flameproof casserole or stock pot, heat oil and cook bacon over low heat for 3 or 4 minutes. Add garlic, onions, leek and carrot; cook for 30 minutes, stirring occasionally.

Add ham hocks, sausages, bay leaves, paprika and beans; add reserved water to barely cover. Bring to a boil; skim off the foam and fat from the top, reduce heat and simmer, partially covered, on very low heat for about

2½ hours, or until beans are tender and juicy. Remove ham hocks and defat surface of stew. Take off meat from ham hocks and return it to the pan. Discard bay leaves. Taste for seasoning. Serve warm, preferably from a clay casserole.

Habas a la Catalana
(Catalan: Faves a la Catalana)
(Fava Bean Stew, Catalan Style)

This is a classic Catalan dish—a wonderful earthy, peasant one, most comforting on a cold day. It is served at many country restaurants in my home region, usually as a small first course; but I have always made it here as a main dish, and a hearty one at that. If it's reheated and served the next day, the flavors will be even better. It is traditionally cooked in a lidded clay pot; this brings out especially good flavor.

Fava beans are more available in Spain than here (see Fava Bean Salad with Mint [Ensalada de Habas a la Hierbabuena]). If you can't find fresh or frozen fava beans, substitute frozen lima beans.

I have enjoyed this dish many times at one of my favorite restaurants, Cal Joan, in Vilafranca del Penedès—one of the warmest, most authentic and finest restaurants in the whole area. Joan Samsó and his wife, María, ran the restaurant until he died recently; now his son, Quico, is the chef. He has added to his father's classic Catalan cooking the innovativeness of a young man who loves to cook.

To serve 8

4 to 6 pounds unshelled fava beans, butter beans or lima beans (4 cups after shelling), or 2 (10-ounce) packages frozen lima beans
2 tablespoons olive oil
½ pound pancetta, sliced medium thin and cut in strips
2 medium onions, chopped
4 large cloves garlic, minced

1 pound white pork sausage (sweet Italian type)
1 pound blood pork sausage, such as Italian blood pudding or boudin noir
3 tablespoons chopped fresh mint
1 large or 2 small bay leaves
1 cup dry white wine
3 cups Chicken Stock

Shell the beans. (If they are not young and their skins are tough, blanch them for 2 or 3 minutes and peel them. When you open the pod, you will know that they are old if the small husk attached to the pod is black.)

In a flameproof lidded casserole, preferably of clay, heat oil and cook pancetta over low heat for about 10 minutes. Remove it and set aside. Add onions and garlic to skillet and sauté until golden, about 20 minutes. Add fava beans and toss for 4 or 5 minutes.

Put about ½ cup water in a skillet and add the sausages. Pierce them with a fork and cook 3 to 5 minutes, until lightly browned. Cut them into 1-inch slices and add to fava beans. Add pancetta, 1 tablespoon chopped mint, bay leaf and wine. Add stock, bring to a boil, reduce heat to low and cook, covered, for 1 hour or more, until beans are quite soft. If you find the sauce too thin, cook, uncovered, for another 15 minutes or until sauce reaches desired consistency; it should be rather soupy. Taste for seasoning. At the last minute, add remaining 2 tablespoons chopped mint, stir and serve.

Callos a la Gallega
(Tripe with Garbanzo Beans, Ham and Sausage, Galician Style)

Tripe is very bland by itself, so it provides an excellent vehicle for all the other good things in this recipe. Best made in a lidded clay pot, it is another of those dishes you can make a day ahead and reheat, for even better flavor. I always serve it as a first course directly from the clay pot, accompanied by Peasant Bread (Pan de Payés) or a good crusty bread to dip in the sauce.

In Galicia the classic preparation includes garbanzo beans. This recipe is an adaptation of that of Moncho Vilas, whose Vilas restaurant in Santiago de Compostela is my favorite in the city. His cooking is down-to-earth home style, enhancing in a simple way the beautiful produce of Galicia.

To serve 8 to 10

2 pounds tripe	1 teaspoon chopped fresh thyme
2 tablespoons olive oil	leaves
1 large onion, finely chopped	1/4 teaspoon hot red pepper
4 large cloves garlic, minced	flakes, or to taste
2 pounds unpeeled tomatoes,	2 teaspoons salt, or to taste
chopped	1/2 teaspoon freshly ground black
1 (1-pound) can garbanzo beans	pepper, or to taste
(chick-peas), drained	2 tablespoons finely chopped
1 (1-pound) ham hock, cracked	fresh parsley leaves
into small pieces	
1/2 pound chorizo-style sausage,	
sliced into 1/2-inch rounds	

Soak tripe in cold water for 1/2 hour. Drain and cut in very thin strips.

Heat oil in a large flameproof casserole, preferably of clay. Sauté onion and garlic until golden, about 20 minutes; add tomatoes and cook until dry. Add beans, ham hock, chorizo, thyme, pepper flakes, salt and black pepper. Cook for 5 minutes and stir in tripe. Simmer very slowly, covered, for at least 2 hours. Remove meat from ham hock bones, and put it back in the casserole. Taste for seasoning. At the last minute, sprinkle parsley on top.

Cocido Catalán
(Catalan: Escudella i Carn d'Olla)
(Meat and Vegetable Stew with a Pasta Soup)

Start preparation the day before, by soaking beans overnight, or use canned beans

Escudella i carn d'olla *is the most typical Catalan dish—a true meal-in-a-pot, in the family of boiled dinners like the French* pot-au-feu *and the Italian* bollito misto. *In the old days, it was the staple meal for those who lived in the country. I remember my grandmother saying that when she was young, they had it five or six days a week! A special* escudella *was reserved for Christmas Day, and today it still is a classic Catalan Christmas dish.*

The idea is to simmer flavorful meats and sausages with vegetables. The broth is served as a first course with pasta—traditionally, the large shell pasta or galets. *The entrée will be the meats and vegetables. And on Christmas, if you can believe it, after that we have the turkey!*

Here is my version of escudella—*subject to any changes according to your taste. For instance, in Spain we pass around some fine olive oil to drizzle over the vegetables; but I enjoy a dab of Garlic Mayonnaise (Allioli) with each item of the stew. Unconventional, maybe, but cooking is an ever-changing art and that's what makes it so exciting.*

To serve 8, with leftovers

1/2 *pound dried or 1 (1-pound) can garbanzo beans (chick-peas)*

2 *tablespoons olive oil*

1/2 *pound pancetta or fresh side pork, diced small*

6 *large cloves garlic, chopped*

1/4 *cup chopped shallots*

1 *pound leeks, thinly sliced, with* 1/3 *of the green part*

3 *stalks celery, chopped*

1 *pound veal or beef knuckle bones (with marrow, if possible), cut up*

1 *(1-pound) ham hock, cracked into small pieces*

1 *pound stewing beef, cut into 1-inch cubes*

1 *stewing hen or large chicken, whole, fat trimmed (see Note below)*

1 *teaspoon salt*

1 *teaspoon freshly ground black pepper*

1 *recipe Meat Ball*

3 *or 4 tablespoons flour*

8 *small turnips, peeled*

8 *small red-skinned potatoes*

1 *small head green cabbage, cored and quartered*

1/2 *pound carrots, peeled and cut into* 1/2*-inch diagonal slices*

2 *pounds assorted pork sausages, including blood sausage and any other flavorful ones*

1/4 *pound large shell pasta*

As a garnish:

Olive oil or Garlic Mayonnaise

(Note: If you can find it, the best is a stewing hen; otherwise, try to get a 5- to 6-pound roasting chicken. The stewing hen should simmer for 2½ hours, whereas the chicken should not cook more than 1½ hours.)

In a bowl, cover garbanzo beans with water and soak overnight. Drain and reserve water. (If you use canned beans, discard water.)

Heat oil in a very large flameproof casserole or stock pot and sauté pancetta over low heat until golden, about 10 minutes. Add garlic, shallots, leeks and celery; cook 15 minutes. Add bones and meats (except meat ball and sausages), garbanzo beans and their water (if using canned beans, add them later); add salt and pepper, and water to cover. Bring to a boil, reduce heat to low and simmer gently, covered, for 2 hours. (If using a chicken, remove it after 1½ hours.) Skim off periodically the scum and fat that rise to the surface.

Divide meat ball mixture in half, and shape it into 2 cylinders about 3 inches in diameter. Sprinkle flour on a board and roll the cylinders in it, coating them with flour all over.

After 2 hours of simmering, add turnips, potatoes, cabbage, carrots, sausages and meat ball cylinders (and canned beans if you are using them). If necessary, add some more boiling water to cover. Simmer for another ½ hour.

Remove meats and vegetables from broth and arrange them on 2 platters; keep warm. Strain broth through a fine sieve and reduce it to about 8 cups. Cook the pasta in the broth, at a rapid boil, until tender. Taste for seasoning.

Serve the broth and pasta as a soup, followed by the vegetables and meats with olive oil or Garlic Mayonnaise (Allioli).

Pelota
(Catalan: Pilota)
(Meat Ball)

Pelota—*Spanish for ball—is a recipe of Arab origin, although originally it did not use pork but other meats, especially lamb. It is part of many classic dishes such as Meat and Vegetable Stew with a Pasta Soup (Cocido Catalán), where it is made into two big cylinders; or Classic Paella with Shellfish, Chicken and Pork (Paella Valenciana de la Ribera), where it is shaped into small balls. These are also delicious simply as an appetizer, sautéed until golden; or cooked in Chicken Stock (Caldo de Pollo) with rice as a soup.*

Makes about 1½ pounds

1 pound medium-ground pork meat
1 cup white bread crumbs, without crusts (see Bread Crumbs*)
2 eggs
3 tablespoons chopped fresh parsley

3 large cloves garlic, minced
1/4 cup pine nuts
1/2 teaspoon salt
1/2 teaspoon freshly ground black pepper
1/8 teaspoon powdered cinnamon

Mix all ingredients in a bowl and shape according to recipe's directions.

Manzanas Rellenas al Horno
(Catalan: Pomes Farcides al Forn)
(Baked Stuffed Apples)

This is one of my favorite dishes at Agut d'Avignon, one of Barcelona's great restaurants. The person who deserves most of the credit for making Agut a culinary star is Ramón Cabau, the flamboyant genius of Catalan cooking. Ramón sold the restaurant in 1983, but continued on as a consultant—and Agut's standards have remained just as high. It features many Catalan dishes, such as these stuffed apples, which are typical of Gerona, north of Barcelona.

To serve 6

6 large thick-skinned baking apples, such as Rome Beauties or Pippins (about 1/2 pound each)

2 tablespoons olive oil
1/4 cup pine nuts
1 medium onion, minced
3 large cloves garlic, minced
3/4 pound precooked boneless lean baked ham, ground
3/4 pound medium-ground pork meat

1/2 cup white bread crumbs, without crusts (see Bread Crumbs*)
1 teaspoon salt
1/2 teaspoon freshly ground black pepper
2 eggs
1 cup dry white wine
1 cup Brown Veal Stock, or more as needed
2 tablespoons sugar

With the stem side down, cut the top quarter off each apple. With a small knife or melon-ball scoop, hollow out a pocket in the bottom three quarters of the apple. Remove seeds and hard core without going all the way through to the bottom of the apple. With a knife, enlarge opening, shaping it like a funnel; reserve apple pieces. Discard seeds and hard core; chop apple pieces and set aside.

Preheat oven to 350 degrees F.

Heat oil in a large skillet and sauté pine nuts until they turn golden. Add onion and garlic, and sauté over low heat until soft and golden—10 to 15 minutes. Add chopped apple pieces; stir and cook until tender, about 10 minutes. Off heat, add ham, pork, bread crumbs, salt and pepper; stir and set aside. Beat eggs lightly in a bowl; add meat mixture and combine well. (It is better to do this with your hands so you can feel that the egg is distributed throughout the meat.)

Mound the stuffing into the apples, packing it inside the pockets; they should look like giant mushrooms. The stuffing will shrink during baking, so don't worry if they look too big; use up all the stuffing. Place apples in an ungreased baking dish, and pour wine around them. Place in the preheated oven and bake for 1¼ to 1½ hours. Baking time will depend on the size and kind of apples; a ½-pound Rome or Pippin apple will take about 1½ hours. Test them with a fork, knife or needle; they should feel soft and pierce easily without resistance. While baking, there should always be a little liquid left in the pan; check periodically and add stock if needed, to make sure the juices don't burn (especially if you have an electric oven).

Remove apples to a serving platter. Add veal stock to baking dish. Cook over high heat until reduced to the desired consistency; it should be a rather light sauce. Meanwhile, caramelize sugar (see Caramelizing*) by cooking it with ½ tablespoon water in a heavy saucepan over medium-high heat, until it turns amber; stir into sauce until caramel dissolves. Serve apples surrounded with the sauce.

Melocotones Rellenos
(Catalan: Préssecs Farcits)
(Peaches Stuffed with Pork and Almonds)

Here is an excellent Catalan combination of fruits and meat—this one comes from my mother's recipe file. It was one of my favorite dishes at home in the summertime, during the height of the peach season. It is interesting and unusual; the flavors mingle with extraordinary harmony.

To serve 6

> *6 large, firm fresh peaches (about 3 pounds), unpeeled*

For the filling:

> *1/3 cup whole almonds*
> *1/4 pound medium-ground pork meat*
> *1/4 cup white bread crumbs, without crusts (see Bread Crumbs*)*
>
> *1 egg*
> *1/2 teaspoon salt*
> *1/4 teaspoon freshly ground black pepper*
> *1/8 teaspoon powdered cinnamon*

For the peaches:

> *2 tablespoons olive oil*
> *2 tablespoons butter*
> *1–2 tablespoons flour*
> *1/4 cup full-bodied Spanish brandy*
>
> *1/4 cup sweet muscat wine, such as Torres Malvasía de Oro*
> *5 whole cloves*
> *2 cups Brown Veal Stock*
> *Salt to taste, if necessary*

Preheat oven to 350 degrees F.

With the help of a knife and melon-ball scoop, remove pits from the peaches, leaving them whole; don't cut them in half. Reserve the pits.

To prepare the filling: Toast almonds in the preheated oven for 15 minutes, and grind them finely. Mix them in a bowl with all the filling ingredients, and stuff peaches with mixture.

To prepare the peaches: Heat oil and butter in a large skillet. Put flour on a dish and dip the stuffed side of each peach into the flour; sauté them over medium heat, stuffing side down, until golden.

Transfer peaches to a flameproof casserole, stuffed side up. Remove fat from the skillet; deglaze with brandy and pour into casserole. Add muscat wine, cloves and veal stock. Bring liquid to a boil, reduce heat to low, add reserved pits and simmer peaches, partially covered, for 3/4 hour.

Arrange peaches on a platter, stuffing side up, and keep warm. Discard pits. Reduce liquid to 3/4 or 1 cup. Taste for seasoning. Pour sauce over peaches and serve.

Carne con Peras
(Catalan: Carn amb Peres)
(Veal with Pears)

This is yet another Catalan dish of meat cooked with fruit, here in a veal stew. It is a recipe from my family's cook, Rosalía, which I remember relishing as a child.

The kind of pears we use in Spain for this dish are very small baking ones; they are not available in North America, but any type of pear, preferably those that are small and suitable for baking, can be substituted. I have made this dish successfully with Winter Nellis, small Bosc, or even Bartlett pears.

To serve 6

6 pears, peeled and cored, leaving stems intact, whole or halved
6 tablespoons pear brandy or full-bodied Spanish brandy
3 pounds boneless veal stew meat, cut into 1 1/2- to 2-inch pieces
3/4 teaspoon salt
3/4 teaspoon freshly ground black pepper
About 6 tablespoons olive oil
3 medium onions, minced
6 large cloves garlic, minced
6 tablespoons pine nuts
1/2 cup dry white wine
2 bay leaves
6 tablespoons sugar

Place pears in a large bowl and pour brandy over them, tossing gently. Cover and marinate at room temperature for at least 30 minutes.

Season veal with 1/4 teaspoon each salt and pepper. In a large skillet, heat 1/4 cup olive oil and, over medium-high heat, sauté veal briefly, in small batches, to sear in the juices. Set veal aside. Add more oil to the skillet if necessary, and sauté two thirds of the chopped onions and garlic until soft, about 10 minutes. Add veal and its juices, cover and cook on very low heat for 30 minutes. Season with remaining 1/2 teaspoon each salt and pepper.

Meanwhile, in a flameproof casserole large enough to hold the pears, sauté pine nuts in 2 tablespoons oil until golden. Remove with a slotted spoon and drain on paper towels. Add remaining onion and garlic and sauté over low heat until soft, about 10 minutes. Add the pears, stem side up, with their marinade, wine, bay leaves and pine nuts; stir gently, bring liquid to a boil and turn heat to very low. Cover and simmer for 20 minutes. Push pears to the sides of the casserole and pour in the veal with its sauce. Cover and simmer for another 30 minutes.

Remove the veal and pears to a serving platter, mounding the meat in the center with the pears surrounding it. Discard bay leaves. Cover and keep warm. Over high heat, reduce the sauce until thickened to desired consistency. Taste for seasoning. Pour over veal.

In a small pan, caramelize sugar (see Caramelizing*) by dissolving it with 2 tablespoons water and cooking over medium-high heat until it turns an amber color. Pour over the pears. Serve immediately.

Filete de Ternera con Salsa de Anchoas
(Catalan: Filet de Vedella amb Salsa d'Anxoves)
(Veal Fillet with Anchovy Sauce)

Tiró Mimet, a tiny family-style bistro in the old part of Barcelona, specializes in traditional dishes from Catalonia, where chef/owner Xavier Grifoll has lived—and cooked—all his life. Xavier serves this elegant dish with Eggplant Tartlets (Tartitas de Berenjena), an accompaniment I find most suitable, as the understated flavor of the eggplant complements the pungency of the anchovies.

To serve 6

For the sauce:

2 tablespoons butter
1 large onion, minced
4 large cloves garlic, minced
1 (2-ounce) can flat anchovy
    fillets, drained and minced
1 tablespoon Dijon-style mustard
1/2 cup full-bodied Spanish
    brandy

1/4 cup amontillado or another
    flavorful dry Spanish sherry
1 1/2 cups Enriched Veal Stock or
    3 cups Brown Veal Stock
1/2 cup heavy cream

For the veal:

3 pounds boneless veal loin,
    T-bone end (about 5 pounds
    before boning—2 or 3 loin
    sections)
1/2 teaspoon salt

1/4 teaspoon freshly ground black
    pepper
1 tablespoon butter
1 tablespoon olive oil

To prepare the sauce: Melt butter in a nonmetallic pan; add onion and garlic and sauté for 10 minutes over low heat. Stir in anchovies and mustard. Add brandy and, when hot, flambé.* Pour in sherry and stock; cook until reduced to 1 1/2 cups. Transfer to a food processor or blender and purée. With the motor running, add cream. Strain through a fine mesh strainer. Taste for seasoning. Reserve.

To prepare the veal: Cut off side flap of meat (use for another recipe or for veal stock, together with the bone). Tie loin at 1-inch intervals, and cut between strings; you will have 12 medallions or little rounds. Season them with salt and pepper. Heat butter and oil in a large skillet and, over medium-high heat, quickly cook meat 2 to 3 minutes on each side or until barely done. Pour sauce over, heat through and serve immediately.

Medallones de Ternera a la Naranja
(Veal Medallions in an Orange Sauce)

Bilbao is a very conservative city, and Guría is a traditional restaurant with an old reputation where Genaro Pildaín, using top-quality ingredients, serves classic Basque dishes like nobody else. His wife, Nati, runs the elegant dining room with the style of a grand Basque lady. This outstanding recipe was inspired by one of Genaro's preparations.

To serve 6

1 tablespoon sugar
1/2 cup Triple Sec or another
   orange liqueur
1 1/2 cups Enriched Veal Stock or
   3 cups Brown Veal Stock
1/2 cup orange juice
1 large orange
2 pounds veal tenderloin or top
   round, trimmed and cut into
   1-inch-thick rounds

1/2 teaspoon salt
1/2 teaspoon freshly ground black
   pepper
2 tablespoons butter
1 tablespoon olive oil
1/2 cup full-bodied Spanish
   brandy

In a saucepan, dissolve sugar in 1 teaspoon water and cook over medium-high heat until sugar melts and caramelizes, turning a dark golden color (see Caramelizing*). Add orange liqueur, stock and orange juice; cook over high heat until reduced to about 2 cups. Set aside.

With a vegetable peeler, peel the orange very carefully to get thin strips with little pith left on them. Cut the peel into thin match-like strips. In a small saucepan, bring about 2 cups water to a boil; add orange peel and cook at a boil for 1 minute. Drain the peel and add it to the sauce; cook for 3 minutes. Set the sauce aside. Cut orange in sections, discarding the membrane; reserve.

Pat veal dry and season with 1/4 teaspoon each salt and pepper. Heat butter and oil in a skillet large enough to hold all of the veal medallions. Add veal and sauté quickly, over medium-high heat, 2 minutes on each side. Pour in the brandy and, when hot, flambé.* When flames subside, add the sauce with orange peel and cook for 5 minutes, coating veal with the sauce. Transfer veal pieces to a serving platter and keep warm. Increase heat to medium-high, and reduce sauce to desired consistency. Season with remaining 1/4 teaspoon each salt and pepper, or to taste. Pour sauce over veal and garnish with the orange sections around.

Lomo de Cerdo a la Naranja
(Pork Loin in an Orange Sauce)

Madrid is full of traditional bistro-style restaurants where you can eat wonderfully; Horno de Santa Teresa has been one of them for over 25 years. Under owners Pepe and Ángeles Iglesias' approving eye, Chef Angel López produces a variety of excellent dishes representative of most Spanish regions. This recipe was inspired by one of his creations.

To serve 6

1 center-cut pork loin, boned
(about 5 pounds before boning,
or 3 to 3 1/2 pounds after;
reserve the bones—see Note
below)
1 1/2 teaspoons salt
3 large cloves garlic, minced
2 cups fresh orange juice
2 cups dry white wine

1 cup Brown Veal Stock,
preferably, or water
1 pound Pippin or Granny Smith
apples, peeled, cored and cut
up
1/4 cup sugar
1/4 teaspoon freshly ground black
pepper

As a garnish:

6 unpeeled orange slices

(Note: Have the butcher bone the loin, and cut the bones in 16 pieces. If there is a tenderloin, reserve it for another dish such as Pork Tenderloin with Grapes [Solomillo de Cerdo con Uvas]. Don't tie up the loin until later, as directed in the recipe.)

Cut a trough about 3/4 inch deep along the length of the loin, on the nonfat side. Season with 1 teaspoon of the salt, rubbing it along the whole loin. Sprinkle the garlic along the trough. Tie loin with string at 1-inch intervals.

Place loin, fat side down, in a heavy-bottomed flameproof casserole and brown it over medium heat, using just the fat from the loin, turning it until golden on all sides. Remove loin and add pork bones, browning them in the fat. Set bones aside and remove fat from casserole. Return loin to the casserole and add bones, orange juice, wine, veal stock and apples. Bring to a boil, immediately reduce heat to low and cook, uncovered, for an hour, turning it from time to time.

Remove loin to a cutting board. Discard bones. Purée sauce in the blender or food processor, and return to the pan. In a skillet, caramelize the sugar dissolved in 1 tablespoon water (see Caramelizing*), until it turns dark golden. Add to the sauce, and stir until dissolved. Increase heat to high and cook sauce until reduced by half, or to desired consistency. Add remaining 1/2 teaspoon salt and the pepper, and taste for seasoning.

Slice pork thinly and arrange on a serving platter. Serve garnished with orange slices, and pass the sauce in a sauceboat.

Lomo de Cerdo Relleno
(Pork Loin Stuffed with Almonds, Mushrooms and Sage)

This delicious pork dish comes from my mother's recipe file. There is one change I made: she used fresh truffles (her special source was much cheaper than here) in the stuffing, which indeed add an extraordinary flavor. But I found that the combination of a fresh herb such as sage with the other ingredients produced an excellent result. You won't miss those expensive, rare fungi!

To serve 8

For the stuffing:

1/4 *pound whole almonds*
1/4 *pound medium-ground pork meat*
1/4 *pound baked ham, finely chopped*
1/4 *pound mushrooms, chopped*
2 *hard-boiled eggs, chopped*

2 *tablespoons finely chopped fresh sage leaves*
1 *teaspoon salt, or to taste*
1/2 *teaspoon freshly ground black pepper, or to taste*
1 *raw egg*

For the pork:

1 *loin of pork, rib end, boned (5 to 6 pounds before boning, or about 3*1/2 *after; see Note below)*

3 *tablespoons olive oil*
1/2 *cup full-bodied Spanish brandy*
2 *cups Brown Veal Stock*

(Note: Ask your butcher to bone the loin, leaving some fat around it, and tie it at 1/2-inch intervals. Then slice the loin between each string, three quarters of the way through, so it opens like a book. Cut bones in about 16 pieces and reserve.)

To stuff the pork: Preheat oven to 350 degrees F. Toast almonds for 15 minutes and grind them finely. Combine them in a bowl with pork, ham, mushrooms, hard-boiled eggs, sage, salt and pepper. Mix well with the egg. Stuff the loin between the strings with this mixture. Tie the loin lengthwise, twice around.

To cook the pork: Heat oil in a casserole and sauté loin over medium heat, turning it around, until golden on all sides. Remove loin and add pork bones, browning them in the fat. Set bones aside. Remove fat from casserole, and deglaze with brandy. Add stock and bones, bring to a boil and add loin. Reduce heat to low, cover and cook for an hour or until done (about 140 degrees on a meat thermometer).

Transfer loin to a cutting board. Discard bones. Reduce sauce by about one third. Taste for seasoning. Remove the strings, slice loin and serve warm, with the sauce on the side.

Solomillo de Cerdo con Uvas
(Pork Tenderloin with Grapes)

La Merced is the finest restaurant in Logroño, capital of La Rioja region, and probably in that whole wine district. Owner Lorenzo Cañas transformed an old palace into this elegant establishment, which he decorated with grand style and impeccable taste. And if that were not enough, the cellar may be the best in La Rioja, with 52,000 bottles from the region alone!

I thought a dish with grapes would be a good one to represent this excellent restaurant.

To serve 6

For the sauce:

> 3 tablespoons olive oil
> 3 large cloves garlic, minced
> 1 small onion, minced
> 1 small leek, chopped, with 1/3 of the green part

> 1 medium carrot, finely chopped
> 1/2 pound seedless red grapes
> 1 bay leaf, middle vein removed, crumbled
> 1/2 cup fresh orange juice

For the pork:

> 2½ pounds pork tenderloin, cut in 18 pieces about 1 inch thick
> 1/2 teaspoon salt
> 1/2 teaspoon freshly ground black pepper

> 2 tablespoons olive oil
> 1/2 cup full-bodied Spanish brandy

For the caramelized grapes:

> 2 tablespoons butter
> 1/4 cup sugar
> 1/2 pound small seedless red grapes
> 1/4 cup dry red wine

To prepare the sauce: Heat oil in a skillet; sauté garlic, onion, leek, carrot, grapes and bay leaf over medium-low heat until very golden, almost brown —about 20 minutes. Transfer to blender or food processor and purée with orange juice. Strain through a fine-mesh strainer. Reserve.

To cook the pork: Gently pound pork pieces to flatten them slightly. Season with salt and pepper. Heat oil in a skillet wide enough to hold the pork. (It will shrink as it cooks, so you can crowd it in the skillet.) When oil is very hot, sauté pork over high heat, 2 minutes on each side. Add brandy and, when hot, flambé* for 1 minute. Douse flames with reserved sauce. Remove pork to a plate and reserve sauce in skillet.

To caramelize the grapes: In another skillet, heat butter and sugar. Cook over medium-high heat, shaking the pan, until sugar starts to turn golden. Immediately add grapes and cook quickly, shaking the pan, until caramel is brown—about 1 minute. Add wine, stir and remove grapes. Cook for another minute over high heat, until it starts to thicken. Stir into reserved sauce. Taste for seasoning. Add pork and cook until done—about 5 minutes. Serve immediately, garnished with grapes.

Chuleta de Cerdo a la Catalana
(Catalan: Costella de Porc a la Catalana)
(Pork Chop Stuffed with Prunes and Pine Nuts, Catalan Style)

As mentioned several times in this book, any "Catalan-style" preparation is bound to have pine nuts and prunes or raisins. Naturally, over the course of my life in Catalonia, I have eaten many a dish with these ingredients—from my mother's Christmas turkey to pigs' feet at Jaume de Provença in Barcelona—but interestingly enough, never pork. Yet I thought the combination should work beautifully with American pork—and indeed it does.

To serve 6

For the stuffing:

3/4 pound pitted prunes   *1/4 teaspoon salt*
3/4 cup port wine   *1/8 teaspoon freshly ground black*
1 tablespoon olive oil   *pepper*
3 tablespoons pine nuts

For the pork:

6 pork chops (1/2 pound each),   *1/2 cup port wine*
* cut with a pocket for stuffing*   *1 cup Brown Veal Stock*
1 teaspoon salt
1/2 teaspoon freshly ground black
* pepper*

To prepare the stuffing: Place prunes in a saucepan and cover with cold water. Bring to a boil, reduce heat and simmer, uncovered, for 20 minutes. Add 1/2 cup port. Bring to a boil, immediately reduce heat to low, cover and simmer for 15 minutes. Drain prunes and reserve prunes and their liquid.

Heat oil in a medium pan and sauté pine nuts until golden. Add prunes, pour in the remaining 1/4 cup port and cook over medium heat until reduced to a glaze. Season with salt and pepper.

To prepare the pork: Stuff pork chops with the filling; if all doesn't fit, reserve it—you can use it later in the sauce. Heat a wide skillet and, over high heat, sear chops 1 minute on each side. Sprinkle with salt and pepper as they cook. Add wine, stock, reserved prune liquid and any leftover filling; cover and cook over low heat for 30 minutes or until done. Transfer chops to a serving platter, together with any filling that oozed out. Increase heat to high and reduce sauce to desired consistency. Pour sauce over chops and serve warm.

CUTTING THE MEAT FROM A LEG OF LAMB

To get the best results in the following lamb dishes, it is a good idea to trim the fat and gristle off the leg of lamb and cut it up yourself; just have the butcher debone the leg for you. It is easy to cut up a leg of lamb, and if you do it according to the following instructions, it will cook much better.

There is a gland that is encased in fat on the leg; remove this carefully, for this gland gives an unpleasant taste to the meat. Remove outer skin and some fat; don't trim all the fat, or the meat will dry while cooking. Separate the meat along the individual muscles; this will give you more solid cubes of meat. You will notice that the meat will divide along its natural seams; some muscle groups are flatter, some thicker. Cut the meat along the line of the muscles, and then across to make pieces about 2 inches square. By not cutting across 2 or 3 muscle groups—as most butchers would do—you will get solid pieces of meat; this is much more important than getting precisely even cubes. Cutting the meat along the muscles ensures as well that all the meat in each muscle will cook uniformly. (This is also important when deboning a larger piece of meat into chops or steaks.)

One small leg of lamb, 5 to 6 pounds, should give you 3 to 3½ pounds of lean meat. This will provide about 6 servings, as indicated in the following recipes.

Pierna de Cordero Rellena de Riñones a la Almendra (Catalan: Cuixa de Xai Farcida de Ronyons a l'Ametlla) (Leg of Lamb Stuffed with Kidneys and Almonds)

For the last few years, La Odisea has been a star in Barcelona. Young owner/chef Antonio Ferrer is as adventurous in his cuisine as his establishment's name suggests. I was fascinated to hear his saga; his love of cooking started in school at eight—he made the sausages there! Now that he's in his early thirties, his passion for experimenting and learning continues, and his talent is reflected in the refined dishes he turns out. His wife, Teresa, is the perfect partner in the dining room.

Among many preparations difficult to reproduce here, he serves a top-quality leg of lamb stuffed with fresh lamb kidneys, which inspired me to develop this recipe. I was very pleased with the outcome—and especially of the fact that it has converted more than one reluctant friend to kidneys! I only hope Antonio would approve my adaptation of his idea.

To serve 6 to 8

For the stuffing:

1/2 cup sliced almonds
2 tablespoons olive oil
10 large cloves garlic, minced
1 large onion, minced
1 pound tomatoes, peeled and
  chopped
2 tablespoons chopped fresh
  parsley
1 tablespoon finely chopped
  fresh thyme

1/2 teaspoon salt
1/2 teaspoon freshly ground black
  pepper
1/4 cup full-bodied Spanish
  brandy
1 pound veal kidneys, fat
  removed, thinly sliced

For the lamb:

1 small (about 5 pounds) leg of
  lamb, boned and butterflied
1/2 teaspoon salt
1/2 teaspoon freshly ground black
  pepper

1 tablespoon olive oil
1/4 cup full-bodied Spanish
  brandy
2 cups Brown Veal Stock

To prepare the stuffing: Preheat oven to 350 degrees F. Toast almonds for 5 minutes. In a large skillet, heat oil and sauté garlic and onion over low heat until soft, about 10 minutes. Add tomatoes, parsley and thyme; cook over medium heat until dry. Season with salt and pepper. Reserve 1 cup of this sauce.

Add brandy to the remaining sauce in the pan and, when hot, flambé.* Cook over high heat until liquid evaporates; turn off heat. Stir in almonds and kidneys. (You may prepare this stuffing ahead of time; if so, let cool before adding almonds and kidneys.)

To prepare the lamb: Lay the lamb flat, skin side down; season with salt and pepper, rubbing it over the meat. Cover with the filling. Bring up the 4 sides of the meat and secure with a metal skewer from top to bottom. With the sides secured, sew up edges to enclose the filling. Don't worry if the shape of the leg isn't perfect, or if some of the filling comes out; it will just add flavor to the sauce.

In a large flameproof casserole, heat oil and brown lamb on all sides. Remove lamb and deglaze casserole with brandy. Add 1 cup stock and reserved tomato sauce. Return lamb to the casserole and bake in preheated 350-degree F. oven, uncovered, for 45 minutes or until it reaches 130 to 150 degrees F. on a meat thermometer inserted into the thickest part of the roast. While cooking, check to see that the sauce in the casserole doesn't burn.

Remove lamb to a cutting board. Pour contents of the casserole into the blender or food processor, add remaining 1 cup stock and purée. Strain through a fine sieve. Taste for seasoning.

Serve lamb sliced with some hot sauce over it, passing the remaining sauce in a sauceboat.

Cordero a la Miel
(Lamb with Honey and Green Peppers)

Start preparation 10 hours ahead or the day before, by marinating lamb

Pepe García Marín, owner of El Caballo Rojo in Córdoba, has done a terrific job of researching the origins of old mozárabe *cooking in Spain, and of adapting the recipes to suit today's palate while keeping their authenticity.* Mozárabes *were the Christians who lived under Arab rule, in conflict; by the tenth century they were being persecuted and had to flee to Christian areas in the north.*

This recipe is one of Pepe's finest achievements, and a classic example of mozárabe *cooking. The blend of flavors with the combination of sweet and sour works out extremely well. I like to serve it with Rosemary-Raisin Wreath Bread (Pan de Romero) or Home-Style White Rice (Arroz Blanco Hervido) as an accompaniment.*

To serve 6

For the marinade:

> About 2 cups dry flavorful
>   Spanish sherry, such as
>   amontillado
> 1 tablespoon Spanish paprika
> 2 teaspoons salt

> 3 to 3½ pounds boneless lamb
>   (from a 5- to 6-pound leg; see
>   directions in Cutting the Meat
>   from a Leg of Lamb*), cut into
>   2-inch pieces

For the lamb:

> 3 or 4 tablespoons olive oil
> 2 medium onions, finely chopped
> 1 large green bell pepper, cored,
>   seeded and chopped
> ½ teaspoon (.2 gram) saffron
>   threads

> ½ cup sherry wine vinegar
> ½ cup eucalyptus honey or
>   another full-flavored honey

To prepare the marinade: In a nonmetallic bowl, combine 1½ cups sherry with paprika and salt. Marinate lamb in it overnight or for at least 8 hours, covered and refrigerated, turning meat occasionally.

Drain lamb from the marinade. Measure liquid and add more sherry to a total of 1½ cups. Reserve.

To prepare the lamb: In a large flameproof casserole, heat 2 tablespoons oil and over medium-high heat sauté the meat quickly, until lightly browned. Set meat aside. Add another 1 or 2 tablespoons oil if necessary, and sauté onions and peppers gently for 10 minutes. Return meat to casserole, add sherry marinade and stir in saffron. Bring to a boil, reduce heat to low, cover and simmer for 1 hour.

Stir in vinegar and honey. Cook, uncovered, on low heat, for 30 minutes. Remove meat to a platter and keep warm. Rapidly cook the sauce in the pan to reduce to about 3 cups. Taste for seasoning. Pour sauce over the lamb. Serve warm.

Cordero Chilindrón
(Lamb in a Mild Dried Pepper Sauce)

Start preparation at least 8 hours ahead, by marinating lamb

Chilindrón *is a preparation for meats—lamb, kid or rabbit—indigenous to the regions of Aragón and southern Navarra, where the palate calls for heartier dishes; the sauce can sometimes be quite hot. It should always include dried red peppers, the* pimientos choriceros *or* del pico, *grown along the banks of the Ebro River. They are used dried because in the spring, when young lamb and goat are in season, there are no fresh peppers in the Ebro gardens; only the dried peppers from the former season are available, preserved the way they were in the old days.*

Pimientos choriceros or del pico *are not available in the United States, but I have found that* ancho *or* pasilla *chiles (also called dried* poblanos *or* pisados*) work very well. If you cannot find these, any other kind of sweet-mild, flavorful dried chile peppers will do. Some* chilindrón *recipes include tomatoes, potatoes, peas, ham, even fresh or canned bell peppers; but traditionally, dried ones should be used.*

This recipe was inspired by the memorable cordero chilindrón *I had at Pamplona's Joselxo restaurant, my favorite in that city. Chef Juan Oscáriz is "supervised" by his mother-in-law, great cook and matriarch Felisa García—nearing 70 and still at the stove every day—who adds the traditional touch to Juan's more inventive, innovative recipes.*

I like to serve this dish with fresh crusty Peasant Bread (Pan de Payés) or Saffron Rice (Arroz con Azafrán).

To serve 6

>   *3 to 3 1/2 pounds boneless lamb*
>   *(from a 5- to 6-pound leg; see*
>   *directions in Cutting the Meat*
>   *from a Leg of Lamb*), cut into*
>   *2-inch pieces*

For the marinade:

>   *1 cup dry white wine*
>   *4 large cloves garlic, peeled and*
>   *crushed*

For the lamb:

>   *3 ancho chile peppers, or another*   *2 large cloves garlic, finely*
>   *type of sweet-mild dried chile*   *chopped*
>   *peppers (see above)*   *2 large onions, chopped*
>   *4 tablespoons olive oil*   *2 cups Brown Veal Stock*
>   *1 1/2 cups dry red wine*   *About 1/2 teaspoon salt*

To marinate the lamb: Place lamb chunks in a nonmetallic bowl with the white wine and garlic cloves. Cover and refrigerate for at least 6 hours or overnight.

To prepare the lamb: Place the chile peppers in a saucepan and cover with water. Bring to a boil and cook over medium heat for 10 minutes. Remove from heat, cover and steep for 45 minutes. Drain peppers; gently stem and seed them. Set peppers aside and discard liquid.

Remove meat from marinade and reserve liquid. In a skillet, heat 2 tablespoons of the oil and over medium heat sauté meat quickly, turning it on all sides until it starts to brown. Transfer meat to a flameproof casserole. Deglaze skillet with 3/4 cup of the red wine and reduce to a glaze; pour over the meat. Wipe the skillet clean and heat 2 more tablespoons oil. Add chopped garlic and onions; sauté until soft, 10 to 15 minutes. Add to the casserole. Pour remaining 3/4 cup red wine into the skillet and deglaze until reduced to a syrup. Add to casserole, together with reserved peppers. Pour reserved marinade with the garlic over the meat. Add stock and bring to a boil; immediately reduce heat to very low and cook, covered, for 1 1/2 hours or until meat is very tender.

Remove meat from the casserole. With a slotted spoon, strain vegetables and purée very finely in the blender or food processor. Increase heat to high and reduce sauce to 3/4 or 1 cup. Return puréed vegetables to the casserole, stir and taste for seasoning; add 1/2 teaspoon salt, or to taste. Add meat and heat through, stirring. Serve immediately.

Cordero a la Pastoril
(Lamb Stew, Shepherd Style)

Start preparation 1 to 3 days ahead, by marinating lamb

Sevilla restaurant is located in Granada, in one of the most colorful parts of this extraordinarily beautiful city: the Alcaicería quarter, in the heart of town, wonderful to explore. Founded in 1930, Sevilla is one of the most typical and traditional restaurants in the city. Owner Juan Mari Álvarez is cheerful and friendly, a true Andalusian at heart. This recipe was inspired by a dish I had there.

To serve 6

> *3 to 3 1/2 pounds boneless lamb
> (from a 5- to 6-pound leg; see
> directions in Cutting the Meat
> from a Leg of Lamb*), cut into
> 2-inch pieces*

For the marinade:

6 large cloves garlic, crushed and
  peeled
1 tablespoon paprika
1 tablespoon dried oregano
2 bay leaves, middle vein
  removed, crumbled

1 teaspoon hot red pepper flakes
1/4 cup sherry wine vinegar or
  red wine vinegar
1/4 cup dry white wine
1 teaspoon salt

For the lamb:

3 tablespoons olive oil
1 cup dry white wine

About 4 cups Brown Veal Stock
Pepper to taste, if necessary

To prepare the marinade: Place lamb pieces in a nonmetallic casserole or bowl. Purée all ingredients for the marinade in a blender or food processor. Toss with the meat and cover. Refrigerate for at least 24 hours or as long as 3 days, turning lamb pieces in the marinade once in a while. Remove meat from the refrigerator 2 hours before cooking.

To prepare the lamb: Heat oil in a large heavy-bottomed skillet. Over medium-high heat, quickly brown lamb pieces lightly, in small batches; do not wipe the marinade from the meat. Reserve the marinade left in the bowl.

Transfer lamb to a flameproof casserole, preferably clay. Pour white wine into skillet and deglaze; cook rapidly to reduce by half. Transfer to casserole. Add stock and reserved marinade, and bring to a boil. Immediately reduce heat to very low and simmer, covered, for 1½ hours or until the meat is very tender. During this time, check periodically to make sure the stew doesn't boil, just simmer.

Transfer meat to a serving platter and keep warm. Cook sauce over high heat until reduced by half or to desired consistency. Taste for seasoning. Pour sauce over meat and serve.

Cordero al Ajillo
(Lamb Stew in a Garlic and Sweet Bell Pepper Sauce)

Start preparation 8 hours ahead or the day before, by marinating lamb

This is another lamb stew recipe inspired by a restaurant in Granada, Los Manueles. Established in 1917, under current owner Ángel de la Plata it has gained a well-deserved reputation for quality and friendliness. It is customary for granadinos to sit below its arches watching the world go by while nibbling on some of its irresistible tapas.

To serve 6

For the marinade:

2 large heads garlic (about 40 cloves), crushed and peeled

1 tablespoon chopped fresh oregano leaves (or 3/4 teaspoon dried)

1 tablespoon chopped fresh thyme leaves (or 3/4 teaspoon dried)

1 cup dry white wine

3 to 31/2 pounds boneless lamb (from a 5- to 6-pound leg; see directions in Cutting the Meat from a Leg of Lamb*), cut into 2-inch pieces

For the lamb:

3 large red bell peppers
About 3 tablespoons olive oil
1 cup dry white wine
11/2 cups Brown Veal Stock

1/2 teaspoon salt, or to taste
1/2 teaspoon freshly ground black pepper, or to taste

As a garnish:

1 head garlic, very thinly sliced, sautéed in olive oil until crisp and golden, drained on paper towels

To prepare the marinade: In a nonmetallic casserole or bowl, combine all ingredients for the marinade and add lamb pieces. Marinate for at least 6 hours, turning lamb in marinade from time to time.

To prepare the lamb: Roast and peel peppers (see Roasting and Peeling Peppers*). Remove stems and seeds, and coarsely chop them. Heat oil in a large heavy-bottomed skillet. Quickly brown lamb lightly over medium-high heat, in small batches; reserve marinade. Transfer lamb to a flame-proof casserole. Add wine to skillet and deglaze; reduce by half. Add to the casserole, together with marinade left in the bowl, peppers and stock. Bring to a boil, immediately reduce heat to low and simmer, partially covered, for 11/2 hours or until meat is tender.

Remove lamb to a serving platter and keep warm. Transfer sauce in casserole with garlic and peppers to a blender or food processor; purée and return to the casserole. Increase heat to high and reduce sauce until thickened to desired consistency. Add salt and pepper, and taste for seasoning. Pour sauce over lamb. Garnish with sliced sautéed garlic on top.

Tronzón de Tudanco al Tresviso
(Beef Steak with Mushrooms in a Blue Cheese Sauce)

This dish was among many interesting ones I had at Risco, the delightful restaurant in Laredo, Cantabria, run by Zacarías and Inés Puente, and it inspired me to develop this recipe.

The region is well known for its excellent blue cheese, Tresviso-Picón, as well as for its beef, tudanco. *Tresviso is a mixture of cow, goat and sheep cheese, similar to the Cabrales-Picón of Asturias and the French Roquefort.* Tudanco *is a breed of ox that lives in the mountains; it has a lot of flavor. The word* tronzón *means large cut, and it is similar to our sirloin.*

To serve 6 to 8

For the sauce:

1/4 pound sharp blue cheese, such as a flavorful Oregon or Danish blue
1/2 cup dry white wine
3 tablespoons butter

1/2 cup heavy cream
2 large cloves garlic, minced
1 pound mushrooms, thinly sliced

For the steak:

1 (3-pound) piece of steak (New York strip or club steak, top sirloin, London broil or butterball)
3/4 teaspoon coarsely ground black pepper

1 teaspoon salt
3/4 cup Enriched Veal Stock or 1 1/2 cups Brown Veal Stock

To prepare the sauce: In a bowl, cream the cheese and wine with a fork. Melt 1 tablespoon butter in a pan; add cheese/wine mixture and cream. Bring to a boil and reduce by one third, stirring. Set aside.

Heat remaining 2 tablespoons butter in a skillet and, over low heat, sauté garlic until soft and golden; add mushrooms and cook until they start to wilt, 6 to 8 minutes. Transfer to the pan with the cheese sauce. (This sauce can be prepared ahead of time, and reheated at the last minute.)

To cook the meat: Shortly before serving time, season both sides of the steak with pepper. Heat a heavy skillet, large enough to hold the steak, until very hot. Sprinkle the salt in the skillet and add steak. Cook the meat quickly, over high heat—it shouldn't burn, but should get dark brown— about 5 minutes on each side, depending on the thickness. The steak should be rare, as it will continue to cook for a few minutes after it is removed from the heat. Transfer meat to a cutting board and let it rest for about 5 minutes.

Meanwhile, pour stock into the skillet where the meat cooked and, over high heat, stir and scrape the bottom and sides of the skillet with a spatula to get all the browned bits of meat left. Cook until reduced to about 1/2 cup. Pour contents into pan with the mushroom sauce. Stir and taste for seasoning.

Cut the meat into thin slices. Pour any juices from the meat into the sauce. Serve steak slices with sauce on top.

Solomillo con Frutas Secas
(Catalan: Filet de Bou amb Fruits Secs)
(Beef Tenderloin with Dried Fruits)

This recipe from the great restaurant El Racó d'en Binu, near Barcelona, is irresistible. The combination of meat and fruits, here again, is classic Catalan; but it takes Francesc Fortí's stroke of genius to put it together. It is a rich, elegant dish, worth every calorie and sure of winning the admiration of your guests.

I prefer to serve it without any accompaniment, just by itself with the fruits; or at the most, with Home-Style White Rice (Arroz Blanco Hervido).

To serve 6

8 figs
18 dried apricots
12 prunes
6 (6-ounce) slices (2 1/4 pounds total) of beef tenderloin, each about 3/4 inch thick, cut from the center of the loin
1 1/2 tablespoons crushed green peppercorns

1 1/2 teaspoons salt
2 tablespoons butter
1/2 cup full-bodied Spanish brandy
1/2 cup heavy cream
1/2 cup Enriched Veal Stock or 1 cup Brown Veal Stock

Place figs, apricots and prunes in a saucepan and cover with boiling water. Let them soak for about 2 hours.

Cut out fat from sides of beef steaks and tie each around with string, to give it a round shape. Cover both sides of the steaks with the peppercorns, and sprinkle them with 1 teaspoon salt. Let them sit, unrefrigerated, for an hour.

Remove fruits from soaking water and cut them into 1/4-inch slices. Over medium-high heat, reduce liquid in saucepan to 1/3 cup.

In a skillet large enough to hold all of the steaks, heat butter and, over medium-high heat, sauté them for 1 minute on each side. Add brandy and flambé*. Set steaks aside. Add fruits, reduced liquid in saucepan, cream and veal stock to the skillet. Increase heat and reduce sauce by one third, or to desired consistency. Add remaining 1/2 teaspoon salt or to taste. Return steaks to the pan and coat them with the sauce. Serve immediately.

VEGETABLES

Calabacines en Escabeche
(Zucchini Marinated in Vinegar and Mint)

This is a very simple escabeche *preparation, the way of marinating foods in lemon or vinegar brought to Spain by the Arabs. Served cold, it makes a very refreshing first course; it can also be served as an accompaniment to cold meats. It is ideal in a summertime buffet.*

To serve 6 to 8

> *3 pounds small zucchini, ends cut off*
> *About 1 tablespoon salt*
> *About 1/2 cup olive oil*
> *12 large cloves garlic, thinly sliced by hand*
>
> *1/4 cup finely chopped fresh mint leaves*
> *1/2 cup finest-quality red wine vinegar, preferably balsamic vinegar*

Cut zucchini in thin slices lengthwise. Layer them on a cloth over a baking sheet; sprinkle salt between each layer. Let them dry in the sun, if possible, for 2 or 3 hours; otherwise, if you have a gas oven, place them in it, unheated, with just the pilot light on, for 2 hours; if you have an electric oven, heat it to 200 degrees F. for 10 minutes, turn it off and leave the zucchini there for 2 hours. And if you are short of time, just let zucchini stand for 1/2 hour and pat them dry.

Heat olive oil in a skillet and sauté garlic slices over medium-low heat until golden. Remove with a spatula and set aside on paper towels. Pat dry zucchini slices and, in the same oil, sauté them over medium heat in small batches, until golden on both sides. Drain on paper towels and layer them in a deep serving platter or wide clay casserole. Sprinkle each layer with garlic and mint; reserve about 1 tablespoon of garlic slices. Pour vinegar over, cover and marinate for at least 3 or 4 hours. At the last minute, sprinkle reserved tablespoon of crunchy garlic slices on top.

"Escalivada"
(Assorted Grilled Vegetables, Catalan Style)

Escalivar *is the Catalan word for cooking over hot embers;* escalivada *is the equivalent of charcoal-grilled vegetables, rubbed with oil and cooked whole. I usually bake them in the oven this way, unless I am already charcoal-grilling.*

Escalivada *is a very common first course all over Catalonia in the summertime—the peak season for red peppers, tomatoes and the flavorful narrow eggplants which are comparable to the Japanese kind available here. You can make* escalivada *with any or all of the vegetables in the following recipe; very often in Spain you would just be served eggplant and red peppers, perhaps with onions. On a platter, they are colorful and attractive, like a mosaic. It also makes a very nice accompaniment for grilled meats or fish, roasts or barbecued chicken. If you are cooking these on a charcoal grill, add the* escalivada; *it will have especially good flavor.*

Carles Camós, *at his Big Rock restaurant in Palamós (Costa Brava), in northern Catalonia, serves as an appetizer* tosta d'escalivada amb anxoves *(Catalan for toast with escalivada and anchovies)—a simple but terrific idea. He toasts thin slices of Peasant Bread (Pan de Payés)—you can also use a good French bread—puts a little bit of* escalivada *of red pepper, eggplant and onion over it, and an anchovy fillet on top. According to Carles, the secret is just to use fresh, ripe, high-quality vegetables.*

To serve 4

2 tomatoes, halved crosswise	**2 white onions**
1 pound small eggplants, preferably the long, thin Japanese variety (see Note in Eggplant, Pepper and Tomato Dip)	**2 baking potatoes, halved lengthwise**
	About 4 tablespoons olive oil
	1/2 teaspoon salt, or to taste
	1/4 teaspoon freshly ground black pepper, or to taste
2 large red bell peppers	

As a garnish:

2 tablespoons chopped fresh parsley leaves

Preheat oven to 350 degrees F.

Rub all vegetables with about 2 tablespoons oil. Place them on a baking sheet (tomatoes, cut side up). Bake about 15 minutes for tomatoes, 45 minutes to 1 hour for eggplant and peppers (depending on size), 1 hour for onions and potatoes.

Peel eggplants and peppers. With your fingers, tear them into very thin strips. Arrange all vegetables on a large platter. Season with salt and pepper, drizzle about 2 tablespoons oil over, and sprinkle with parsley. Serve warm or at room temperature.

"Ceballots"
(Baked Young Onions or Leeks)

Springtime in Catalonia brings on the calçotada—*a special fiesta held in the town of Valls that celebrates the arrival of* calçots *or* ceballots, *tender young onions about the size of small leeks.* Calçotadas *are outdoor gatherings where these seasonal delicacies are grilled on open wood fires—traditionally we use grapevine prunings which have been cut in the winter—until they are completely charred on the outside. You peel away the burned skins, douse them with the* romesco-style *sauce* salbitxada *and feast away. Meanwhile, there is plenty of music, wine and lots of merriment. Sometimes we dance the traditional Catalonian folk dance known as the* sardana.

Since ceballots *are not available in America, I have found that the recipe works very well with leeks. They are best cooked on an outdoor charcoal grill, which provides great flavors; but they are also delicious cooked on an indoor grill, or even baked in the oven.*

Ceballots *or leeks combine perfectly with any* romesco *sauce; but I think the recipe for Romesco-Style Sauce for Grilled Vegetables (Salbitxada), from Pere Valls of El Celler del Penedès restaurant, goes particularly well.*

To serve 6

3 bunches young leeks, trimmed
   of all but 2 or 3 inches of the
   green part
About 1/2 cup olive oil

1/2 recipe Romesco-Style Sauce
   for Grilled Vegetables

Cut leeks in half lengthwise down to within 1 inch from the bottom or root end. Rub leeks quite generously with olive oil, and cook them (over a charcoal grill, on an indoor grill or in a preheated 425-degree F. oven) until they are very tender and golden. Depending on their size and cooking method, they may take from 30 to 60 minutes. Turn them over occasionally while cooking.

Serve the leeks warm, with the sauce on the side.

Cebollitas a la Crema y al Perfume de Tomillo
(Catalan: Cebetes a la Crema i al Perfum de Farigola)
(Pearl Onions in a Cream and Thyme Sauce)

I had these delicious onions at Can Boix, the Pyrenean restaurant in Martinet where Josep Boix handles with perfection the local produce of the bountiful Catalan district La Cerdanya: in this case, the baby onions and the fresh mountain thyme, which abounds there. In fact, it imparted an extraordinary fragrance to an after-lunch hike!

To serve 4 to 6

1¹/2 pounds pearl onions (see Note below)	*1¹/2 cups Brown Veal Stock or Chicken Stock*
2 tablespoons butter	*1/2 cup heavy cream*
1/2 cup full-bodied Spanish brandy	*1/4 teaspoon salt, or to taste*
1 teaspoon chopped fresh thyme (or 1/4 teaspoon dried)	

(Note: Pearl or cocktail-size onions are particularly good for this dish; they can be time-consuming to peel, but following the directions below will make the job much easier—and they are so good, it is truly worth it. You can also make this dish with the smallest white boiling onions. Allow 3 or 4 onions per person, in that case.)

Peel the onions by dipping them in a pan of boiling water for 5 to 10 seconds. Immediately drain and, when cool, cut out the bottom with a sharp knife. Squeeze onion out of its outer layer; it will pop out peeled.

Melt butter in a medium skillet and, over medium-high heat, sauté onions quickly for 4 to 5 minutes, shaking the pan, until they start to color. Add brandy and when hot, flambé.* Add thyme and stock, and bring to a boil; reduce heat to low and cook, uncovered, for 15 minutes or until onions are barely done but still crisp.

With a slotted spoon, transfer onions to a platter and reserve. Increase heat to high and reduce stock in the skillet to just about 2 tablespoons. Add cream, stir and cook over medium heat to thicken a little. Add onions and salt; cook over medium-low heat until tender, about 5 more minutes. Taste for seasoning. Serve immediately.

Confit de Cebollas
(Catalan: Confit de Cebes)
(Onion Relish)

Roig Rubí *is Catalan for ruby red—and also the name of a small restaurant in Barcelona run by chef/owner Mercedes Navarro, her daughter Imma and son Juan. They opened in 1982, named it after the color of fine red wine and set out to serve authentic Catalan home-style cooking. The restaurant's setting, with its charming umbrella-covered patio, provides the pleasant feeling of being in someone's private residence.*

Mercedes's food shows her innovative approach to simple ideas. This relish makes a delightful, tangy condiment which may be served hot to accompany roast meats or poultry—it is excellent with Veal Medallions in an Orange Sauce (Medallones de Ternera a la Naranja) or Game Hens in a Sweet and Sour Sauce (Capones al Agridulce)—as well as cold with pâtés, cold meats or sausages.

To serve 4

4 tablespoons butter
2 pounds yellow onions, thinly
  sliced
1½ cups medium-bodied dry red
  wine

½ cup sherry wine vinegar or
  red wine vinegar
¼ teaspoon salt, or to taste
2 tablespoons honey

Heat butter in a skillet with high sides. Add onions and cook over low heat, very slowly, until soft and golden; it should take about 45 minutes. Add wine, vinegar and salt; cook over medium heat until liquid is absorbed by onions. Add honey and cook slowly until honey begins to caramelize. Taste for seasoning. Serve warm or at room temperature.

Espinacas a la Catalana
(Catalan: Espinacs a la Catalana)
(Spinach with Pine Nuts and Raisins, Catalan Style)

You will find this classic Catalan vegetable dish—again with pine nuts and raisins—in the menus of many regional restaurants. A favorite of mine is Quo Vadis's preparation, because they get such good fresh spinach from nearby La Boquería market, the best in town, in Barcelona's old Ramblas promenade. That's about all there is to the dish; the idea is quite simple, yet ingenious and very tasty. It will be the perfect accompaniment for pork or game.

To serve 4

4 small bunches spinach (about 3
  pounds), stemmed
2 tablespoons olive oil
½ cup pine nuts

¼ cup dark raisins
¼ teaspoon salt, or to taste
¼ teaspoon freshly ground black
  pepper, or to taste

Rinse spinach well and place in a large saucepan. Cook over medium heat, covered, with only the water that clings to the leaves, just until wilted— about 10 minutes. Toss spinach with 2 spoons from time to time. Drain and squeeze dry. Chop coarsely.

Heat olive oil in a large skillet. Add pine nuts and raisins; sauté over medium-high heat until pine nuts are golden and raisins plump up, 3 or 4 minutes. Add spinach, salt and pepper, and gently toss until well mixed. Taste for seasoning. Serve warm.

Pastelitos de Espinaca
(Spinach Timbales)

These spinach/potato flans make a very nice accompaniment for any meat entrée. The potato makes for a less rich, more nutritious vegetable combination than a cream sauce, adding an interesting texture without any of the heaviness.

To serve 6:   Makes 6 (1/2-cup) timbales

1/2 pound potatoes	2 eggs, beaten
2 tablespoons butter	1/4 cup milk
1/2 cup chopped onion	1/2 teaspoon salt
1 bunch spinach (about 1 pound), stemmed and chopped	1/4 teaspoon freshly ground black pepper, or to taste
1/2 cup grated Asiago, Gruyère or Emmenthaler cheese	About 1/4 cup finely grated Parmesan cheese

Boil, peel and mash potatoes finely, with a potato ricer, masher or fork (don't use a food processor or blender). While still warm, mix in 1 tablespoon butter with a fork.

In a medium skillet, sauté onion in 1 tablespoon butter until soft. Add spinach and cover; cook until wilted, about 3 minutes. Transfer to a bowl and combine with mashed potatoes, grated cheese, eggs and milk. Mix well with a fork. Add salt and pepper; taste for seasoning.

Preheat oven to 350 degrees F.

Oil muffin tins or individual timbale molds. Flour and shake out excess; sprinkle with some Parmesan cheese, just to coat. Fill with the spinach mixture.

Place molds inside a larger pan filled with boiling water halfway up the molds. Bake in the preheated oven until the mixture puffs up, about 30 minutes.

Preheat broiler.

When cool, run a knife around the edges of the timbales and unmold onto a serving platter. Sprinkle remaining Parmesan over tops. Place under broiler for a few moments, until golden. Serve immediately.

Tartitas de Berenjena
(Catalan: Pastissets d'Albergínia)
(Eggplant Tartlets)

These attractive little tartlets are an idea from Tiró Mimet restaurant, where chef Xavier Grifoll serves them as an accompaniment to his Veal Fillet with Anchovy Sauce (Filete de Ternera con Salsa de Anchoas). The sharp taste of the eggplant provides an interesting contrast to any meat dish with a sauce.

To serve 8

For the tartlets:

> 1 recipe Press-in Pastry

For the filling:

> 3 tablespoons olive oil
> 1 pound eggplant, preferably the long, thin Japanese variety (see Note in Eggplant, Pepper and Tomato Dip), peeled and cut into 1/4-inch cubes
> 2 tablespoons minced onion
> 1 tablespoon minced garlic
> 1 small red or green pepper
> (preferably red), seeded and finely chopped (about 1/2 cup)
> 1 pound tomatoes, peeled, seeded and chopped
> 1/2 teaspoon salt, or to taste
> 1/4 teaspoon freshly ground black pepper, or to taste
> 1 egg, beaten
> 1/2 cup heavy cream

To prepare the tartlets: Preheat oven to 425 degrees F.

Divide dough into 8 equal parts and line 8 ungreased 1/2-cup ramekin molds or muffin tins; press the dough into the molds and up on the sides, distributing evenly. Refrigerate for at least 15 minutes. Immediately bake in the preheated oven for 10 to 15 minutes, or until golden. When slightly cooled, gently remove pastry from molds and set aside. Reduce oven temperature to 375 degrees F.

To prepare the filling: In a large skillet, heat 2 tablespoons oil and sauté eggplant over medium heat, stirring, for 10 minutes. Set eggplant aside. Add remaining tablespoon oil to the skillet and sauté onion and garlic over low heat for 5 minutes. Add peppers and cook 10 minutes. Add tomatoes and cook until dry. Return eggplant to the pan, stir and cook, covered, another 10 minutes. Season with salt and pepper, and taste for seasoning. Let cool slightly. In a bowl, mix egg and cream with vegetables.

To assemble the tartlets: Fill prepared tart shells with the mixture. Bake on a baking sheet in the 375-degree F. oven for 15 minutes. Serve immediately.

Tortilla de Berenjenas
(Eggplant Omelet)

The idea for this eggplant omelet comes from my good friend Mercedes Molina, who is from Murcia, one of the main vegetable-growing regions in Spain. I've enjoyed tortilla de berenjenas *at her home, as a first course or even as a light supper; I often serve this and Spanish Potato Omelet (Tortilla Española) for lunch, together with Bread with Tomato, Catalan Style (Pan con Tomate).*

To serve 6

6 tablespoons olive oil
1 large onion, chopped
2 pounds eggplant, preferably
  the long, thin Japanese variety
  (see Note in Eggplant, Pepper
  and Tomato Dip), peeled and
  diced small

6 eggs
1 teaspoon salt
1/2 teaspoon freshly ground black
  pepper

Heat 4 tablespoons olive oil in a wide skillet and sauté the onion slowly for 10 minutes. Add eggplant and cook over medium-low heat until very tender, stirring often with a spatula—about 15 or 20 minutes. In a bowl, beat the eggs with the salt and pepper; stir in the eggplant.

Heat remaining 2 tablespoons oil in an 8- or 10-inch nonstick skillet. When quite hot, pour in the eggplant mixture, reduce heat to low and cook, shaking the skillet occasionally, until set on the bottom and halfway through the omelet—15 to 20 minutes. Place on top of the skillet an inverted plate slightly larger than the skillet, and turn out the omelet onto it; slide the omelet back into the skillet. Cook until firm and set all the way through—about 5 minutes. Slide omelet onto a serving platter. Serve warm or at room temperature.

Flanes de Verduras
(Catalan: Assortiment de Flams de Llegums)
(Green Pea and Red Pepper Flans)

El Racó d'en Binu, the very special restaurant in Argentona, near Barcelona, serves these colorful flans made with whatever vegetables are in season. I have found that green peas and red peppers work best here, and they make a very lovely combination—both color- and taste-wise. Served together or individually, they are a perfect accompaniment to poultry dishes, such as Chicken Flavored with Sherry, in a Sherry Sauce (Pollito de Grano al Vino de Jerez).

To serve 6

For the green pea flan:

1 1/2 cups (or 10 ounces) fresh or
  frozen shelled peas
1/2 cup half-and-half
3 eggs

1/2 teaspoon salt
3/8 teaspoon freshly ground
  white pepper

For the red pepper flan:

1 1/2 pounds red bell peppers (or
  1 1/2 cups canned roasted sweet
  peppers)
1/2 cup half-and-half

3 eggs
3/4 teaspoon salt
1/4 teaspoon freshly ground
  white pepper

Preheat oven to 350 degrees F.

To prepare the green pea flan: Cook peas in a small amount of boiling water until tender—5 minutes for frozen and 15 for fresh. Drain them and purée in the blender or food processor; add all remaining ingredients and blend well.

Generously butter 6 individual 1/2-cup flan molds, especially the bottom, and fill them three-quarters full with the pea mixture. Cover with foil and place them in a baking pan, pouring hot water around them to halfway up the sides of the molds. Bake in the preheated oven for 35 minutes; when done, they should feel slightly firm to the touch.

Let them cool, so they firm up a little more, before unmolding. Then run a knife around the rim of each mold and invert onto a serving plate, giving it a whack to unmold the flan. Serve warm; if made ahead, cover with foil and reheat in the oven.

To prepare the red pepper flan: Place peppers on an ungreased baking sheet in the oven and roast them for 45 minutes to an hour, turning them around until the skin is blackened and blistered. When cool enough to handle, peel and seed them, squeezing them dry with your hands; reserve the juices. Purée the peppers and add remaining ingredients, proceeding as for the pea flan recipe.

Place pepper juices in a saucepan and cook over high heat until reduced to just about 1 tablespoon. Pour around the unmolded flans on the platter. (After the flans are unmolded, some liquid will ooze out from the peppers; this will blend with the reduced juices, making a nice sauce.)

Flanes de Setas
(Catalan: Flams de Rovellons)
(Mushroom Flans)

This is an elegant, subtle but flavorful first course, worthy of your finest dinner parties. The recipe was inspired by a dish from El Racó d'en Binu, the excellent restaurant in Argentona, near Barcelona.

In his classic style, chef Francesc Fortí has taken the idea from a traditional Catalan dish—the delicious mushrooms rovellons, which usually are simply grilled and sprinkled with fresh garlic and parsley. We don't have those special mushrooms here, but I have found that some flavorful dried ones result in a dish pretty close to his rendition.

This recipe yields 4 cups of flan mixture, so you will need 8 (1/2- or 2/3-cup) molds or ramekins.

To serve 8

For the flans:

1 ounce flavorful dried
  mushrooms, such as
  chanterelles or porcini (1/2 cup
  packed, after soaking)
2 tablespoons butter
3 large cloves garlic, minced
3/4 pound fresh mushrooms,
  thinly sliced
1 tablespoon finely chopped
  parsley leaves

1/2 teaspoon salt
1/4 teaspoon freshly ground
  white pepper
1/3 cup full-bodied Spanish
  brandy
4 egg yolks
3 whole eggs
1 cup half-and-half

For the sauce:

2 tablespoons butter
1/2 cup minced shallots (about 6
  large)
1/2 pound fresh mushrooms,
  thinly sliced
1/4 cup amontillado or another
  flavorful Spanish sherry

1 cup Brown Veal Stock
1/2 cup heavy cream
1/2 teaspoon salt, or to taste
1/2 teaspoon freshly ground
  white pepper, or to taste

To prepare the flans: Soak dried mushrooms in 1½ cups lukewarm water for 30 minutes. Drain them, and reserve liquid.

Preheat oven to 350 degrees F.

Melt butter in a skillet and add garlic, fresh and dried mushrooms, and parsley. Sauté on low heat until the mushrooms are soft, 10 to 15 minutes. Season with salt and pepper. Add brandy and, when hot, flambé.* Continue sautéeing for 2 or 3 more minutes, until dry. Pour mushroom mixture into the blender or food processor, and purée. Beat in egg yolks and eggs. Stir in half-and-half, and blend well. Strain through a medium sieve.

Butter sides and bottoms of 8 flan molds, and pour in flan mixture. Place molds in a baking pan filled with boiling water one third of the way up the sides of the molds. Cover molds with foil and bake in the preheated oven for about 40 minutes, or until a cake tester comes out clean.

To prepare the sauce: Melt butter in a skillet, add shallots and sauté over medium-low heat until soft, about 5 minutes. Add sliced mushrooms and continue cooking until mushrooms are soft, about 10 minutes. Strain reserved liquid from soaking dried mushrooms and add it; increase heat and cook rapidly until liquid is reduced by half, about 5 minutes. Transfer to a blender or food processor and purée very finely with the sherry, stock and cream. Strain through a fine sieve into a skillet, and heat through. Add salt and pepper, and taste for seasoning.

To assemble the dish: Serve each flan on an individual dish, pouring hot sauce over and around.

Alcachofas con Piñones
(Artichoke Stew with Pine Nuts)

Since it was founded in 1925 by Pepe Sánchez-Gómez, Rincón de Pepe has undoubtedly become the best restaurant in Murcia, the southeastern region which is home of the Huerta Murciana, Spain's main vegetable "garden." Current owner Raimundo González-Frutos has done a fantastic job of researching and developing a great variety of delicious regional recipes. Many use the Huerta's fresh produce, such as these baby artichokes. Since excellent baby artichokes are available from California, this recipe works very well here.

I usually serve this dish as a first course, in a bowl; but it is also a nice accompaniment to grilled chicken or meats.

To serve 4 to 6

1/2 cup red or white wine vinegar
36 fresh baby artichokes, or
   artichoke hearts (3 1/2 pounds)
2 tablespoons olive oil
1/4 pound pancetta, finely diced
1 large onion, minced
3 large cloves garlic, minced

1 pound ripe tomatoes, peeled,
   seeded and chopped
3 cups Chicken Stock
1 teaspoon salt, or to taste
1/4 teaspoon freshly ground black
   pepper, or to taste
1/4 cup pine nuts

In a nonmetallic bowl, combine vinegar with 1 quart water. Remove outer leaves from each artichoke; trim top and bottom. Lay artichoke on its side and, with a small knife, cut away from the bottom toward the top on a slant, to form points. This is a pretty way of cutting the artichokes—the edges look scalloped, the bottoms are round and the tops pointed. As you trim each artichoke, immediately plunge it into the vinegar water.

Heat olive oil in a nonmetallic pan. Add pancetta and cook over medium-low heat for 10 minutes, until golden. Add onion and garlic and cook for 5 minutes. Add tomatoes and cook over medium heat for 10 to 15 minutes, until dry. Add stock, salt and pepper; bring to a boil. Drain artichokes and add to the pan. Reduce heat to a simmer and cook, covered, for 30 minutes.

Transfer artichokes to a tureen or clay casserole and keep warm. Bring liquid to a boil and reduce to about 1 cup. Taste for seasoning.

Meanwhile, toast pine nuts in a heavy skillet over low heat, stirring, until golden. Pour sauce over artichokes and sprinkle with pine nuts.

Pastel de Col
(Cabbage Torte)

This is an excellent recipe from my mother's files, traditionally Catalan in style.

To serve 6

1 large head green cabbage
3 tablespoons olive oil
1/4 pound pancetta, finely diced
1/2 pound medium-ground pork
2 medium onions, minced
3 eggs, beaten
1/2 cup white bread crumbs,
    without crusts (see Bread
    Crumbs*)

1/4 cup milk
1 cup grated Parmesan cheese
1 teaspoon salt, or to taste
1 teaspoon freshly ground black
    pepper, or to taste
2 pounds tomatoes, peeled,
    seeded and chopped
1 tablespoon tomato paste

Cut cabbage in half and cook in boiling salted water for 20 minutes, covered; drain and set aside.

Heat 1 tablespoon oil in a skillet and, over medium-low heat, sauté the pancetta until golden, about 10 minutes. Add pork and cook, stirring, for 3 minutes or until cooked. Remove the pork and pancetta and reserve. Add onions to the skillet and sauté over medium-low heat for 15 minutes or until very soft.

Preheat oven to 350 degrees F.

In a bowl, soak bread in milk. Stir in eggs, pancetta, pork, onions, cheese, 1/2 teaspoon salt and 3/4 teaspoon pepper, or to taste.

Butter an 8-inch springform pan. Separate the cabbage leaves and arrange a third to cover the bottom and sides of the baking pan, overlapping the edges. Spread half of the pork mixture on top. Cover with another third of the cabbage leaves, and spread remaining filling on top. Cover with the remaining cabbage, bringing the overhanging leaves up over the top. Bake in the preheated oven for 40 minutes.

To prepare the tomato sauce: Heat remaining 2 tablespoons oil in a skillet and cook tomatoes over medium heat until reduced to a sauce consistency—15 to 20 minutes. Add tomato paste, remaining 1/2 teaspoon salt and 1/4 teaspoon pepper. Taste for seasoning.

Unmold the cabbage onto a serving platter. Spread tomato sauce on top. Serve hot.

RICE, POTATOES AND PASTA

Arroz Blanco Hervido
(Home-Style White Rice)

The rice we use in Spain is the short-grain type, the equivalent of the Italian Arborio, which is thicker and tastier than the long-grain. It is essential to prepare any of my rice recipes, and much better than long-grain to accompany sauce dishes.

This is the way Rosalía, our family cook, always prepared it at home. You will find it retains its fluffiness and does not stick together, so it is not necessary to add any butter. A nice way to present it as an accompaniment to any entrée (especially those with sauce) is in individual molds, as directed below.

To serve 6

> *1 teaspoon salt*
> *1 1/2 cups short-grain rice (see*
> *above)*
> *2 lemon slices*

In a heavy pot, bring 3 quarts water to a boil; add salt. Add rice and lemon slices. Stir rice with a wooden spatula at the beginning, so it doesn't stick to the bottom. Boil rice, uncovered, over medium heat for 10 minutes or until grains are not hard.

Remove lemon slices; strain rice through a colander and run under cold water, to stop the cooking.

To serve: Rinse a 1/3- or 1/2-cup flan mold or individual muffin tin in cold water and pack the rice firmly in it, up to 1/4 inch from the top. Invert mold onto a serving platter and tap against the surface; it will come out in a neat mound. Repeat until you use up all the rice, rinsing mold each time; arrange rice attractively on platter. Before serving, cover with foil and warm up in the oven.

Arroz con Azafrán
(Saffron Rice)

This flavorful rice will be a fine accompaniment to many of the meat, poultry or fish dishes in this book.

To serve 8

4 tablespoons butter
1 large onion, minced
3 large cloves garlic, minced
3 cups Chicken Stock
1/2 teaspoon (.2 gram) saffron threads (or 1/4 teaspoon powdered saffron)

1 teaspoon salt
1/4 teaspoon freshly ground black pepper
11/2 cups short-grain rice (see Home-Style White Rice)

Heat butter in a wide saucepan with high sides. Sauté onion and garlic over low heat until soft, 10 to 15 minutes. Meanwhile, bring stock to a boil in a small saucepan; stir in saffron, salt and pepper. Add rice to onion mixture and cook for 1 minute, stirring. Add boiling stock; bring liquid to a boil again, reduce heat to low and simmer, covered, for 18 minutes. Remove from heat and let stand for 5 to 10 minutes before serving.

Arroz con Pasas y Piñones a la Catalana
(Catalan: Arròs amb Panses i Pinyons a la Catalana)
(Rice with Raisins and Pine Nuts, Catalan Style)

Here is a traditional "Catalan-style" rice—with pine nuts and raisins—the way I have had it as an accompaniment at El Racó d'en Binu, the great restaurant in Argentona, near Barcelona. It makes a perfect complement for any meat or poultry dish, especially those with a sweet touch such as Game Hens in a Sweet and Sour Sauce (Capones al Agridulce) or any dish cooked with fruits.

To serve 6

2 tablespoons butter
1/4 cup pine nuts
6 tablespoons raisins

2 teaspoons salt
11/2 cups short-grain rice (see Home-Style White Rice)

In a large pan, heat butter and add pine nuts and raisins; sauté over medium-low heat, stirring, until raisins plump up and pine nuts turn golden. Meanwhile, bring 3 cups water to a boil with the salt. Add rice to pine nuts and raisins; stir and scrape the bottom, to get the brown bits attached to the pan.

Add boiling water to rice; reduce heat to low and cook, uncovered, for 15 minutes. Taste for seasoning. Turn off heat and cover with a cloth for 5 minutes. Serve immediately.

Paella Valenciana de la Ribera
(Catalan: Paella Valenciana de la Ribera)
(Classic Paella with Shellfish, Chicken and Pork)

Paella is, indeed, perceived in America as the "national dish" of Spain. There are as many recipes for paella as there are cooks in Valencia—or in Spain. This "classic" recipe comes from one of my favorite restaurants in the region: Galbis, located in L'Alcudia de Carlet, a little town 20 miles south of Valencia.

Chef Juan Carlos Galbis deserves credit for breaking paella-making records by cooking this dish for 2,500 people, in a huge paella pan 13 feet in diameter. He explained to me that the first giant paella was made for 1,000 people in March 1979, and it originated from a bet made after many bottles of wine. . . . It required 1,100 pounds of firewood and, among other ingredients, 220 pounds of rice.

The classic Paella Valenciana always has snails—the fresh flavorful ones from the local mountains. But unless you can find them fresh, I recommend you omit them.

To serve 8

1 (3- to 4-pound) chicken, cut into small serving pieces
1 pound lean pork meat, diced
2 1/2 teaspoons salt
1 1/2 teaspoons freshly ground black pepper
2 tablespoons olive oil, or more as needed
1/2 recipe Meat Ball
8 large prawns, in their shells
1 1/2 pounds squid, cleaned and cut into rings (see Rice in a Casserole with Shellfish)
1 large red bell pepper, stemmed, seeded and cut into thin strips lengthwise (if red peppers are not available, use green pepper —or 2 to 3 canned pimientos)

4 large cloves garlic, minced
1 large onion, minced
3 pounds tomatoes, peeled, seeded and chopped
8 live small clams, shells scrubbed
8 live mussels, shells scrubbed (if mussels are not available, use 16 clams)
3 cups short-grain rice (see Home-Style White Rice)
3/4 pound green beans, ends trimmed, cut into 1-inch pieces
1 teaspoon (.4 gram) saffron threads (or 1/2 teaspoon powdered saffron)
2 dozen fresh snails, in the shell (optional)

As a garnish:

1 or 2 lemons, cut into 8 wedges

Pat dry chicken and pork. Season them with 1 teaspoon salt and 1/2 teaspoon pepper. Heat oil in a large skillet or paella pan; add chicken and sauté over medium-high heat until golden. Remove chicken to a colander (pour drippings back into skillet). Add pork to hot oil and sauté until just golden; set aside. Make meat ball mixture into small, walnut-size balls and sauté until golden; set aside. Pat dry prawns and squid; season squid with 1/4 teaspoon each salt and pepper. Sauté prawns until just colored; set aside. Finally, add squid and sauté for 2 or 3 minutes, stirring; set aside.

Reduce heat to medium, add more oil if necessary and sauté pepper until golden; set aside. Add garlic and onion and sauté until soft. Add tomatoes and cook quickly until dry.

In a large pot with about 1 cup water, steam clams and mussels on a rack until they open—4 or 5 minutes for mussels, 5 to 10 for clams. Discard any that do not open. Strain the cooking liquid through a fine-mesh strainer. Measure liquid and add enough water to make a total of 6 cups.

About 45 minutes before serving, bring the 6 cups of liquid to a boil. Meanwhile, add rice to the tomato sauce; stir and add pork, meat balls, squid, green beans, saffron, snails if desired and remaining 1 1/4 teaspoon salt and 3/4 teaspoon pepper. Sauté for 2 or 3 minutes, stirring. Add chicken pieces; push them down and distribute them evenly.

Add boiling liquid and cook over medium-low heat for 20 minutes. (Cooking this dish evenly throughout the skillet is essential. The rice should simmer with small bubbles, but not boil; stir a bit on the sides and turn the skillet around to prevent overcooking in the center.) Five minutes before cooking time is up, add shellfish and peppers on top, arranging them attractively.

Turn off heat and place a cloth over the skillet. Let it sit for 10 minutes. Arrange lemon wedges around and serve immediately. Never let more than 20 minutes pass before eating; as the Spanish saying goes, rice doesn't wait for you—*you* wait for it!

Arroz al Horno de Verano
(Catalan: Arròs al Forn d'Estiu)
(Baked Rice with Summer Vegetables)

Arròs al forn *(baked rice) is probably the oldest of all Valencian rice dishes. It is also called* arròs passejat *or walked rice, from the days when households had no ovens, so the wife would take the casserole to the local baker and cook it in his oven.*

This is another of the many outstanding rices I relished at Galbis restaurant near Valencia. Juan Carlos Galbis, whose father started the restaurant-inn in 1939, is a "born" cook; he has done more than anybody I know to research and develop traditional Valencian recipes. I especially liked this rice because it can be perfectly reproduced with American ingredients, and it is easy to put together. Like all baked rices, it is traditionally cooked in a shallow clay casserole. For this recipe I use one 12 inches in diameter.

To serve 8

3 tablespoons olive oil
1/4 pound pancetta, finely diced
3 ounces chorizo or another
flavorful spicy pork sausage
with paprika, casing removed,
cut into 3/4-inch rounds
1/2 pound pork blood sausage,
such as Italian blood pudding
or boudin noir, casing
removed, cut into 3/4-inch
rounds
4 large cloves garlic, minced
2 large red bell peppers,
stemmed, seeded and cut
lengthwise into thin strips
11/2 pounds ripe tomatoes, peeled
and chopped, unseeded

1 pound green beans, ends
trimmed, cut into 1-inch pieces
1 (10-ounce) package frozen baby
green peas
2 cups short-grain rice (see
Home-Style White Rice)
1 teaspoon Spanish paprika
1 teaspoon turmeric
1/2 teaspoon (.2 gram) saffron
threads (or 1/4 teaspoon
powdered saffron)
1 teaspoon salt
1 teaspoon freshly ground black
pepper

In a large pan, heat 1 tablespoon olive oil and add pancetta, chorizo and blood sausages. Cook over low heat for 10 minutes.

Heat remaining 2 tablespoons oil in a skillet. Add garlic and peppers; cook over medium heat for 8 to 10 minutes, or until peppers start to turn golden. Add tomatoes and cook until dry. Transfer to pan with the sausages. Add green beans and 4 cups cold water. Bring to a boil, reduce heat to low and cook for 10 minutes, uncovered. Drain through a colander into a large shallow ovenproof casserole (preferably of clay). Measure liquid, and if it is less than 4 cups, add water to equal 4 cups. Stir remaining ingredients into the casserole.

Preheat oven to 400 degrees F.

(One of the good things about this rice dish is that it can be prepared ahead of time up to this point, as Juan Carlos Galbis told me: "in the morning, before you go to the beach; and then when you come home, just add the water, put it in the oven, let it cook by itself and it is ready to eat!")

Bring the 4 cups of liquid to a boil. Add to the casserole and place in the preheated oven for 20 to 30 minutes, or until rice is cooked. (Timing will depend on the oven, especially whether it is electric or not. If the rice gets dry before it's cooked, add a little more water.)

Remove rice from the oven, cover with a cloth and let it sit for 10 minutes. Serve immediately.

Arroz Caldoso de Monte
(Catalan: Arròs Caldós de Muntanya)
(Rice with Rabbit in Broth)

This dish is literally named mountain rice, because it is made from the produce of the Valencian mountains: rabbit, rosemary—and snails. Again, as in the paella recipe, I have left these optional, for I feel that unless they are fresh they don't contribute much. Rabbit is not essential either; you can substitute chicken.

This was my favorite of all the excellent rices I had at La Venta del Toboso, an old restaurant in the city of Valencia which Javier de Zárate acquired in 1983. He and chef Rafael Haba set out to serve some of the most traditional dishes of Valencian cuisine, of which this is indeed one.

Typically, this rice dish is made in a wide flameproof clay pot, but it can also be made in a paella pan or a casserole. The dish is not a paella, though, because it has more liquid; it should have the consistency of a stew.

To serve 6 to 8

> 1 rabbit, cut into small serving
> pieces
> 2 teaspoons salt, or to taste
> 1 teaspoon freshly ground black
> pepper, or to taste
> 1/4 cup olive oil
> 1 pound mushrooms, thinly
> sliced
> 1 pound green beans, ends
> trimmed, cut into 1-inch pieces
> 1 1/2 pounds tomatoes, peeled,
> seeded and chopped
> 3 large cloves garlic, minced

> 1 teaspoon finely chopped fresh
> rosemary
> 1 teaspoon Spanish paprika
> 1/2 teaspoon (.2 gram) saffron
> threads (or 1/4 teaspoon
> powdered saffron)
> 2 cups short-grain rice (see
> Home-Style White Rice)
> 2 dozen fresh snails, in the shell
> (optional)
> 8 cups Chicken Stock, preferably,
> or water

Pat dry rabbit pieces, and season with 1/2 teaspoon salt and 1/4 teaspoon pepper. Heat oil in a large flameproof casserole (or paella pan) and sauté rabbit over medium heat until golden. Set rabbit pieces aside. Add mushrooms to the casserole and sauté for 5 minutes. Add beans and cook another 5 minutes. Add tomatoes and garlic, increase heat and cook quickly until dry. Stir in rosemary, paprika, saffron, remaining 1 1/2 teaspoons salt and 3/4 teaspoon pepper. Taste for seasoning.

Stir in rice and snails, if desired, and return meat to casserole. Bring stock or water to a boil and pour it in. Return to a boil, reduce heat to medium-low and cook for 18 to 20 minutes, or until rice is just slightly underdone. Turn off heat and let rice sit for 5 minutes, or until cooked to the right consistency.

Since this dish is meant to be soupy, it should be served immediately or the rice will overcook.

Arroz a la Cazuela con Marisco
(Catalan: Arròs a la Cassola amb Marisc)
(Rice in a Casserole with Shellfish)

The recipe for this classic Catalan rice dish is inspired by the superb rendition I had at Els Perols de L'Empordà (The Pots of L'Empordà), a tiny home-style restaurant in Barcelona which specializes in the cuisine of the district of L'Empordà. Owners Reinaldo and Juli Serrat are from Palamós, a fishing town in the heart of that area, where they lived until opening the restaurant in 1982. She cooks and he runs the dining room; they are the staff. And her cooking faithfully features some of the best recipes of their home district, prepared with love and care and great enthusiasm.

The dish is traditionally cooked and served in a shallow clay casserole; I use one 12 inches in diameter. It is a fisherman's rice, always a little soupy, and typically served with Garlic Mayonnaise (Allioli) on the side—although I find it doesn't really need it.

To serve 8

For the *sofrito*:

> 1/4 cup olive oil
> 1 pound red onions, minced

> 21/2 pounds ripe tomatoes, peeled, seeded and chopped

For the *picada*:

> 2 large cloves garlic, minced
> 2 tablespoons chopped fresh parsley leaves
> 1/2 teaspoon (.2 gram) saffron threads (or 1/4 teaspoon powdered saffron)

> 3/4 teaspoon salt, or to taste
> 3/4 teaspoon freshly ground white pepper, or to taste

For the rice and shellfish:

> 2 pounds squid
> 16 small live clams, shells scrubbed
> 16 small live mussels, shells scrubbed
> 2 tablespoons olive oil

> 11/2 cups short-grain rice (see Home-Style White Rice)
> About 4 cups Fish Fumet
> 16 large prawns, in their shells
> 1/2 pound large scallops

As a garnish (optional):

> 8 lemon wedges
> 1/2 recipe Garlic Mayonnaise (make whole recipe and use half)

To prepare the sofrito: Heat oil in a large flameproof casserole, preferably of clay. Add onions and sauté slowly on low heat, stirring from time to time, until onions are brown and almost caramelized; add small amounts of water if necessary, so they don't burn. It may take 45 minutes or more—

the longer the better, as it will add more flavor to your dish. Add tomatoes and increase heat to medium; cook until dry.

To prepare the picada: In the food processor or with a mortar and pestle, finely mash garlic, parsley, saffron, salt and pepper. Set aside.

To clean the squid: Pull out head and discard the cuttlebone and internal organs from each squid body; rinse well under running water. Cut off tentacles from head; remove the beak by pressing the tentacle base so it pops out. Remove the purplish skin from the body sacs, and cut bodies (with fins attached) into rings. Set aside body rings and tentacles.

To steam the clams and mussels: In a large pot, bring about ½ cup water to a boil and steam clams and mussels on a rack until they open—4 to 5 minutes for mussels, 5 to 10 minutes for clams. Set them aside. Discard any that do not open. Strain broth through a fine-mesh strainer. Reserve.

To cook the rice and shellfish: In a skillet, heat oil; add squid rings and tentacles. Sauté for 2 or 3 minutes, stirring. Add squid and its juices to casserole with *sofrito.* Stir in rice and *picada.*

Measure reserved broth and add enough fish fumet to make a total of 4½ cups. Bring to a boil in a pan. Add to casserole and cook gently over medium heat for 10 minutes. Add prawns and scallops, pushing them down into the casserole so they are covered with the broth. Cook another 8 minutes (altogether the rice should cook 18 minutes; it will be underdone). Turn off heat. Arrange mussels and clams on top. Cover casserole with a cloth and let it sit for 5 minutes, or until rice is the right consistency.

Serve immediately, so the rice doesn't overcook (since it is meant to be a little soupy, if you wait the rice will continue to cook). If desired, garnish with lemon wedges, and pass the Garlic Mayonnaise (Allioli) in a sauceboat.

Arroz Negro con Calamares Rellenos
(Catalan: Arròs Negre amb Calamars Farcits)
(Black Rice with Stuffed Squid)

"Black rice," in a sauce made from the squid's own ink, is a dish originally from the Catalan district of L'Empordà, but found all along the Mediterranean coast of Spain. I had an especially good arroz negro con chipirones *(black rice with tiny squid) at El Plat, one of Valencia's finest restaurants specializing in rice dishes. The ink not only makes it totally black, but also contributes an unusual, wonderful flavor.*

Spanish squid have more ink than American, because they are caught with bait. So, to obtain more ink, it is a good idea to buy extra squid—double the amount—which you can use for other recipes such as Classic Paella with Shellfish, Chicken and Pork (Paella Valenciana de la Ribera) or Shellfish Stew, Barcelona Style (Zarzuela de Mariscos); squid freezes well. Cleaning and obtaining the ink from the squid is rather time-consuming, but well worth it.

To serve 6 to 8

For the squid:

> 1½ pounds small squid,
>   uncleaned, with their ink sacs
>   (see above—best buy 3
>   pounds)
> 1 cup Fish Fumet

For the filling:

> 2 tablespoons olive oil
> 2 large onions, minced
> 6 large cloves garlic, minced
> 2 tablespoons chopped fresh
>   parsley
> 1 teaspoon chopped fresh
>   oregano (or ⅓ teaspoon dried)

> ¼ cup pine nuts
> ¼ cup white bread crumbs,
>   without crusts*
> 1 hard-boiled egg, coarsely
>   chopped
> 1 raw egg

For the *sofrito*:

> 1 pound unpeeled ripe tomatoes,
>   chopped
> 2 large red bell peppers,
>   stemmed, seeded and chopped

> ⅛ teaspoon hot red pepper
>   flakes
> 1 bay leaf

For the rice:

> 3 cups Fish Fumet
> 2 cups short-grain rice (see
>   Home-Style White Rice)

> ½ teaspoon salt, or to taste
> ½ teaspoon freshly ground black
>   pepper, or to taste

As an accompaniment (optional):

> ½ recipe Garlic Mayonnaise
>   (make whole recipe and use
>   half)

To obtain ink from squid: Pull the heads of the squid from their bodies and carefully lift the long, silvery ink sacs from the inner section of the tail. Don't worry if you get some of the inner section along with them, for they will be sieved anyway. Place the ink sacs in a small fine sieve over a bowl. Pour 1 cup fumet over the ink sacs; the sieve should rest in the fumet, so the ink sacs soak at least a couple of hours. From time to time, press and stir the ink sacs with a spoon against the sieve to extract as much ink as possible. At first the liquid will be just grayish, but it will become black after a while.

To clean the squid: Discard the cuttlebone and internal organs from each squid body; rinse well under running water. Cut off tentacles from head; remove the beak by pressing the tentacle base so it pops out. Remove the purplish skin from the body sacs, and pull the fins off; you will be left with a small white pouch. Finely chop the fins. Set fins, pouches and tentacles aside separately.

To prepare the filling: In a medium skillet, heat oil and, over low heat, sauté onions and garlic until soft. Set aside half. Add chopped fins, parsley and oregano; stir and cook for 5 minutes. Transfer to a bowl. Toast pine nuts in a small dry skillet over medium heat, shaking it, until golden. Stir them into the bowl, together with bread crumbs and eggs.

To stuff the squid: Fit a pastry bag with a wide tip and put filling in it. Stuff squid bodies only half full, otherwise they will burst, since squid shrinks as it cooks. Close tops with a toothpick. Prick squid bodies once or twice with a toothpick.

To prepare the sofrito: Arrange stuffed squid in a large shallow flame-proof clay casserole with a flat bottom, or in a large skillet with high sides. Stir in reserved garlic/onion, tomatoes, red peppers, pepper flakes and bay leaf; cook over medium heat until dry, 20 to 30 minutes.

To cook the rice: Bring to a boil 3 cups fumet with the 1 cup "ink" fumet. Stir reserved squid tentacles, rice, salt and pepper into casserole. Add boiling liquid and cook over medium heat for 20 minutes; gently move rice around so it cooks evenly throughout the casserole. Turn off heat and cover casserole with a cloth for 10 minutes.

Remove bay leaf and toothpicks, and serve immediately. If desired, pass the Garlic Mayonnaise (Allioli) separately in a sauceboat.

Patatas Aliñadas con Gambas
(Potato Salad with Prawns)

Potatoes are served very often as a tapa in Spain, and that's how I had these at Don Peppone, a homey restaurant in the charming village of Puerto de Santa María, near Jerez. Its pleasant garden and patio provide an ideal summer luncheon or informal dinner spot after a day at the nearby beach. And José Luis Gómez-Heredia is always there, welcoming his patrons like a perfect host in his own home.

I find the combination of potatoes with prawns, peppers and tomatoes in this recipe irresistible, whether as a first course on a hot day, as a light luncheon entrée accompanied by a salad, or as an anytime potato salad.

To serve 6 to 8

For the prawns:

1/2 cup dry white wine
2 or 3 sprigs parsley
1 bay leaf
6 black peppercorns
1/4 teaspoon hot red pepper
 flakes

10 coriander seeds
1 pound medium prawns, in
 their shells

For the dressing:

3/4 cup olive oil
3 tablespoons sherry wine
  vinegar, or more to taste

1 teaspoon salt, or to taste
1 teaspoon freshly ground black
  pepper, or to taste

For the salad:

2 pounds potatoes, preferably
  small red-skinned ones
1 cup finely chopped red bell
  pepper
6 tablespoons chopped fresh
  parsley leaves

2 medium unpeeled tomatoes,
  seeded and diced (by hand)
1/2 cup chopped red onion

To cook the prawns: In a large pan, bring to a boil 1 cup water with all ingredients for the prawns, except prawns themselves. Add prawns, reduce heat to low and cook for about 4 minutes or until prawns are pink. Drain, and discard liquid. Peel prawns.

To prepare the dressing: In a large salad bowl, combine all dressing ingredients, beating with a fork.

To prepare the salad: Boil potatoes in salted water to cover until they are tender. Drain.

While potatoes are still warm, cut them into 1-inch pieces (or into quarters if they are small) and immediately toss them with the dressing in the bowl. Let stand for about 1/2 hour.

Add prawns and remaining ingredients to potatoes in bowl; toss to combine well. Taste for seasoning. Allow flavors to mingle for at least 2 or 3 hours. Serve at room temperature.

Pastel de Patata con Romero
(Potato, Onion and Rosemary Cake)

The flavor of rosemary in this cake mingles very well with any Catalan meat dish cooked with fruit, such as Stuffed Peaches with Pork and Almonds (Melocotones Rellenos). It can also be served as a light luncheon entrée with a seafood salad.

To serve 8 to 10

6 tablespoons butter
1 1/2 pounds onions, peeled and
  thinly sliced
2 pounds new potatoes
1 teaspoon salt

1/2 teaspoon freshly ground black
  pepper
3 tablespoons coarsely chopped
  fresh rosemary leaves
1 cup half-and-half

In a skillet, heat butter and sauté onions over low heat for about 30 minutes, stirring occasionally. They should become very soft and lightly golden, but not brown.

Preheat oven to 350 degrees F.

Butter a 9- or 10-inch round baking dish or pie plate. Peel potatoes and slice them very thinly by hand. Place them individually in a layer, sprinkle with some salt and pepper, arrange a thin layer of onions on top, and sprinkle some rosemary over. Continue with alternate layers, ending with rosemary. Pour half-and-half over and around.

Cover with a piece of aluminum foil and bake in the preheated oven for 1 hour. Remove foil and cook another 20 to 30 minutes, or until top turns golden. Serve immediately.

Tortilla Española
(Spanish Potato Omelet)

This is the most classic omelet in Spain, and although it translates as "Spanish omelet" it has no peppers or tomatoes in it. Mexican tortillas *are practically unknown in Spain;* tortilla *always means omelet, and unless you order a* tortilla francesa *(French omelet) you are bound to get a round one cooked like an Italian* frittata, *as in this recipe.*

It is particularly interesting to note that the person credited with "inventing" the French omelet was a Spaniard, Francisco Martínez Montiño; he picked up the idea from a Spanish convent and took it to the court of King Philip III, for whom he was the chef, in the early seventeenth century. Our "Spanish omelet" is of more recent origin, well into the nineteenth century.

Practically every bar in Spain serves tortilla española *as a* tapa, *cut into small squares or wedges. At home we had it often for supper accompanied by Bread with Tomato, Catalan Style (Pan con Tomate)—a great combination. It also makes a perfect picnic or lunch dish, served at room temperature. Although it can be made ahead, I prefer to eat it shortly after making it, while it is still warm.*

Traveling around Spain, you will find omelets made with anything and everything, from seasonal vegetables to fish, meat and sausages. Worth mentioning is the tortilla sacromonte, *typical of Granada, made with calf's brains and testicles. I wouldn't dare give you the recipe—although it can be quite delicious.*

To serve 6

> *2 pounds potatoes, peeled and sliced into thin nickel-size rounds (can do this in food processor)*
> *3/4 teaspoon salt*
>
> *1/2 teaspoon freshly ground black pepper*
> *1/2 cup olive oil*
> *2 large onions, thinly sliced*
> *6 eggs*

Season potatoes with 1/2 teaspoon salt and 1/4 teaspoon pepper. Heat 1/4 cup oil in a nonstick skillet, add potatoes and cook over medium heat until golden brown and crispy. Toss the potatoes around with a spatula so they don't clump together; but if they stick a bit, don't worry. Meanwhile, heat 2 tablespoons oil in another pan and sauté onions until soft and golden, about 20 to 30 minutes.

In a bowl, beat eggs; stir in remaining 1/4 teaspoon each salt and pepper, and onions. Set potatoes aside, wipe the skillet clean and heat remaining 2 tablespoons oil. Stir potatoes into the egg mixture, and pour into the skillet. Reduce heat to low and cook until lightly golden on the bottom, about 8 to 10 minutes.

Place on top of the skillet an inverted plate slightly larger than the skillet, and turn out the omelet onto it; slide the omelet back into the skillet. Cook until the eggs are set, 3 or 4 more minutes. Serve warm, preferably.

Pasta Casera
(Basic Homemade Pasta)

Making pasta at home is very easy and great fun, especially if you have a food processor—and even more so if you have a pasta machine. It certainly is worth it; freshly made pasta is a treat in itself.

Yields about 1 pound

2 cups flour	*1 teaspoon salt*
3 eggs	*1 tablespoon olive oil*

Put all ingredients into a food processor. Whirl until the dough forms a ball or pulls away from the sides of the bowl. Remove dough from processor, shape into a ball and place on a floured board. Cover with a towel and let it rest for 15 minutes.

Divide the dough into quarters and roll 1 quarter at a time, keeping the remaining dough covered. I prefer to roll the dough out with a straight rolling pin without handles, as it allows more control. If you have a pasta machine, process the dough according to the directions that come with the machine.

If you do it by hand, roll the dough as thin as possible. Always roll away from you, flipping the dough over from time to time. Add flour to the board if the dough becomes sticky. Cut the dough as directed in the recipe you are using. Let pasta dry before cooking it.

To dry the pasta, I always hang it on the back of a chair. Allow it to dry to a nonsticky state but not until it becomes brittle, or it will crack when you cut it. The timing will depend on the humidity and temperature —about 1/2 hour.

If the dish you are preparing does not require the full amount of this recipe, it is best to make the whole recipe anyway and save the rest for another time; or the trimmings can be cut into noodles, allowed to dry and stored airtight for use anytime in the future.

Canelones de Espinacas
(Catalan: Canalons d'Espinacs)
(Spinach Cannelloni)

I always enjoyed this dish at home; my parents' cook, Rosalía, often made it as a first course on Sundays. I was thrilled to find a very special rendition at an equally special restaurant in Barcelona, Jaume de Provença, and I have adapted Rosalía's recipe accordingly.

To serve 8:   Makes 20 to 25 cannelloni

For the pasta:

> *1 recipe Basic Homemade Pasta*
> *1 tablespoon salt*
> *1 tablespoon oil*

For the filling:

> *4 bunches spinach, stems*
> *removed*
> *1 tablespoon olive oil*
> *2 large cloves garlic, minced*
> *1 medium onion, minced*
> *1/2 pound prosciutto, chopped*

> *2 (7-minute) boiled eggs,*
> *coarsely chopped*
> *1/2 teaspoon freshly ground black*
> *pepper, or to taste*
> *1/2 teaspoon nutmeg, or to taste*

For the white cheese sauce:

> *3 tablespoons butter*
> *3 tablespoons flour*
> *3 cups milk*

> *1/2 pound Gruyère or*
> *Emmenthaler cheese, grated*

To prepare the pasta: Roll dough into thin strips 4 inches wide, either by hand or by using a pasta machine (No. 5 on a manual pasta machine). Cut strips into 4-inch squares. Allow them to dry for about 1/2 hour.

Bring a large pot of water to a boil, with salt and oil. Drop pasta squares in the water, one at a time; after the water has returned to a boil, cook for 3 minutes. Drain and immediately plunge them into a bowl of cold water. Lay pasta flat on clean towels to drain.

To prepare the filling: Place spinach in a large pot, with just the water that clings to the leaves after washing it. Cook on low heat, covered, until wilted. Drain and squeeze it dry; chop and set aside.

In a skillet, heat oil and add garlic, onion and prosciutto. Cook on low heat for 15 minutes or until golden. Add chopped spinach, eggs, pepper and nutmeg. Taste for seasoning.

To prepare the sauce: Melt butter on low heat; add flour and stir until well mixed. Add milk all at once, stirring constantly with a whisk or wooden spoon, until mixture comes to a boil and thickens slightly—about

5 minutes. (This should be a light white sauce.) Turn off heat and stir in half the grated cheese.

Preheat oven to 400 degrees F.

To assemble the dish: Stir 3/4 cup sauce into spinach mixture. Distribute filling evenly on the cannelloni squares; roll each like a cigar and place them on an ovenproof platter. Pour sauce over cannelloni, and sprinkle remaining cheese on top. Bake in preheated oven for 30 minutes. At the last moment, place under the broiler for a few minutes, until cheese turns golden and bubbly.

Lasagna de Salmón a la Salsa de Vino Blanco (Catalan: Lasagna de Salmó a la Salsa de Vi Blanc) (Salmon Lasagna in a White Wine Sauce)

The idea of combining a salmon mousse with freshly made pasta comes from one of my favorite restaurants in Barcelona, Azulete. I found the dish extremely delicate, the blend of flavors enhanced by a light, very complementary sauce.

For this recipe you will need a 5-cup rectangular terrine. I use a 3 × 10-inch lidded terrine; you can also use a 9 × 5-inch loaf pan.

To serve 8

For the pasta:

> 1/2 recipe Basic Homemade Pasta
> 1 tablespoon salt
> 1 tablespoon oil

For the salmon mousse:

> 1 pound skinned and boned
>   fresh salmon, cut into chunks
>   (about 1 1/2 pounds with skin
>   and bones)
> 2 egg whites
> 1 teaspoon salt

> 1/2 teaspoon freshly ground
>   white pepper
> 1 cup heavy cream
> 1/4 cup salmon caviar (or a
>   2-ounce jar)

For the sauce:

> 2 tablespoons butter
> 2 medium carrots, finely chopped
> 3 medium stalks celery, finely
>   chopped
> 1 medium onion, minced
> 1 large red bell pepper, finely
>   chopped
> 1 cup dry white wine

> 1/2 teaspoon salt
> 1/4 teaspoon freshly ground
>   white pepper
> 1/2 cup heavy cream
> 1/2 cup Fish Fumet

To prepare the pasta: Roll out the pasta dough, cutting the sheets to approximately fit the size of the terrine. (The pasta will stretch as you cook it, so you can cut the sheets smaller. They will have to be trimmed to size later anyway.) You will need at least 5 pieces of pasta, and up to 8 or 9 if you wish. Let pasta dry for about 30 minutes.

Bring a large pot of water to a boil, with salt and oil. Drop pasta pieces in the water, one at a time; after the water has returned to a boil, cook for 3 minutes. Drain and immediately plunge them into cold water. Remove from the water and place on clean towels to drain. Using as a pattern a piece of wax paper to fit the bottom of the terrine, cut the sheets to size.

To prepare the salmon mousse: In the food processor, purée the salmon with the egg whites, salt and pepper until smooth. With the motor running, pour in the 1 cup cream. Stop the motor and scrape down the sides of the bowl. Whirl again. Remove to a bowl and fold in the salmon caviar.

To prepare the terrine: Preheat oven to 350 degrees F. Butter the terrine. Place a piece of pasta on the bottom. Spread one quarter of the salmon mousse on top (if you are using more than 5 pasta skins, use less mousse per layer). Continue alternating layers of pasta and mousse, ending with a piece of pasta on top.

Cover the terrine with a lid or foil. Place inside a larger pan filled with boiling water halfway up the terrine. Bake in the preheated oven for 30 minutes. To unmold, run a knife around the lasagna and turn out onto a board. Cover to keep warm.

To make the sauce: Melt butter in a skillet and add carrots, celery, onion and red pepper; cook slowly for 20 minutes. Pour in white wine; cook for 10 minutes. Add salt and white pepper. Transfer to a blender or food processor; purée with the 1/2 cup cream and the fumet. Strain through a fine-mesh strainer into a saucepan. Taste for seasoning and heat through.

To assemble the dish: Cut lasagna into 8 serving pieces. Pour some sauce over, and pass the rest in a sauceboat.

"Fideuà"
(Thin Pasta Noodles Cooked in a Fish Fumet)

Fideuà is a Valencian dish made with noodles, which in Catalan are called fideus. *Its origin is picturesque: a group of friends went on a picnic with the intention of making a rice dish, but they forgot the rice. Fortunately, they had some noodles on hand, so they used them instead, and to their delight, the dish turned out to be great!*

Eugenia and Josep Pedrell—he represents the third generation of a fishing family— own Eugenia restaurant in the little coastal town of Cambrils, near Tarragona, where I ate the best fideuà *in my memory. Cooking noodles this way was an old tradition with the fishermen along the Valencian and Catalan coast.*

The trick here is to sauté the dry noodles in olive oil before cooking them in the stock, until they acquire a rossejat *(Catalan for golden) color. It is important to use a good fish fumet; a substitute such as commercial broth or clam juice won't be as good. This was the sound advice that Eugenia's chef, Blas Moreno, gave me as I watched him in the kitchen while he sautéed the noodles, stirring all the time until they turned golden brown. Then he beamed—"See,* now it is rossejat"—*and went on adding ladles of his wonderful fish stock, little by little, until it was totally absorbed by the noodles.*

To serve 4 to 6

3 tablespoons olive oil
4 large cloves garlic, chopped
1½ pounds unpeeled tomatoes, chopped
6 cups Fish Fumet
½ teaspoon (.2 gram) saffron threads

8 ounces coiled fedelini (very thin dried pasta noodles rolled into coils) or dried angel hair pasta
½ teaspoon salt, or to taste

As a garnish:

1 lemon, cut into 4 or 6 wedges

In a 2-quart saucepan, heat 1 tablespoon olive oil and add garlic. Cook until soft and add tomatoes; cook for 3 minutes, stirring. Add fumet, bring to a boil and reduce to 4 cups. Add saffron threads; cover and set aside.

Heat remaining 2 tablespoons oil in a wide flameproof clay casserole or a nometallic pan. Add the pasta, breaking it up with your hands in about 3-inch pieces as you add it. Over medium heat, stir the pasta with a wooden spatula for a few minutes, until it is golden brown (the more color the pasta acquires, the more flavor it will give to this dish; but be careful not to burn it).

Bring fumet to a boil, and pour into the pan with the noodles. Add salt and continue cooking rapidly, stirring all the time, until the liquid is absorbed by the pasta. Cooking time will vary according to the size and material of the pan—probably 10 to 15 minutes. Taste for seasoning.

If you have used a clay casserole, surround the *fideuà* with the lemon wedges and serve directly from the casserole. Have guests squeeze a little lemon juice over their servings.

Breads and Pastry Doughs

I recommend the use of unbleached flour when making breads and doughs. Chemicals are used to bleach flour, and as a health-conscious person I feel it is important to avoid any unnecessary chemicals in our diets. These chemicals were originally introduced because bleached flour produces a better machine-made dough for mass production.

On a trip to San Sebastián, I visited the bakery of Luis Galparsoro, who is justifiably proud of his excellent, healthful breads and rolls. He uses Manitoba flour in making his products. This Canadian flour and some U.S. flours—such as those of Deaf Smith, of Texas—are made from hard grains and produce a high-gluten flour, which makes a light, well-aerated dough. High-gluten flours are available in many health food stores. Gluten makes dough elastic, which is wonderful for breads but not good for puff pastry or for any pastries, really—gluten tends to make the pastry tough.

I never sift flour. To measure it, carefully scoop it up in a measuring cup and gently slide a knife over the top of the cup to remove excess flour; do not shake the cup to level the top of the flour. Even with careful measurement, sometimes you must add more flour or liquid to a recipe to make it turn out correctly. The moisture content of flour varies greatly, which makes it difficult always to follow a recipe exactly. You must get a "feel" for the dough you are working with.

For the following recipes I always use a food processor; it is especially invaluable in making bread doughs—it saves time and energy.

Pasta Prensada
(Press-In Pastry)

This is a quick and easy pastry dough, great to use for tarts and tartlets, as it avoids having to roll out the pastry—you just press it into the mold.

Yields about 3/4 pound dough

> 1½ cups all-purpose flour
> 8 tablespoons chilled unsalted
>   butter, cut into 1-inch cubes
> 1 egg

In the food processor, mix together flour and butter; pulse to blend until flour acquires the consistency of cornmeal. Add egg and whirl until a ball forms. Press the pastry into the molds. Keep pastry at room temperature for ease in pressing.

Always refrigerate this pastry for at least 15 minutes before baking. This will keep it from shrinking during baking.

Pasta Brisa
(Pie Pastry)

This recipe is excellent for baking savory as well as sweet pastry dishes—quiches, sweet tarts, etc. It is a basic pastry dough, not flaky rich but thin and crispy.

Makes 1 pound dough

> 1½ cups all-purpose flour   1 egg yolk
> 8 tablespoons frozen unsalted   1/2 teaspoon salt
>   butter, cut into 1/2-inch pieces   5 tablespoons ice-cold water

In a food processor, mix together flour and butter. Pulse to combine until it reaches a cornmeal consistency.

In a bowl, mix together egg yolk, salt and water; add to flour and butter. Whirl until a ball forms. (If a ball doesn't quite form, remove dough from food processor and knead with your hands for a short while—about 1/2 minute.)

Shape into a ball, place in a plastic bag and refrigerate for about 30 minutes.

Pasta de Hojaldre
(Puff Pastry)

This recipe dispels the idea that making puff pastry is only for professionals. It is not difficult to make, and a real treat for those special recipes.

You can buy puff pastry at the store, but it will never taste as good as homemade—especially if you use good, fresh sweet butter.

Makes 1 pound dough

1 cup minus 1 tablespoon all-
purpose flour
1 tablespoon cornstarch
3/4 teaspoon salt

1/2 pound chilled unsalted butter,
cut into 1/2-inch pieces
1/4–1/2 cup ice-cold water
Flour for sprinkling

In a bowl, combine flour, cornstarch and salt. With your hands, work butter and flour together; the butter pieces should flatten a bit but not be completely incorporated into the flour. Work quickly; the butter must not get warm. (If you are working in warm weather, refrigerate the dough for 10 minutes at this point.) Pour in enough ice water to pull flour and butter together. The dough should stick together, but not in a neat ball—in fact, it will be a mess. Gather it into a mound in the bowl.

Flour a pastry board or marble, as well as your hands and rolling pin. Put dough on the board, and roll it out to about 18 × 6 inches. It will not be a neat rectangle at this point; there will probably be holes, which you can patch. It will help to use a dough scraper, as the dough will stick to the board. It is very important to roll only back and forth, not sideways or diagonally. Work quickly; overworking the dough raises the gluten in the flour and makes it too elastic to work with. Keep your board and rolling pin well floured.

Fold the top of the dough one third of the way down toward you, and then fold over again—as if folding a business letter. Turn the open flap to your left, and roll the dough straight up the board into another 18 × 6-inch piece; it will be a neater rectangle this time. Each roll and fold of the dough is called a turn. Fold the dough again the same way as before—that is, do one more turn. Place the flat piece of dough in a plastic bag, and refrigerate for 30 minutes.

Remove from the refrigerator and do 2 more turns. Refrigerate for another 30 minutes.

Do 2 more turns. Now roll it out in any direction you want, to cut as directed in your recipe. Always cut puff pastry with a sharp knife, making a clean cut; the less you touch it with your fingers, the better it will rise.

Puff pastry, covered, will keep in the refrigerator for a week, and for 1 month in the freezer.

Pasta Akelaŕe
(Crisp Pastry Crust)

I named this crusty, nutty dough after Akelaŕe restaurant in San Sebastián, where I had it in a delicious wild strawberry tart. We don't have those delicate berries here, but this crust will make any fresh fruit tart special. I use it in my Aunt Oriola's Lemon Tart (Tarta de Limón Oriola), and also filled with some ice creams such as Date-Nut Honey Ice Cream (Helado de Miel con Nueces y Dátiles) with Chocolate Sauce (Salsa de Chocolate) on top— why not! Rich, sinful and plain yummy.

Makes a 9-inch pie crust

> 1/3 cup whole almonds
> 4 tablespoons unsalted butter, at
>   room temperature
>
> 1 cup flour
> 2 tablespoons sugar

Preheat oven to 350 degrees F.

In the food processor, grind almonds finely. Add remaining ingredients, pulsing until there are no lumps of butter.

Press dough into an ungreased 9-inch removable-rim pan or pie plate; make a thin, even layer. Place in the preheated oven and bake for 20 minutes, or until golden brown.

Pan de Payés
(Catalan: Pa de Pagès)
(Peasant Bread)

This is the bread you find most often in Catalonia, just as you find sourdough bread in San Francisco. It is simple to make with a food processor, and homemade bread is a great addition to any dinner.

Yields 2 small loaves

> 1 tablespoon (or 1/2 ounce) dry
>   active yeast
> 1 tablespoon sugar
> 2 cups lukewarm water (105 to
>   115 degrees F.)
>
> 1 tablespoon salt
> 5 1/2 cups all-purpose flour

In the food processor bowl, dissolve yeast and sugar in the lukewarm water; don't stir, just let it sit for 5 to 10 minutes, to activate the yeast (when the yeast starts popping to the top, that means it is ready to work). Immediately add salt and 1/2 cup flour; whirl to combine well. Add all remaining flour; process for 2 minutes. Oil a bowl and place dough in it, turning to coat all sides with oil. Cover with a cloth and put the bowl in a warm place for about 1 hour, or until dough has doubled in size.

Punch down dough to release the air, and let it rest for 3 or 4 minutes. Oil a large baking sheet. Shape dough into 2 round mounds and place them on the baking sheet. Using a razor blade or a very sharp knife, make 3 parallel slashes on the tops. Cover again with a cloth and let them rise in a warm place for 20 to 30 minutes, or until they again double in size.

Preheat oven to 400 degrees F.

Place a pan of hot water on the bottom of the oven, or on the bottom rack if it is electric. Just before baking, spray dough with water to obtain a harder crust. Bake for 30 to 35 minutes, or until loaves are golden and sound hollow when thumped on the top. Remove to a rack and let cool.

Pan de Molde
(Loaf Bread)

This is the bread Koldo Lasa uses to make his Prawn Toast (Tosta de Gambas). It not only is perfect for that dish, but also makes great toast. It's fun and easy to make, especially with a food processor.

Makes 2 standard-size loaves (about 31/2 × 8 inches)

1 tablespoon (or 1/2 ounce) dry active yeast	*1 cup milk*
1 tablespoon sugar	*2 tablespoons butter*
13/4 cups lukewarm water (105 to 115 degrees F.)	*1 teaspoon salt*
	51/2 cups all-purpose flour
	1 egg

In the food processor bowl, dissolve yeast and sugar in the lukewarm water; don't stir, just let it sit for 5 to 10 minutes, to activate the yeast (when yeast starts popping to the top, that means it is ready to work). Meanwhile, heat milk to lukewarm (about 115 degrees F.), add butter and salt and set aside. As soon as the yeast is activated, add 1 cup flour and whirl for 1 minute. Add milk mixture and egg, and pulse to combine. Add remaining 41/2 cups flour and whirl until the dough pulls away from the sides of the bowl.

Oil 2 loaf pans. Divide dough in half and put into pans, pressing gently along the sides and corners to even out the surface somewhat. Cover with a cloth and let it rise for 1 hour, or until doubled in size.

Preheat oven to 425 degrees F.

Place loaf pans in the oven and bake for about 30 minutes, or until they are golden on top and the bread pulls away from the sides of the pans. Immediately remove bread from the pans and place on a rack to cool.

Bollos de Pan con Café
(Whole Wheat Bread Rolls with Ground Coffee)

These bread rolls were the perfect accompaniment to a memorable lunch at Arzak restaurant in San Sebastián; I just had to go to the bakery that afternoon to get the recipe. Owner Luis Galparsoro was delighted not only to share it with me but to proudly show me around his bakery—indeed an impressive, modern establishment which also happens to make great bread.

You will not notice any coffee flavor in these rolls; the ground coffee just provides an interesting texture, which I couldn't figure out until Luis told me what it was. The rolls are not strongly flavored, so they will complement any dish.

Makes 12 medium dinner rolls

2 tablespoons (or 1 ounce) dry
  active yeast
3 tablespoons honey
1½ cups lukewarm water (105 to
  115 degrees F.)
1 tablespoon salt

1 tablespoon ground coffee
3 tablespoons vegetable oil
2 cups all-purpose flour
2 cups whole wheat flour
About 3 tablespoons cracked
  wheat

In the food processor bowl, dissolve yeast and honey in the warm water; don't stir, just let it sit for 5 to 10 minutes, to activate the yeast (when the yeast starts popping to the top, that means it is ready to work). Immediately add salt, ground coffee, oil and 1 cup white flour; whirl to combine well. Add whole wheat flour and remaining cup white flour; process for 2 minutes or until the dough pulls away from the sides of the bowl.

Oil a bowl and place dough in it, turning to coat all sides with oil. Cover with a damp cloth, put in a warm place and allow it to rise until doubled in size, about 1 hour.

Punch down the dough. Divide it into quarters, and each quarter into 3 equal pieces. Form a ball with each piece, folding it over to make it smooth. Put the cracked wheat in a dish. Oil a large baking sheet (or 2). Holding each ball at the bottom with your fingers, dip it into the cracked wheat and place well apart on the oiled sheet(s). Cover rolls with a cloth, put in a warm place and allow them to rise again for 30 minutes.

Preheat oven to 425 degrees F.

Bake rolls in the oven for 20 minutes or more, until they are dark brown and crusty. Remove to a rack and let cool.

Rollos de Pan
(Bread Rings)

The idea for these cute rolls shaped like a ring came from the Sevilla restaurant in Granada, where I had some that were similar to accompany their tasty Lamb Stew, Shepherd Style (Cordero a la Pastoril). The rings are great fun to make, and complement all the lamb dishes in this book as well as any meat or fish stew.

Makes 12 medium bread rings

*1 tablespoon (or ½ ounce) dry
  active yeast
1 tablespoon sugar
1 cup lukewarm water (105 to
  115 degrees F.)*

*2 tablespoons olive oil
1 teaspoon salt
2½ cups all-purpose flour*

For basting:

*3 tablespoons olive oil
1 or 2 teaspoons coarse salt
  (optional; see Note at end of
  recipe)*

In the food processor bowl, dissolve yeast and sugar in the lukewarm water; don't stir, just let it sit for 5 to 10 minutes, to activate the yeast (when the yeast starts popping to the top, that means it is ready to work). Immediately add olive oil, salt and 1 cup of the flour; whirl for 1 minute. Add remaining flour and whirl until a ball forms or the dough pulls away from the sides of the bowl. Continue to whirl for 1 minute.

Oil a bowl and place dough in it, turning to coat all sides with oil. Cover with a cloth and let it rise in a warm place until doubled in size, about 1 hour.

Punch dough down to release the air. Divide it into quarters, and then divide each quarter into 3 equal pieces. Work with 1 piece at a time and keep remaining dough covered. With your hands, roll each piece of dough, making it into a 12- to 14-inch-long roll. Press the edges together to form a ring. Place rings on 2 oiled baking sheets, setting them 2 inches apart. Cover them with a cloth and let rise for another 30 minutes.

Preheat oven to 375 degrees F.

Place rings in the preheated oven and bake for 5 minutes. Brush with the olive oil. Bake for 10 more minutes. Brush with oil again; if desired, sprinkle with salt. Bake for another 5 to 10 minutes, or until the rings are golden brown. Remove to a rack and let cool.

(Note: If the dish to be accompanied by these bread rings will not blend well with their salty flavor, don't add the coarse salt. A dish such as Lamb in a Mild Dried Pepper Sauce [Cordero Chilindrón], for example, will go very nicely with these bread rings without the salt.)

Pan de Mollete
(Chignon Bread)

These delicious rolls, shaped to resemble the back of a woman's head with a bun or chignon at the nape of the neck, are so unusual-looking your guests will love them. I took the idea from the great Galician restaurant Chocolate, where Josefa Cores serves them with all her wonderful food. She told me they are typical of Galicia because so many women wear their hair in a low bun—a style that, in this region, is called mollete.

This recipe will yield 16 medium rolls, so you may want to cut it in half. But if you have a large food processor or mixer, why not make them all? Surely you will have requests for seconds, and they are just as good warmed up the next day.

Makes 16 medium rolls

1/2 cup butter, at room temperature	2 tablespoons sugar
2 cups milk	2 teaspoons salt
2 tablespoons (or 1 ounce) dry active yeast	2 eggs
	6 1/2 cups all-purpose flour

In a saucepan, melt butter with the milk over low heat until lukewarm (105 to 115 degrees F.).

This bread can be easily made in a large food processor, or in a heavy-duty mixer. In the food processor or mixer bowl, dissolve yeast and sugar in about 1/2 cup of the lukewarm milk/butter mixture; don't stir, just let it sit for 5 to 10 minutes, to activate the yeast (when the yeast starts popping to the top, that means it is ready to work). Immediately add salt, eggs, remaining milk/butter and 1 cup of the flour; whirl to combine well. Gradually add remaining flour; the dough will be sticky, but it doesn't matter—the less flour you use, the lighter the bread will be.

Oil a bowl and place dough in it, turning to coat all sides with oil. Cover with a cloth and let it rise in a warm place until doubled in size, about an hour.

Punch the dough down to release the air. Divide it into quarters, and each quarter into 4 equal pieces. Work the dough with your fingers into 16 smooth round balls. Place them on 1 or 2 oiled baking sheets. Cover with a cloth and let them rise again for about 40 minutes.

Preheat oven to 375 degrees F.

Form the rolls to resemble the back of a woman's head with a bun at the nape of the neck. Pinch up a small ball from each roll, working just off center from the top of the roll (as if the woman's head were face down), to make it look like a chignon. The rolls will deflate a little, but don't worry; they will puff right up in the oven.

Bake in the preheated oven for 25 to 30 minutes, until golden and crusty. Remove to a rack and let cool.

Pan de Romero
(Rosemary-Raisin Wreath Bread)

This bread is especially wonderful with lamb or meat dishes cooked with fruits—as in the Catalan recipes in this book. The aromatic pungency of the rosemary blends very well with any sauce that has a touch of sweetness. The bread will also look very nice on a buffet dinner table, decorated with rosemary sprigs.

Yields 1 large wreath

1 tablespoon (or 1/2 ounce) dry
    active yeast
1 teaspoon honey
1 cup lukewarm water (105 to
    115 degrees F.)
1 cup milk

2 tablespoons coarsely chopped
    fresh rosemary leaves
1/2 cup dark raisins
51/2 cups all-purpose flour
2 tablespoons fruity olive oil
11/2 teaspoons salt

As a garnish (optional):

A bouquet of fresh rosemary
    sprigs

In a food processor bowl, dissolve yeast and honey in the warm water; don't stir, just let it sit for 5 to 10 minutes, to activate the yeast (when the yeast starts popping to the top, that means it is ready to work). Meanwhile, heat the milk in a small saucepan until warm; set aside. In a small bowl, toss the chopped rosemary and raisins with 1/2 cup of the flour and set aside.

As soon as the yeast is activated, mix in the warm milk (it should be at 105 to 115 degrees F.), olive oil, salt and 1 cup of the flour; whirl for 1 minute. Add the remaining 4 cups of flour and process until dough pulls away from the sides. Turn the dough out onto a floured board and knead in the raisins and rosemary with their flour. Continue to knead until these are evenly distributed throughout the dough, and the surface is shiny and elastic.

Oil a bowl and place dough in it, turning to coat all sides with oil. Cover with a cloth and let rise in a warm place until doubled in size, about 1 hour.

Oil a pizza pan. Punch the dough down to release the air. Lift it and, holding it in both hands, punch your thumbs through the middle of the dough and pull it apart to make a large doughnut-shaped bread, about 12 inches in diameter. Be sure to make the hole in the center quite large; it will close up as the bread bakes. Place on the oiled pizza pan, and slash it around the edges with a sharp knife or razor blade, to make it resemble a braided wreath. Brush the top with olive oil, and let it rest for 5 minutes.

Place the loaf in a cold oven, turn oven to 400 degrees F. and bake for

35 minutes, or until the crust is browned and the bread sounds hollow when tapped on the top.

Let bread cool on a rack. Serve it on a wooden board, garnished, if desired, with the rosemary sprigs.

Pan con Tomate
(Catalan: Pa amb Tomàquet)
(Bread with Tomato, Catalan Style)

The idea for this bread couldn't be more simple—and yet I have found it only in Catalonia, usually served at country-style restaurants instead of plain bread. Sometimes it is accompanied by some Catalan anchovies (those from La Scala, on the Costa Brava, are the best), cold local sausages or cured ham.

That's how I serve it at home—as an appetizer with anchovies, prosciutto, salami or other cold sausages; I slice the bread very thin, and cut it in small pieces. I also find it a winner for a light lunch with Spanish Potato Omelet (Tortilla Española) and/or Eggplant Omelet (Tortilla de Berenjenas). At home we often had it like that for supper on Sundays, when the cook had been off in the afternoon and had to whip up something quick! In fact, you can serve this bread anytime.

To serve 4

8 thin, large slices of Peasant
  Bread, sourdough or French-
  style white bread
2 large cloves garlic, peeled and
  cut in half lengthwise
  (optional)

2 large, very ripe tomatoes, cut
  in half crosswise
2 tablespoons olive oil
Salt and freshly ground black
  pepper to taste

Toast the bread on both sides. If desired, rub garlic, cut side down, on bread. Cupping ½ tomato in your palm, rub 2 pieces of bread with each tomato half; squeeze the tomato so that not only the juice and seeds ooze onto the bread but also some of the pulp.

Drizzle olive oil over, and sprinkle with salt and pepper to taste. This bread is best served while still warm.

Coca de Tomate y Pimiento
(Catalan: Coca de Tomàquet i Pebrot)
(Flat Bread with Tomato and Pepper Topping)

The name coca *is given to a number of different breads or pastries in Catalonia. There are two basic kinds: savory and sweet. The first have a bread base; they are particularly traditional in the northeastern regions of Catalonia, such as L'Empordà and Maresme. These bread* cocas *are usually long and oval; they are often toasted, rubbed with half a fresh tomato—or with garlic—and sprinkled with olive oil and salt, in the style of the preceding recipe.*

At L'Olivé restaurant in Barcelona, which specializes in traditional Catalan cuisine, coca del Maresme torrada amb tomàquet (Catalan for toasted coca from Maresme with tomato) is served with your meal instead of bread, much like Bread with Tomato, Catalan Style (Pan con Tomate). In the old days, this plain bread coca or coca de forner (baker's coca) was also called in Catalan pa de torn or return bread, because it was given "in return" as change for a purchase at the bakery.

Sweet cocas are used in a very different way—for breakfast, midday snack or dessert; they are usually covered with candied fruit, pine nuts and sugar. Most of them have a religious connotation; perhaps the best known is coca de San Juan, eaten on St. John's Day, June 24. To me, they are a little too sweet, especially when they have sugar and candied fruit on top. Some are covered with only pine nuts and sugar, which I love; then they are more like my Pine Nut Tart (Tarta de Piñones).

The savory cocas sometimes have on top different local produce such as herring or anchovies, peppers, pitted olives, cooked eggs or cold cuts. The following version makes a great party dish or, cut in squares, a convenient appetizer. It is best served warm (reheated at the last minute). For greater effect, serve it on a large wooden board and cut it at the table.

Makes 1 10 × 15-inch flat bread (or about 15 individual portions)

For the crust:

1 tablespoon (or 1/2 ounce) dry active yeast
1 teaspoon sugar
1/2 cup lukewarm water (105 to 115 degrees F.)
1/4 cup olive oil

1/2 cup finely chopped onion
1/2 cup dry white wine, at room temperature
2 teaspoons salt
31/2 cups all-purpose flour

For the topping:

3 tablespoons olive oil
10 large cloves garlic, sliced or coarsely chopped
1 pound green peppers, seeded and cut into 1/2-inch dice
4 pounds tomatoes, peeled, seeded and chopped

1 teaspoon salt, or to taste
3/4 teaspoon freshly ground black pepper, or to taste
1/4 cup pine nuts

To prepare the crust: In the food processor bowl, dissolve yeast and sugar in the lukewarm water; don't stir, just let it sit for 5 to 10 minutes, to activate the yeast (when the yeast starts popping to the top, that means it is ready to work). Meanwhile, in a skillet heat the oil and, over low heat, sauté onion until soft.

As soon as yeast is activated, whirl in the wine, salt and 1 cup of the flour. Add the onion with its oil and another cup of the flour; mix well. Add all remaining flour; whirl for 2 minutes. Oil a bowl. Remove dough from food processor and place in the bowl, turning to coat all sides with oil. Cover with a cloth and let rise in a warm place until doubled in size, about 1 hour.

To prepare the topping: In a skillet, heat olive oil and add garlic; cook over medium heat until garlic is golden and crunchy. Add peppers and cook for a couple of minutes, stirring so the garlic won't burn. Add tomatoes and season with salt and pepper. Cook briskly for 10 to 15 minutes, or until tomatoes are reduced to a thick sauce. Taste for seasoning.

Preheat oven to 400 degrees F.

Punch down the dough to release the air. Grease a 10 × 15-inch jelly roll pan or cookie sheet. Press the dough into the pan, shaping the edges up to make a border. Pour the topping over the dough and spread to cover. In a small dry pan, toast pine nuts over low heat, stirring, until they color. Sprinkle pine nuts over the top of the *coca*.

Bake in the preheated oven for 25 to 30 minutes, or until the dough edges are golden brown. Remove to a rack and let cool.

Roscón de Reyes
(Catalan: Tortell de Reis)
(Three Kings' Sweet Bread with Almond Filling)

Start preparation at least 6 hours in advance, or the day before

Tortells are a most popular dessert in Catalonia; they are always round, shaped like a doughnut, and filled with anything rich and sinful—whipped cream, chocolate, pastry cream. At home we had them on Sundays; we would go to the pastry shop, which was invariably crowded, after mass. In Spain nobody makes tortells *at home; they always come from a pastry shop.*

Just like cocas *(see preceding recipe), some* tortells *have religious ties. A memorable one is the* tortell de Sant Antoni, *eaten on his feast day, January 17. He is the patron saint of animals—and affectionately nicknamed "St. Anthony of the Donkeys" because of his reputed ability to cure the maladies of people and animals. Even today, in the memory of this St. Anthony, on January 17 a parade is organized in Barcelona and other towns all over Catalonia, where the farmers take their animals to the church to be blessed. Inside the church,* tortells de Sant Antoni *are sold and also given to the animals after they are blessed.*

Tortell de Reis is probably the one tortell *eaten not only in Catalonia but elsewhere in Spain (where it is known as* Roscón de Reyes) *on January 6, Epiphany or Three Kings' Day. The tradition of eating this* tortell *has very ancient roots, dating back to the fifteenth century, in France as well as in Spain. The celebration was also called Fiesta de la Haba or festivity of the fava bean, because a dried fava bean was hidden in the filling. In the old days, the fava bean was a symbol of bad luck; but later it lost its negative connotation, and whoever found it in his or her piece was the king or queen of the festival!*

Even today, it is traditional to hide inside the filling a fava bean and/or a little prize or goody, usually a tiny white ceramic piece—something silly like a duck or a shoe. I remember, as a child, buying tortells *hoping to find the prized fava bean and goody. And I still keep in Spain my enviable collection of prizes gathered over the years.*

This recipe is adapted from one of my favorite delicatessen/pastry shops in Barcelona, Mantequerías Tívoli. Sadurní Val proudly features a selection of sweet and savory pastries, party dishes, cheeses and wines.

This tortell *can be served as a dessert or as a teatime cake, and it is also superb for breakfast with a little sweet butter. For this to be a true* tortell de reis, *you must have a little ceramic or plastic goody—how about a tiny Spanish bull?—to insert in the filling. The finder gets a kiss!*

To serve about 8:   Makes 1 (12-inch) ring

For the dough:

1 tablespoon (or 1/2 ounce) dry active yeast	*3 eggs*
1/2 cup sugar	*1/2 teaspoon salt*
1/4 cup lukewarm water (105 to 115 degrees F.)	*1 teaspoon vanilla extract*
3/4 cup unsalted butter, at room temperature	*2 tablespoons orange zest**
	21/2 cups all-purpose flour

For the filling:

1/2 pound blanched almonds, finely ground	*6 tablespoons fresh orange juice*
2/3 cup sugar	*1/4 teaspoon almond extract*

For the garnish:

1 egg
1/2 cup sliced almonds

To prepare the dough: In a small bowl, dissolve yeast and 1/4 cup sugar in lukewarm water; don't stir, just let it sit for 5 to 10 minutes, to activate the yeast (when the yeast starts popping to the top, that means it is ready to work). Meanwhile, in the food processor or mixer, beat remaining 1/4 cup sugar with butter, eggs, salt, vanilla and orange zest. Add yeast as soon as it is ready, and mix well. Add 1 cup of the flour and beat vigorously. Add remaining 11/2 cups flour and continue to whirl until well mixed.

Transfer to a bowl (if you used a food processor), cover with a cloth and allow the dough to rise in a warm place until doubled in size. It may take as long as 2 hours.

Stir down the dough with a spoon or your fingers (this is a sticky dough) to release the air. Refrigerate for at least 2 hours and up to 3 days (it will also rise in the refrigerator).

To prepare the filling: In the food processor, grind almonds and sugar until the mixture starts to move up the sides of the bowl. Gradually add the orange juice, and flavor with the almond extract. (If you make this ahead of time, keep it covered in the refrigerator.)

To assemble the sweet bread: Stir down the dough again. Flour your hands and a board, and roll the dough into a 30-inch-long log. Pat the log flat to about 5 inches wide. Spread the filling all the way down the center of the log, to within 1 inch of the side edges. At this point, remember to insert a little "goody" inside the filling!

Pinch sides of the dough up and over the filling. Pinch log ends together to form a circle. Place bread, seam side down, on a buttered pizza pan or a large baking sheet.

To garnish the tortell: Beat the egg in a small bowl and brush the top of the bread with it. Pat sliced almonds all over. Allow the bread to rise, uncovered, for 20 minutes.

Preheat oven to 400 degrees F.

Bake bread in the preheated oven for 25 minutes. Serve warm.

Empanada de Anchoas
(Anchovy and Onion Pie)

Empanadas *are classic seafood or meat pies from Galicia. I had one of the best at my favorite Galician restaurant in Madrid, Combarro. Manuel Domínguez, a Galician, has faithfully taken to Spain's capital the classic fish and shellfish dishes of his region, with great success.*

In this recipe I've used an anchovy filling—an idea of Manuel's—which works perfectly with the other ingredients. The dough using cornmeal is inspired by a unique corn empanada *I had at Chocolate, the terrific Galician restaurant near Pontevedra.*

To serve 8

For the dough:

1/2 cup yellow or white cornmeal
1 teaspoon salt
1 tablespoon olive oil
1 tablespoon (or 1/2 ounce) dry active yeast
2 teaspoons sugar
1 1/2 cups all-purpose flour

For the filling:

3 tablespoons olive oil
2 large onions, thinly sliced
3 cloves garlic, minced
1 tablespoon Spanish paprika
1 1/2 (2-ounce) tins flat anchovy fillets (or 13–14 large fillets), drained and chopped
1/2 teaspoon freshly ground black pepper, or to taste
1 pound unpeeled tomatoes, puréed
2 hard-boiled eggs, chopped
1/4 cup dark raisins

For the crust:

1 tablespoon milk
1 tablespoon cornmeal

To prepare the dough: Bring 1/2 cup water to a boil and pour over the cornmeal. Stir in salt and oil. Let cool.

In the food processor bowl, dissolve yeast and sugar in 1/4 cup lukewarm water (105 to 115 degrees F.). Don't stir, just let it sit for 5 to 10 minutes, to activate the yeast (when the yeast starts popping to the top, that means it is ready to work). As soon as the yeast is ready and the cornmeal has cooled to at least 115 degrees F., add cornmeal and flour to the yeast. Whirl to combine well, until dough pulls away from the sides of the bowl or forms a ball. Oil a bowl and put dough in it, turning to coat on all sides with oil. Cover and put in a warm place until doubled in size, about 1 hour.

To prepare the filling: Meanwhile, heat the oil in a large skillet; sauté onions and garlic slowly for 20 minutes over low heat. Add paprika, anchovies and pepper; cook, stirring, for 5 minutes. Add tomatoes and cook for 2 minutes, stirring. Off heat, stir in hard-boiled eggs and raisins. Taste for seasoning.

Punch down the dough and divide it in half. On a floured board, roll out half the dough into a circle about 12 inches in diameter. Place this circle of dough on an oiled baking sheet and spread filling over, to within 1 inch of the sides. Roll out remaining half of the dough into another 12-inch circle and cover the filling. Roll up edges, pinching dough and turning pie around to seal it, so that edge resembles a coiled rope. Brush the top of the pie with the milk and sprinkle with the cornmeal. Allow the pie to rest in a warm place, uncovered, for 20 minutes.

Preheat oven to 450 degrees F.

Place pie in the preheated oven and bake for 20 to 25 minutes, until golden. Serve warm, cut into wedges.

STOCKS AND SAUCES

Stocks will keep for 3 or 4 days in the refrigerator, or for six months frozen. It is better to freeze them in small batches—1 or 2 cups—for easier use.

It is a good idea to keep a bag of chicken and veal parts in your freezer, adding to it whenever you have spare pieces. When you have accumulated several pounds, make a stock.

It is best not to season basic stocks, but rather to do so in the final recipe. The following stock recipes can also be used as is for a soup—in that case with seasonings added.

After the fat has been removed, the stock may be cooked over medium-high heat and reduced by half to produce a very rich stock, which will add great flavor to sauces. Then you may freeze it in ice cube trays, remove it from the trays and keep in a plastic bag.

Caldo de Pollo
(Chicken Stock)

This stock recipe is a basic one to keep on hand in your freezer. It will add richness to your dishes, without extra calories!

Yields about 3 quarts

5 or 6 pounds of chicken backs, necks and/or wing tips
1 pound onions, sliced or coarsely chopped
1 pound carrots, topped but unpeeled, sliced or coarsely chopped
2 or 3 leeks, sliced or coarsely chopped, with 2/3 of the green part

1 cup dry white wine
1 large bay leaf
3 sprigs parsley
8 black peppercorns
1 sprig fresh thyme (optional)

Preheat oven to 450 degrees F.

Put chicken pieces, onions, carrots and leeks in a large roasting pan. Bake in the preheated oven for 1 hour, turning meat and vegetables occasionally.

Transfer contents of roasting pan to a stock pot. Add wine, and let it boil for 3 or 4 minutes to evaporate the alcohol. Transfer this liquid to the stock pot; add remaining ingredients, and cover with about 3 quarts water. Bring to a boil and immediately reduce heat to low.

Remove scum that forms on top. Simmer stock, partially covered, for about 3 hours. During this time, it is a good idea to remove the scum occasionally as it rises to the top; but don't worry about the fat on the surface, you will be able to remove that easily after the stock is chilled.

Strain the stock through a colander, and then through a fine sieve. Let cool at room temperature, and refrigerate overnight. Then it will be easy to remove the fat from the surface, after it has hardened; lift it carefully, as it may not be too hard. The stock is now ready to use as is, or to be reduced in order to make a richer stock. (Never boil a stock that has not had the fat removed from it, or the fat becomes a part of the stock and is impossible to remove.)

Caldo de Ternera
(Brown Veal Stock)

This is a dark stock which will provide a lot of flavor for your meat dishes and sauces.

Yields about 6 cups

4 or 5 pounds veal bones and/or
  veal breast (see Note below)
3/4 pound carrots, topped but
  unpeeled, sliced or coarsely
  chopped
1 large onion, sliced or coarsely
  chopped
2 leeks, sliced or coarsely
  chopped, with 2/3 of the green
  part

1 (4- to 6-inch) piece of celery,
  with the leaves
1/4 cup chopped shallots
1 cup dry white wine
1 bay leaf
4 sprigs parsley
1 teaspoon whole black
  peppercorns

(Note: Veal breast is often available on special, and it is excellent for making stocks. It is usually sold by the piece, about 2 or 3 pounds; if you can find it, get another 2 pounds of veal bones. The best bones for making a stock are knuckle and marrow bones. Ask your butcher to cut the bones and the breast in small pieces.)

Preheat oven to 450 degrees F.

Put the bones/breast, carrots, onion, leeks, celery and shallots in a large baking pan. Place in the preheated oven for 1¼ hours, or until bones and vegetables are browned. Turn them from time to time, especially toward the end of the cooking, so as not to burn the vegetables in the corners.

Transfer contents of the roasting pan to a stock pot. Add wine to the roasting pan; over medium heat, stir and scrape bottom and sides to get all the browned bits of vegetables and veal left in the pan. As you scrape, let wine boil for 4 to 5 minutes to evaporate the alcohol.

Add this liquid to stock pot. Add remaining ingredients and 2 quarts water, or to cover. Bring to a boil, and immediately reduce heat to low. Continue as directed in Chicken Stock (Caldo de Pollo) recipe.

Mi Salsa Española
(Enriched Veal Stock)

Salsa española, or sauce espagnole in French, is an enriched brown stock thickened with flour. But I don't care for floury sauces, because flour doesn't add any flavor—only thickness and calories. It is worth the effort to use a more flavorful stock instead, enriched by making a double veal stock (that is, using a veal stock to make it, instead of water) and fresh vegetables. This, then, is my version of salsa española; *you will see the difference when you use it as directed in several recipes of this book.*

Yields about 4 cups

1 pound veal bones, cracked into small pieces
1 ham hock, cracked into 4 or 5 pieces
2 medium leeks, sliced or coarsely chopped, with 2/3 of the green part
1 stalk celery, sliced or coarsely chopped
2 medium onions, sliced or coarsely chopped
1/2 pound carrots, topped but unpeeled, sliced or coarsely chopped

2 cups dry Spanish sherry
4 cups Brown Veal Stock
1 bay leaf
1 pound unpeeled tomatoes, chopped
1 sprig fresh rosemary
1 sprig fresh thyme (or 1/2 teaspoon dried)
6 black peppercorns
1 (2-inch) stick cinnamon

Preheat oven to 450 degrees F.

Place the bones, ham hock, leeks, celery, onions and carrots in a large baking pan. Bake in the preheated oven for 1¼ hours, or until meat and vegetables are browned. Turn them from time to time. Transfer to a stock pot. Deglaze the baking pan with sherry, stirring and scraping, until reduced by half; pour into the stock pot. Add veal stock and remaining ingredients. Bring to a boil, and immediately reduce heat to low. Simmer, covered, for about 2 or 3 hours. Continue as directed in Chicken Stock (Caldo de Pollo) recipe.

Caldo de Pescado
(Fish Fumet)

A good fish stock, or fumet, is essential for many fine seafood dishes. Bottled clam juice is not a good substitute; it is salty and will never add the flavor of a fumet.

This recipe is quick and easy to make. All you need are fish heads and bones, which you will find at many markets or you can order ahead of time. To make a good fumet, it is important to use only white fish—any sole/flounder type, halibut, red snapper, lake trout, spike, whiting, ocean perch, rockfish, etc. Do not use oily fish such as bluefish. When preparing it, remove skins and fins, for they are oily.

Yields about 2 quarts

3 pounds fish heads, collars and/
    or bones
1/4 cup olive oil
2 large or 3 small leeks, sliced or
    coarsely chopped, with 2/3 of
    the green part
1 large onion, sliced or coarsely
    chopped
1 medium carrot, topped but
    unpeeled, sliced or coarsely
    chopped

2 cups dry white wine
1 or 2 sprigs parsley, with plenty
    of stems
1 or 2 bay leaves
2 or 3 sprigs fresh thyme (or 1
    teaspoon if dried)

Rinse fish bones and heads thoroughly; unless they are absolutely fresh, soak them in cold water for 10 to 15 minutes. Drain.

Heat oil in a large stock pot. Add leeks, onion and carrot; sauté for about 5 minutes, stirring, until they start to color. Add wine, and boil for 5 minutes to evaporate the alcohol. Add fish heads/bones, herbs and 6 cups cold water; bring to a boil, immediately reduce heat to very low and remove scum on the surface. Simmer slowly, partially covered, for 30 minutes. During this time, skim off 2 or 3 times any scum that rises to the surface.

Strain the fish stock through a colander, gently pressing down the bones and vegetables with a spoon, and then through a fine-mesh strainer into the container where you will store it. Let cool before refrigerating or freezing.

ROMESCO

Romesco is truly indigenous to Catalonia, specifically to the city of Tarragona and its surroundings. An annual festival associated with its preparation is held there on the arrival of summer, the prime season for the vegetables which are essential to the sauce. A competition is then organized, based on cooking the best *romesco;* the winner is awarded the title of Mestre Major Romescaire, or Grand Master *Romesco* Maker.

The origin of *romesco,* in fact, is not as a sauce but as a dish: Fish Stew, Tarragona Style (Romesco de Pescados). It was a simple way to cook fish for fishermen all along the coast from Vilanova—a fishing village 20 miles south of Barcelona—to Valencia. They made it when out at sea, using their lesser-quality catch (naturally saving the best to sell), with a strong sauce, which became known as *romesco.* Later on, the sauce came to be made separately, and today is served mainly to accompany grilled, poached or deep-fried fresh fish. Purists maintain, though, that *romesco* is not a sauce but a dish.

Romesco is based on primary Catalan ingredients: hazelnuts or almonds, red peppers, garlic, onions, tomatoes, herbs or spices and—most important —a very good, fruity olive oil.

Many restaurants in Catalonia will serve you a little bowl of *romesco* as well as Garlic Mayonnaise (Allioli), especially with grilled or fried fish, even without asking for it. Often, both sauces are blended together.

I have selected here a few of my favorite *romesco* sauces from different chefs in Catalonia. They can be combined with recipes in this book as well as with almost anything—salads, grilled meats or vegetables, pasta, rice, and so on.

The ingredients in a *romesco* sauce should be finely ground, which in the old days was done with a mortar and pestle; today it can be done much more efficiently in a food processor. All *romescos* should rest at room temperature for at least 3 to 4 hours before serving, for the flavors to mingle.

Salsa Roja
(Catalan: Salsa Vermella)
(Romesco-Style Sauce for Grilled Fish)

Salsa vermella, *as Eugenia Pedrell—owner of Eugenia restaurant in Cambrils, near Tarragona—calls this sauce in Catalan, translates as "red sauce." It is a light, fresh and zesty* romesco-*style sauce. It goes particularly well with grilled fish.*

Yields about 2 cups

1 large (1/2-inch) slice of white
   bread
1/4 cup red wine vinegar
1/2 cup whole almonds
1/2 pound unpeeled ripe
   tomatoes, chopped

2 teaspoons Spanish paprika
1/2 teaspoon salt
1/2 cup fruity olive oil

Preheat oven to 350 degrees F.

Soak the bread in the vinegar to soften. Toast almonds in the preheated oven for 15 minutes. Grind them finely in the food processor. Add remaining ingredients except the oil, and purée. With the motor running, add the oil slowly. Taste for seasoning.

"Xató"
(Romesco-Style Sauce for "Xatonada")

Xató is a sharp and nutty romesco-style sauce, with a buttery smoothness. It is traditionally served with Catalan Tuna Salad ("Xatonada"), as Pere Valls does at his El Celler del Penedès restaurant—but I find it wonderful with just about anything.

Makes about 2½ cups

> 1 cup whole almonds
> 1 medium red bell pepper
> 3 large cloves garlic, coarsely
>   chopped
> 1 tablespoon fresh parsley leaves

> ½ teaspoon salt
> ¼ teaspoon freshly ground black
>   pepper
> ½ cup red wine vinegar
> ¾ cup fruity olive oil

Preheat oven to 350 degrees F. Toast almonds for 15 minutes; grind them finely in the food processor. Roast red pepper over a flame or in the oven (see Roasting and Peeling Peppers*) until skin starts to blacken; peel, seed and cut it up.

Add red pepper, garlic and parsley to the food processor; purée. Add salt, pepper and vinegar, whirling until they form a smooth paste. With the motor running, gradually add the oil in a thin stream. Taste for seasoning. The sauce should have a thick consistency and very sharp flavor. Depending on the strength of the vinegar used, you may need more or less oil.

"Salbitxada"
(Romesco-Style Sauce for Grilled Vegetables)

This version of romesco is typically served with Baked Young Onions or Leeks ("Ceballots") or other grilled vegetables. The color is a beautiful light terracotta, and the flavors a harmonious, rich blend of all its ingredients. Pere Valls serves an excellent salbitxada at his El Celler del Penedès restaurant, from which I adapted this recipe.

Yields about 2 cups

> 1 tablespoon olive oil for frying
> 1 large (½-inch) slice of white
>   bread
> ½ cup whole almonds
> ¼ teaspoon hot red pepper
>   flakes
> 3 large cloves garlic
> ½ pound unpeeled ripe tomatoes

> 1 (4-ounce) can pimientos,
>   drained (⅓ cup packed)
> ¼ teaspoon Spanish paprika
> ¼ teaspoon salt, or to taste
> ½ teaspoon freshly ground black
>   pepper, or to taste
> ¼ cup red wine vinegar
> ½ cup fruity olive oil

Preheat oven to 350 degrees F.

Heat the 1 tablespoon oil in a small skillet and, over medium heat, fry bread slice until golden on both sides.

Toast almonds in the preheated oven for 15 minutes. Grind them finely in the food processor, together with bread, pepper flakes and garlic. Add tomatoes, pimientos, paprika, salt and pepper; purée until they form a smooth paste. Add vinegar and whirl. With the motor running, add oil slowly, in a thin stream. Taste for seasoning.

Romesco de L'Olivé
(Romesco Sauce with Ancho Chiles, Onion and Paprika)

The following are two of my favorite romesco *sauces, both from restaurants in Barcelona which specialize in classic Catalan cuisine: L'Olivé, tiny and new; and Cal Isidre, traditional and home style. I have simply given their recipes the name of the restaurant. They both use* nyoras, *the dried red peppers similar to our* ancho *or* pasilla *chiles (see Fish Stew, Tarragona Style [Romesco de Pescados]) and hazelnuts as well as almonds, which provide earthy full flavors. Josep Olivé uses onion and paprika, which contribute a rounder, milder taste; and Isidre Gironés bakes the vegetables for a sweeter, tangier flavor.*

Both sauces are excellent with lamb, barbecued pork or chicken, or any grilled meats.

Yields about 3 cups

2 medium ancho (pasilla) *chile peppers*
1/2 cup whole almonds
1/2 cup hazelnuts (filberts)
1 tablespoon olive oil for frying
1 large (1/2-inch) slice of white bread
3 large cloves garlic
1/2 cup chopped onion

1/2 pound unpeeled ripe tomatoes, cut up
2 teaspoons Spanish paprika
3/4 teaspoon salt
1/4 teaspoon freshly ground black pepper
2 tablespoons red wine vinegar, or to taste
1/2 cup fruity olive oil

Preheat oven to 350 degrees F.

Cover chiles with water in a saucepan. Bring to a boil and cook for 10 minutes over medium-low heat. Turn off heat, cover and steep for 30 minutes. Remove stems and seeds, and discard water. You should have 1/4 cup packed peppers.

While the chiles steep, toast the nuts separately in the preheated oven for about 15 minutes. Rub hazelnuts in a damp cloth to remove most of the skins.

Heat the 1 tablespoon oil in a small skillet and, over medium heat, fry the bread slice until golden on both sides.

In the food processor, grind the nuts finely with the garlic and bread. Add chiles, onion, tomatoes, paprika, salt and pepper. Purée until they form a smooth paste. Add vinegar and whirl. With the motor running, pour in the oil slowly, in a thin stream. Taste for seasoning.

Romesco de Cal Isidre
(Romesco Sauce with Ancho Chiles and Baked Garlic/Tomato)

Yields about 2 cups

2 medium ancho (pasilla) chile
  peppers
1/4 cup whole almonds
1/4 cup hazelnuts (filberts)
1 large head garlic
1 large unpeeled ripe tomato
1 tablespoon olive oil for frying

1 large (1/2-inch) slice of white
  bread
1/4 teaspoon hot red pepper
  flakes
1/4 cup red wine vinegar
1/2 teaspoon salt
1/2 cup fruity olive oil

Preheat oven to 350 degrees F.

Cover the chiles with water in a saucepan. Bring to a boil and cook 10 minutes over medium-low heat. Turn off heat, cover and steep for 30 minutes. Remove stems and seeds; you should have 1/4 cup packed peppers. Reserve 2 tablespoons of the water.

Toast the almonds and hazelnuts separately in the preheated oven for about 15 minutes. Rub hazelnuts in a damp cloth to remove most of the skins.

Put the whole head of garlic and the tomato on an ungreased baking sheet. In the 350-degree F. oven, bake garlic for 45 minutes and tomato for 20 minutes. Cut off about a quarter of the garlic head top, and squeeze the pulp out. Peel the tomato.

Heat the 1 tablespoon olive oil in a small skillet and, over medium heat, fry the bread until golden on both sides. Grind it finely in the food processor, together with the nuts and pepper flakes. Add tomato, garlic pulp and chiles; whirl until they form a smooth paste. Add vinegar, salt and 2 tablespoons reserved water from cooking the chiles; whirl to combine. With the motor running, add the oil slowly, in a thin stream. Taste for seasoning.

Salsa Mayonesa
(Mayonnaise)

Yields 1 1/2 cups

1 whole egg, at room
  temperature
1 egg yolk, at room temperature
1 1/4 teaspoons prepared Dijon-
  style mustard
1 cup safflower oil or another
  vegetable oil

1/2 cup extra virgin olive oil
1 tablespoon plus 2 teaspoons
  lemon juice
1/4 teaspoon salt, or to taste
Pinch of cayenne

In a blender or food processor fitted with a metal blade, combine the whole egg, egg yolk and mustard. Mix the oils and lemon juice together in a pouring jar and add slowly, with the motor running, in a thin stream; the mixture will thicken and become a mayonnaise. Season with the salt and cayenne.

If the mixture separates or does not thicken, you can correct it as follows: pour all but 1 tablespoon of the separated mayonnaise into another container. Add 1 tablespoon water to the tablespoon of mayonnaise left in the blender or food processor. With the motor running, add the separated mayonnaise slowly; the mixture should attain the right consistency—if not, try again. It will work!

Keep sauce refrigerated until ready to use.

Allioli
(Garlic Mayonnaise)

Best to prepare this sauce a day ahead.

Yields about 1¹/₂ cups

1¹/₂ tablespoons minced garlic	1 cup safflower oil or another
1 egg, at room temperature	vegetable oil
¹/₂ cup extra virgin olive oil	1 tablespoon lemon juice

In a blender or food processor fitted with the metal blade, purée garlic with egg. Mix the oils with the lemon juice in a pouring jar. With the motor running, add slowly in a thin stream. Whirl an additional 10 seconds. Transfer to a bowl, cover and refrigerate.

You may use the *allioli* immediately, but I prefer it the next day, after the flavors mingle and mellow.

Allioli de Miel
(Catalan: Allioli de Mel)
(Honey Garlic Mayonnaise)

This and the next allioli *recipe are a creation of Montse Guillén and typical of her inventiveness: adding a "new" note to an old traditional Catalan recipe such as* allioli. *Both sauces are featured at her Barcelona restaurant. Montse likes to serve them to accompany grilled meats, such as lamb chops.*

Makes 1¹/₂ cups

1 egg	3 tablespoons honey
2 tablespoons minced garlic	¹/₂ teaspoon salt
1 cup olive oil	

In a food processor or blender, purée egg with garlic. With the motor running, gradually add the oil in a thin stream until it thickens like a mayonnaise. Add honey and salt, whirl to mix and taste for seasoning. Keep refrigerated until serving time.

Allioli de Manzana
(Catalan: Allioli de Poma)
(Apple Garlic Mayonnaise)

In addition to the serving suggestions mentioned in the former recipe, I find this apple allioli goes very well with Rabbit and Prune Terrine (Terrina de Conejo con Ciruelas) and with the pork loin recipes in this book.

Makes 2¹/₂ cups

> 1 pound tart cooking apples,
>   such as Pippin or Granny
>   Smith, peeled, cored and cut
>   into 1-inch pieces
> 1 teaspoon minced garlic

> ²/₃ cup olive oil
> ¹/₄ teaspoon salt, or to taste
> ¹/₄ teaspoon freshly ground
>   white pepper, or to taste

Place apples in a saucepan and cover with water. Bring to a boil, reduce heat to low, cover and simmer until tender—about 30 to 45 minutes. Drain apples and place them in a food processor or blender. Add garlic and purée finely. With the motor running, gradually add the oil in a thin stream. Add salt and pepper, and taste for seasoning. Keep refrigerated until serving time.

Salsa de Chocolate
(Chocolate Sauce)

If you like chocolate, this is the ultimate sauce. It is especially delicious over ice cream, as in Caramelized Nut Ice Cream with Hot Chocolate Sauce (Helado de Frutos Secos al Caramelo con Salsa de Chocolate) or with fresh fruit. I also love to marinate strawberries in an orange brandy liqueur (such as Gran Torres or Grand Marnier) and dip them in this chocolate sauce.

Makes about 1¹/₂ cups

> 1 cup heavy cream
> 2 ounces unsweetened baking
>   chocolate
> ³/₄ cup semi-sweet chocolate
>   chips

> 1¹/₂ tablespoons finest-quality
>   Spanish brandy
> 1 teaspoon vanilla extract

Heat the cream in the top of a double boiler over boiling water, or in a heavy-bottomed small saucepan. Melt chocolates in the cream, stirring over very low heat, until combined into a smooth sauce. Off heat, add brandy and vanilla. Serve hot.

If you make this sauce ahead, reheat it in a double boiler, stirring, so it does not separate.

DESSERTS

Tocinillos de Cielo
(Egg Caramel Tarts)

The name of these rich, mellow tarts of silky texture literally translates as "little pigs from heaven." They are found all over Spain, in restaurants as well as in bakeries. They may be small tarts or made in only one mold, in which case it is called tocino de cielo.

Actually, this dessert originated in the south of Spain; history has it dating back to 1611, in Jerez. The winemakers in that area used a lot of egg whites for filtering their wines, and they had no use for the yolks. King Philip III decided to give them to the Clarisas order of nuns, which he had founded. They first used them in a dessert still made all over Spain, natillas, *a light custard consisting of egg yolks, milk and sugar. According to records, this went on for quite a while—until one day the head cook became ill, and another nun had to take over. She mistakenly omitted the milk, so the* natillas *came out firm like flans. When she served them, one nun started using her knife and fork to eat them, joking that she "had to cut this dessert like a pig"—to which another nun retorted, "but a pig from heaven, because it is so delicious!"*

Even today, popular belief has it that in order to ensure fine weather for a special party, one should send 2 or 3 dozen eggs to the Clarisas nuns because their prayers have an influence over the elements.

For this recipe you need 6 (1/3-cup) molds—either muffin tins, flan molds or ramekins. Don't fill them to the top; they will be easier to unmold. This is such a rich dessert that you will probably want to serve just 1 tocinillo *per person.*

To serve 6

For the caramel:

>6 tablespoons sugar

For the tarts:

1 cup sugar	6 egg yolks
1 (2- or 3-inch) stick cinnamon	2 whole eggs
Peel of 1 lemon	

As an accompaniment:

>1/2–1 cup whipped cream

To caramelize the molds: In a small heavy-bottomed pan, dissolve sugar with 1 or 2 tablespoons water and cook over medium heat until sugar melts and turns golden. To facilitate caramelizing, have molds warm by the time the caramel is ready. Distribute caramel into molds; it must coat the bottom and most of the sides of the molds. This may be a little tricky, as caramel gets very hot. Work quickly, 1 or 2 molds at a time, using potholders and turning the molds around to coat the sides; a little spoon may also help. (If the caramel should harden in the molds before you have a chance to coat the sides, you may soften it by placing the molds in a pan with boiling water.)

To prepare the tarts: Dissolve sugar with 1/4 cup water in a heavy-bottomed saucepan, preferably one with a pouring lip. Add cinnamon stick and lemon peel. Cook over medium heat to 230 degrees F. on a candy thermometer, or thread consistency. Remove from heat and set aside for 1 minute. Discard cinnamon stick and lemon peel.

While the sugar mixture is cooking, beat egg yolks and whole eggs with a fork in a medium bowl; do not beat to a froth. Add sugar syrup to the eggs in a very thin stream, stirring with a fork, so egg yolks won't curdle. Strain through a fine-mesh strainer into a pouring jar, and pour into the caramelized molds.

To prepare the tocinillos: This is the most delicate part, for the tarts must be steamed, not baked. If you have a steamer, it is easier to do it on top of the stove because this will give you better control. Place tarts on the steamer rack, making sure the water is below the rack level. The water should boil, otherwise it won't produce enough steam to cook them. Place a double-layered cloth on top of the pot, and cover tightly with a lid.

(You can also cook them in the oven, inside a large pan with about 1 inch boiling water. The molds must not touch the water, however; place them on a rack and, if necessary, put the rack on top of a folded cloth. Form a tent of foil and cover the entire pan so that the steam will stay under the tent. Bake in a preheated 350-degree F. oven.)

Cook for about 15 minutes, or until a cake tester comes out clean and the surface is firm and puffed up. Be very careful when opening the lid of the steamer (or the foil tent over the pan)—steam will scald you very easily!

To assemble the dish: As soon as the molds are cool enough to handle, unmold them onto a serving platter or individual plates. To unmold, pass a knife around the edges and tap the mold against the plate; they will come out easily. With a spoon, scoop out as much as possible of the liquid caramel in the mold, and drip it over the *tocinillos.* Serve garnished with whipped cream.

Flan de Coco al Caramelo
(Caramelized Coconut Flan)

Flans are classic Spanish desserts, and the following two are favorite recipes from my mother's file. The first is light and subtly flavored with the coconut; the second mingles together the full taste of apples with a light, interesting texture—and of course, coming from my family, they both are enhanced by a dash or so of fine brandy!

Coconut is often eaten raw in Spain, and the summer stands on the boulevards of the seaside resorts usually sell it cut into wedges, side by side with other children's delights such as sugar-coated almonds and cotton candy. As a child, I remember relishing this crunchy refreshment on balmy Mediterranean afternoons.

To serve 8

For the caramel:

> *1/2 cup sugar*

For the flan:

> *4 cups milk*
> *1 vanilla bean, split in half*
> *   lengthwise*
> *Peel of 1 lemon*
> *5 egg yolks*

> *5 whole eggs*
> *3/4 cup sugar*
> *3 tablespoons finest-quality*
> *   Spanish brandy*
> *1/2 cup packed shredded coconut*

For the garnish:

> *1/4 cup packed shredded coconut*

To prepare the caramel: In a small heavy saucepan, dissolve the 1/2 cup sugar in 2 tablespoons water. Cook over medium-high heat until sugar melts and turns medium brown. Don't stir, just shake pan around. Immediately pour caramel into a 5-cup ring mold. With oven mittens on both hands, rotate mold gently, swirling caramel to cover bottom and some of the sides; keep moving mold around until caramel is almost set.

To prepare the flan: Preheat oven to 350 degrees F.

Combine milk, vanilla bean and lemon peel in a saucepan and cook over low heat for 10 minutes. Cover and set aside for 15 minutes. In a blender or food processor, beat egg yolks, eggs and sugar, until light and foamy. Discard vanilla bean and lemon peel. Pour hot milk into egg mixture in a slow steady stream, beating constantly. Stir in brandy and 1/2 cup coconut. Immediately pour mixture into mold, and place it inside a larger pan filled with boiling water halfway up the mold. Bake in the preheated oven for 50 minutes, or until a cake tester comes out clean.

Let flan cool at room temperature, and chill. Meanwhile, in a dry skillet toast 1/4 cup coconut for the garnish, stirring, until golden.

To assemble the dish: Unmold flan onto a dessert platter with a rim. Spoon caramel left in mold on top of the flan. Garnish with toasted coconut around the top of the flan. Serve at room temperature or chilled.

Flan de Manzana al Caramelo
(Caramelized Apple Flan)

To serve 6 to 8

For the caramel:

> 1/3 cup sugar

For the flan:

> 3 tablespoons butter
> 2 pounds Pippin or Granny
>   Smith apples, peeled, cored
>   and coarsely chopped
> 1/2 cup finest-quality Spanish
>   brandy

> 6 eggs
> 1/2 cup sugar
> 1 teaspoon powdered cinnamon

As a garnish:

> 1 cup heavy cream
> 2 tablespoons confectioner's
>   sugar

> 1/2 teaspoon vanilla extract
> 1/4 teaspoon powdered cinnamon

To prepare the caramel: Caramelize a 5-cup ring mold with the 1/3 cup sugar and 1 or 2 tablespoons water, proceeding as directed in Caramelized Coconut Flan (Flan de Coco al Caramelo).

To prepare the flan: Preheat oven to 350 degrees F.

In a heavy skillet, heat butter and cook apples over medium-low heat, covered, for 15 minutes. Add brandy; when hot, flambé.* Cook for 2 or 3 minutes, shaking the skillet. In a bowl, beat eggs with 1/2 cup sugar and 1 teaspoon cinnamon. Stir in apples.

Pour apple mixture into caramelized mold, and place in a larger pan filled with boiling water halfway up the mold. Bake in the preheated oven, uncovered, for 45 minutes or until a cake tester comes out clean.

To prepare the garnish and assemble the dish: Whip cream with confectioner's sugar and vanilla. As soon as flan is cool enough to handle, unmold it onto a serving platter. Spoon caramel over flan. Mound cream into center of the flan, sprinkling the top with cinnamon. Serve warm or at room temperature.

Flan de Moras con Salsa de Moras
(Catalan: Flam de Móres amb Salsa de Móres)
(Blackberry Flan with a Blackberry Sauce)

If you like blackberries and can get them fresh during their short season, don't miss making this flan, a creation of Neichel restaurant in Barcelona. Jean-Louis Neichel, an Alsatian, is one of my favorite chefs in the city; his way of handling the finest ingredients is impeccable, always enhancing their freshness with unusual, new-style personal ideas.

To serve 6 to 8:   Makes 1 (5-cup) flan

For the flan:

1 cup milk
1 teaspoon vanilla extract
1/2 cup sugar
4 egg yolks
1 envelope (or 1/4 ounce) unflavored gelatin

1/2 cup crème de cassis liqueur
1 pound fresh blackberries
1 cup heavy cream

For the sauce:

1/2 pound fresh blackberries
1/3 cup sugar

2 tablespoons crème de cassis liqueur

To prepare the flan: In a heavy-bottomed saucepan, combine milk, vanilla, sugar and egg yolks. Heat gently and cook over low heat, stirring constantly, until the custard thickens and coats the back of a spoon; it will take about 15 minutes.

In a small saucepan, dissolve gelatin in cassis liqueur, stirring over low heat until the gelatin is dissolved. Add to the custard. Refrigerate custard until it begins to set—about 45 minutes.

Meanwhile, with a fork or potato ricer, crush 1/2 cup of the blackberries and mix it with the remaining whole berries. Whip the cream until it forms stiff peaks. Remove the custard from the refrigerator; fold in the blackberries and the cream. Pour mixture into a 5- to 7-cup flan or ring mold. Refrigerate for at least 3 or 4 hours before serving.

To prepare the sauce: In a food processor or blender, purée blackberries with sugar and cassis liqueur. Strain through a fine-mesh strainer.

To assemble the dish: Unmold the flan by dipping it into a pan or sink filled with hot water for 5 or 6 seconds. Invert mold onto a serving platter, and pour some sauce around the flan. Pass remaining sauce in a sauceboat. Serve chilled.

Flan de Fresas con Su Salsa de Fresas Frescas (Catalan: Flam de Maduixes amb Salsa de Maduixes Fresques) (Strawberry Flan in a Fresh Strawberry Sauce)

I enjoyed this strawberry flan, among other good things, at Hostal del Priorato, a quaint Catalan country restaurant in Banyeres, south of Barcelona. Chef/owner Miguel Puig prepares excellent traditional dishes, some of them with a "new" approach, such as this one.

When I tried it at home, it was delicious—but after boiling the strawberries to get a concentrated syrup, the color was grayish and unappealing. As I looked through my kitchen window mulling over the problem, the hummingbirds picking at my fuchsias gave me an idea: they wouldn't mind if I took one drop of the red food color I use to tint the syrup for their feeding, would they? (Naturally, I didn't need to tell my guests either.) Well, the flan came out great, and also looking pretty.

Makes 1 (5-cup) flan

For the flan:

1 cup sugar
1/2 cup sweet muscat wine, such as Torres Malvasía de Oro
1 tablespoon lemon juice
1 1/2 pounds fresh strawberries, stemmed

8 eggs
1 drop red food color, either No. 3 or No. 40 (optional; see above)

For the sauce:

1 pound fresh strawberries, stemmed
1/3 cup sugar

2 or 3 tablespoons raspberry liqueur, or to taste

Preheat oven to 350 degrees F.

To prepare the flan: In a large saucepan, combine sugar, wine, lemon juice and strawberries. Bring to a boil, and boil vigorously for 5 minutes. Strain through a medium sieve or food mill into a bowl. Beat eggs well and strain them through a fine-mesh strainer into the bowl with the strawberry mixture. If desired, add drop of red food color. Pour into a 5- or 6-cup flan mold, cover with foil and place inside a larger pan filled with boiling water halfway up the mold. Bake in the preheated oven for 40 minutes. Let cool at room temperature, and chill.

To prepare the sauce: In the food processor or blender, purée strawberries with sugar and liqueur. Strain through a fine-mesh strainer.

To assemble the dish: Unmold flan onto a serving platter. Spoon some of the sauce over it, and pass remaining sauce in a sauceboat.

Corona de Naranja
(Catalan: Corona de Taronja)
(Orange Flan in a Crown)

Nicolás is a tiny restaurant in the colorful quarter of Chamberi in Madrid—near Malasaña, one of the most animated districts in the city at night. José Antonio Méndez opened this family-run place in 1984. He features home-style, well-made dishes; among them a simple but delightful orange flan which inspired me to develop this recipe.

I find this flan makes a perfect combination with Orange Ice Cream (Helado de Naranja); I make it in a ring mold and put the ice cream balls in the center, surrounding the flan with the whipped cream garnish. Or it can be served with the garnish alone—it's delicious either way.

To serve 4 to 6:   Makes about 3 1/2 cups

For the caramel:

>   1/2 cup sugar

For the flan:

>   1 cup fresh orange juice
>   1 cup sugar
>   6 eggs

As a garnish:

>   1 cup heavy cream
>   2 tablespoons orange liqueur,
>   such as Gran Torres or Grand
>   Marnier
>   1 tablespoon sugar

To prepare the caramel: Caramelize a 4- or 5-cup ring mold with 1/2 cup sugar, proceeding as directed in Caramelized Coconut Flan (Flan de Coco al Caramelo).

Preheat oven to 350 degrees F.

To prepare the flan: In a bowl, beat well orange juice, sugar and eggs. Pour mixture into caramelized mold. Cover with foil and place inside a larger pan filled with boiling water halfway up the mold.

Bake in the preheated oven for about 40 minutes, or until a cake tester comes out clean. (You can also feel it with your fingertip; the surface should be slightly firm.)

To prepare the garnish and assemble the dish: When cold, unmold the flan onto a round serving dish. Whip the cream until it forms soft peaks.

Add liqueur and sugar and whip a little more, until stiff. Using a pastry bag, pipe cream decoratively around the sides of the flan.

Tarta de Limón Oriola
(Aunt Oriola's Lemon Tart)

This is an old recipe from my Aunt Oriola, a dessert I often asked her to make for me when she offered to bring something to my parties. It is not new-style cuisine or low in calories— rather, it's sinfully rich and worth every bite.

I have made one change: she used a pâte sucrée *as a crust, which is a French recipe; I use instead Crisp Pastry Crust (Pasta Akeláre), which I actually find much tastier—and certainly more Spanish!*

To serve 10 or 12

For the pastry:

> **1 recipe Crisp Pastry Crust**

For the custard:

> **4 eggs, separated, at room temperature**
> **1 (14-ounce) can sweetened condensed milk**
>
> **3/4 cup fresh lemon juice**
> **1 1/2 tablespoons lemon zest***
> **1/2 cup milk**

Preheat oven to 350 degrees F.

To prepare the pastry: Prepare the crust as directed in the recipe, using an 8- or 9-inch removable-rim tart pan or pie plate. Push dough up the sides to about 1 1/2 inches; try to make it very thin on the bottom, and thicker on the sides. Bake in the preheated oven for 30 minutes, or until golden.

To prepare the custard: In a large bowl, beat the 4 egg yolks with the condensed milk, lemon juice and lemon zest. Stir in milk. Beat egg whites until stiff but not dry. Fold them carefully into the mixture.

To prepare the tart: Pour custard into the crust and bake in the 350-degree F. oven for 35 to 40 minutes, or until top starts to get golden and a cake tester comes out clean. (During the baking process the filling will rise, but after it comes out of the oven it will fall to the crust level.) Serve at room temperature.

Tarta Templada de Limón
(Catalan: Pastís Tebi de Llimona)
(Warm Lemon Tart)

The idea for this zesty tart came from chef Toya Roqué of Azulete restaurant in Barcelona. It has a delightful balance of sweet and tart, rich and tangy.

To serve 6 to 8

For the pastry shell:

> *1 recipe Pie Pastry*

For the filling:

> *6 tablespoons unsalted butter, at room temperature*
> *1 cup sugar*
> *1 tablespoon lemon zest**
>
> *5 eggs, separated, at room temperature*
> *1/2 cup lemon juice*

To prepare the pastry shell: Preheat oven to 425 degrees F.

Roll out pastry thinly to fit a 10- or 11-inch removable-rim tart pan with low sides. Place a piece of foil over the pastry, and fill it with rice or beans. Bake in the preheated oven for 15 minutes.

Pick up the foil from the pastry by its edges and carefully lift it out of the pastry shell. Bake another 5 or 10 minutes, until lightly golden. Reduce oven temperature to 375 degrees F.

To prepare the filling: While pastry cooks, cream butter and sugar with lemon zest in the food processor until sugar is dissolved. Whirl in egg yolks, and then lemon juice.

Whip egg whites until stiff but not dry. Fold them into lemon mixture, and pour into the baked crust. Bake in the 375-degree F. oven for 35 to 40 minutes, or until golden on top. Serve warm. (If you make it ahead of time, warm it up for 10 minutes in a preheated 350-degree F. oven at the last moment.)

Tarta de Espinacas
(Sweet Spinach Tart)

This was my favorite among an array of irresistible desserts at Jolastoky, a superb restaurant in the Basque city of Bilbao owned by Sabino and Begoña Arana. Your most discriminating guests will be delighted with the combination of flavors in this tart. And although it looks fancy, it really is not difficult to make.

To serve 6 to 8

For the pastry shell:

>*1 recipe Puff Pastry, chilled*

For the custard:

>*2 cups milk*
>*Peel of 1 lemon*
>*1 cup sugar*
>*6 egg yolks*
>*1 (10-ounce) package frozen chopped spinach, thawed and drained*
>
>*1 tablespoon lemon juice, or to taste*
>*1/2 teaspoon freshly grated nutmeg*

For the meringue:

>*4 egg whites, at room temperature*
>
>*Pinch of salt*
>*1/3 cup sugar*

Preheat oven to 425 degrees F.

To prepare the pastry shell: Roll out pastry and cut it into 2 (10-inch) rounds (use a removable-rim pie bottom or a plate as a pattern). Cut your rounds cleanly with a knife; do not tear the pastry, or it will not rise properly. Using a sharp pointed knife, draw a circle on 1 of the rounds 2 inches from the edge (don't cut all the way through the dough, however, for better rising). Dip your finger in water and moisten a 2-inch area around the edge of the other round. Place round with the circle on top of the one with the moistened edge; lay it down carefully, but don't press down the dough or adjust the edges with your fingers, or pastry won't puff properly.

Immediately bake in the preheated oven for 10 minutes. (If you don't bake it immediately, keep it refrigerated.) Reduce heat to 375 degrees F. and bake for an additional 20 minutes, or until pastry is golden and the bottom starts to darken.

Remove pastry from oven and immediately cut, with a sharp knife, through the inner circle you made earlier, carefully lifting out the "lid." If there is any soft puff pastry inside the shell, scoop it out so you will be left with a neat round "box." Discard the lid (if you can resist having it as a snack).

This shell can be made up to 3 days ahead, and warmed up at the last moment in a preheated 300-degree F. oven for 5 minutes.

To prepare the custard: Heat milk with lemon peel in a saucepan. Cover and set aside for 10 minutes. In a bowl, beat together sugar and egg yolks. Discard lemon peel and add egg yolks/sugar to the hot milk. Cook over low heat, stirring constantly, until the mixture thickens enough to coat the back of a spoon. Squeeze spinach dry; stir it into the custard. Add lemon juice and nutmeg; taste for seasoning. Set aside.

To prepare the meringue: Beat egg whites with pinch of salt until stiff. Gradually beat in sugar.

To assemble the dish: Raise oven temperature to 425 degrees F.

Just before serving, heat the spinach custard gently and cook for about 5 minutes, stirring. Pour custard into the pastry shell and arrange meringue on top, spreading it to the edges of the filling. Fluff the surface with the bottom of a fork to make little peaks. Bake in preheated 425-degree oven for about 5 minutes, or until meringue is slightly golden. Serve immediately.

Tarta de Músico
(Catalan: Pastís de Músic)
(Musician's Tart)

Postre de músic, or musician's dessert, is one of Catalonia's simplest desserts—nothing more than a mixture of dried fruits and nuts. The name comes from the old days when musicians, usually young and poor, traveled around the countryside. They were not paid much but always got some food, and if their music was really good, a dessert treat: raisins, filberts, almonds, pine nuts—whatever the farmer had on hand.

Tarta de músico is a sophisticated version of that humble dessert made into a delicious tart.

To serve 8:   Makes 1 (10-inch) round tart

For the pastry shell:

> *1 recipe Pie Pastry, chilled*

For the filling:

> *1 cup (or 8 ounces) dried figs, Calimyrna or another moist type, stemmed*
> *1/2 cup (or 4 ounces) pitted dates*
> *1/2 cup (or 3 ounces) black raisins*
> *1/2 cup (or 3 ounces) golden raisins*
> *2 tablespoons unsalted butter*

> *1 tablespoon flour*
> *1 cup cold milk*
> *3/4 cup sugar*
> *3 egg yolks*
> *1/2 cup finest-quality Spanish brandy*
> *1/4 cup lemon juice*

For the topping:

> *1/3 cup hazelnuts (filberts)*
> *1/3 cup blanched almonds*

> *1/3 cup walnuts*
> *1/3 cup pine nuts*

As a garnish:

> 1 cup heavy cream
> 2 tablespoons finest-quality
>   Spanish brandy
> 1 tablespoon sugar

To prepare the pastry shell: Preheat oven to 425 degrees F.

Roll out chilled pastry dough to fit a 10-inch removable-rim tart pan. Place a piece of foil over the pastry, and fill the foil with pie weights, rice or beans. Bake in the preheated oven for 15 minutes. Pick the foil up by its edges and carefully lift it out of the pastry shell.

To prepare the filling: In a saucepan, combine dried fruits with 1½ cups water. Bring to a boil, reduce heat to low, cover and cook for 10 minutes. Uncover, increase heat to medium-high and cook, stirring, until there is no liquid left in the pan. Purée fruit in a blender or food processor.

Reduce oven temperature to 350 degrees F.

In a medium saucepan, melt butter; add flour and stir. Add cold milk and sugar, stir and cook over medium heat until sugar is melted. Meanwhile, in a bowl beat egg yolks with brandy; add to the hot milk and cook over low heat, stirring constantly, until the custard thickens, about 15 minutes. Add puréed fruits and lemon juice; taste to see if it has enough lemon juice and brandy. Pour mixture into prepared crust.

To prepare the topping: Toast hazelnuts in the 350-degree F. oven for 12 minutes. Rub them inside a damp cloth, so most of the skins come off. Toast almonds for 10 minutes, or until they start to color. Increase oven temperature to 375 degrees F. Sprinkle filberts, almonds, walnuts and pine nuts over the tart, and pat them down with your hand. Bake in 375-degree F. oven for 45 minutes, or until nuts and piecrust are golden.

To prepare the garnish: In a bowl, beat cream to soft peaks. Mix in brandy and sugar.

Serve at room temperature or slightly warm, accompanying each slice with a dollop of the cream.

Tarta de Piñones
(Catalan: Pastís de Pinyons)
(Pine Nut Tart)

Start preparation 5 or 6 hours ahead

Here is another classic Catalan idea: a tart of pine nuts over cabell d'angel *or angel's hair, a filling used very often for sweets in Catalonia. I had always wondered what* cabell d'angel *was made from—well, it's the equivalent of our spaghetti squash! And if you've never cooked one of these, you are in for a treat; they are really fun to do.*

You can usually buy little pine nut tartlets at pastry shops all over Catalonia, but I have had this exquisite tart, homemade, only at one of Barcelona's most elegant restaurants, Vía Veneto. José Monje, an enthusiastic and enterprising restaurateur, acquired it in 1980 and took on a noted young cook, Josep Bullich; together they set out to bring their cuisine to the top rank. I must add, it is my father's favorite when he wants to entertain someone lavishly—that's where he took my mother recently for their fiftieth wedding anniversary!

To serve 6 to 8

1 medium spaghetti squash	**1 cup sugar**
(about 3 pounds)	**1 cup pine nuts**
1/2 recipe Puff Pastry, chilled	
(make the whole recipe and	
freeze half)	

Steam the squash over boiling water until tender when pierced with a fork; it will take about 30 or 40 minutes.

To prepare the pastry: Roll out puff pastry to a 12 × 7-inch rectangle (or longer, if you have a long enough plate to serve it on). Cut out the rectangle with a sharp knife, making a clean cut; handle the pastry as little as possible. Place it on a baking sheet, prick the bottom all over with a fork and refrigerate for at least 1/2 hour.

Preheat oven to 350 degrees F.

To prepare the filling: Cut squash in half and discard the seeds (try to remove only the seeds and not the stringy part to which the seeds are attached). With a fork, scrape the sides of the squash interior and scoop out the "spaghetti," leaving only the skin.

In an oven pan, combine spaghetti squash with sugar and bake in the preheated oven, stirring occasionally, until squash is very tender and starts to brown from caramelizing; it should lose all its crunch and become a dark golden color. This may take 3 to 4 hours. Toward the end, you may want to cook it on the stove so you can watch better.

Increase oven temperature to 400 degrees F.

While squash cools, bake puff pastry for 12 minutes. During this time, prick it with a fork once or twice.

To assemble the dish: Spread squash filling over the pastry, leaving a border all around. Place pine nuts on top, pressing them into the filling. Bake in the 400-degree F. oven for about 30 minutes, or until nuts are golden. Serve barely warm or at room temperature.

Tarta de Santiago
(Santiago Almond Torte)

Can be made 1 or 2 days ahead

I enjoyed this torte at several restaurants in Madrid, and was puzzled to see that it was exactly the same every time—until I found out the story behind it from Félix Colomo, who serves it at his colorful Posada de la Villa. A "little old lady," Purita, used to make them at a restaurant she owned, which did not prosper; so she now prepares them at home and supplies them to other restaurants.

Tarta de Santiago is named after the Galician city of Santiago de Compostela. And sure enough, later on I found it all over Galicia, one of the best at the excellent Vilas restaurant in Santiago.

As this torte is not too sweet, it makes a delicious afternoon cake as well as a dessert. It goes very well with a glass of fine sherry or red wine, or even with a sharp cheese and fruit as dessert.

Makes 1 (9-inch) torte

1/4 pound unsalted butter, at
    room temperature
1 cup sugar
1 tablespoon lemon zest*
4 eggs, at room temperature

2 tablespoons finest-quality
    Spanish brandy
2/3 cup flour
1 1/2 cups whole almonds, finely
    ground

As a garnish:

About 3 tablespoons
    confectioner's sugar

Preheat oven to 350 degrees F.

Cream butter and sugar together until light in color. Add lemon zest and eggs; beat until smooth. Stir in 1/2 cup water and the brandy, add flour and mix well. (If batter curdles, don't worry about it). Fold in the almonds.

Butter a 9-inch springform pan and pour batter into it. Bake in the preheated oven for about 40 minutes, or until the center springs back when pressed lightly with your finger and the cake pulls away from the sides. Let stand for 10 minutes; then remove torte from mold and cool on a rack. When completely cooled, sprinkle top of the cake with finely sifted confectioner's sugar.

This torte can be prepared ahead of time, and will last for at least a week, if kept in a tin. If you make it ahead of time, sprinkle sugar on top at the last minute.

Bizcocho de Chocolate con Crema Inglesa
(Chocolate Torte with a Light Cream Custard)

These days there is as much of a passion for chocolate in Spain as there is in the United States, and most restaurants feature some kind of chocolate torte. I had one that left particularly fond memories at El Amparo, the outstanding restaurant in Madrid, and it inspired this recipe: it is chocolate-chocolate at its best. The light custard and candied orange peel make this a most distinctive dessert, but the torte stands very well on its own.

Serves 12:   Makes 1 (8- or 9-inch) torte

For the torte:

> 1/2 cup unsalted butter, at room
>   temperature
> 2/3 cup sugar
> 1/4 teaspoon salt
> 1/2 teaspoon vanilla extract
> 3 eggs
> 3/4 cup minus 1 tablespoon flour
> 1 tablespoon cornstarch
> 1/4 cup white bread crumbs,

> without crusts (see Bread
> Crumbs*)
> 11/2 ounces unsweetened baking
> chocolate
> 3/4 cup semi-sweet chocolate
> chips
> 2 tablespoons orange liqueur,
> such as Gran Torres or Grand
> Marnier

For the glaze:

> 4 tablespoons unsalted butter
> 2 ounces unsweetened baking
> chocolate

> 1/4 cup semi-sweet chocolate
> chips
> 1 tablespoon orange liqueur

For the custard:

> 13/4 cups half-and-half
> 4 egg yolks

> 2/3 cup sugar
> 2 tablespoons orange liqueur

For the candied orange peel:

> 12 strips orange peel, about 1/16
>   inch wide and 21/2 or 23/4
>   inches long (as directed below)
> 1 cup sugar

Preheat oven to 350 degrees F.

To prepare the torte: In a mixer or food processor, cream butter and sugar together with salt and vanilla. With the motor running, beat in the eggs. Combine flour, cornstarch and bread crumbs; beat into the mixture.

In a small heavy pan, melt chocolates together with liqueur, stirring over very low heat. As soon as they melt, remove from heat and blend into the torte mixture.

Butter an 8- or 9-inch cake pan or a springform pan. Line bottom with buttered parchment or brown bag paper.

Pour batter in and bake torte in the preheated oven until surface feels firm to the touch, about 25 minutes for an 8-inch mold and 20 minutes for a 9-inch mold. The center of the cake should seem a little underdone. Leave cake in the pan for 30 minutes. Invert onto a rack to cool. Remove paper from surface.

To prepare the glaze: While the torte cools, melt butter in a small heavy pan. Add chocolates and liqueur; slowly melt them together over very low heat, stirring. As soon as they melt, remove from heat.

Place cake on a rack over a plate, and pour glaze over. Smooth quickly with a spatula, spreading the glaze over the top and around the sides of the cake.

To prepare the custard: Scald the half-and-half in a nonmetallic pan. In a heavy-bottomed pan, beat egg yolks with sugar; cook over low heat, stirring, until slightly warm. Whisk in the half-and-half; stirring constantly, cook until the custard thickens enough to coat a spoon; it will take about 15 minutes. Add liqueur and whisk briskly to cool.

Pour custard through a fine-mesh strainer into a bowl. Place this inside a larger bowl filled with ice cubes. Stir the custard with a whisk until it is cool (it should be cooled immediately, so it will end up thick and smooth). Cover and refrigerate until serving time.

To prepare the candied orange peel: Using a small sharp knife, peel the orange in strips from pole to pole. Remove the strips with your fingers. From these, cut 12 even long and narrow strips, about 1/16 inch wide and 2½ or 2¾ inches long (they should be just a little under the length of the torte slice). Remove all pith, so you are left with only the thin orange part of the peel.

Combine sugar and 1 cup water in a saucepan, and bring to a boil. Add orange peel strips and cook them at a simmer, but not a boil, for 30 minutes. Remove peel to an oiled plate and let cool. The peel should be pliable, not brittle.

To assemble the torte: Cut the torte into 12 pieces. Pour custard onto a large round serving platter. Place pieces of torte over, in a circle, like flower petals. Arrange a piece of candied orange peel on top of each piece of torte, lengthwise.

(This torte can be prepared a day ahead, but it should be assembled with the cream sauce at the last minute so the bottom of the torte does not get soggy.)

Filloas con Piña y Salsa de Naranja
(Thin Pancakes with Pineapple in an Orange Sauce)

Filloas are a typical Galician dessert: thin pancakes filled with cream pastry and sautéed in oil. I had never cared for them until I tasted this version at Madrid's delightful Sacha restaurant. Owner Pitila Mosquera, who is from Galicia, adds a touch of originality to all her traditional recipes, and this is a fine example of her cooking talent.

To serve 4 to 6   Makes 12 to 14 pancakes

For the pancakes:

> 3 eggs
> 3/4 cup flour
> 3/4 cup milk
> 1/2 tablespoon sugar

> 1 teaspoon vanilla extract
> About 2 tablespoons butter for
>   cooking

For the filling:

> 2 egg yolks
> 1/3 cup sugar
> 1 1/2 tablespoons flour
> 3/4 cup milk

> 1/2 cup canned crushed pineapple
>   in its own juice (no sugar
>   added), drained

For the sauce:

> 1/4 cup sugar
> 1/3 cup finest-quality Spanish
>   brandy

> 1/3 cup orange liqueur, such as
>   Gran Torres or Grand Marnier
> 2/3 cup orange juice

To prepare the pancakes: In a blender or food processor, combine all pancake ingredients except the butter, and blend until very smooth. Let batter rest for about 30 minutes before cooking.

Prepare pancakes as directed in Thin Pancakes Stuffed with Crab (Crêpes de Txangurro) recipe. You should have 12 to 14 pancakes.

To prepare the filling: In a bowl, beat together egg yolks, sugar and flour until well mixed. Heat the milk in a small saucepan. Add milk to the egg mixture in a thin stream, stirring. Pour back into the saucepan and cook over low heat, stirring, until the custard thickens and coats the back of a spoon. Fold in the pineapple.

To assemble the pancakes: Spread 1 heaping tablespoon of the filling over each pancake, on the side that didn't get golden. Roll it like a cigar. Line *filloas* on a platter and reserve. (The *filloas* may be prepared up to this point and refrigerated until needed.)

To make the sauce: In a pan large enough to hold all the *filloas*, dissolve sugar in 1 tablespoon water. Cook over medium-high heat until it caramelizes and turns golden brown. Watch so it doesn't burn—but don't stir the pan, just shake it gently. Add brandy and orange liqueur; it will hiss, but don't worry. Ignite and flambé*—be careful not to burn yourself! Pour the orange juice into the pan to dowse the flames. Cook quickly over medium heat, stirring with a wooden spatula, until thickened and reduced a little— about 1 or 2 minutes (the sauce will continue to thicken when the *filloas* are added, so don't reduce too much now). Reduce heat to low and add *filloas*, basting them with the sauce until heated through.

Serve 2 or 3 *filloas* to each guest, with some of the sauce on top.

Terrina de Frutas con Muselina de Almendras (Fruit Terrine with Almond-Buttercream Filling)

Prepare one day in advance, or at least 10 hours ahead

This terrine, with the colorful fruits—strawberries, kiwi and papaya or mango—encased in a fluffy filling and surrounded by liqueur-soaked sponge cake, is one of the most visually attractive desserts in my repertoire. On my trips around Spain I've had similar renditions several times in Madrid, Barcelona and the Basque Country; but Peñas Arriba, the exceptional new-style restaurant in Madrid run by "Chiqui" Seco and chef Javier Otaduy, gave me the best recipe.

To make this cake you will need a 9 × 5-inch bread loaf pan and a 10 × 15-inch cookie sheet—and a little art to place the fruits so they come out in a colorful triangle when the slices are cut. The sponge cake, while easy to make, can be replaced by ladyfingers; you will need 2 (3-ounce) packages.

To serve 8 to 10

For the sponge cake:

> 4 eggs (2 whole and 2 separated)
> 3/4 teaspoon baking powder
> 1/4 teaspoon salt
> 3/4 cup sugar
>
> 1 teaspoon vanilla extract
> 3/4 cup flour
> 1/2 cup orange liqueur, such as
>   Gran Torres or Grand Marnier

For the filling:

> 13/4 cups (71/2 ounces)
>   confectioner's sugar
> 10 tablespoons unsalted butter,
>   at room temperature
> 1 cup blanched almonds, very
>   finely ground
> 11/4 cups heavy cream, whipped
>   to stiff peaks
> About 8 large strawberries,
>   stemmed
>
> 1 large kiwi (4 or 5 ounces),
>   peeled and quartered
>   lengthwise
> 1/2 large ripe papaya, peeled,
>   seeded and cut in 4 pieces
>   lengthwise (you can substitute
>   mango)

To prepare the sponge cake: Preheat oven to 400 degrees F. In the food processor or blender, beat 2 whole eggs and 2 egg yolks, baking powder, salt, sugar and vanilla until thick, about 2 minutes. Add flour; pulse a few times, just enough to blend—don't overmix. Transfer to a bowl. Whip 2 egg whites until stiff; fold them into batter lightly, without overfolding.

Butter a 10 × 15-inch cookie sheet or jelly roll pan, and line it with buttered wax paper. Pour in batter, evening it out with a spatula. Bake in the preheated oven for 8 to 10 minutes, just until it starts to color and feels firm to the touch; don't let it get golden. Turn it out onto a clean towel and carefully remove the wax paper while still warm. Cut off the edges.

Cut out cake into 2 rectangles: one as wide as the length of your bread loaf pan, and long enough to cover the long sides and bottom of it (9 × 9 inches). Cut out another rectangle to cover the top of the loaf pan (9 × 5 inches). Sprinkle both rectangles with the liqueur. Line sides and bottom of the loaf pan with the first rectangle and reserve the second.

To prepare the filling: Cream sugar and butter together. Add almonds and blend until thoroughly mixed. Transfer to a bowl. Fold in the whipped cream.

To assemble the terrine: Put a layer of filling over the bottom of the pan lined with the sponge cake. Cut off the tips and tops of strawberries and arrange them in a continuous line along the center of the pan; press the fruit down with your fingers into the filling, lining it up evenly. Cover with another layer of filling. Cut off tips and tops of the kiwi and papaya pieces. Arrange kiwi and papaya in 2 continuous lines next to each other, both cut side down, on top of the filling along the edges of the pan. Mound remaining filling on top, evening out with a spatula. Cover with reserved rectangle of the sponge cake, pressing down gently.

Cover pan with foil and place a weight on top. Refrigerate overnight or at least 9 hours before serving (in fact, it can be made up to 4 days ahead).

Serve on individual plates, cut into 3/4-inch slices, so that each colorful slice shows the pattern of the fruit.

Pudín de Frutas Secas al Licor de Naranja
(Dried Fruit Pudding with Orange Liqueur)

The next three recipes are all from my Aunt Oriola. They are great home-style fruit desserts (this one with dried, the others with fresh fruits); each has a distinctive touch that seems very Spanish to me. And naturally, they all use some of my family's products—whether wine, brandy or orange liqueur.

To serve 6 to 8

For the caramel:

  1/2 cup sugar

For the pudding:

  2 cups milk
  2 tablespoons unsalted butter
  2 cups white bread crumbs,
    without crusts (see Bread
    Crumbs*)
  1 cup orange liqueur, such as
    Gran Torres or Grand Marnier

  1/2 pound mixed dried fruits
    (light and dark raisins,
    apricots, dates, figs), chopped
  3 eggs, beaten

As a garnish:

  1 cup heavy cream, whipped
    with 2 tablespoons sugar and 1
    tablespoon orange liqueur

Preheat oven to 350 degrees F.

To prepare the caramel: Caramelize a 5-cup mold with 1/2 cup sugar, proceeding as directed in the recipe for Caramelized Coconut Flan (Flan de Coco al Caramelo).

To prepare the pudding: Bring milk to a boil and add butter, stirring until it melts. Combine with the bread in the food processor and whirl to form a thin paste. Transfer to a bowl and mix in the liqueur, fruits and beaten eggs. Pour into the prepared ring mold.

   Place mold inside a larger pan filled with boiling water halfway up the mold. Bake in the preheated oven for 40 minutes, or until a cake tester comes out clean.

To assemble the dish: Let cool 10 or 15 minutes before unmolding onto a round serving plate. Garnish with whipped cream, mounding it in the center.

Pinchitos de Fruta al Licor de Naranja
(Baked Fruit on Skewers Sprinkled with Orange Liqueur)

This dessert is a perfect, light end to a fine meal. In fact, I think this recipe works better in North America than in Spain, because my aunt used canned pineapple and we can get such good fresh ones here.

   For this recipe you will need 12 (10-inch-long) bamboo or wooden skewers. Soak them in water for 1/2 hour before using them, so they won't burn during broiling.

To serve 6

> 1/2 large pineapple, peeled, cored
> and cut into 4 (1/2-inch) slices,
> each cut into 1-inch wedges
> 4 medium bananas, cut into 1/2-
> inch slices
> 4 large seedless oranges, peeled
> and sectioned, with the
> membrane

> 1 teaspoon powdered cinnamon
> 1/4 cup sugar
> 2 1/4 cup orange liqueur, such as
> Gran Torres or Grand Marnier

Preheat broiler.

Skewer fruit, beginning and ending each skewer with pineapple, until you use up all the fruit.

Line a baking pan with aluminum foil and arrange skewered fruit in it. Mix cinnamon with sugar in a bowl, and sprinkle over fruit.

Broil fruit as close to heat source as possible, turning once, until browned—about 3 to 5 minutes. Remove from oven and sprinkle 1 teaspoon liqueur over each skewer. Serve immediately.

Peras al Vino Tinto
(Pears in Red Wine with Strawberry Sauce)

You can't go wrong with pears cooked in red wine—but these are the best ever. The natural tartness of the wine is perfectly balanced with the sweetness of the strawberry sauce.

To serve 6

For the pears:

> 6 large ripe, firm pears, such as
> Bartlett or Bosc
> 1 (750 ml) bottle full-bodied dry
> red wine

> 1/2 cup sugar
> 2 (2 1/2-inch) sticks cinnamon

For the filling:

> 3 ounces cream cheese, at room
> temperature
> 1/4 cup sugar

> 1/4 cup whipped cream
> Dash of finest-quality Spanish
> brandy

For the sauce:

> 3/4 pound fresh strawberries
> 1/4 cup sugar

To prepare the pears: Peel the pears and core them whole, from bottom to top, making a cylindrical hole. In a saucepan, bring wine with sugar and cinnamon to a boil. Turn heat to low and simmer pears in the wine for about 1/2 hour, or until they are very tender but not mushy. Keep basting pears with wine while simmering, so that they will take on the color of the wine. Remove pears from the pot and discard cinnamon sticks. Bring liquid to a boil and reduce it to 3/4 or 1 cup. Set aside.

To prepare the filling: Mix cream cheese with sugar in the food processor or blender. Transfer to a bowl and fold in whipped cream. Stir in dash of brandy, to taste.

With a pastry bag, pipe filling into pears. Place them in a bowl. Pour reduced wine over. Chill.

To prepare the sauce: Purée strawberries with the sugar in a blender or food processor until sugar dissolves completely. Chill.

To assemble the dish: At the last minute, cover pears with the strawberry purée, or pass sauce in a sauceboat.

Manzana Gratinada
(Catalan: Poma Gratinada)
(Apple Gratin)

I fell in love with this surprisingly simple, flavorful dessert at Azulete restaurant in Barcelona. The kind of apples chef/owner Toya Roqué uses in Spain are similar to our Golden Delicious, but I find that Pippin and Granny Smith work even better. Don't use Rome Beauties or other baking apples, as they are not firm enough.

To serve 6

For the apples:

2–21/2 pounds Pippin or Granny Smith apples	1 tablespoon lemon juice
	1 cup sugar

For the topping:

1 cup blanched almonds	4 tablespoons butter
1/2 cup sugar	2 eggs

To prepare the apples: Peel, core and cut the apples into thin crescents. Put them in a bowl with water to cover, acidified with lemon juice to keep them from browning.

In a pan large enough to hold all of the apple slices, combine the 1 cup sugar with 11/2 cups water; bring to a boil. Drain the apple crescents and add them to the pan. Cook at a boil for 5 minutes.

Butter a gratin dish or a small pie plate. Remove the apple slices from the syrup with a slotted spoon, and pile them into the baking dish.

Preheat oven to 425 degrees F.

To prepare the topping: Finely grind almonds and sugar in the food processor. Cut the butter into small pieces and add to mixture; whirl until smooth. Add the eggs and whirl to blend. Pour this mixture over the apples.

Bake in the preheated oven for 15 minutes or until top is puffed and golden. Serve warm.

Nueces Caramelizadas con Nata
(Caramelized Walnuts with Whipped Cream)

Baeza is a little village in Andalucía, 30 miles northeast of Jaén, just off the road from Madrid to the south. I had been told it was "worth the detour" to go for lunch at Juanito, a truck-stop restaurant owned by Juanito and Luisa Salcedo and their son, Damián. Luisa's good old peasant country cooking has become famous, and the roadside restaurant has received numerous awards.

So I decided to get up early one day and go there for lunch, on a trip from Madrid to Córdoba. It was packed—I learned later that it always is—and fortunately, it was worth it. Luisa has rescued traditional recipes from that part of Andalucía, which she executes with down-to-earth perfection. This dessert, in its simplicity, is a winner.

To serve 6

1 cup heavy cream	1½ cups (or 5 ounces) walnut
1 tablespoon sugar	halves
3 tablespoons honey	

Whip cream until it forms soft peaks; add sugar and whip to stiff peaks.

In a skillet, cook honey over medium heat until it starts to foam. Add walnuts and cook, stirring, until walnuts turn a dark golden color from the caramelized honey.

Place a mound of whipped cream in the middle of each individual serving plate or bowl. Arrange walnuts, right out of the pan, on top. Serve immediately, while walnuts are still hot. The whipped cream will just start to melt, with a very nice visual effect and a great texture contrast.

Pan de Higos y Chocolate
(Fig and Chocolate Loaf)

Excellent figs are produced in the area around Alicante, south of Valencia. One of the desserts I had at Els Capellans, in Elche, was pan de higos, which literally translates as fig bread; but rather than figs in a dough, this merely consisted of some wonderful local dried figs, pressed into the shape of a loaf of bread, with the addition of some powdered sugar. That gave me the idea for this easy yet terrific recipe. It is quite rich indeed, so this "loaf" will go a long way; a thin slice per serving may be more than enough. The good news is, it will keep for 2 or 3 weeks or even a month, in an airtight tin. It would also make a delightful little Christmas gift!

Serves about 12:   Yields 1 medium loaf

> 1 cup whole almonds
> 6 ounces semi-sweet chocolate
>   chips
> 1 pound small moist dried black
>   Mission figs, stemmed and cut
>   up

> About 1/4 cup confectioner's
>   sugar

Preheat oven to 350 degrees F. Toast almonds for 15 minutes. Immediately grind them finely in the food processor; add chocolate and whirl to mix. The chocolate will melt from the heat of the almonds and all will stick together. Add figs to food processor and whirl to combine well.

Butter a springform pan and sift in about 1 tablespoon confectioner's sugar. Coat pan with the sugar, and shake out the excess. (If you don't have a springform mold, line your loaf pan with a piece of foil, so it will be easier to unmold.)

Press the fig mixture firmly into the pan. Unmold onto a serving plate and sift some more confectioner's sugar over the top of the loaf. Serve at room temperature.

Higos Pasos Rellenos
(Figs Stuffed with Chocolate and Nuts)

At the end of a memorable meal and several desserts at La Muralla, the gastronomic haven in Huelva, in western Andalucía, I was served these figs as an after-lunch treat—and found myself going back for more. You can't go wrong with figs, nuts and chocolate; but the combination here is truly irresistible.

Makes 24 stuffed figs

For the figs:

> 1/4 cup sugar
> 1/2 cup orange liqueur, such as
>   Gran Torres or Grand Marnier

> 24 dried Calimyrna figs, or
>   another moist type

For the stuffing:

> 3 1/2 ounces bittersweet chocolate
> 1/4 cup shelled pistachio nuts
> 1/4 cup shelled walnuts

For the garnish:

> 24 walnut halves

To prepare the figs: In a saucepan, combine sugar with liqueur and 2 cups water. Bring to a boil and boil for 1 minute. Add figs, reduce heat to low and cook at a simmer for 10 to 15 minutes, or until the figs have softened slightly. Turn off heat and let figs steep in the syrup for ½ hour to an hour. Remove figs and reserve. Cook syrup over medium-high heat until just before it reaches thread consistency (220 to 225 degrees F. on a candy thermometer).

To prepare the stuffing: In a food processor, finely grind together the chocolate, pistachios and walnuts. Stir 1 tablespoon of the fig syrup into the chocolate mixture. Discard remaining liquid.

Preheat oven to 350 degrees F.

To assemble the dish: Cut off stem ends from the figs. With your finger, poke a hole in the stem end of each fig to make a pouch. Fill with some of the stuffing. Close up the fig opening by pinching it together firmly (don't worry if the figs don't close all the way).

Place figs, stem side up, on an ungreased baking sheet. Push them down slightly to make them stand upright. Press a half walnut into the opening of each fig. Bake for 12 minutes and serve immediately, while still warm, or at room temperature.

Tejas Gigantes
(Giant Tile Cookies)

Tiles are fun cookies to make, but these are particularly distinctive because of their size. I first had them at one of Madrid's fanciest restaurants, Zalacaín, where they bring you one giant tile on a silver platter as a treat with coffee, and the waiter breaks it into pieces with a spoon. Tile cookies are quite popular in Spain—especially in the Basque Country, for they originated in the town of Tolosa, near San Sebastián. Maybe that's why they are so special at Zalacaín, whose owner Jesús María Oyarbide is a Basque.

You will need three things to make these giant tiles successfully: (1) a dry day, (2) 2 (12-inch) pizza pans and (3) 1 empty 1.5-liter (magnum) Bordeaux-shaped wine bottle. Of course, I don't have much of a problem there because my family makes 3 wines—Viña Sol, Sangre de Toro and Coronas—in this size. So the worst that can happen is that you have to go to the liquor store, buy a magnum and then drink it before you can make these wonderful cookies—it will be worthwhile!

The reason you need a dry day is because in damp weather these tejas *will get soggy very quickly. I have made them, however, on a rainy day in Sausalito pretty close to dinnertime and they were still crisp when I served them. They won't last much longer; but that's not a big problem anyway, as it is unlikely there will be any left over.*

Makes 3 (10-inch) tiles

½ cup sliced almonds
½ cup slivered almonds
⅔ cup sugar
6 tablespoons flour
1 tablespoon cornstarch

Pinch of salt
1 teaspoon vanilla extract
2 egg whites
8 tablespoons unsalted butter

Preheat oven to 350 degrees F.

In a bowl, mix together almonds, sugar, flour, cornstarch, salt, vanilla and egg whites. Melt the butter in a small pan; don't let it get too hot. Stir butter into bowl and combine well.

Butter a 12-inch pizza pan. Pour one third of the batter in the middle of the pan. Using a fork, spread the batter so it covers a circle 2 inches from the sides of the pan. Spread as thinly as possible; if there are some holes don't worry, they will fill in during the baking.

Bake in the preheated oven for 8 to 10 minutes. After 7 or 8 minutes, watch carefully; the cookie should be golden in the middle and brown on the sides, but don't let it burn.

To form the tiles, have a 1.5-liter wine bottle ready by the time the cookie is baked. Use a long metal spatula to loosen it from the pan. Put the second pizza pan on top and flip it over. Holding the pan with one hand and the bottle with the other, flip the cookie gently over the bottle (the reason for flipping from one pan to the other is so that the better-looking side of the cookie will be on top).

The cookie will cool quickly and take the shape of the bottle—a giant tile. Leave it over the bottle for just a couple of minutes (if left too long, it tends to stick to the glass) and then remove the bottle, letting the cookie stand on its own.

Make the second and third tiles in the same manner. Make sure the pizza pan is very clean before buttering it again, and wipe off the bottle each time.

Even on a dry day, these *tejas* should be done not more than a few hours before serving time, as they are fragile and will absorb moisture. However, if they do lose their crunchiness, just reheat them in the oven and form them again. If you don't succeed in making a perfect tile the first time and it breaks, just put it on the buttered pizza pan again, reheat in the oven and re-form it.

"Panellets"
(Catalan Fall Cookies)

Halloween is a festivity unknown in Spain; however, we do celebrate November 1 as All Saints' Day. This is a national holiday—and a particularly important date for those whose name is not in the registry of saints, as they celebrate their saint's day November 1. You see, birthdays pass almost unobserved in Spain—in fact, it is considered impolite to congratulate a lady on her birthday—but saints' days are important festivities. So for instance, if your name is Theresa, you would have your saint's day on St. Theresa's day, October 15. But if your name is, say, Eve, since Eve was not a saint your saint's day will be November 1.

You may wonder what all this has to do with food. Well, Spaniards have a tendency to associate any religious holiday with something to eat, and panellets *(little breads, in Catalan) are a traditional treat on All Saints' Day. They are made only at this time of the year, when yams are in season. I have fond memories of spending many a cozy November 1 afternoon around a fireplace with a group of friends, eating more* panellets *than I should have, with yams and chestnuts roasted over a wood fire.*

The most typical panellets, panellets de piñones, *are made with the basic dough and just covered with pine nuts; similar confections can be found in the rest of Spain under the name* empiñonados, *literally translated as "covered with pine nuts." But there are many different kinds, and we traditionally serve a selection of them. I have chosen here a few favorites and given different quantities, which you may adapt according to your taste. I suggest you make the full* panellet *dough recipe and then 2 or 4 different flavors—the way we would do it in Spain.*

Panellet Dough:

Makes about 2 cups, or 1½ pounds

> *1 small yam or sweet potato (¼*
> *pound)*
> *1 cup sugar*
> *1½ cups blanched almonds,*
> *finely ground*
>
> *1 egg yolk*
> *½ teaspoon vanilla extract*
> *1 teaspoon lemon zest**

Boil yam until tender (about 30 minutes, depending on size). Peel and mash it; you should have about ½ cup. In a food processor, mix yam together with the rest of ingredients, until dough is soft. Let it sit for at least ½ hour before using in any of the following recipes.

Panellets de Piñones (Pine Nut *Panellets*)

Makes 18 to 20 cookies

> *½ recipe* Panellet *Dough*
> *About 1 cup pine nuts*
> *1 or 2 tablespoons milk*

Preheat oven to 350 degrees F.

Make small walnut-size balls and coat them with pine nuts. Brush them lightly with milk. Place on an oiled baking sheet, 1 inch apart. Bake in the preheated oven for 15 minutes.

Panellets de Chocolate (Chocolate *Panellets*)

Makes 15 to 18 cookies

> *¼ cup unsweetened ground*
> *chocolate or cocoa (preferably*
> *Dutch process cocoa)*
>
> *½ recipe* Panellet *Dough*
> *About ¼ cup ground blanched*
> *almonds or hazelnuts (filberts)*

Preheat oven to 350 degrees F.

Mix chocolate powder with dough. Shape dough into walnut-size balls and roll them in the ground almonds or hazelnuts. Place on an oiled baking sheet, 1 inch apart. Bake in preheated oven for 10 to 15 minutes, just until they start to color.

Panellets de Castañas (Chestnut *Panellets*)

Makes about 20 cookies

> 6 ounces chestnuts, peeled
> 1 cup milk
> 1/2 recipe Panellet *Dough*
>
> Pinch of nutmeg
> About 1/4 cup ground blanched
>   almonds or hazelnuts (filberts)

Preheat oven to 350 degrees F.

Simmer chestnuts in milk for 35 minutes, covered. Grind chestnuts with milk in the food processor; add dough and nutmeg. Shape dough into walnut-size balls and coat with ground almonds or hazelnuts. Bake as directed in Chocolate *Panellets* recipe.

Panellets de Café (Coffee *Panellets*)

Makes 8 to 10 cookies

> 1/4 recipe Panellet *Dough*
> 1 teaspoon instant coffee
>
> About 1 tablespoon sugar
> 8–10 whole coffee beans

Preheat oven to 350 degrees F.

Mix dough with instant coffee, shape into walnut-size balls and roll them in sugar. Put 1 coffee bean on top of each cookie, pressing it in slightly. Bake as directed in Chocolate *Panellets* recipe.

Panellets de Avellanas (Hazelnut *Panellets*)

Makes 10 to 12 cookies

> 1/4 recipe Panellet *Dough*
> 1/2 cup toasted hazelnuts
>   (filberts), peeled and finely
>   ground
>
> About 1 tablespoon sugar
> 8–10 whole hazelnuts (filberts),
>   toasted and peeled

Preheat oven to 350 degrees F.

Mix the dough with ground hazelnuts, shape in walnut-size balls and roll them in sugar. Place a whole hazelnut in the center of each cookie. Bake as directed in Chocolate *Panellets* recipe.

Panellets de Clavo (Clove *Panellets*)

Makes 8 to 10 cookies

> 1/4 recipe Panellet *Dough*
> 1/4 teaspoon ground cloves
> About 1 tablespoon sugar

Preheat oven to 350 degrees F.

Mix dough with ground cloves. Shape into walnut-size balls and roll them in sugar. Bake as directed in Chocolate *Panellets* recipe.

Panellets de Coco (Coconut *Panellets)*

Makes 10 to 12 cookies

> *1/4 recipe* **Panellet** *Dough*
> *1/2 cup sweetened shredded*
> *coconut*
> *About 1 tablespoon sugar*

Preheat oven to 350 degrees F.

Mix dough with coconut. Shape into walnut-size balls and roll them in sugar. Bake as directed in Chocolate *Panellets* recipe.

Pelotitas del Profesor
(Hazelnut Meringue Cookies)

The name of these cookies actually translates as "professor's little balls"—and naturally, there is a story behind it. When I had these meringue cookies at Madrid's Asturian restaurant La Máquina, former director Eduardo Méndez Riestra explained to me that the recipe comes from a bakery in a little Asturian town named Salas, whose owner was affectionately called "the professor." These cookies had no name, but one day a tourist who went to buy them asked the "professor" for his pelotitas—*a word she probably associated with the shape of the cookies. He naturally found that quite amusing, and from then on the cookies had a name. The "professor" died long ago, and today the cookies are still made at the same bakery by his niece.*

If you make these on a damp day, don't leave them uncovered or they might get soggy. Keep them in a tightly closed tin and they will last for quite a while.

Makes about 15 small cookies

> *1 cup hazelnuts (filberts)*   *1/2 teaspoon vanilla extract*
> *1/4 cup sugar*   *2 egg whites*

Preheat oven to 350 degrees F. Toast nuts for 15 minutes. Rub them inside a damp cloth, to remove most of the skins.

Grind nuts very finely, together with sugar, vanilla and 1 of the egg whites. Beat remaining egg white until very stiff (you should be able to turn the bowl over without the egg white falling out). Fold egg white into nut mixture until well mixed. Increase oven temperature to 400 degrees F.

Line a baking sheet with buttered parchment or brown bag paper. Using two teaspoons, drop small mounds of the batter onto the baking sheet, spacing them 1 or 2 inches apart. Bake in the 400-degree F. oven for 10 to 15 minutes, or until they start to brown.

"Carquinyolis"
(Hard Almond Cookies)

Carquinyolis *are typical Catalan cookies, found in different versions in most pastry shops of the region. They have one thing in common: they are always hard—sometimes too much so for my taste. These are just delightfully crunchy.*

Makes about 50 to 60 cookies

1¹/2 cups (¹/2 pound) blanched
  almonds
3 cups flour
1 cup sugar
1 tablespoon baking powder
¹/2 teaspoon salt

2 tablespoons lemon zest*
8 tablespoons chilled unsalted
  butter, cut into small pieces
3 eggs
1 teaspoon vanilla extract
1 teaspoon almond extract

Preheat oven to 350 degrees F. Toast almonds for 10 minutes (they will bake later with the cookies, so don't let them turn golden). Set aside.

In a food processor, combine flour, sugar, baking powder, salt and lemon zest. Cut butter into the dry ingredients with just a few pulses. Add eggs, vanilla and almond extract. Pulse a few times; don't overmix, the dough should not be too smooth. Transfer to a bowl and fold almonds into the dough quickly with your hands, until evenly distributed.

Butter a cookie sheet. Shape dough into 3 logs lengthwise on the cookie sheet; they should be about 2 to 2¹/2 inches wide and ³/4 to 1 inch high. The dough will spread during baking, so leave 1 inch between each log.

Bake in the preheated oven for about 25 to 30 minutes, or until dough starts to turn golden. Remove from oven and immediately, while still hot, cut logs into ³/4-inch-thick slices. Place the slices, cut side down, on the cookie sheet and return to the oven. Bake for another 15 to 20 minutes, or until golden.

These delicious cookies will keep for quite a while, stored in a tightly closed tin—but I've never been able to make them last more than a week!

ICE CREAMS AND SHERBETS

There are few better treats for an ice cream lover than homemade ice cream and sherbet. And indeed, with one of the excellent ice cream makers available today, the difference will be worthwhile. In the following ice cream and sherbet recipes, I have assumed that you have such a machine; but here are the directions if you don't have one.

To prepare ice cream without a machine: Refrigerate the mixture in a bowl until completely chilled. Freeze until firm about 1 inch from the edge of the bowl. Beat with an electric mixer to blend thoroughly. Cover and freeze until partially firm. Repeat process twice more. Freeze until set.

Sorbete de Vino Tinto a la Hierbabuena
(Catalan: Xarrup de Vi Negre a la Menta)
(Red Wine Sherbet with Mint)

This is an idea from Cal Joan, the quaint country restaurant in Vilafranca del Penedès—home of my family's winery. Naturally, Joan and now his son, Quico, have always used one of our wines, Coronas, to make this sherbet, and that's what I use myself. In any case, the secret to this recipe is to use a fine medium-bodied dry red wine; a harsh red will give you a harsh, unpalatable sherbet.

Makes 5 to 5½ cups

> 1 cup sugar
> 5 fresh mint leaves
> 1 (750 ml) bottle fine medium-
>   bodied dry red wine
>
> ½ cup fresh orange juice
> 3 tablespoons lemon juice

In a small pot, combine sugar and mint leaves with ½ cup water. Bring to a boil, and boil for 1 minute. Let cool and remove the mint leaves.

Pour wine into a nonmetallic bowl. Add sugar syrup, orange and lemon juice, and stir. Chill and make into sherbet according to the instructions for your ice cream machine.

Sorbete de Apio
(Celery Sherbet)

This is an understated, refreshing sherbet, perfect as a palate cleanser between courses. The idea came from Madrid's Cabo Mayor restaurant; owner Víctor Merino created it because he likes celery so much. Its success was a surprise even to him!

Makes 3 cups

> 1½ pounds celery, with leaves,
>   cut into ½-inch pieces
>
> ¼ cup lemon juice
> ¾ cup sugar

In a nonmetallic pan, bring to a boil 6 cups water with all the ingredients. Reduce heat to low and cook, covered, for 25 minutes.

Strain through a fine sieve, pushing the celery down with a spoon; return strained liquid to pan and cook over high heat until reduced to 3 cups. Chill and make into sherbet according to the instructions for your ice cream machine.

If you have kept the sherbet in the freezer, leave it out for 15 to 20 minutes before serving it, so it will not be frozen hard. Serve it in a wine or sherbet glass, for greater effect.

Sorbete de Gazpacho con Gambitas
(Gazpacho Sherbet with Bay Shrimp)

Gazpacho is such a refreshing, healthy vegetable combination, it is a natural to make a sherbet out of it. The idea comes from José Carlos Capel, the Madrid writer who has taught me a lot about Andalusian gastronomy. He has written about gazpachos, too, and while commenting on that subject over dinner one evening, he told me how delicious his gazpacho sherbet with tiny prawns was. And he was right!

This will make a perfect palate freshener between courses, whetting your appetite for the main dish, or before dessert, instead of a salad.

Makes 4 cups

For the gazpacho:

> 1 pound unpeeled ripe tomatoes,
>   cut up
> 2/3 cup chopped onion
> 1 teaspoon chopped garlic
> 1/4 English-type cucumber,
>   peeled and cut up
> 1 small red bell pepper, cored,
>   seeded and coarsely chopped

> 1 (12-ounce) can tomato juice
> 2 tablespoons sherry wine
>   vinegar or red wine vinegar
> 1 tablespoon finest-quality olive
>   oil, extra virgin if possible
> 3/4 teaspoon salt
> 1 or 2 tablespoons hot red salsa
>   picante or salsa jalapeña

As a garnish:

> 1/2 pound cooked bay shrimp or
>   small peeled cooked prawns
> 1 teaspoon olive oil
> 1/2 tablespoon sherry wine
>   vinegar or red wine vinegar

> 1/2–1 tablespoon hot red salsa
>   picante or salsa jalapeña
>   (optional)

To prepare the gazpacho: In a blender or food processor, purée tomatoes, onion, garlic, cucumber and red pepper. Add tomato juice, vinegar, oil, salt and 1 tablespoon *salsa.* Whirl to combine well. Taste for seasoning.

Strain gazpacho through a medium sieve. Measure and add water to equal 4 cups. Chill and make into sherbet according to the directions for your ice cream machine.

To prepare the garnish: If the shrimp or prawns you have bought are salty, rinse them under running water and pat them dry. Toss them in a bowl with the oil and vinegar. Taste for seasoning and add *salsa,* if desired. Let shrimp marinate for 1 to 5 hours. Drain shrimp on paper towels. Garnish each sherbet serving with a few of the shrimp.

Sorbete de Manzana con Pasas
(Apple Sherbet with Raisins)

Start preparation at least 6 hours in advance

Luis Irizar is considered by many the father of "New Basque Cuisine." After living and cooking in San Sebastián for many years, he moved to Madrid and in October 1982 opened Irizar restaurant. His classic Basque recipes have a personal, interesting approach to cooking; an example is his apple sherbet, which inspired me to develop this recipe. It can be served between courses or as a light dessert, maybe accompanied by some of the cookies in this book.

Makes 6 to 7 cups sherbet

> 1/2 cup dark raisins
> 1/2 cup dark rum
> 2 pounds tart apples, such as
>   Gravenstein or Granny Smith

> 2/3 cup sugar
> 4 cups apple cider

Soak raisins in the rum for at least 4 or 5 hours.

Peel, core and quarter apples; place in a saucepan with sugar and cider. Cook over medium heat, uncovered, until very tender; it should take about 30 minutes. Strain apples through a medium sieve or a food mill. Stir in raisins and rum.

Chill and make into sherbet according to the directions for your ice cream machine. (Because of the consistency of the apples, it may take this sherbet a little longer to freeze.)

Sorbete de Moras
(Blackberry Sherbet)

Blackberries make wonderful ice creams or sherbets. I had a memorable sorbete de moras *at Josetxo—my favorite restaurant in Pamplona, capital of Navarra—which inspired this recipe. It made a perfect, light dessert after an excellent summer lunch.*

Makes about 4¹/₂ cups

> **1 pound fresh blackberries**
> **1¹/₂ cups sugar**

> **1 tablespoon lemon juice**
> **1 cup heavy cream**

Purée the blackberries in a food processor or blender. Combine sugar with 7 cups water in a large pan and add blackberry purée. Bring to a boil and cook over high heat until reduced by half. Strain to remove the seeds. Let cool. Add lemon juice and cream.

Chill and make into sherbet according to the directions for your ice cream machine.

Leche Merengada
(Meringued Milk Sherbet)

This is my version of leche merengada. *The one you find all over Spain in bars and ice cream and coffee houses during the summertime has no liquor in it, but I find it much better this way! It would make a lovely dessert on a hot summer evening, perhaps accompanied by Hard Almond Cookies ("Carquinyolis").*

The origin of leche merengada *is traced to Valencia, from where it went to Catalonia. It appeared for the first time in 1747, and was very popular throughout the nineteenth century, along with other iced drinks and ice creams. My favorite place to have it is at Chocolatería de Santa Catalina (St. Catherine's Chocolate House) in Valencia. Don't miss it if you are there in the summertime.*

Makes about 1¹/2 quarts

1/2 cup sugar
Peel of 1 lemon
1 (2¹/2-inch) stick cinnamon
6 tablespoons orange liqueur,
    such as Gran Torres or Grand
    Marnier

1 quart half-and-half
2 egg whites, at room
    temperature
1/4 cup finest-quality Spanish
    brandy, or to taste

As a garnish:

Powdered cinnamon

In a saucepan, mix sugar, lemon peel, cinnamon stick, orange liqueur and half-and-half. Cook over low heat for 10 minutes. Cover and steep for 15 minutes. Transfer to a bowl. Discard lemon peel and cinnamon stick.

Beat the egg whites until stiff. Fold them into half-and-half mixture. Add brandy to taste. Chill. Make into sherbet according to the directions for your ice cream machine.

Sprinkle the top with powdered cinnamon and serve.

Helado de Miel con Nueces y Dátiles
(Date-Nut Honey Ice Cream)

Jockey, the great Madrid restaurant, serves a honey ice cream which inspired this recipe. I thought some dates and walnuts would go well here; and they surely do.

Makes 5 to 6 cups ice cream

4 cups milk
4 whole eggs
1/2 cup honey

1 cup pitted, chopped dates
1/2 cup chopped walnuts

In a large heavy-bottomed pan, beat together milk, eggs and honey. Heat mixture and cook over low heat, stirring constantly, until it thickens—about 15 minutes. (If it should curdle, don't worry; it won't be noticeable after processing the ice cream.) Chill.

Fold dates and nuts into the custard. Make into ice cream according to the directions for your ice cream machine.

Helado de Naranja
Catalan: Gelat de Taronja
(Orange Ice Cream)

I've had orange ice cream at several restaurants in Barcelona, perhaps the most memorable at Florián, a small refined establishment where Rosa Grau presents a very personal, imaginative cuisine. She and her husband, Javier García-Ruano, opened Florián in 1980 and have since built up an excellent reputation for their quality and uniqueness.

Rosa's orange ice cream inspired me to develop this recipe, acclaimed by many guests as the most delicious ice cream they've ever had. Hers didn't have candied orange rind, but I find it contributes a particularly interesting texture which combines very well with the richness of the ice cream and the freshness of the orange juice. (It is important to use fresh orange juice.)

This ice cream goes particularly well with Orange Flan in a Crown (Corona de Naranja). A nice way to serve it is by scooping balls of ice cream into the center of the flan ring.

Makes about 1 quart

For the candied zest:

1 cup sugar
About 2 tablespoons finely
  chopped orange zest*

1 cup freshly squeezed orange
  juice, strained

For the ice cream:

2 egg yolks
1/2 cup half-and-half

Pinch of salt
1 cup heavy cream

To prepare the candied zest: Combine sugar and orange zest in a saucepan with 1/2 cup water. Bring to a boil and continue to cook at a boil until the syrup darkens or reaches 250 degrees F. on a candy thermometer (firm-ball consistency). Remove from heat and immediately add orange juice to the syrup. Stir well; the caramelized zest will stick together in a candied lump. Pour through a fine sieve into a container, reserving the orange juice syrup. Spread the candied zest on a small buttered dish to let it dry.

To prepare the ice cream: Beat egg yolks, half-and-half and salt together in a small heavy saucepan. Cook over low heat, stirring all the time, until the mixture thickens enough to coat the back of a spoon; it will take about 15 minutes. Add reserved orange juice syrup to the egg mixture. Pour through a fine sieve into a bowl, and chill.

Beat heavy cream until it forms stiff peaks; fold it into the custard mixture. Don't worry about the lumps of cream you will probably get; they will disappear when processing the ice cream. Chop candied zest and add to the ice cream mixture.

Make it into ice cream according to the directions for your ice cream machine.

Helado de Crema Catalana con Salsa de Avellanas
(Catalan: Gelat de Crema Catalana amb Salsa d'Avellanes)
(Catalan Caramel Custard Ice Cream with Hazelnut Sauce)

Crema Catalana *is a delicious custard served very often as dessert in Catalonia. The nicest thing about it is the caramelized sugar on top, which is made by sprinkling sugar over the custard and burning it with a red-hot iron plate. In the old days it was done with the central iron circle in the wood stoves used in the homes. These stoves had iron tops, built into concentric circles; you would take out with a handle as many circles as necessary to fit the size of your pan. The central circle would be about 3 inches in diameter, and this was used to burn the sugar top. You raised it with a handle and just touched the surface of the sugar so it would caramelize.*

These days such iron plates are sold commercially in Spain, but are seldom found in the United States. Instead, you can use a flat metal spatula and heat it on a gas stove or another heating element with a flame. Or you can caramelize the sugar and make "angel hair" to top each ice cream mold, as directed below.

The idea of making crema catalana *into an ice cream comes from the always imaginative Jaume Bargues, chef/owner of Jaume de Provença restaurant in Barcelona. This is characteristic of his talent: taking a very old, classic Catalan recipe and adding his personal touch to make it into a creation of his own.*

To serve 8:   Makes 16 (1/4-cup) molds, or about 1 quart

For the ice cream:

> *3 cups half-and-half*
> *1 cup heavy cream*
> *1 vanilla bean, split in half*
> *   lengthwise*
> *Peel of 1 lemon*

> *8 egg yolks*
> *2/3 cup sugar*
> *6 tablespoons finest-quality*
> *   Spanish brandy, or to taste*

For the sauce:

> *1/3 cup hazelnuts (filberts)*
> *2 cups milk*

> *4 egg yolks*
> *1/4 cup sugar*

For the caramel topping:

> *4 or 5 tablespoons sugar*

To make the ice cream: In a nonmetallic pan, heat half-and-half and cream gently with vanilla bean and lemon peel until just before it boils; cover and set aside for 10 to 15 minutes. Remove and reserve lemon peel and vanilla bean.

In a heavy-bottomed saucepan, beat egg yolks and sugar with a whisk. Slowly whisk cream mixture into eggs. Cook over low heat, stirring constantly, until the mixture thickens and coats the back of a spoon; it should take about 15 minutes. Remove from heat and briskly whisk to cool off.

Stir in brandy. Let cool at room temperature. Chill and make into ice cream according to the directions for your machine.

Fill 16 (1/4-cup) molds with the ice cream, cover and store in the freezer for at least 1/2 hour. Run a knife around the edges of each mold. Dip molds for just a few seconds in hot water and unmold onto a baking sheet. Put them back in the freezer until the last minute; they must be frozen very hard by serving time.

To prepare the sauce: Preheat oven to 350 degrees F. Toast hazelnuts for 12 minutes. Rub them in a damp cloth to remove most of the skins. Grind them very finely in the food processor.

Heat milk with reserved lemon peel and vanilla bean until just before it boils; cover and set aside. In a saucepan, beat egg yolks and sugar; make custard in same manner as above. Discard lemon peel and vanilla bean. Stir in ground hazelnuts (if they form lumps, blend in food processor until smooth). Refrigerate until serving time.

To assemble the dish: Just before serving, pour about 2 tablespoons of the sauce on each plate. Place a metal spatula over stove flame until red hot (unless you are making "angel hair" as directed below). Sprinkle about 1 teaspoon sugar on the flat top of each ice cream mold, and immediately burn sugar with the red-hot metal spatula. Place 2 ice cream molds on each plate, and serve immediately.

Alternatively, to make "angel hair" caramel topping: Caramelize 4 tablespoons sugar with 1 tablespoon water, proceeding as directed in the Caramelized Coconut Flan (Flan de Coco al Caramelo) recipe. Do not let the caramel get dark; remove from heat as soon as it turns light golden, since the caramel will continue to cook and darken.

Stir caramel with a fork to cool. After 1 or 2 minutes, lift the fork from the caramel; when you see that threads begin to form, "string" the threads over each ice cream mold, working quickly with the fork. The caramel topping should not be thick—just a thin latticework of "angel hair" over each one.

Helado de Pasas al Pedro Ximénez
(Raisin Ice Cream with Cream Sherry)

The idea of combining a raisin ice cream with sherry would have to come from Jerez—of course! Outside the Sherry district I've had it with Chocolate Sauce (Salsa de Chocolate), which is a nice dessert too; but only in the south have I tasted it with a dash of cream sherry. The first time was at El Faro, one of Cádiz's most colorful restaurants. Gonzalo Córdoba started the restaurant as a small eating spot in the old part of the city where he served fresh fish from the bay, plainly cooked. Today his menu is quite extensive, still featuring some of the best seafood from the nearby waters, based on traditional recipes from the area.

Another restaurant worth mentioning which features this ice cream is the charming, casual Bigote (Moustache, the nickname of the founder) in Sanlúcar de Barrameda. This is a tavern-style eatery where Bigote's sons, Paco and Fernando Hermoso, serve the simplest fisherman-type cooking for their top-quality local fish. After a feast of seafood, nothing could have been better than their raisin ice cream.

Makes about 7 cups

1 cup dark raisins
1/2 cup finest-quality Spanish
   brandy
1 quart milk
1 cup sugar

8 egg yolks
About 1 ounce per person of a
   fine Spanish cream sherry, or a
   Pedro Ximénez

Soak raisins in the brandy for at least 2 to 3 hours.

Scald milk in a saucepan. In a bowl, beat sugar together with egg yolks. Beat into the hot milk, stirring. Cook over low heat, stirring all the time, until it thickens and coats the back of a spoon; it should take about 15 minutes. Set aside.

Drain the raisins, reserving the brandy. Chop the raisins very finely in the food processor or blender; add them with the brandy to the custard. Let cool to room temperature and chill. Make into ice cream according to the directions for your ice cream machine.

Serve in individual bowls, pouring sherry on top.

Helado de Frutos Secos al Caramelo con Salsa de Chocolate
(Caramelized Nut Ice Cream with Hot Chocolate Sauce)

Wallis is a new, very "in" restaurant in Madrid, with an elegant decor and most interesting cuisine. Chef/owner Iñaki Izaguirre blends very innovative ideas with some old classics from his home region, the Basque Country where he was born, and Navarra, where he lived and cooked for a long time. After tasting an impressive array of his specialties, he recommended his copa Don Ignacio for dessert, which I loved, and it gave me the idea to develop this recipe.

Makes 5 1/2 cups

1/2 cup blanched almonds
1/2 cup hazelnuts (filberts)
1 cup sugar
1/2 cup walnuts or walnut pieces
4 cups milk
1 (2-inch) stick cinnamon

8 egg yolks
1/2 cup finest-quality Spanish
   brandy
1/4 cup honey
1 recipe Chocolate Sauce

Preheat oven to 350 degrees F. Toast almonds and hazelnuts for about 12 minutes, or until almonds start to color. Rub hazelnuts in a damp cloth to remove most of the skins.

In a skillet, caramelize 1/2 cup sugar (see Caramelizing*) by dissolving it with 1 or 2 tablespoons water. Cook over medium heat, until it starts to turn golden. Add almonds, hazelnuts and walnuts; stir with a wooden spoon, until nuts are coated with caramel and acquire a dark, golden color. Transfer caramelized nuts to a large buttered plate, spreading them out. When they have cooled and hardened, grind them very finely in the food processor. Set aside.

In a saucepan, scald milk with the cinnamon stick. Meanwhile, in a bowl, beat egg yolks together with remaining 1/2 cup sugar. Whisk egg mixture into the hot milk and cook on low heat, stirring constantly, until custard thickens and coats the back of a spoon—about 15 minutes. Turn off heat; stir in brandy, honey and ground nuts. Let cool at room temperature. Chill. Make into ice cream according to the directions for your ice cream machine.

Serve in individual bowls, pouring hot chocolate sauce on top.

BEVERAGES

Sangría
(Red Wine and Fruit Punch)

This is my personal recipe for sangría, the refreshing, popular Spanish punch. It is a very colorful drink for a party, great for the summertime. I serve it in a large glass bowl, and peel the lemons and oranges leaving the skins in one piece, so they look like festive spirals hanging from the sides of the bowl.

The quantities of brandy, orange liqueur and gin can be adjusted at your discretion; I always pour rough amounts, depending on my mood—and my guests. If you find you went overboard, just add more wine, fruits, soda, etc., and make more of it. I never have any left over!

I must add that it is much against the will of my brother Miguel, our perfectionist winemaker, that I give out this recipe. It is his strong feeling that wine should never be mixed with soda and fruit—and he is right, in fact. But I remember our teenage summer parties when he would skillfully mix healthy amounts of our winery products into tasty punches, which kept everybody going merrily until hours later than our parents would have liked. Well, that's what sangría is about—a drink not to be taken seriously, but just for the fun of it.

To serve 8 or more

3 (750 ml) bottles full-bodied dry
  red wine
2 large lemons, peel cut in one
  long spiral, sliced thin
2 large oranges, peel cut in one
  long spiral, sliced thin
2 large peaches (when in season),
  cut in sections
3 tablespoons sugar, or to taste
1/2 cup finest-quality Spanish
  brandy, or to taste

1/2 cup orange liqueur, such as
  Gran Torres or Grand Marnier,
  or to taste
1/4 cup gin, or to taste
Any other fresh fruits such as
  strawberries and grapes (except
  melon)
2 or 3 (10-ounce) bottles club
  soda
Ice cubes

Place all ingredients, except soda and ice cubes, in a large glass bowl or pitcher. Stir well. Taste to adjust ingredients if necessary. Cover and refrigerate for at least 4 hours before serving. At the last minute, add soda and ice cubes. (If you make it more than 6 hours before serving, add fruits like strawberries at the end, so they don't get mushy.)

Zurracapote
(Spiced Red Wine)

Prepare at least two days in advance

I learned about this zesty wine drink from José Ramón Aguiriano at the historic restaurant Dos Hermanas (Two Sisters) in Vitoria, founded by his grandmother and grandaunt more than a century ago. Today José Ramón continues their fine cooking tradition.

Vitoria is the capital of the southern Basque province of Álava, home of the fine red wines of Rioja Alavesa. I have had zurracapote *there cold and warm, mild and explosive —depending on the proportions of wine, fruits and their grape alcohol,* aguardiente—*but always a treat.*

To serve 4 to 6

(Yields about 1 quart)

1 (750 ml) bottle medium-bodied
  dry red wine
1/4 cup sugar
3 (2 1/2-inch) sticks cinnamon

Peel of 1 lemon
1/3 cup finest-quality Spanish
  brandy

Bring one third of the wine slowly to a boil with the sugar, cinnamon and lemon peel. Simmer for 15 minutes over low heat. Turn off heat; add remaining wine and the brandy, and stir.

Transfer to a plastic or glass container, cover and leave at room temperature for at least 48 hours to mature.

Serve at room temperature, strained into glasses.

"Cremat"
(Catalan Hot Coffee and Brandy)

This is a very old, classic recipe from the Catalan fishermen of the Costa Brava, the coastal area north of Barcelona. They have traditionally prepared this comforting beverage to warm their bodies as well as their spirits while singing their sensual songs, habaneras.

Toward the end of the nineteenth century, many Catalans emigrated to Cuba to seek their fortunes; when they came back, full of good memories of the "Caribbean Pearl"—as they called it—and its beautiful women, they sang melancholy songs evoking days past, named habaneras *after the city of Havana. They had discovered* cremat *there, the great combination of Antilles rum and Cuban coffee; and back home they continued to enjoy the beverage—often substituting the local brandy for the rum—together with their nostalgic songs. After the long day's work at sea, the* cremat's *flames provided the perfect accompaniment for the evening.*

Today there are performances of habaneras *held during the summer in the Costa Brava; the fishermen sing them while* cremat *flows abundantly.* Habaneras *reflect the exuberant flavor of the tropical island: lyrical hymns to distant dreams, nostalgia and love. Perhaps one of the most popular is "La Bella Lola" ("Beautiful Lola"), and the lyrics illustrate those feelings:*

> *After a year without seeing land,*
> *because the war prevented it,*
> *I went to the port to find*
> *the one that I adored.*
> *Ah! what a pleasure I felt*
> *when at the beach she waved her handkerchief at me,*
> *then she came to me and hugged me,*
> *and in that embrace I thought I'd die.*

In Catalonia, cremat *is traditionally prepared in a wide, flameproof casserole—as I've had it at L'Avi Pau in Cunit, a restaurant famous for its theatrical presentation of* cremat. *This beverage is more fun to prepare in front of your guests; it can be heated over a chafing dish burner.*

To serve 6 to 8:   Yields about 6 cups

1¹/₂ cups finest-quality Spanish brandy	*5 cups freshly brewed, strong hot coffee*
¹/₄ cup sugar	*1 tablespoon coffee beans*
1 (2- or 3-inch) stick cinnamon	
3 strips each lemon and orange peel, cut with a vegetable peeler from pole to pole	

In a wide flameproof casserole, preferably of clay, heat brandy with sugar, cinnamon, lemon and orange peels. When hot, ignite with a match and flambé* for about 1 minute, stirring with a ladle. Dowse the flames with the coffee. Add coffee beans and serve immediately, ladling into coffee cups.

"Euskal Akaita"
(Basque Coffee with Brandy and Prunes)

The recipe for this traditional Basque coffee was given to me by Juan José Lapitz, the gastronomic writer who has been my main guide and mentor throughout my visits to Basque Country. He prepared it for me at the Basque Gastronomic Society in San Sebastián—where only men are members and cooks—after a dinner cooked by him and the society's president. It was indeed the finishing touch of a superb meal!

Makes 8 (3/4-cup or 6-ounce) servings

1 1/2 cups plum brandy, such as
  slivovitz, or a fine-quality
  Spanish brandy
1/3 cup dark brown sugar
4 cups freshly brewed strong hot
  coffee

8 dried prunes, pitted
1 cup heavy cream, slightly
  whipped, just to give it some
  body
1 teaspoon powdered instant
  coffee

In a jug, mix brandy and sugar; stir. Add hot coffee. Place a prune in each glass or snifter, and pour in coffee mixture. Float the cream on top and sprinkle instant coffee over the cream.

Queimada
(Witch's Brew)

Catalonia has cremat, Basque Country has euskal akaita—and Galicia has queimada. And in the good Galician tradition, this drink has a background of superstition. It is the brew around which goblins and meigas (Galician for witches) are conjured up while the cauldron flames in the dark and bewitching songs are chanted in low, monotonous tones.

That's the story, as was told to me by a cheerful group of Galicians around a midnight queimada at Galloufa, a cozy restaurant in the little village of Villagarcía de Arosa. Just about every Galician has a recipe for queimada, and one thing you cannot reproduce here is Galloufa's excellent grappa-style spirit.

After all I've said, obviously this is a great drink to prepare in front of your guests, so I have adapted the recipe accordingly. And if possible, serve it from a wide, shallow flameproof clay casserole—the effect will be even more spectacular.

To serve 8

6 tablespoons sugar
2 cups grappa or a fine-quality
  Spanish brandy
2 cups medium-bodied dry red
  wine

Peel of 1 large lemon
1 large Pippin or Golden
  Delicious apple, peeled, cored
  and cut in wedges
1 tablespoon coffee beans

In a heavy-bottomed skillet, dissolve sugar with 1 or 2 tablespoons water; cook over medium-high heat until sugar caramelizes and turns dark gold. Add the grappa or brandy (it will hiss, but don't worry) and scrape with a spatula to dissolve the caramel. Meanwhile, heat wine in a separate pot. Transfer caramel/brandy mixture to a round clay casserole or whatever container you are serving from. Add lemon peel, apple and coffee beans.

Right away, so the brandy stays hot, take the casserole to the room where your guests are. Ignite with a match and flambé.* Now you can turn off the lights and invoke the witches! Stir the *queimada* with a long spoon for a few minutes, while flames beautifully light the room in the dark. . . .

When you have had enough of a show, dowse flames with hot red wine. Serve very warm in small glasses or cups.

A Tour of
SPAIN'S
FINEST
WINE
REGIONS

To understand Spanish wine, it is important to realize that *everybody* in Spain drinks it. Wine for Spaniards is a staple, the way milk is for Americans; it is not a luxury, as it is here. Spain's per capita consumption is 15 gallons—compared to 2.3 gallons in the United States.

The Phoenicians and the Greeks, in the fifth and fourth centuries B.C., were the real initiators of wine growing in Spain. Later on, 2,000 years ago, the Romans established and extended the cultivation of the vines. At that time, more than 100 varieties of *Vitis vinifera* wine grapes were grown in the Iberian Peninsula.

Spain has 4.2 million acres of land planted in vineyards—more than any other country in the world. Yet the average annual wine production in the last decade has been about 800 million gallons, so it is only the number four producer after France, Italy and the Soviet Union.

There are 30 wine-growing areas in Spain covered by an Appellation of Origin (Denominación de Origen), or specific regions controlled by legislation which regulates their viticulture and winemaking practices—equivalent to the French Appellation Contrôlée or the Italian Denominazione d'Origine Controlata. This chapter will be a tour only of the main regions, those I feel produce today the most interesting wines.

Very broadly, Spain can be divided into three main wine-producing areas: (1) The south, with the highest temperatures and most sun, is the home of the great aperitif and dessert wines in areas such as Sherry, Montilla-Moriles and Málaga. (2) The drier, arid central zone makes a wide range of sound but less delicate wines for everyday drinking. (3) The northern belt of Spain—Galicia, Upper Duero, Rioja and Catalonia—for reasons of soil as well as climate produces the great Spanish table wines.

RIOJA

The Denominación de Origen Rioja is part of the upper valley of the Ebro River; it gets its name from one of its tributaries, the Oja River (Río Oja). North and south of the Ebro the land is rugged, with few but fertile plains, making it one of the best agricultural areas of Spain. The rivers play an important role in Rioja; besides the Oja, there are several Ebro tributaries. The gentle slopes rising above the rivers are the home of many of the region's vineyards.

The Tirón, the Oja and the Najerilla rivers form the Rioja Alta (High Rioja). Farther east, from the cities of Logroño to Alfaro, four more Ebro tributaries—the Iregua, the Leza, the Cidacos and the Alhama—form the Rioja Baja (Low Rioja). From the mouth of the Tirón River to that of the

Alhama, the Ebro descends 725 feet, so there is a big change in climate and vegetation between these two areas. The western region, or High Rioja, is influenced by the Atlantic Ocean; whereas the eastern, Low Rioja, has a Mediterranean climate.

A third region is named Rioja Alavesa after the province of Álava, north of Rioja Alta. According to Professor Antonio Larrea, enologist and Rioja historian, Rioja Alta produces better wines for aging, because of the climate; whereas the wines of Rioja Alavesa are softer and with less acidity, better for earlier drinking.

The Grapes

There may have been vineyards in Rioja 5,000 years before Jesus Christ, but the heyday of Rioja came after the phylloxera plague started in France in the 1860s. As the great vineyards of Bordeaux became infested with the insect, some French winemakers went to Spain and established themselves in Rioja, which is only 300 miles south. They introduced their vinification and aging methods, most significantly the use of oak. Eventually phylloxera also hit Rioja and the rest of Spain, until at the turn of the century, the method of grafting onto American phylloxera-resistant rootstock was developed and the vineyards were replanted.

These same grapes continue to be grown today. The reds are mostly Tempranillo and Garnacha (the French Grenache), which make up 30 and 40 percent of Rioja's vineyards respectively, with tiny quantities of Graciano and Mazuelo. For the whites, it is mainly Viura (the Macabeo of Catalonia) with 13 percent of the total. The noble European grapes, such as Cabernet and Merlot, have been planted only experimentally and are not authorized for wines bearing the Denominación de Origen Rioja.

The total vineyard acreage in Rioja is 100,000 acres. Most of the wineries don't own vast vineyards; the largest is probably owned by CUNE, with over 1,000 acres, and Domecq with 700 to 800 acres planted. There are 60 *bodegas* which make wine and label it, and about 40 of them export some of the wine they produce. In a normal year, the total Rioja production is 29 million gallons. Harvest rarely starts there before mid-October, whereas in Catalonia or Jerez, for example, it usually starts in early September.

The Expansion of the Seventies

The late sixties saw the beginning of the arrival of outside capital in Rioja. Some of the large *bodegas* of Jerez came into the area, acquiring old established wineries such as Paternina and Franco Españolas. But the great expansion came between 1970 and 1973; several new wineries were built, among them Domecq, Olarra, Marqués de Cáceres, Berberana, Lan, Montecillo, Lagunilla, Alavesas and Palacio.

A Winery Tour of Rioja

We will start our tour in the town of Haro, capital of Rioja Alta, and then move east to Rioja Alavesa, ending in Logroño, following the course of the Ebro River all the way.

The most striking impression when you visit the wineries in Rioja is how different one can be from another. Cold fermentation is used by almost all the large *bodegas* today, and many employ the latest technology— yet 15 to 25 percent of the wine is still crushed by stomping! There is contrast in the aging, too: some wineries will age their red wines no longer than two years in oak, whereas others—such as López de Heredia—keep them up to seven years. The cooperage used is mostly American white oak, except for a few French barrels.

LÓPEZ DE HEREDIA
Haro (Rioja Alta) — (941) 310127 and 310244
Founded in 1877 by Rafael López de Heredia and today run by his grandson, Pedro, López de Heredia is one of the most conservative wineries in Rioja. A relatively small, family-owned business (under 50 employees), it prides itself on the traditional style and craftsmanship of its wines. The winery has its own cooper's shop and, faithful to the past, still ferments its wines in oak and ages them in old barrels for a long time—the whites 4 to 5 years, and up to 7 for their red Reservas. The top wine is Viña Tondonia, named after a vineyard on its 420-acre estate. Most of the production is sold in Spain; only 25 percent is exported, the United States being the main market.

LA RIOJA ALTA
Haro (Rioja Alta) — (941) 310346 and 310467
Established in 1890, this is another medium-sized winery making excellent wines in the traditional Rioja style. Its finest wine, in memory of that date, is called Reserva 890—a wine of limited production, just about 1,000 cases, of which very little is exported. The second label is Reserva 904, available at select wine stores in the United States. The '70 vintage is a classic Rioja with an elegant oaky character.

The most widely sold brands in the United States are Viña Ardanza, a Reserva wine of good structure and balance which makes up 50 percent of sales, and Viña Arana. The '76 and '78 vintages, respectively, are good representatives of these wines.

COMPAÑÍA VINÍCOLA DEL NORTE DE ESPAÑA (C.V.N.E.)
Haro (Rioja Alta) — (941) 310650
One of the first exporters of Rioja to the United States, CUNE (its pronounceable acronym) has been well known in this country for its white Monopole as well as for its reds, Viña Real Plata and Viña Real Oro, the

latter considered in Spain one of the best Rioja Reservas. The founding family still retains control of the winery, which was established in 1879. It was greatly expanded in 1940, when it was the first in Rioja to use cement vats for wine storage; it was further enlarged in 1970 and 1980.

Though the winery owns over 1,000 acres of vineyards, it also buys grapes from local farmers. Its wines have been awarded numerous prizes in international competitions, dating back to 1885.

BODEGAS BILBAÍNAS
Haro (Rioja Alta) — (941) 310147
Founded in 1901 by Santiago Ugarte, a Basque from Bilbao, Bilbaínas is today one of the wineries with longest-standing tradition in Rioja. The Ugarte family still retains control, and third-generation Santiago Ugarte is one of the directors.

A medium-sized company, its emphasis is on consistent quality. It owns 625 acres of vineyards, mostly in Rioja Alta around Haro, which provide it with about 25 percent of its needs. The vinification plant is modern and efficient—a sign that the current generation is working toward establishing a prestigious, high-quality image for the winery.

The United States is one of its main export markets, where it was among the first to establish its brand as a quality Spanish wine. The semi-sweet Brillante white and rosé, dry whites Viña Paceta and Cepa de Oro, reds Viña Zaco and Viña Pomal, and especially the red Reservas, Vendimia Especial and Gran Reserva (aged in oak for 4 years), are excellent representatives of its style. It also produces a very pleasant sparkling wine, Royal Carlton, available in small quantities in the United States.

BODEGAS MUGA
Haro (Rioja Alta) — (941) 310498 and 311825
Isaac Muga's winery, founded by his father in 1932, is not large: he makes 40,000 to 45,000 cases a year of premium wines, in the fine old style. The wines, neither pasteurized nor cold-treated, are aged 2 to 4 years mostly in American oak and some French Limousin; they are clarified with egg whites and filtered to a minimum if at all; the bottles are packed horizontally in wooden cases as well as in cartons. Respect for tradition and craftsmanship works for him to produce elegant red wines, with great personality. Muga exports some of his production, and the good news is that in 1984 the first shipments reached U.S. shores.

GRANJA REMÉLLURI
Labastida (Rioja Alavesa) — (941) 331274
In the mid-sixties Jaime Rodríguez-Salís, a Basque industrialist from Irún, acquired the Remélluri farm (granja) in Labastida. With its eighteenth-century farmhouse and 170 acres of land, the farm had once belonged to the convent of Monte Toloño Monastery. From the back garden you can see

the Toloño mountain, and off the front balcony the most marvelous view of the entire Rioja, its vineyards sprawling endlessly in the distance.

An enthusiast of Rioja wines, Jaime embarked on the task of building a château-style winery. From 10,000 bottles in the first vintage, 1971, Granja Remélluri is now producing over 200,000. The wines are aged 3 years in American and French Limousin oak, and at least 1 year in the bottle before release.

Granja Remélluri's wines, unfortunately, are not exported. But if you find yourself in Rioja, don't miss a visit to the château; it will be well worth it.

BODEGAS DOMECQ
Elciego (Rioja Alavesa) — (941) 106001
The great Jerez family set out in 1973 to enter the Rioja wine business by acquiring 750 acres of vineyard land and building a most impressive winery with the latest technology.

Their production is now about 400,000 cases, mostly from their own grapes. All the vineyards planted since '73 are trellised, something fairly unusual in Rioja. Their reds are aged in American oak, from 1½ years for the regular wines to 2½ for the Reservas; they look for fruit and varietal character, rather than for oak. Their white, made from Viura, has no oak at all but fresh, clean fruit. Their reds are well made, round and consistent in quality.

Domecq is very export-minded, and 30 percent of its sales go abroad. In the United States it sells under the Privilegio label—a wine with a story behind it. In 1773 there was a dispute between two Rioja towns over the right to plant vineyards: the grape growers of Laguardia were opposed to new plantings in Elciego. The Elciegans took the case to the Supreme Court of Castile, which ruled in their favor, based on a "privilege" (privilegio) awarded to the town by King Sancho of Navarre in the year 1165; hence the full name of the wine is Privilegio del Rey Sancho.

MARQUÉS DE RISCAL
Elciego (Rioja Alavesa) — (941) 106000
Founded in 1860 by the Marquis of Riscal, Camilo Hurtado de Amézaga, this is the oldest winery in Rioja. Its underground cellar—built in 1860—keeps an outstanding library of old vintages, dating back to the founding years. Winemaker Javier Salamero attributes their longevity partly to the fact that in those days they had Cabernet Sauvignon in them.

The fine quality of Riscal wines probably goes back to 1868, when the Marquis hired the services of a respected French enologist, Jean Pinau, to make his wines. As early as 1895, the wines of Riscal were awarded the first medal ever won by a Spanish wine—which has been shown on their label since—and at a Bordeaux exposition no less, in competition with the local French wines.

Everything surrounding Riscal has great history—including the town where it is located, Elciego (the Blind Man), named after a roadside inn owned by a blind man where travelers stopped to rest on their way to Basque Country. At some point, 50 or 60 years ago, the entire village was dependent on Riscal. The winery may be considered the last remnant of a good feudalism, where a nobleman created an enterprise and was able to instill in the families and workers around him the same devotion and enthusiasm he had. Today the workers are shareholders, and their attachment to the winery is still strong.

BODEGAS RIOJANAS
Cenicero (Rioja Alta) — (941) 454050

Founded in 1890, Bodegas Riojanas has been controlled for several generations by the Artacho family. It exports 50 percent of its production, although the United States is not a very big market. Here it sells the Monte Real and Viña Albina labels, both white and red Reservas. Viña Albina is made in a lighter style than Monte Real, and on the label it shows several prizes the wine has won over the years.

MARQUÉS DE CÁCERES
Cenicero (Rioja Alta) — (941) 454000

Enrique Forner, a native of Valencia who owns Château Camensac and Larose Trintaudon in Bordeaux, came down to Rioja in 1968 and decided to create his third "château" there.

His first vintage, 1970—the year the winery was completed—was released in 1975. Forner's philosophy of winemaking is indeed quality-oriented, and it shows in the classic style of the wines. His basic red as well as the Reserva are good exponents of a new ideology in Rioja winemaking, happily blending tradition with the latest technology. Cáceres white is fresh and with fine floral aromas, yet intense and complex. The reds are aged for a maximum 18 months in oak, American and French Limousin, which contributes an elegant trace of spiciness in perfect balance with the fruit from the Tempranillo grape.

BODEGAS MONTECILLO
Fuenmayor (Rioja Alta) — (941) 440125

Established in 1874 by brothers Alejandro and Celestino Navajas, the winery was family-owned until sold in 1973 to the Jerez family firm of Osborne. The existing structure was expanded, and new vinification and aging plants were built. Under the keen direction of winemaker Gonzalo Causapé and with an enthusiastic, highly professional team, the winery has evolved from a small quality business to a prestigious 300,000- to 400,000-case-a-year operation.

The red wines—Viña Cumbrero, Viña Monty and Montecillo—all have great character and good balance between fruit and oak; the Gran

Reservas are especially fine, the best being a '73 Montecillo black label. The white Viña Cumbrero is fresh and crisp, without any trace of oak.

FAUSTINO MARTÍNEZ
Oyón (Rioja Alavesa) — (941) 110701

The Martínez family had been making wine since the 1850s, but it was in 1930 that Faustino Martínez decided to bottle his products. His son, Julio Faustino Martínez, carries on the family tradition. Today the winery owns about 600 acres of vineyards, and it is the number one exporter of Reserva and Gran Reserva wines in Rioja. In the United States it sells Faustino I and the premium Faustino V, as well as a young Faustino V white.

The evolution of Faustino Martínez is astonishing. Here is a family of grape growers who one day decided to make wine—and not only did they succeed, but they have become one of the top wineries in Rioja.

MARQUÉS DE MURRIETA
Castillo de Ygay, Logroño (Rioja Alta) — (941) 258100

This is an old prestigious name representative of quality wines from Rioja in the United States as far as 20 or 30 years ago. It was in 1872 that the Marquis Luciano Murrieta acquired the Ygay estate near Logroño, and began making fine wines in the style of Bordeaux. Today the beautiful château-style winery owns 350 acres of vineyards, and the wines are all estate-bottled.

Murrieta was one of the first wineries in Rioja to export its wines, despite the small production: 90,000 cases/year, of which about 50 percent are sold abroad. The white is made from Viura and the reds from Tempranillo, the latter aged 2 or 3 years in American oak. Its red Reserva, Castillo Ygay, is a particularly good exponent of the quality of Murrieta wines, and the old vintages occasionally found at specialty stores are proof of their long life.

BODEGAS OLARRA
Logroño (Rioja Alta) — (941) 235299 and 235388

This is probably the most California-style winery in Rioja. It was built in 1972 by a Basque industrialist, Luis Olarra; he recently sold the winery, but winemaker Ezequiel García has stayed on.

Olarra is a wonder of technology and efficiency, different from anything else in Rioja. Yet it has maintained the best of Rioja's tradition, blending it with the most modern enological advances.

Olarra has looked for a style of its own. The whites and reds, especially the Reserva Cerro Añón, have been a hit ever since the first vintage, 1970. Its marketing team is highly professional and consumer-oriented, and the sales—300,000 cases in '83—are one-third export, including the United States. Despite the winery's youth, the wines have won numerous awards because of their elegance and personality.

GALICIA

Winemaking in Galicia goes back to the eleventh century. But it was in the fourteenth century that the British, always searching for areas which could produce fine wine, came to Galicia, and they made a good white port-style wine for a while. Unfortunately, in the sixteenth century they were forced to leave—the Catholic Church became fearful that the trade with "heretics" would corrupt the locals' souls. So they went farther south, to Portugal; they established themselves in Oporto, and the history of port began.

About 65 percent of the wines made in Galicia are red, yet the best are white. The reds are consumed locally; they are generally rough and quite acidic. The best whites, all consumed locally, can be elegant and delightful. Because the consumption is twice the amount produced, a lot of grapes, and even wine, are imported from other areas—and sold as native. Fraud is quite common, aided by the fact that Galicians distrust labels; they believe a bottle with a label is a clear indication that the wine was made "chemically." Thus good wine is hard to find; and when you do, it's very expensive.

While winemaking is rudimentary, the grapes are grown with immense care; nothing else is tended with such devotion in Galicia. To avoid cryptogamic diseases caused by the abundant rains, vines are planted on arbors. The best vineyards are located on the sunny slopes above the rivers; altitude hurts quality because of the scarce sun in the region, and the plains give large quantities of mediocre grapes.

After phylloxera struck Galicia, most of the vineyards were replanted with the white Palomino grape from Jerez—called Jerez in Galicia—because it is heartier than the indigenous varieties and produces a larger yield. And this is the only area in Spain where I've seen hybrid grapes. The variety, called Catalam, is originally from California and produces bountiful crops of ordinary white and red wines. Fortunately, an effort is being made to bring back the noble local varieties as the basis for the great wines of Galicia.

Alvarinho is the best Galician grape, and the price paid for it is the highest in Spain. Alvarinho is a Specific Appellation or Denominación Específica, applicable to any wine made from that grape regardless of the area, rather than a Denominación de Origen such as the Galician regions Ribeiro or Valdeorras. Treixadura and Torrontés are the finest varieties in Ribeiro, and Godelho in Valdeorras.

The Alvarinho variety seems related to the Alsatian and German Riesling, brought back via the Camino de Santiago (the pilgrim route described in the section on Galicia in "The Flavor of Spain"). Of course, some maintain that it was actually the other way around: Alvarinho was taken from

Galicia to northern Europe and there it became Riesling. And indeed, at its best it has the fruit and elegance of a fine European Riesling.

A Winery Tour of Galicia

ASOCIACIÓN DE COSECHEROS DE ALVARINHO
Sisam, Cambados (Pontevedra) — (986) 710052

The co-op system in Galicia works very differently from co-ops in other areas of Spain; here it plays a very important role in the quality improvement of the wines. President Daniel Casalderrei is enthusiastic about the new installations at this co-op as well as about further plans underway, and is proud of the results already obtained.

The winery is indeed a model of cleanliness and efficiency. With 17 members in the *Asociación*, the production is only about 300,000 bottles; so unlike the big co-ops, Casalderrei can control the growers who turn their grapes in for vinification. Faithful to tradition, he seldom labels the wines —the members want it that way! Regardless, he turns out some lovely bottles, with delicate and elegant aromas. And naturally, he proudly feels that Alvarinho makes the best wines in the world.

PAZO DE BAYÓN
Villagarcía de Arosa (Pontevedra) — (986) 500789

Pazo is the Galician word for farmhouse—but this is more like a château. Situated near the delightful town of Villagarcía de Arosa, Pazo de Bayón is in a movie-style setting, with its castle rising over the estate, its vineyards and trees and little paths sprawling over the lush valley. Justo Álvarez de la Fuente, an industrialist from Ávila, is a most friendly host who takes pleasure in showing a wine lover around. And if all this were not enough, Pazo de Bayón makes a terrific Alvarinho; only 80,000 bottles a year, most sold locally, but well worth searching for.

SANTIAGO RUIZ
Sam Miguel de Tabagom (Pontevedra) — (986) 610568

Nestled in the far southwest corner of Galicia, where the Minho River flows into the Atlantic Ocean, forming a natural boundary with Portugal, is the district of O Rosal, producer of some truly charming Alvarinhos. At the very southern tip of O Rosal is the village of Sam Miguel, where Santiago and Isabel Ruiz make the most renowned Alvarinhos in the area.

Santiago's family has been making wine at that property since the 1700s. His production has not increased much from that time: in 1984—an excellent year—he made 15,000 bottles!

Santiago Ruiz makes wine as his father and grandfather did: with great love and care, the old way, in a tiny cellar behind his home, next to a museum of memorabilia and old wine artifacts. Right there is his "bottling machine"—the same one his grandfather had used since 1908. Yet he ferments in stainless steel and uses a modern pressing machine to crush the grapes. Heralded by connoisseurs and wine writers in Spain, his wine is not only very difficult to obtain but also quite expensive.

Watching the sunset from his deck, with a marvelous view of the Minho River and Portugal in the distance, Santiago will sing for you the praises of Galician wines—definitely the best in the world. And while tasting his, you will agree!

COOPERATIVA DEL RIBEIRO
Ribadavia (Orense) — (988) 470175

This cooperative is a far cry from the one in Alvarinho. It has about 1,000 members, produces 4 to 5 million bottles a year, and the members' input varies from 22 pounds to 88,000!

The varieties planted are the indigenous Treixadura and Torrontés, plus a lot of the lesser Palomino. One of the problems there is that the grapes have always been harvested in large plastic bags, in which they may sit in the sun for a day until the harvest truck comes by to pick them up. The growers were up in arms when the co-op stopped selling the bags to discourage such practice. Now the finest varieties are harvested in boxes, and the members are encouraged by financial incentives to plant more of the better varieties.

About 80 percent of the co-op's wines are sold with a label. Its top brand is Bradomín, a 100 percent Treixadura and Torrontés varietal of lovely golden color, with fine aromas reminiscent of banana and tropical fruits. Viña Costeira is pale, fresh and crisp, with a touch of bubbliness, made mostly from the two indigenous varieties with some Palomino.

CASTILLA-LEÓN

This is a vast area with various wine-growing districts, but probably the finest wines are made in the only 2 regions covered by a Denominación de Origen: Rueda and Ribera del Duero, the last a D.O. only since 1982. Both are located on the banks of the upper Duero River. The first is best known for its white wines, the second for its reds—notably the legendary Vega Sicilia.

Ribera del Duero is an area of extraordinary beauty. During the cold, rigorous winters, the snow-covered mountains in the background seem to want to protect the vineyards sprawling in the valleys. In an October visit there, the fall colors were spectacular. The vineyards had taken on a fiery red hue due to the early frosts—one of the main problems for the vineyards in the area—and the landscape exuded a certain peaceful serenity.

The main grapes planted in the district are Tinto Fino (same as Rioja's Tempranillo), Garnacha and three French varieties: Cabernet Sauvignon, Merlot and Malbec. Ribera del Duero and Penedès, in Catalonia, are the only two D.O.s which authorize foreign grapes to be used in their wines.

Rueda's vineyards are mostly planted with Verdejo, a white grape indigenous to the region. Viura and Palomino are also grown; they make harder, less elegant wines. At its best, Verdejo produces wines of pale golden color, dry, almost austere, with character and individuality, finishing off with a slightly grassy, refreshing aftertaste.

A Wine Tour of the Upper Duero

VEGA SICILIA
Valbuena de Duero (Valladolid) — (983) 300393 and 220318

For decades, any lover of Spanish wines has known about the great wine of Vega Sicilia—probably since Sir Winston Churchill proclaimed it his favorite. Today, under the surveillance of Jesús Anadón, the wines continue to have an enviable level of quality and a well-deserved prestige throughout Spain as well as abroad.

The winery is located on the right bank of the Duero River, 25 miles east of Valladolid. The estate dates from 1864, when Eloy Lecanda brought the French vines Cabernet Sauvignon, Merlot and Malbec down from Bordeaux and planted them alongside various Spanish varieties.

All Vega Sicilia wines are estate-bottled; the production is quite limited, although in 15 years it has gone from 30,000 bottles to 200,000 in 1984. The property has about 300 acres of prime soil planted with vineyards along the gentle slopes rising from the Duero: 70 percent Tinto Fino, 20 percent Cabernet Sauvignon and 10 percent Malbec/Merlot. The winery exports some of its production, but only 200 cases reach the United States annually—hardly enough to satisfy the curiosity and appreciation for the wine in this country!

The wines are made following the traditional methods handed down from Vega Sicilia's first winemaker, the notable "Chomín." They spend between 3 and 10 years in oak, mostly American, plus 1 or 2 in the bottle before release. Those with bigger potential are first kept 3 to 4 years in large wooden vats.

The premier label is the Vega Sicilia "Único," an elegant, complex red, with exceptional character reminiscent of a great Bordeaux yet with its very own personality. The other red, Valbuena, is velvety and soft, with a deep bouquet and excellent balance between fruit and oak.

To me, Vega Sicilia has achieved a mythical reputation thanks to the unique character of its wines—something similar to what Château Latour has done in Bordeaux. You may like one vintage more than another; but they all have that unmistakable individuality which is the mark of a great wine. For that, and for showing the world how fine a Spanish wine can be, Vega Sicilia deserves the utmost respect.

ALEJANDRO FERNÁNDEZ
Pesquera de Duero (Valladolid) — (983) 881023
Alejandro is a man in his fifties who has always loved wine. After amassing a sizable fortune in his business, in 1970 he decided to build a winery in Ribera del Duero and to produce the best red wine in the world. Today he has 70 acres, planted mostly with the finest local grape, Tinto Fino.

The first vintage, 1974, was released in 1976. Alejandro makes about 100,000 bottles of two reds, Pesquera Tinto and Gran Reserva, which have recently won many prizes—and when I tasted the '80 Gran Reserva, I realized why. Three years in American oak had mellowed out its intense, robust body; the nose was rich with breed and character, and the lingering aftertaste had enough good tannin to augur a long life.

MARQUÉS DE GRIÑÓN
Rueda (Valladolid) — (983) 868116
A recent newcomer to Rueda is Carlos Falcó, Marquis of Griñón. In 1974 he and his partner, Antonio Sanz, built a winery equipped with the latest winemaking technology.

Their white, sold under the label Marqués de Griñón, is made exclusively from the Verdejo grape. They produce 15,000 to 18,000 cases and are already exporting to the United States and other countries. It is a dry, aromatic wine, with abundant fruit and marked varietal character; with no wood aging, it is a fine example of the elegant whites that can be produced in the area.

Also very exciting are the red wines they are making from a 35-acre Cabernet Sauvignon vineyard near Toledo. Their '82 and '83, tasted out of the cask, showed great promise and fine Cabernet fruit in the nose. They will be released after 2 years' aging in American oak and, despite the small output, some will be shipped to the United States.

CASTILLA–LA MANCHA

This is the largest wine-producing region of Spain, accounting for 70 to 75 percent of the country's wine production. There are four Denominaciones de Origen in the area, the main ones being La Mancha—which by itself makes up about 40 percent of Spain's total—and Valdepeñas; the other two are Almansa and Méntrida.

Driving through the miles and miles of vineyards in La Mancha, you will admire the endless rows of tidy, well-kept vines tended lovingly like gardens. Here and there a windmill sprinkles the landscape with a dot of white, as in Don Quijote's time.

La Mancha is an immense plateau, with an average altitude of 2,000 feet and 1.2 million acres planted—the largest vineyard concentration in the world. There are in La Mancha about 2,000 wineries, making a total of

400 million gallons of wine per year. The climate is dry and extreme, with sparse rainfall and temperatures that reach −10 degrees F. in the winter and 110 degrees F. in the summer.

Valdepeñas is a much smaller district, planted with 86,000 acres of vineyards; it was part of La Mancha until 1968, when it became a separate Denominación de Origen. Valdepeñas wines are more stable—owing to their own natural constitution—and travel better than those from the rest of the region; therefore the district has been Madrid's traditional wine purveyor since the eighteenth century.

Valdepeñas is quite a wine town; with a population of 25,000 or 30,000, it has 400 wineries—and they all look alike! The village is full of caves, housing the traditional huge *tinajas,* 4,200-gallon earthenware jars with conical bottoms, shaped like the ancient Roman amphoras; wine has been made, stored and even transported in them since time immemorial. In fact, *tinajas* are the next best thing to temperature-controlled fermentation. They dispel the heat produced during the process as the air circulates around inside the container, producing a natural ventilation which cools the fermenting grape juice.

Although *tinajas* are typical of all La Mancha, their largest concentration has always been in the Valdepeñas district. Today, with modern enological techniques, they are falling into disuse—but most wineries still have some. Since 1982, the attractive boulevard leading into Valdepeñas, Avenida del Vino, has 126 *tinajas* lining the sides of the street—a clever idea of Mayor Esteban López, who rescued them as they were thrown away by wineries that had no more use for them.

The region of Castilla–La Mancha produces three types of wine: white from the Airén grape, reds mostly from Cencibel (yet another name for Rioja's Tempranillo) and *claretes* from a mixture of 85 percent white and 15 percent red. The reason for the existence of these *claretes* is that Cencibel is much more expensive than Airén, which has a higher yield and characteristically produces soft wines, low in acidity.

Traditionally, La Mancha has been the big producer of ordinary wines in Spain, much of it shipped in bulk abroad or to other Spanish wine districts for blending. But in the last 5 to 10 years, a handful of pioneering wineries have been applying new production methods and moving away from *claretes.* They are making some crisp, young whites with clean fruit from the Airén grape, and light, fruity reds from Cencibel; both are excellent values for the money. Fortunately, they are changing the idea—so deeply rooted in yesterday's Spain—that the higher the alcohol content and the older the vintage, the better the wine.

The cooperatives play an important role in the area. There are 86 of them in La Mancha, making about 60 percent of all the district's wines. Their storage capacity is staggering: anywhere between 2 and 10 million gallons each. With these figures in mind, it is easy to understand that La Mancha has enormous surpluses of wine—which the government subsidizes by buying vast amounts at minimum prices for distillation into alcohol. Lately, however, steps have been taken in the right direction. A "Quality Plan" has been established, giving financial help to wineries to help them introduce temperature-controlled fermentation and other technological improvements.

A Winery Tour of Valdepeñas and La Mancha

LUIS MEGÍA
Valdepeñas (Ciudad Real) — (926) 320600
Founded in 1947 by Luis Megía, the winery was recently sold to a leading Spanish bank, although Luis and his team have stayed on. The change has, in fact, been very positive for the quality of the wines, as large sums of capital have been invested in the company. This is encouraging, and speaks for the success of these new higher-quality wines.

Megía is the most technologically advanced producer in Valdepeñas. Fermentation is done under controlled temperature in stainless-steel tanks, with selected yeasts; yet *tinajas* are still used to clarify the wines. Production is 3 million gallons per year, of which some is exported—soon to the United States.

COOPERATIVA LA INVENCIBLE
Valdepeñas (Ciudad Real) — (926) 320458
This is the largest and oldest co-op in Valdepeñas, an incredible operation with over 1,000 members which produces 30 percent of all the district's wine—about half bottled and half in bulk. The smallest member brings in 11 tons of grapes, and the biggest 550 to 750 tons. During harvest time, it is an amazing sight to watch the long row of tractors lining up at day's end to deposit their load of grapes at the winery; the line goes on and on through the streets of Valdepeñas.

The vinification is handled with great efficiency. The tractors go through a station at the entrance where a sample of the must is extracted and the sugar content measured; the computer prints a card which will be the receipt for the grape grower at profit-sharing time. As the grapes are unloaded into the presses, the whole transaction has taken just about five minutes!

FÉLIX SOLÍS
Valdepeñas (Ciudad Real) — (926) 322400
Since Félix Solís established the small winery Bodega del Cura (priest's cellar) in 1925, it has become one of the largest and most modern wineries in Valdepeñas, as well as the number one exporter and bottled wine producer in the area. Mr. Solís is still president of the family-owned company.

The winery produces fresh, young cold-fermented whites and clean, pleasant reds. The red Reservas are aged in *tinajas* and in American oak for 1 year or longer, which contributes their creamy, vanilla-like character. All in all, their price/quality ratio is excellent; few regions in the world can match it.

VINÍCOLA DE CASTILLA
Manzanares (Ciudad Real) — (926) 610450
In 1976, the former conglomerate Rumasa went all out to build the ultimate winery in La Mancha: a technologically advanced, quality-oriented operation which would take full advantage of the vast potential of La Mancha wines.

General Manager Alfonso Monsalve and winemaker Alberto Pérez have great confidence in the future of the district's wines. Very export-oriented, they started shipping to the United States in 1983, mostly with the labels Viña Bonita, Espada and Señorío de Guadianeja.

Of particular interest are their experimental plantings (50 acres) of Cabernet Sauvignon, for which Alberto believes there are great microclimates in La Mancha. And indeed, I was impressed with the fruit displayed by the young '84. Their '79 Reserva, a blend of 90 percent Cencibel and 10 percent Cabernet aged in American oak, has good balance and a nice touch of vanilla in the finish. In general, their wines are clean, honest and well made, a terrific value for the price.

COOPERATIVA NUESTRO PADRE JESÚS DEL PERDÓN
Manzanares (Ciudad Real) — (926) 610309
This modern co-op was the first in La Mancha to attempt, back in 1970, a change in the vinification of white wines toward more emphasis on the fruit. It has over 700 members and a capacity of 8.2 million gallons.

Pascual Herrera oversees the production, assisted by young cellar master Pepe Casalderrey. As we tasted the wines, I could see how they look for youth and freshness in the whites, and for clean fruit in the reds.

JEREZ

To me, the wines of Jerez have an aura of mystery about them. It still is something of an enigma why the *flor* (flower), or layer of yeast that grows spontaneously on the surface of the wine, appears in this privileged Denominación de Origen.

Few wines in the world can boast as illustrious a literature as *jerez,* or sherry. And such prestige is due to the excellence of their wines, achieved through centuries of fine winemaking. "If I had a thousand sons," said Shakespeare's Falstaff, "the first humane principle I would teach them should be, to forswear thin potations, and to addict themselves to sack [sherry]."

Fino sherry is *the* aperitif wine in Spain, yet its consumption is limited. The *jerez* drinker is usually sophisticated, and also very loyal—somewhat like the classical music lover. In southern Spain *jerez* is part of the lifestyle, and in Madrid it is the most popular aperitif; but in the rest of Spain, the habit of serving it is not as deeply rooted.

During my last visit to Jerez, I tried to understand why sherry is not more popular in the United States. And it occurred to me that maybe the problem is the same as in northern Spain: people don't know when to serve it. Yet it should fit the American lifestyle so well! A fino, for example, is a refreshing aperitif which entices the palate for the meal to come. And after dinner, an old amontillado or a fragrant oloroso are certain to enhance any dessert.

One possible reason for confusion, I believe, is that the label usually reads "sherry" rather than *jerez*. Many people don't realize that the *true* sherry, *jerez*, comes only from a relatively small region—50,000 acres—in southwest Spain, in the triangle formed by the towns of Jerez de la Frontera, Sanlúcar de Barrameda and Puerto de Santa María. Furthermore, Spain is the only country that can use the word "sherry" alone on the label. California, Australia, Chile, South Africa or Cyprus must have the name of the region or country preceding the word sherry—as in California or Australian sherry. Unfortunately, many consumers associate true Spanish sherry with the sweet, less expensive, poorer quality product from other countries.

Another problem is that a delicate fino or manzanilla does not have a long life in the bottle—at the most, 1 or 2 years—and since it has no vintage, it is difficult to be sure that the bottle you buy is at its peak. Finally, I find that even the U.S. wine critics often have some confusion about *jerez*. I hope the following pages will shed some light as well as add to the enjoyment of the wine.

The Grapes and the Soil

The main grape in Jerez is Palomino, planted in 92 percent of the district's soil. Pedro Ximénez accounts for another 5 percent, and Moscatel 2 percent.

The soil in Jerez is the famous white, chalky *albariza,* found mainly on gentle slopes. With a high calcium carbonate content, it is very absorbent and, when it dries out, it reflects the heat and keeps the humidity in the plant's roots. Thus the vines can overcome the torrid Andalusian summer, with its 110-degree F. temperatures.

The Flor

The key factor in *jerez* wines is the *flor,* or film of saccharomyces yeast which protects the wine from oxidation and transforms the alcohol into aldehyde, giving sherry much of its flavor, aroma and character. The *flor* has been transferred to other areas of the world, but it grows spontaneously only in the Spanish Sherry, Montilla and Upper Duero districts, and in the French Jura.

Several yeasts produce *flor*, but the quality one is formed by *Saccharomyces ellipsoideus*. This thrives on oxygen, glycerin and alcohol, and it develops perfectly at around 60 degrees F.—the fall and spring temperature in Jerez—in wines of an alcohol content around 15.5 percent. The wine, right after fermentation, is transferred to *botas* or butts (the 130-gallon casks of American oak used in Jerez), which are not filled to the top, in order to encourage development of the *flor*. For some unexplained reason, the *flor* will not develop in every *bota*. Whether or not it does determines which classification of sherry will be produced.

The Classification: Finos, Olorosos and Amontillados

From December through January, the cellar master or *capataz* will watch the development of every butt, periodically tasting each one by dipping the *venencia* (a long, narrow cup at the end of a rod) with a clean, swift stroke, to extract a sample. Those butts marked with *una raya* (1 stripe) will be selected for finos. Those marked with *dos rayas* (2 stripes) will usually be destined for olorosos. The classification goes down to 4 stripes, for wines that can be used only for distillation into brandy. If the classification is undetermined, the *capataz* will mark the butt with *raya y punto* (stripe and dot).

After this, the young wines are fortified with alcohol accordingly, in order either to encourage or to eliminate further growth of the *flor:* the finos up to 15.5 percent to encourage it, and the olorosos to 18 percent to kill it off. Those butts marked as undetermined will be tasted again after 5 or 6 months; their definitive trend will then be established and they will be fortified accordingly.

In order for a wine to be a fino, it has to stay in the butt with the *flor* for at least a year. If a fino is allowed to age, it will evolve into an amontillado. In the finos, the film of *flor* is pale yellow; in the amontillados it is thinner and grayish, and it dies after 2 to 3 years, falling to the bottom of the butt.

Finos are light, very dry wines of pale straw color, with clean pungent aroma and a special, almost green-olive taste; they should be drunk cold. Amontillados have an elegant amber color, more body and fullness, a marked dry palate and a nutty quality reminiscent of hazelnuts.

Most of the olorosos on the market are semi-sweet, but there also exist excellent dry ones. They are scarce, though, because a good one needs to be 8 years old. At its best, a dry oloroso will have an old-gold amber color, acquired after the long aging in wood. The bouquet will be intense and clean, and on the palate it will display a luscious first impression—due to the high glycerin content—evolving into a complex aftertaste, somewhat like walnuts.

The Solera System

The wines of Jerez are aged by the traditional method of *soleras,* which is aimed at maintaining consistency in the quality. *Soleras* are the bottom-row butts (thus *soleras,* from *suelo* or floor); those on top, the *criaderas* (from *criar,* or nurture), contain the younger wine. As the sherry is drawn from the *soleras* for bottling or shipping—a maximum of one third from each butt per year—the *solera* is refilled with new wine from the butts right above, called *primera* (first) *criadera;* the new wine will then acquire the characteristics of the older wine. The *primera criadera* in turn will be refilled with wine from the *segunda* (second) *criadera,* or the butts on the third tier, and so on. (This process is known as "refreshing" the *solera.)*

Obviously, *jerez* is a blended wine; a specific brand is usually made of a special blend of *soleras,* which will determine the style of the wine characteristic of that particular winery.

Manzanilla

The town of Sanlúcar, right on the Atlantic Ocean, has a peculiarity: the wines made there as finos come out as manzanillas. If the same wine is taken to age in Jerez, in 2 or 3 months it will become a fino. The name manzanilla means chamomile, and the wine is soft, very aromatic, with that slight appealing bitterness and pale straw color of chamomile tea. The *flor* in Sanlúcar grows differently from the *flor* in Jerez—although the towns are only 15 miles apart—because of the proximity of the ocean, which imparts to the wine a subtle and complex bouquet reminiscent of the ocean breeze.

Manzanilla must be made in old oak butts—some are up to 300 years old—so it does not acquire the flavor of wood. In spring and fall, as the *flor* grows more abundantly, it sinks down to the bottom of the butt and naturally clarifies the wine, turning it paler in color; then some more *flor* forms on the surface.

Some Jerez wineries—such as Valdespino, Domecq and González Byass—also have *bodegas* in Sanlúcar and produce a manzanilla; but only those with the ideal conditions can grow it. A manzanilla can hold for 1 or 2 years if the temperature doesn't go above 80 degrees F.; if it leaves Sanlúcar, however, it turns into a fino soon afterward.

An aged manzanilla will evolve into a manzanilla *pasada,* just as a fino will develop into an amontillado, after the *flor* dies.

Pedro Ximénez and Cream

The Pedro Ximénez grape takes its name from a Spanish translation of Peter Siemens, the German soldier in Charles V's army who allegedly brought it to Spain from the Rhine. It is harvested in a different way from Palomino. In order to obtain a high concentration of sugar, the bunches of grapes are left out in the sun for two weeks, until they reach a concentration of 26 to 28 degrees Brix. (Actually, a more efficient method is used today by most wineries to increase the sugar content without exposing the grapes to rains and night moisture; but the theory is the same.) After the grapes are crushed, the grape juice or "must" is fortified before the fermentation ever takes place.

A certain amount of Pedro Ximénez is added to oloroso to produce cream sherries, which have the body of an oloroso with the lusciousness of the P.X. grape. Wines made from 100 percent P.X. are rare, but they exist; they have the color of mahogany and are mellow and velvety, almost like a nectar, with the unmistakable "burnt" character of the variety.

Palo Cortado
Palo cortado is a rare variety of oloroso that grows no *flor* but is very delicate, with certain characteristics of an amontillado, especially a fresher aroma and a hazelnut-like scent. Its name means "cut stripe," because the *capataz* will mark the butt with a stripe and a line through it. An authentic palo cortado is considered by experts to be the "king" of *jerez*.

The New White Wines of Jerez
An interesting phenomenon is occurring in Jerez: a few wineries—notably Barbadillo—have started to produce crisp, fresh wines from Palomino. Cold-fermented and released early to capture the fruit of the grape, they are finding a good market locally as well as in the rest of Spain.

A Winery Tour of Jerez
The wineries in Jerez are grand, and their owners friendly and hospitable. They are well prepared to receive visitors, who are welcomed with a style and flair unique to this area.

GONZÁLEZ BYASS
Jerez de la Frontera (Cádiz) — (956) 340000
This is one of the largest wineries in Jerez, founded in 1835 by Manuel María González. His uncle, José Ángel de la Peña—affectionately called "Tío Pepe"—owned a *bodega* in Sanlúcar and initiated Manuel into the fascinating world of *jerez* wine. Uncle Pepe requested that a few butts be set aside for his private use in his nephew's *bodega;* and that's what gave the name to the firm's most popular sherry, Tío Pepe, the largest selling fino in the United States. Today, the Gran Bodega Tío Pepe contains 75,000 butts of *soleras* for this fino alone, which accounts for about 80 percent of the winery's sales.

Another great cellar there is Las Copas. Built in 1974, it has the most modern vinification plant in Jerez, crushing 2,000 tons per day. Altogether, González Byass's facilities occupy an area of 133 square miles, and the estate has 3,000 acres of vineyards—the largest vineyard property owned by a single *bodega* in Jerez.

Extremely well organized to receive visitors, the winery is certainly worth a tour. And don't miss the unusual attraction of the oloroso-loving mice, which have been drinking the wine for 40 years by climbing up a mouse-size ladder to a sherry glass!

PEDRO DOMECQ
Jerez de la Frontera (Cádiz) — (956) 331800

The firm was established in 1816 by a French nobleman, Pierre Domecq-Lembeye, a true wine lover who came to Jerez from London and built the first Domecq winery. He appropriately changed his name to Pedro and started a dynasty which to this day is one of the most prestigious in Jerez. In 1823 King Ferdinand VII visited the winery and, impressed by what he saw, made Domecq a nobleman and allowed him to use the royal crown in the family and company crest.

Today Domecq is an empire, still 75 percent controlled by the family. José Ignacio Domecq—affectionately called "The Nose" because of the size and great gustatory qualities of his—is chairman of Domecq International. His son, José Ignacio Domecq, Jr. ("The Nose, Jr."), who learned from his father the art of tasting, is in charge of production and quality control. There are 261 Domecq first cousins in the current seventh generation, but only 8 in the business—one of them the managing director, Ramón de la Mora Figueroa Domecq. A cousin, Michael Domecq, lives in New York and handles their U.S. importing company.

Domecq offers a wide range of wines. Fino La Ina is the top-selling brand—about 40 percent of its sherry sales. It is a delightful aperitif, with a clear, pale topaz color and a delicate aroma of mature flowers and fruits. The Primero Amontillado is excellent, complex and very dry, available in the United States in small quantities. So is Río Viejo Oloroso, mellow and luscious. Celebration Cream and the 100 percent P.X., Viña 25, are classics of the style. Domecq's Double Century sherries are its standard line—fino, amontillado, oloroso and cream—at very good prices. And on the expensive end, the Rare Sherries are extraordinary: Sibarita Amontillado, Palo Cortado, Imperial Oloroso and Venerable P.X.

Finally, there are the brandies. Fundador is one of the top-selling brands in Spain; but in the United States, Domecq's best-seller is Presidente, made in Mexico. Also from Spain are Tres Cepas, the more expensive Carlos I and the top of the line, Marqués de Domecq.

SANDEMAN
Jerez de la Frontera (Cádiz) — (956) 331100

El Hombre de la Capa Negra ("The Man with the Black Cape") or "The Don Figure" is a familiar sight in Spain and Portugal, but its history is less well known. It goes back to 1790, when George Sandeman founded the House of Sandeman in London and shipped the first true vintage port. The sherries have been shipped from Jerez since 1809. In 1980 the company was acquired by Seagram's, but the Sandeman family is still involved in the business, with David Patrick Sandeman as the chairman.

"The Don Figure," their trademark since 1928, is a figure dressed in a stylized Portuguese student's cape, sporting a wide-brimmed hat such as those still worn by the *caballeros* (noblemen) of Jerez.

Sandeman's best-selling sherry in the United States is Dry Don, a medium-dry amontillado which fills your mouth with a mellow, nutty flavor. Character is a medium-dry oloroso, versatile and complex, with a lingering pleasant aftertaste. Don Fino is dry and light, fresh in the nose and deliciously fragrant. Armada Cream, with the touch of lusciousness from Pedro Ximénez, is full-bodied and much more complex than most cream sherries on the market.

WILLIAMS & HUMBERT
Jerez de la Frontera (Cádiz) — (956) 331300

Dry Sack—a blend of oloroso, amontillado and Pedro Ximénez—is the largest-selling sherry in the United States bottled in Spain. And for good reason; it is not too dry despite the name, the "sack" packaging is smart and attractive, it is easy to drink chilled or on the rocks and Williams & Humbert has put an excellent promotional effort behind it.

Exported to 140 countries, Dry Sack accounts for 95 percent of the firm's sales; but its Pando Fino and Canasta Cream are best-sellers too. Pando is a light, very pleasant fino, fresh and dry. Canasta Cream, named after the basket in which the bottle is cradled, is a smooth, mellow, classic cream. The rare Dos Cortados is a palo cortado of medium amber color, deep and subtle bouquet, dry and elegant.

VALDESPINO
Jerez de la Frontera (Cádiz) — (956) 331450

I owe this old winery many a nice time over a glass of its rare oloroso, amontillado and palo cortado, which are available at some specialty stores in the United States. Its Hartley & Gibson line of sherries—manzanilla, fino, amontillado and cream—are terrific values, and I always have a bottle on hand at home. I was also delighted to find that Manuel de Argüeso, the Pedro Ximénez I had used with great results to enhance my Raisin Ice Cream with Cream Sherry (Helado de Pasas al Pedro Ximénez), was Valdespino's brand, too!

Brothers Rafael and Miguel Valdespino are the current generation of the oldest family of Spanish origin in Jerez. Their roots go back to 1264, when King Alfonso X, the Wise, knighted 24 families in Jerez and granted them land. The company was established in 1877, although the Valdespinos had been making wine at their *bodega* since 1430. They have one of the oldest cellars in Jerez, dating back to the 1600s, which has been kept almost the same. Everything at Valdespino, even today, breathes age and tradition!

OSBORNE
Puerto de Santa María (Cádiz) — (956) 855211
Osborne is the major *jerez* winery in Puerto de Santa María. You can't miss the two big iron bulls at the entrance of the town by the gate of their Bodegas del Tiro. In fact, all over Spain you can't miss the brave-looking black bull, always strategically placed on top of a hill—the clever ad for Osborne's Veterano brandy. The bull logo comes from the association with the family's cattle-raising business. The bullring of Puerto de Santa María, one of the most beautiful and famous in the world, was built by Tomás Osborne, son of the founder.

The company was established in 1772 by Thomas Osborne, a British merchant. Today, fourth-generation Enrique Osborne is president of the board of directors. But the current heart of the winery is Manuel Robles, the enterprising general manager since 1978.

Osborne's Veterano, the number one selling brandy in Spain, is also exported to the United States. Its sherries are sold here under the Duff Gordon label, notably the No. 28 semi-dry oloroso.

ANTONIO BARBADILLO
Sanlúcar de Barrameda (Cádiz) — (956) 360352
A tour of Jerez would be incomplete without visiting the home of manzanilla: Sanlúcar, the charming port on the Costa de la Luz (Coast of Light) just northwest of Jerez. And in Sanlúcar, *the bodega* to visit is Barbadillo, quite large yet family-run. Antonio Pedro "Toto" Barbadillo is at the helm of the company; he and cousin Juan Carlos represent the fifth generation of this old family to run the company since it was founded by Benigno Barbadillo in 1821.

Unfortunately, Barbadillo wines are not sold in the United States. But if you find yourself near there, I highly recommend you try some of their manzanillas—or better yet, stop by and visit the winery. I can assure you that you will receive a warm, hospitable welcome!

CATALUNYA (CATALONIA)

In exploring the wines of Catalunya, or Catalonia—home of my family's winery—I enlisted the help of my friend Mauricio Wiesenthal, author of several books on Spain, its art, peoples and lifestyle, as well as about other Latin cultures. He is also an authority on wines and gastronomy, and contributing editor to a Spanish food and wine magazine.

Catalan wines today are a far cry from what they were just a few years ago. As in many other wine areas of Spain, quantity rather than quality had been the determining factor in the past. Toward the end of the nineteenth century, the most typical rural industry in Catalonia was the distillation of brandy and spirits, or *aguardientes.* But in recent years, the vineyard acreage has decreased while the quality of the wines has improved proportionally. The Catalan winemakers' determination has brought the most modern technology, and their creativity has prompted them to experiment in the adaptation of new grape varieties (Cabernet Sauvignon, Chardonnay, Pinot Noir, Riesling, Gewürztraminer, etc.) to their soil and climate.

As a result, the wines have reached such a level of quality that they now rank with the finest in the world at international competitions. Yet they have not lost their local character; there is a certain unity among Catalan wines, a style they have in common even if each district—and winemaker—has a distinct personality. There are seven different Denominaciones de Origen in Catalonia, and they all have something in common which sets them apart from the rest of Spanish wines. The whites are aromatic, fresh and elegant; the reds are well aged, round and full-bodied.

The commercial "discovery" of these Catalan wines dates from the 1970s; but winemaking is an old art in Catalonia. Back in the first half of the fourteenth century, some lovely sparkling wines were made which the writers of the time called "subtle" and "tingling." The full-bodied, soundly structured wines of Priorato were made by the monks in the medieval monasteries. And the pale wines of Alella, brilliant and delicate, were very popular in Barcelona at the turn of the century. Catalonia has always had a certain universal vocation which enabled it to adapt to the changes of the times with great flexibility. And today its wines have adapted themselves to the tastes of a period which enjoys youth and natural elegance over heaviness and excess oak.

The Denominaciones de Origen
One important factor in Catalonia is the diversity of its climate and soil. The Mediterranean provides the area with mild temperatures, yet the high mountains of the Catalan coastal system contribute the cold winters and cool summer nights which are ideal for growing white aromatic grapes and making fresh, fragrant white wines.

The seven Catalan Denominaciones de Origen are: Alella, Ampurdán–Costa Brava, Conca de Barberá, Priorato, Penedès, Tarragona and Terra-Alta. There are other small districts which produce wines of great quality, such as Raimat, near Lérida; and most important, the cavas or sparkling wines produced by the méthode champenoise, which is a Denominación Específica or Specific Appellation, physically located 98 percent in Penedès but not part of the Denominación de Origen.

A special mention must be made of Catalan brandies, which have created a style of their own. They are made from the distillation of the area's white wines in copper pot stills—some by the charentais process of double distillation used in Cognac—and aged in American or French Limousin oak.

Alella

Located just north of Barcelona, Alella is well known for its white wines of pale straw color, aromatic and fruity. The main wineries are Cooperativa de Alella, producer of the Marfil brand of dry and semi-dry white, rosé and red; and Bodegas Alta Alella, which markets the white Marqués de Alella label. The latter uses very modern winemaking methods, fermenting the musts under controlled temperatures to make young, fresh and lively wines.

Ampurdán–Costa Brava

This district's vineyards, located north of Gerona, bordering France, are probably the most ancient in Catalonia. One of the oldest enology manuals in Europe was written in 1130 by the monk Ramón Pere de Novàs at the monastery of Sant Pere de Roda, its ruins rising today over the rugged Mediterranean coastline. Most of Ampurdán's wines are fresh, young rosés, made primarily from the Garnacha and Cariñena grapes.

The most important winery is Cavas del Ampurdán, established in 1930 and located in the historic fourteenth-century Perelada castle. It produces white, rosé and red wines, as well as *cavas* and a slightly carbonated, very pleasant and refreshing white, Blanc Pescador, made from Parellada and Macabeo grapes.

Another grower, Cellers Santamaría, has had a family winemaking tradition since the nineteenth century. In the village of Capmany it produces a high-quality rosé and red in small quantities.

Conca de Barberá

This is a district full of medieval legends, vineyards and almond orchards. Situated just north of Tarragona, it produces fine, aromatic and fruity rosés. The Knight Templars and the Cistercian monks began growing grapes here as early as the twelfth century. The historic heart of the area is the grandiose Monastery of Poblet, where the kings and queens of Catalonia and Aragón were buried. It is still possible to visit the Gothic cellar where Poblet wines were produced and aged. It is said that the monks had already discovered modern winemaking techniques; they fermented their wines at cool temperatures, sprinkling the tanks with water pumped from a well.

The area's white wines, made from Parellada and Macabeo grapes, are light and aromatic; they are sold mostly for the production of sparkling wine to firms in San Sadurní de Noia. My family feels the district's wines have a bright future, and in our Milmanda Castle estate near Poblet we have already planted some noble European grapes—Chardonnay, Pinot Noir and Cabernet—which we believe will soon produce high-quality wines.

Priorato

This is another historic area, once under the jurisdiction of the Carthusian Scala Dei order of monks. The impressive ruins of the monastery still rise among the vineyards, just west of Tarragona. Garnacha was the classic grape variety of the aromatic, full-bodied and slightly sweet Priorato red wines. Today, however, the vineyards are planted mainly with Cariñena, which gives a sturdy wine, suitable for aging. Most of the district's wines are made from a blend of both grapes; they are rich in color and alcohol. When they are well made, the softness and aroma of Garnacha is nicely coupled with the powerful structure of Cariñena. The best-known firms are Bodegas Müller and Scala Dei.

Tarragona

The land of the old Tarraco, of ancient Roman history, has a serene and classic beauty. Olive, almond and hazelnut trees stretch over the landscape among the vineyards. The area's wines were already famous at the Roman tables, and highly appreciated in the days of Emperor Augustus. Its production is so bountiful that the wines are exported throughout the world; such abundance has sometimes affected the quality required by their historic reputation. The main varieties planted are Macabeo, Xarel-lo and Parellada for whites, and Tempranillo and Cariñena for reds.

The best-known winery is Bodegas Müller, established in 1851; it produces mostly young, fresh white wines. It is also famous for its sweet wine for the Holy Mass, made according to the canons dictated by the Vatican.

Penedès

This is the wine-producing district par excellence in Catalonia. It not only makes the finest table wines, which constitute one of the great enological achievements in the second half of this century, but also is the home of the renowned Spanish *cavas* or sparkling wines. Grapes have been growing here since the fourth or fifth century B.C. The Penedès Denominación de Origen covers an area of 385,000 acres, of which about 62,000 are planted with vineyards. The D.O.'s capital is Vilafranca del Penedès, 30 miles southwest of Barcelona.

The Penedès climate and soil are very diverse. In less than 20 miles, the vineyards climb from sea level to an altitude well over 2,000 feet; this provides dramatic landscapes and a great variety of microclimates. The area is divided into 3 sub-zones: Low Penedès, with vineyards planted up to 400 feet; Middle or Central Penedès to 1,300 feet; and High Penedès, where vines grow at an elevation of 2,300 feet. Such variation allows the acclimation of very different grape varieties.

The traditional red grapes—Cariñena, Garnacha, Tempranillo and Monastrell—are grown mostly in the Low Penedès, along the Mediterranean. The Middle Penedès produces the classic whites from Xarel-lo and

Macabeo, which are the basis for the area's sparkling wines. It is also most suitable for the noble European red varieties Cabernet Sauvignon, Cabernet Franc, Pinot Noir and Merlot, and for the whites Chardonnay and Sauvignon Blanc. The High Penedès, with its rainy and cooler climate, is ideal for growing the fine, elegant local white Parellada and the French Sauvignon Blanc, as well as the aromatic Alsatian and German varieties Riesling, Gewürztraminer and Muscat d'Alsace.

In the Penedès, good winemakers grow their own grapes, select the vine stocks and varieties, oversee their pruning and study the adaptation of the prime grapes. A tour of the area provides a picturesque sight of well-kept trellised vineyards on neatly worked, clean soil. From the large cooperatives to the small family wineries in the traditional Catalan *masías* (farmhouses), a wide range of wines is made: whites full of youth and aroma or well-aged and buttery, occasionally reminiscent of honey; fresh, fruity rosés; reds complex and noble or full-bodied and sturdy; lively spritzy whites and elegant sparkling *cavas;* or aperitif and dessert wines, including the maderized *rancio* wines and the traditional sweet *malvasía* of Sitges, itself an institution among Spanish dessert wines.

Typical of the Catalan character is the will to create, change and improve, and many vineyards are continually in a state of change, trying new grapes, new methods and new blends.

The *bodegas* of Penedès fall into two categories: those that are introducing more and more noble grapes from Europe and producing wines of a more international character, rather than traditionally Spanish; and those *bodegas* that are content with the grapes and the wines they have always grown. In the middle are a number of wineries that are trying new varieties while relying on those they already have. Fortunately they can exist side by side, each making some very successful wines.

The Sparkling Cava Wines

The small town of San Sadurní de Noia, 7 miles from Vilafranca del Penedès and about an hour's drive from Barcelona, has been the headquarters for the sparkling wine industry in Spain since 1872, when José Raventós brought the *méthode champenoise* to his family *bodegas,* Codorníu, and to Spain.

The grapes used in *cava* wines are generally a mixture: Parellada for elegance and suppleness, Macabeo for aroma and finesse, and Xarel-lo for body and freshness. The red grapes Garnacha and Monastrell are used for the rosés.

Today there are over 100 *cava* wineries in Spain, 83 of them in Penedès. The Consejo Regulador del Cava (Regulatory Council of Cava), an organization under the Ministry of Agriculture, plays a very important role in controlling the quality of *cava* wines. Its regulations are strict; the name *cava* appears only on bottles produced by the *méthode champenoise* (the method used for Champagne), which means that the wine has become sparkling as a result of undergoing a secondary fermentation in the bottle. The cheaper Charmat process (known in France as *cuve close,* and in Spain as *granvas)* can never produce the same quality. The Council also sets controls for the minimum 9-month aging of the base wine or *cuvée* (if vintage-dated, minimum aging is 3 years) and for other areas, such as the compulsory bottling date on the cork.

Most Americans wonder why Spanish *cava* wines can be sold for such a low price, given their quality. First of all, the price of the wine before the second fermentation is not high. But it is mainly due to the technology, introduced by Codorníu in 1972, when José María Raventós was manager of the company. The Raventós family was committed to the *méthode champenoise,* and while others—in Spain and France—were trying to perfect the cheaper Charmat process, Codorníu set out to mechanize the *méthode champenoise* and bring down the cost.

It used to take skilled specialists 3 to 6 weeks to complete the task of "riddling," or turning each bottle a little bit every day until the sediment produced by the second fermentation settles in the cork end, prior to expulsion. Now, at the larger wineries, this operation is accomplished manually by a *girasol* (sunflower) or mechanically by a *giropallet,* a huge crate with an octagonal base which holds 504 bottles and tilts them a bit every 8 hours.

Such automation, however, can be done only at the large wineries; the smaller ones cannot afford it. With 45 million bottles of *cava* produced in 1984, the Codorníu group is the world's largest *champenoise*-method producer of sparkling wines. Second in Spain comes Freixenet, with 34 million bottles, and third is Castellblanch (now part of the Freixenet group) with 6 million.

The story of the small *cava* producers is also a happy one: they are making excellent wines and easily selling them in the domestic market at pretty high prices. They are mostly vineyard owners who make their *cava* with little mechanization, family style. The largest of them is Monistrol, with 2 million bottles in '84, followed by Juvé i Camps with about 1 million; the rest make under 1 million—and are happy to stay that way.

A Winery Tour of Catalonia

JEAN LEON
Plà del Penedès (Barcelona) — (93) 899-5033
Representative of those winemakers seeking to explore new and exciting techniques is Jean Leon. Born in Spain, he went to America in the fifties and eventually opened La Scala restaurant in Beverly Hills. In 1962 he acquired a 375-acre vineyard in Plà del Penedès, 3 miles from Vilafranca, with a small farmhouse which he turned into a winery. He then obtained cuttings of Cabernet Sauvignon, Cabernet Franc, Chardonnay and Pinot Noir from France, and proceeded to adapt them to his estate. At present

one third of his vineyard is in full production, planted with Cabernet Sauvignon and Chardonnay, and the quality of his grapes is among the best.

All of Jean Leon's wines are made from his own grapes and aged in a beautiful underground cellar. His production is about 200,000 bottles per year, mostly sold locally and in the United States.

HEREDAD MONTSARRA
Torrelles de Foix (Barcelona) — (93) 892-2897
This winery is located in a historic sixteenth-century farmhouse built over the ruins of more ancient constructions, as evidenced by its Roman underground cellar. The estate belonged to the aristocratic family of the Marquis of Spain until it was acquired by the Balaguer family in 1748.

José María Balaguer began in 1974 to bottle and label varietal wines made from the indigenous white grapes of Penedès: Parellada, Macabeo and Xarel-lo. Today the estate has 250 acres of vineyards planted with these varieties, as well as some Chardonnay in the experimental stages. None of the wines are aged in wood, most are bottled young and each tastes of the grape from which it is made. The winery's Parellada is the most interesting varietal, a wine with lovely aroma, fine fruit and crisp finish.

MONT MARÇAL
Castellví de la Marca (Barcelona) — (93) 891-8281
Established in 1975 by Manuel Sancho, Mont Marçal has acquired a well-deserved reputation among wine lovers in the few years of its existence.

Its 150 acres of vineyards are planted with the traditional Penedès varieties—Parellada, Xarel-lo and Macabeo—as well as with some noble European grapes such as Chardonnay and Cabernet Sauvignon; Sylvaner is also in the experimental stages. The wines are made with the most modern technology, in cold-fermented stainless-steel tanks, and the reds are oak-aged. Their production, sold in Spain and also exported to Europe and the United States, includes whites, reds and *cava*. Of particular interest are their fresh and aromatic white Vi Novell (Catalan for new wine), another white made with some Chardonnay, and their Reserva red, with great character and breed.

MASÍA BACH
San Esteve de Sesrovires (Barcelona) — (93) 771-4052
Two enterprising brothers, Pere and Ramón Bach, after making their fortune in the textile industry in the twenties, decided to become winemakers. They acquired a beautiful 850-acre estate near San Sadurní, planted it with vineyards and olive trees, built a great mansion (a Catalan *masía)* and established Masía Bach in 1929. Unfortunately, after the Spanish Civil War the winery went into decline, until it was acquired by Codorníu in 1975. Under the auspices of winemaker Ángel Escudé, they set out to revive the old

bodega—a task that has been accomplished well. The renovated mansion today enjoys its splendor once more, with the charming modernist, wood-paneled salons decorated with beautiful stained glass and tiles, and a superb Florentine-style staircase. Truly worth a visit!

The firm owns 85 acres of the original estate and buys most of the grapes for its wines, made from the traditional Penedès varieties. A special point of interest is their 1/2-mile-long, 80-foot-deep cellar, built in 1924, destined for oak aging of their red wines.

The firm's legendary brand is the white Gran Reserva Extrisímo, a luscious, mellow, well-aged sweet white wine of silky texture. Extrisímo Seco is a fine dry white, characteristic of Penedès, with the fresh aroma of the Parellada variety. Masía Bach wines are exported, among other countries, to the United States and Canada.

MARQUÉS DE MONISTROL
Monistrol de Noia (Barcelona) — (93) 891-0276
A great enologist and promoter of Spanish agriculture, José María Escrivá de Romaní, Marquis of Monistrol, established this winery in 1882 and around it grew the picturesque village of Monistrol de Noia, near San Sadurní.

Monistrol's whites, rosés, reds and *cava* wines are produced according to the most modern technology, vinified in stainless steel and aged in impressive underground cellars. Among their top brands are the white Blanc de Blancs, fresh and fruity, with a pleasant hint of carbonation; and Blanco Seco, dry and delicate, made with the traditional Penedès varieties. Both are available in the United States.

HEREDAD SEGURA VIUDAS
San Sadurní de Noia (Barcelona) — (93) 899-5111
This estate, which dates back to the eleventh century, is today part of the Freixenet group. Its 270 acres of vineyards sprawl along the banks of the Noia River, with the legendary Montserrat mountains in the background. Besides Segura Viudas, two other wines, Conde de Caralt and René Barbier —a historic label established in 1880—are made at the winery.

The facilities are modern and efficient, with a beautiful bottling plant, large groups of horizontal presses and long underground, multileveled aging cellars. In addition, a wine library keeps a collection of the estate's best Reservas over the years.

The sparkling wines are sold under the brand name Segura Viudas; Conde de Caralt are white wines, and René Barbier whites and reds, the latter including some well-aged Reservas. All of them are made from the traditional Penedès grapes.

RAIMAT
Raimat (Lérida) — (973) 724008
Established in 1914 by the Raventós family, this impressive winery ranks high today among the first-quality wine producers of Catalonia. They have succeeded in reviving viticulture in an area of drier and warmer climate than Penedès, which traditionally had not been devoted to vineyards.

The estate includes close to 2,000 acres of vineyards, planted with the Catalan grapes Parellada, Macabeo, Garnacha, Cariñena and Tempranillo, as well as with some noble European varieties such as Cabernet Sauvignon, Chardonnay and Merlot.

The winery, designed in 1922 according to the classic modernist turn-of-the-century style, is worthy of a visit. The wines are made with the latest technology, using temperature-controlled stainless-steel tanks, and the reds are carefully aged in oak casks. Among the various brands, their varietal Cabernets and Chardonnays are especially notable: the reds complex and velvety, the whites fresh and aromatic, and both with great character.

CODORNÍU
San Sadurní de Noia (Barcelona) — (93) 891-0125
The main building of the Codorníu *bodega* is a nineteenth-century "national monument" of fascinating architecture, set in beautiful gardens just outside San Sadurní. The winery dates from 1551 and has belonged to the Raventós family since 1659, when the Codorníu heiress, María Ana, married Miguel Raventós. Today its vast 5-tier underground cellar is the longest in the world; it winds around for 15 miles and holds more than 100 million bottles. The current managing director is Manuel Raventós, representing the fourth generation since José Raventós started to make sparkling wines in 1872.

If you are near Barcelona or Tarragona, a visit to Codorníu is a wine lover's must. Not only the wines but the cellars, the museum of old wine presses, the gardens, the entire tour is memorable—including the 500-year-old oak tree which welcomes you at the entrance.

Codorníu wines are smartly packaged and have an individual style. Several brands are sold in the United States, all of them vintage-dated; the best known are Blanc de Blancs, Brut Clásico and the top of the line, Gran Codorníu.

FREIXENET
San Sadurní de Noia (Barcelona) — (93) 891-0125
Freixenet is the number-one-selling sparkling wine imported into the United States. Its characteristic black bottle (which everybody remembers even if they can't pronounce the name) and its aggressive marketing have made it the leader. Besides the Cordón Negro brand in the black bottle,

also sold here are the less expensive Carta Nevada, the premium brand Brut Nature, and the top of the line Brut Barroco.

The estate of La Freixeneda (ash grove in Catalan) has belonged to the Ferrer family since the thirteenth century. In 1889, Pedro Ferrer, nicknamed "Freixenet," started to make sparkling wine. His son José Ferrer is the current president.

After Freixenet's recent purchase of the sparkling wines Castellblanch, Segura Viudas, Conde de Caralt and René Barbier—once owned by the holding company Rumasa—it is now a close second to Codorníu in size. The winery has kept up almost constant expansion in an attempt to fill the phenomenal demand.

During the Rumasa days, a large investment was made to transform Segura Viudas into one of the most modern sparkling wine *bodegas.* The entire operation is mechanized, and their cellars house about 10 million bottles. Besides the Segura Viudas label, it produces the Paul Cheneau brand exclusively for the American market.

TORRES
Vilafranca del Penedès (Barcelona) — (93) 890-0100 and 890-2504
It is appropriate to end this tour of Spanish wineries with a visit to my family's *bodega,* sharing our history and what I feel we have contributed to Spanish viticulture.

My family has owned vineyards and made wine since the seventeenth century, but our entry into the world market actually had its beginnings in 1858, when Jaime Torres set off for America to make his fortune. Eventually settling in Havana, Cuba, he worked and saved diligently for seven years and in 1865 invested his savings in a fledgling oil company. Shortly thereafter, a world-wide oil boom made him a wealthy man.

Jaime reinvested in oceangoing sailing ships and organized the first shipping line between Barcelona and Havana. Then he returned to Barcelona and began construction of the large wine cellar, inaugurated in 1870. Upon his death in 1906, his brother Miguel took over the winery operation. Miguel's eventual successor was Juan Torres, father of the present owner, Miguel Torres—my father.

Miguel was only twenty-three when his father died in March 1932; but assisted by his mother, Josefa, he took charge of the winery management. Those were difficult days in Spain, and all over Europe. The Spanish Civil War started in July 1936 and lasted three years. In January 1939, during an air raid in Vilafranca del Penedès, several bombs hit our winery. A huge 160,000-gallon vat, full of wine, was destroyed during the explosions. The streets became real rivers of wine; the damage was overwhelming. The efforts of three generations lay in ruins.

However, from the ashes and the debris arose, firm and powerful, the will to rebuild. There was no capital, so Miguel applied for credit. In spite of the difficulties of that time, the reconstruction began very soon and was finished in early 1940.

While former generations had always exported wine and brandy in bulk, it was Miguel who decided to embark on the estate-bottling venture and to create prestige for each Torres label.

To this day, my father remembers with nostalgia and pride his first selling activities in Barcelona. He would personally visit restaurants and retail stores; if the buyer was busy with customers, he would apologize and wait patiently. Then he would pull out of his briefcase some samples of wine or brandy and coerce the prospective buyer into tasting them, while explaining with enthusiasm the history of their production and aging. By the late fifties, Torres brandy had acquired a small but influential patronage. Compared with the Sherry brandies, Miguel's was different: it had a softer bouquet and a French style.

In the mid-sixties, my brother Miguel, Jr.—our winemaker—started to experiment with adapting to our soil and climate the noble European grapes. First he planted Cabernet Sauvignon and Pinot Noir, then Chardonnay, Sauvignon Blanc, Riesling, Gewürztraminer, Muscat d'Alsace and Cabernet Franc. All these varietals are today blended to produce our wines, and experimental plantings are still going on with other grapes such as Merlot and Petite Sirah, which we also expect to use for our wines in the future.

These noble grapes have changed the whole picture of Penedès wines. Today many fine winemakers in Spain—not only in Catalonia but in other Spanish wine regions as well—are following the path set by my brother since the 1960s.

In 1973, our winery pioneered in Spain the use of temperature-controlled fermentation for white wines; keeping the temperature low to ensure a slower fermentation produces more aromatic and fruity wines. At the same time, we also began using stainless-steel tanks to ferment our reds. Many wineries all over Spain are now using these methods to make their wines.

Perhaps the main contribution my family has made to Spanish viticulture has been to change the concept of wine appreciation in Spain. Today most Spaniards realize that wine does not necessarily need to be old in order to be good; that the varietal character and the nobility of the grape is extremely important; that Spanish wines do not have to be an imitation of French, they can have their own personality and the winemaker's individual style, which makes them different from all others.

Today, Torres is the largest individually owned producer of premium wines in Spain; they can be found, under only one label, in 85 countries all over the world.

In the United States, Torres is the number-one-selling Spanish table wine. Since 1975, our sales here have gone from 15,000 cases a year to over 100,000. The secret of our success is brand image, personal approach and our own, personal style. The quality of a wine is determined by four factors: climate, soil, grape variety and—most important—the winemaker. In our case, I feel we have found the right combination of the four, led by a winemaker who is not only innovative and creative but has one attribute that is fundamental: he is never content with the results obtained in the last harvest and always looks forward to doing better next year.

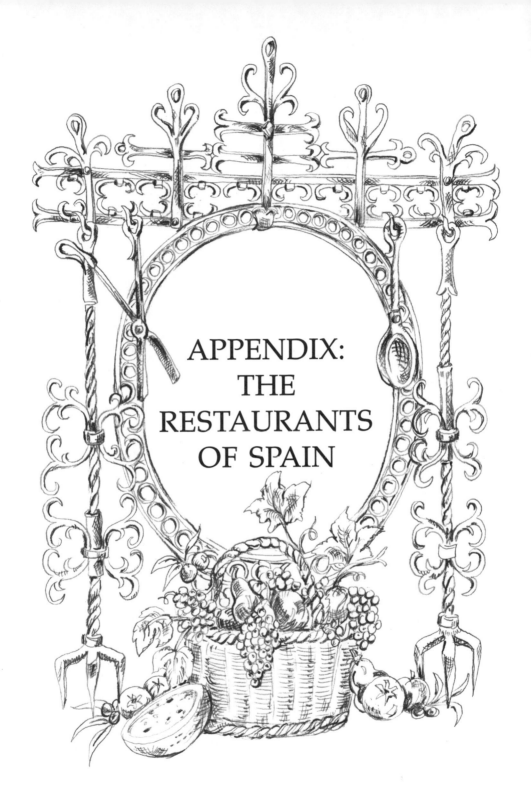

APPENDIX:
THE
RESTAURANTS
OF SPAIN

Throughout my travels in Spain I visited hundreds of restaurants, the finest of which gave me the ideas to develop most of the recipes in this book. Below is a list of these restaurants, as well as the region and town where they are located and the recipes they inspired. They are all worth a visit, so I hope the list will be a helpful reference when planning your next trip to Spain.

CATALUNYA

TOWN	RESTAURANTS	RECIPES
Vilafranca del Penedès	**El Celler del Penedès**	Caracoles Picantes (Snails in a Piquant Sauce)
		"Xatonada" (Catalan Tuna Salad with a *Romesco*-Style Sauce)
		"Xató" *(Romesco*-Style Sauce for "Xatonada")
		"Salbitxada" *(Romesco*-Style Sauce for Grilled Vegetables)
	Cal Joan	Habas a la Catalana (Fava Bean Stew, Catalan Style)
		Sorbete de Vino Tinto a la Hierbabuena (Red Wine Sherbet with Mint)
Barcelona	**Azulete**	Tartaletas de Caracoles a las Hierbas Aromáticas (Snail Tarts with Mushrooms and Aromatic Herbs)
		Ensalada Templada de Lentejas y Conejo al Curry (Warm Curried Lentil and Rabbit Salad)
		Silla de Conejo Rellena con Verduras (Stuffed Rabbit Saddle with Vegetables)
		Mollejitas a la Salsa de Miel y Vinagre de Jerez (Sweetbreads in a Honey and Sherry Vinegar Sauce)

TOWN	RESTAURANTS	RECIPES
		Lasagna de Salmón a la Salsa de Vino Blanco (Salmon Lasagna in a Light Cream Sauce)
		Tarta Templada de Limón (Warm Lemon Tart)
		Manzana Gratinada (Apple Gratin)
	Montse Guillén	Crema de Tomillo (Thyme Cream Soup)
		Allioli de Miel (Honey Garlic Mayonnaise)
		Allioli de Manzana (Apple Garlic Mayonnaise)
	L'Olivé	Ensalada de Col Lombarda con Boquerones (Red Cabbage Salad with Anchovies)
		Coca de Tomate y Pimiento (Flat Bread with Tomato and Pepper Topping)
		Romesco de L'Olivé (Romesco Sauce with Ancho Chiles, Onion and Paprika)
	Tritón	"Esqueixada" (Catalan Shredded Codfish Salad)
	Cal Isidre	Langostinos a la Crema de Perejil (Shrimp in a Parsley Cream)
		Romesco de Cal Isidre (Romesco Sauce with Ancho Chiles and Baked Garlic/ Tomato)
	Jaume de Provença	Bacalao a la Catalana con Pasas y Piñones (Catalan-Style Codfish with Pine Nuts and Raisins)
		Bacalao a la Mousse de Allioli (Codfish in an Allioli Mousse)
		Chuleta de Cerdo a la Catalana (Pork Chop Stuffed with Prunes and Pine Nuts, Catalan Style)

TOWN	RESTAURANTS	RECIPES
		Canelones de Espinacas (Spinach Canneloni)
		Helado de Crema Catalana con Salsa de Avellanas (Catalan Caramel Custard Ice Cream with Hazelnut Sauce)
	Neichel	Salmón al Vapor con Salsa de Vino Tinto (Fresh Salmon in a Red Wine Sauce)
		Flan de Moras con Salsa de Moras (Blackberry Flan with a Blackberry Sauce)
	Casa Costa	Zarzuela de Mariscos (Shellfish Stew, Barcelona Style)
	Reno	Capones al Agridulce (Game Hens in a Sweet and Sour Sauce)
	Tiró Mimet	Pato con Aceitunas (Duck with Olives)
		Filete de Ternera con Salsa de Anchoas (Veal Fillet with Anchovy Sauce)
		Tartitas de Berenjena (Eggplant Tartlets)
	Quo Vadis	Perdiz con "Farcellets" de Col a la Ampurdanesa (Partridge with Cabbage Croquettes, L'Empordà Style)
		Espinacas a la Catalana (Spinach with Pine Nuts and Raisins, Catalan Style)
	Agut d'Avignon	Pato con Higos (Duck with Figs)
		Manzanas Rellenas al Horno (Baked Stuffed Apples)
	La Odisea	Pierna de Cordero Rellena de Riñones a la Almendra (Leg of Lamb Stuffed with Kidneys and Almonds)

TOWN	RESTAURANTS	RECIPES
	Roig Rubí	Confit de Cebollas (Onion Relish)
	Els Perols de L'Empordà	Arroz a la Cazuela con Marisco (Rice in a Casserole with Shellfish)
	Mantequerías Tívoli	Roscón de Reyes (Three Kings' Sweet Bread with Almond Filling)
	Vía Veneto	Tarta de Piñones (Pine Nut Tart)
	Florián	Helado de Naranja (Orange Ice Cream)
Argentona	El Racó d'en Binu	Sopa de Tomate y Hierbabuena con Almendras (Cold Tomato Mint Soup with Almonds)
		Solomillo con Frutas Secas (Beef Tenderloin with Dried Fruits)
		Flanes de Verduras (Green Pea and Red Pepper Flans)
		Flanes de Setas (Mushroom Flans)
		Arroz con Pasas y Piñones a la Catalana (Rice with Raisins and Pine Nuts, Catalan Style)
Figueras	Ampurdán	"Garum" (Roman Dip)
		Terrina de Conejo con Ciruelas (Rabbit and Prune Terrine)
		Mousse de "Escalivada" (Eggplant, Pepper and Tomato Dip)
		Ensalada de Habas a la Hierbabuena (Fava Bean Salad with Mint)
		Rodaballo Soufflé a la Albahaca (Turbot with Basil Soufflé)
Palamós	Big Rock	Mousse de Endibias con Salsa de Cabrales (Endive Mousse with Blue Cheese Sauce)

TOWN	RESTAURANTS	RECIPES
		"Suquet" de Pescado (Fish Stew with Potatoes, Costa Brava Style)
		"Escalivada" (Assorted Grilled Vegetables, Catalan Style)
Martinet	**Can Boix**	Crema de Hinojo (Cream of Fennel Soup)
		Cebollitas a la Crema y al Perfume de Tomillo (Pearl Onions in a Cream and Thyme Sauce)
Meranges	**Can Borrell**	Tarta de Puerros (Leek Tart)
		Crema de Tomillo (Thyme Cream Soup)
Sitges	**Mare Nostrum**	Sopa de Pescadores (Fishermen's Soup, Mediterranean Style)
Pals	**Sa Punta**	Ensalada de Endibias y Aguacates a la Salsa de Cabrales (Endive and Avocado Salad with a Blue Cheese Sauce)
		Guisantes Estofados a la Menta Fresca con Almejas (Pea Stew with Fresh Mint and Clams)
Sant Felíu de Guixols	**Eldorado Petit**	"Trinxat" de Rape (Catalan Shredded Monkfish Salad)
		Langosta con Pollo "Mar y Montaña" (Lobster and Chicken with Nuts and Chocolate)
Cunit	**L'Avi Pau**	Pescado "A l'All Cremat" (Fish in a Burned Garlic Sauce)
		"Cremat" (Catalan Hot Coffee and Brandy)
Torredembarra	**Casa Morros**	Romesco de Pescados (Fish Stew, Tarragona Style)
Vilanova i la Geltrú	**Peixerot**	Zarzuela de Mariscos (Shellfish Stew, Barcelona Style)

TOWN	RESTAURANTS	RECIPES
Cambrils	Eugenia	"Fideuà" (Thin Pasta Noodles Cooked in a Fish Fumet)
		Salsa Roja *(Romesco*-Style Sauce for Grilled Fish)
Banyeres	Hostal del Priorato	Flan de Fresas con su Salsa de Fresas Frescas (Strawberry Flan in a Fresh Strawberry Sauce)

VALENCIA

Elche	Els Capellans	Ensalada de Naranja y Aguacate (Orange and Avocado Salad)
		Pan de Higos y Chocolate (Fig and Chocolate Loaf)
Valencia	El Plat	Arroz Negro con Calamares Rellenos (Black Rice with Stuffed Squid)
	La Venta del Toboso	Arroz Caldoso de Monte (Rice with Rabbit in Broth)
	Chocolatería de Santa Catalina	Leche Merengada (Meringued Milk Sherbet)
L'Alcudia de Carlet	Galbis	Paella Valenciana de la Ribera (Classic *Paella* with Shellfish, Chicken and Pork)
		Arroz al Horno de Verano (Baked Rice with Summer Vegetables)

MURCIA

Murcia	Rincón de Pepe	Ensalada de Zanahoria al Jerez (Carrot Salad with Sherry)
		Alcachofas con Piñones (Artichoke Stew with Pine Nuts)

TOWN	RESTAURANTS	RECIPES
	ANDALUCÍA	
Sevilla	**Las Golondrinas**	Zanahorias Aliñadas (Carrots Seasoned with Herbs)
Puerto de Santa María	**El Fogón**	Ajo Blanco de Málaga (Cold White Gazpacho from Málaga with Garlic and Almonds)
		Crema de Remolacha (Beet Cream Soup)
	Don Peppone	Patatas Aliñadas con Gambas (Potato Salad with Prawns)
Córdoba	**El Caballo Rojo**	Salmorejo de Córdoba (Thick Gazpacho from Córdoba)
		Cordero a la Miel (Lamb with Honey and Green Peppers)
Dúrcal (Granada)	**El Molino**	Atún Mechado al Horno (Braised Tuna Studded with Anchovies)
Granada	**Sevilla**	Cordero a la Pastoril (Lamb Stew, Shepherd Style)
		Rollos de Pan (Bread Rings)
	Los Manueles	Cordero al Ajillo (Lamb Stew in a Garlic and Sweet Bell Pepper Sauce)
San Roque	**Los Remos**	Ensaladilla de Bonito (Bonito Salad with Peppers, Onions and Tomatoes)
		Rape con Nueces (Monkfish in a Walnut Cream Sauce)
Huelva	**La Muralla**	Hojaldre de Mollejas al Aroma de Alcaparras (Sweetbreads in Puff Pastry with a Caper Sauce)
		Higos Pasos Rellenos (Figs Stuffed with Chocolate and Nuts)
Baeza	**Juanito**	Nueces Caramelizadas con Nata (Caramelized Walnuts with Whipped Cream)

TOWN	RESTAURANTS	RECIPES
Cádiz	El Faro	Helado de Pasas al Pedro Ximénez (Raisin Ice Cream with Cream Sherry)
Sanlúcar de Barrameda	Bigote	Helado de Pasas al Pedro Ximénez (Raisin Ice Cream with Cream Sherry)

MADRID

Madrid	Sacha	Pâté de Salmón Ahumado (Smoked Salmon Pâté)
		Filloas con Piña y Salsa de Naranja (Thin Pancakes with Pineapple in an Orange Sauce)
	El Amparo	Mousse de Salmón y Aguacate (Salmon and Avocado Mousse)
		Pollito de Grano al Vino de Jerez (Chicken Flavored with Sherry, in a Sherry Sauce)
		Bizcocho de Chocolate con Crema Inglesa (Chocolate Torte with a Light Custard)
	La Máquina	Pâté de Cabrales a la Manzana (Blue Cheese Pâté with Apples)
		Pelotitas del Profesor (Hazelnut Meringue Cookies)
	El Cenador del Prado	Crema Fría de Melón a la Hierbabuena (Cold Melon Cream Soup with Mint)
	Zalacaín	Zanahoria Rallada con Naranja y Piñones (Shredded Carrot Salad with Orange and Pine Nuts)
		Tejas Gigantes (Giant Tile Cookies)
	La Gabarra	Ensalada de Aguacate con Tomate (Avocado and Tomato Salad)
	Wallis	Ensalada de Aguacate y Pimientos Rojos (Avocado and Red Pepper Salad)

TOWN	RESTAURANTS	RECIPES
		Helado de Frutos Secos al Caramelo con Salsa de Chocolate (Caramelized Nut Ice Cream with Hot Chocolate Sauce)
	Cabo Mayor	Ensalada de Aguacate y Pimientos Rojos (Avocado and Red Pepper Salad)
		Ensalada de Verduras con Dos Gustos de Salmón (Vegetable Salad with Fresh and Smoked Salmon)
		Sorbete de Apio (Celery Sherbet)
	O'Pazo	Trucha Escabechada (Trout Marinated in Vinegar with Onions and Carrots)
	Príncipe de Viana	Bacalao al Ajoarriero (Codfish in a Tomato and Red Pepper Sauce)
	Jockey	Pescado Braseado en Hojas de Col con Salsa al Cava (Braised Fish Wrapped in Cabbage Leaves with a Champagne Sauce)
		Helado de Miel con Nueces y Dátiles (Date-Nut Honey Ice Cream)
	Peñas Arriba	Escalopas de Salmón con Vieiras y Pimientos Verdes (Salmon with Scallops in a Green Pepper Sauce)
		Terrina de Frutas con Muselina de Almendras (Fruit Terrine with Almond–Buttercream Filling)
	Horno de Santa Teresa	Lomo de Cerdo a la Naranja (Pork Loin in an Orange Sauce)
	Combarro	Empanada de Anchoas (Anchovy and Onion Pie)
	Nicolás	Corona de Naranja (Orange Flan in a Crown)
	Posada de la Villa	Tarta de Santiago (Santiago Almond Torte)

TOWN	RESTAURANTS	RECIPES
	Irizar	Sorbete de Manzana con Pasas (Apple Sherbet with Raisins)

CASTILLA-LEÓN

TOWN	RESTAURANTS	RECIPES
Aranda de Duero	Mesón de la Villa	Pollo Escabechado (Chicken Marinated in Vinegar and Wine, Spices and Herbs)
Valladolid	La Fragua	Lengua Empiñonada (Braised Tongue with Pine Nuts)

GALICIA

TOWN	RESTAURANTS	RECIPES
Vilaxoán	Chocolate	Fideos con Almejas (Noodles with Clams)
		Pan de Mollete (Chignon Bread)
		Empanada de Anchoas (Anchovy and Onion Pie)
Santiago de Compostela	Vilas	Callos a la Gallega (Tripe with Garbanzo Beans, Ham and Sausage, Galician Style)
		Tarta de Santiago (Santiago Almond Torte)
Villagarcía de Arosa	Galloufa	Queimada (Witch's Brew)

ASTURIAS

TOWN	RESTAURANTS	RECIPES
Oviedo	La Máquina	Fabada Asturiana (Bean Stew with Sausages, Asturian Style)

CANTABRIA

TOWN	RESTAURANTS	RECIPES
Laredo	Risco	Pâté de Anchoa con Caviar (Anchovy Pâté with Caviar Mayonnaise)
		Tronzón de Tudanco al Tresviso (Beef Steak with Mushrooms in a Blue Cheese Sauce)

TOWN	RESTAURANTS	RECIPES
	PAÍS VASCO	
San Sebastián	**Akelaŕe**	Caracoles sin Trabajo con Salsa de Berros (Effortless Snails in a Watercress Sauce)
		Ensalada Templada de Bonito (Warm Bonito Salad with Vegetables)
		Rape con Romero (Monkfish with Rosemary)
		Mollejas de Ternera al Oporto (Veal Sweetbreads in a Port Sauce)
		Pasta Akelaŕe (Crisp Pastry Crust)
	Bar Oquendo	Tartaletas de Riñones (Kidney Tartlets)
	Panier Fleuri	Tarta de Cebolla (Onion Tart)
	Arzak	Pastel de Krabarroka (Basque Fish Mousse)
		Crêpes de Txangurro (Thin Pancakes Stuffed with Crab)
		Bollos de Pan con Café (Whole Wheat Bread Rolls, with Ground Coffee)
	Rekondo	Pimientos Rellenos de Bacalao (Red Peppers Stuffed with Cod)
	Kokotxa	Chicharro con Juliana de Verduras (Mackerel with Julienned Leeks and Carrots)
	Casa Alcalde	Hígado Glaseado con Manzana y Naranja (Glazed Liver with Apple and Orange)
Bergara	**Hostal Lasa**	Tosta de Gambas (Prawn Toast)
		Pan de Molde (Loaf Bread)
Vitoria	**Dos Hermanas**	Bacalao al Ajoarriero (Codfish in a Tomato and Red Pepper Sauce)

TOWN	RESTAURANTS	RECIPES
		Zurracapote (Spiced Red Wine)
Beasaín	Castillo	Riñones al Jerez (Kidneys in a Sherry Sauce)
Bilbao	Guría	Medallones de Ternera a la Naranja (Veal Medallions in an Orange Sauce)
	Jolastoky	Tarta de Espinacas (Sweet Spinach Tart)

NAVARRA

Pamplona	Josetxo	Bacalao al Ajoarriero (Codfish in a Tomato and Red Pepper Sauce)
		Cordero Chilindrón (Lamb in a Mild Dried Pepper Sauce)
		Sorbete de Moras (Blackberry Sherbet)

LA RIOJA

Logroño	La Merced	Solomillo de Cerdo con Uvas (Pork Tenderloin with Grapes)

INDEX

Mar Cantábrico

Océano Atlántico

La Coruña

Santiago de Compostela

GALICIA

Lugo

ALVARINHO

Pontevedra

RIBEIRO

Orense

Valdeorras

Río Miño

ASTURIAS

Oviedo

CORDILLERA CANTÁBRICA

PICOS DE EUROPA

CANTABRIA

Santander

Loredo

León

CASTILLA - LEÓN

Burgos

Ha

Río Ebro

Palencia

Ribera del Du

Zamora

Valladolid

Rueda

Río Duero

Salamanca

Segovia

Ávila

MADRID

Madrid

Guad

PORTUGAL

Río Tajo

Cáceres

CASTILLA - LA MANCH

Toledo

Ciudad Real

Río Guadiana

Badajoz

EXTREMADURA

Valdepeñas

SIERRA MORENA

Jabugo

Córdoba

Río Guadalquivir

Jaén

Huelva

Sevilla

ANDALUCÍA

Granada

Si

Sanlúcar de Barrameda

Jerez de la Frontera

Puerto de Santa María

Cádiz

Málaga